Criminal Visions
Media representations of crime and justice

Edited by

Paul Mason

WILLAN
PUBLISHING

Published by

Willan Publishing
Culmcott House
Mill Street, Uffculme
Cullompton, Devon
EX15 3AT, UK
Tel: +44(0)1884 840337
Fax: +44(0)1884 840251
e-mail: info@willanpublishing.co.uk
website: www.willanpublishing.co.uk

Published simultaneously in the USA and Canada by

Willan Publishing
c/o ISBS, 5824 N.E. Hassalo St,
Portland, Oregon 97213-3644, USA
Tel: +001(0)503 287 3093
Fax: +001(0)503 280 8832
e-mail: info@isbs.com
website: www.isbs.com

First published 2003

ISBN 1-84392-013-1 (paperback)
ISBN 1-84392-014-X (hardback)

British Library Cataloguing-in-Publication Data
A catalogue record for this book is available from the British Library

Project management by Deer Park Productions
Typeset by GCS, Leighton Buzzard, Beds
Printed and bound by T.J. International, Padstow, Cornwall

Contents

Part Two: Criminal Representations: Crimes and Criminals

Part Three: Criminal Decisions: Agencies and Agents

Acknowledgements

People say that editing a book is a poison chalice. They are, of course, completely right: I will die happy if I never have to set another margin or indent another quote in my life. That said, this book has given me the opportunity to meet with some excellent academics who I knew by reputation alone, and others of whose work I was previously unaware. To my eternal shame this includes Deborah, who has been working at my institution for three years and whose work I had never come across. My thanks, then, to all the contributors who have delivered what they promised. For his patience and faith in the final delivery of the manuscript, I am grateful to Brian Willan who showed enthusiasm for the book from the very start.

I would also like to thank those whose inspiration and academic excellence were the reason I have been so interested in this field: Professors Martin Barker, Robert Reiner and Frank Leishman; the latter an outstanding colleague and friend, I also thank for his incisive and thoughtful comments on earlier drafts of this book. As always, the love and support of my parents at The Set has been paramount.

Finally, I would thank my students whose constant whingeing about the lack of a course textbook was the reason I decided to put this publication together and it is to them that I dedicate this book.

List of tables and figures

Contributors

Jessica Allen, having previously worked at the London School of Economics, is currently a researcher and evaluator at the American Museum of Natural History, New York. Publications include (with Sonia Livingstone and Robert Reiner) 'True lies: changing images of crime in British post-war cinema' *European Journal of Communications*, 1998.

Ian Conrich is Senior Lecturer in Film Studies, at the University of Surrey Roehampton. He is co-editor of *New Zealand – A Pastoral Paradise?* (Kakapo, 2000), *New Zealand Fictions: Literature and Film* (Kakapo, 2002), *The Technique of Terror: The Films of John Carpenter* (Flicks Books, 2003) and *Musical Moments: Film and the Performance of Song and Dance* (Flicks Books, 2003).

Steve Greenfield is Senior Academic, School of Law University of Westminster. He is co-author of *Film and the Law* (Cavendish, 2001, with Guy Osborne and Peter Robson) and *Regulating Football* (Pluto, 2001, with Guy Osborne).

Chris Greer is Senior Lecturer in Criminology at Northumbria University. He is author of *Sex Crime and the Media: Sex Offending and the Press in a Divided Society* (Willan, 2003). He has also published in the areas of policing and human rights and crime and the media.

Mark Hayes is Senior Lecturer in Criminology at Southampton Institute. He is co-editor of *Republican Voices* (Seysu, 2001) and author of *The New Right in Britain: An Introduction to Theory and Practice* (Pluto, 1994).

Martin Innes is Lecturer in Sociology at the University of Surrey. He is the author of *Investigating Murder: Detective Work and the Police Response to Criminal Homicide* (Oxford University Press, 2003) and is currently conducting work on the use of forensic evidence in long-term unsolved homicide investigations, signal crimes and contemporary logics and practices of social control.

Deborah Jermyn is a Senior Lecturer in Film Studies at The University of Surrey, Roehampton. She is co-editor of *Understanding Reality Television* (Routledge, 2003), *The Audience Studies Reader* (Routledge, 2002), and *Hollywood Transgressor: The Cinema of Kathryn Bigelow* (Wallflower Press, 2002).

George S. Larke is Lecturer in Film at University of Northumbria. She has recently completed her PhD at the University of Sunderland on contemporary film and cultural theories with regard to articulations of ethnicity and masculinities in postclassical gangster films.

Sonia Livingstone is Professor of Social Psychology at the London School of Economics. Her publications include *Making Sense of Television*, Routledge, 1998.

Guy Osborn is Senior Lecturer in Law at the University of Westminster. Recent publications include *Film and the Law* (Cavendish, 2001, with Steve Greenfield and Peter Robson) and *Regulating Football* (Pluto, 2001, with Steve Greenfield).

Paul Mason is Reader in Criminology and Director of the Centre for Crime, Conflict and the Media at Southampton Institute. He is co-author, with Frank Leishman, of *Policing and the Media: facts, fictions and factions* (Willan, 2003) and *The Impact of Electronic Media Coverage of Court Proceedings at the ICTY* (2000), a report for the United Nations on cameras in court.

Rob C. Mawby is Head of the Centre for Public Services Management and Research at Staffordshire University, from where he has undertaken criminal justice research since 1993. He has written many papers on policing and the media and is the co-author of *Practical Police Management* (Police Review Publishing, 1998) and author of *Policing Images: policing, communication and legitimacy* (Willan, 2002).

Michael McCahill is Lecturer in Criminology at the University of Hull. He is currently working as UK Research Officer on a two-year research project funded by the European Union. The URBANEYE project is a comparative study of the use of CCTV surveillance systems in seven European capital cities. His most recent publications include: *The Surveillance Web: The Rise of Visual Surveillance in an English City* (Willan, 2002).

Julian Petley is Senior Lecturer in Media and Communications Studies at Brunel University. His most recent publications are *Ill Effects: the Media Violence Debate* (2nd edn, Routledge, 2002), edited with Martin Barker, and *British Horror Cinema* (Routledge, 2001). He is also chair of the Campaign for Press and Broadcasting Freedom.

Jonathan Rayner is Lecturer in English and Film at the University of Sheffield. He is author of *The Films of Peter Weir* (Cassell, 1998), *The New Zealand and American Films of Geoff Murphy* (Kakapo, 1999) and *Contemporary Australian Cinema: An Introduction* (Manchester University Press, 2000).

Robert Reiner is Professor of Criminology in the Law Department, London School of Economics. He is author of *The Politics of the Police* (3rd edn, Oxford University Press, 2000) and editor with Mike Maguire and Rod Morgan of *The Oxford Handbook of Criminology* (3rd edn, Oxford University Press, 2002).

Daniel Stepniak is Lecturer in the Faculty of Law, University of Western Australia, Solicitor of the Supreme Court of Queensland and Barrister and Solicitor of the Supreme Court of Victoria. He is author of *Electronic Media Coverage of Courts* (Federal Court of Australia, 1999), an evaluation of electronic media coverage of court proceedings around the world.

Visions of crime and justice

Paul Mason

This book was put together for several reasons but one, I must confess, is selfish. While teaching crime and the media units on law and criminology degrees, it has often struck me how disparate work on crime, criminals and the media has been. Although media representations of criminal justice and deviance have been the subject of a long-running criminological debate (see for example Cohen, 1971, 2002; Ericson *et al.*, 1987, 1991; Innes, 2003; Leishman and Mason, 2003; Mawby, 2002; Reiner, 2002; Sparks, 1992), publication of volumes seeking to offer an overview of the key contemporary themes in the field has been limited. Although there have been important works on the interaction between criminology, popular culture and the media as well as more specific research on representations and content analyses of particular aspects of crime and justice,[1] collections of work on televisual and cinematic representations have been relatively sparse both in Britain (Kidd-Hewitt, 1995; Brown, 2003) and in the United States (Bailey and Hale, 1997; Ferrell and Websdale, 1999; Rafter, 2000).

In any edited collection, deciding which topics to cover and which to omit is a difficult balancing act. Indeed, the title of the book has proved equally problematic. *Criminal Visions: Media Representations of Crime and Justice* was chosen to evoke a sense of the visual – the consumption of images – as well as the mediated constructions of criminal deviance. The title also connotes insight and, perhaps, notions of future develpments in the field. Both of these ideas, I hope viewers will share on reading the contributions. 'Representations' is used deliberately here, for as Dyer rightly argues:

> Reality is always more extensive and complicated than any system of representation can possibly comprehend and we always sense that this is so – representation never 'gets' reality which is why human history has produced so many different and changing ways of trying to get it. (Dyer, 1993: 3)

Representations of crime and justice are relative to the individuals who produce and consume them. There are no neutral, objective representations, hence notions of 'reality' and 'authenticity' are relative, although, as O'Shaughnessy observes, 'We may decide that one set of representations are true or that they are more true than others' (O'Shaughnessy, 1999: 40). Any assessment of our 'para-experience' (Perlmutter 2000: xi) of crime and justice through the media must take into account the viewer's own knowledge and experience of crime and justice. Although this knowledge may have been acquired through some direct experience, having been the victim of a crime or contact with the police or courts, it is likely to be heavily supplemented with information gleaned from newspapers, television, radio, film and the Internet. Successive British Crime Surveys (BCS) have borne out this fact, and Levenson (2001) further notes that one of the most recent BCS reports that just 6 per cent of the public consider their principal source of information to be inaccurate. This perhaps suggests that audiences tend to accept as true those parts of a drama that are beyond their experience,[2] what Hurd (1981) and Mawby (Chapter 11, this volume) refer to as the completion of 'the half-formed picture' (Hurd, 1981: 57).

The aim of *Criminal Visions* has been to collect together contemporary writing to explore what can be termed 'representations of crime and justice'. The choice has been, naturally, subjective, but we attempt to offer more than simply an eclectic anthology of essays. The rationale for the book's structure and content is driven by a desire to provide for the reader both broad perspectives and specific analysis of mass-mediated constructions of criminal deviance and law enforcement agencies. The media in this book consist, for the most part, of television and film as there already exists a number of excellent works on crime news (see for example Chibnall, 1977; Ericson et al., 1987, 1991; Howitt, 1998; Surette, 1998; Wykes, 2001). However, both Robert Reiner et al. in Chapter 1 and Martin Innes in Chapter 3 offer excellent syntheses and analysis of crime news research, as well as providing new perspectives of this work.

Criminal Visions is divided into three thematic sections. In Part One, 'Criminal Visions In Context', the contributions of Robert Reiner, Sonia Livingstone and Jessica Allen, Julian Petley and Martin Innes appraise some of the principal matters that have preoccupied the British media. In

Chapter 1, Reiner *et al.* offer a comprehensive analysis of crime news reporting since 1945, highlighting Surette's 'law of opposites' in the shift in crime news content from stories concerning law breaking and enforcement to what they term the orchestration of 'virtual lynch-mobs'. In Chapter 2, Julian Petley outlines the arguments surrounding video violence. In particular, he traces the troubled release of the film *The Last House of the Left* and the problematic interpretation of the Obscene Publications Act 1959 and Video Recordings Act 1984 following public concern about the effects of videos like *Child Play III*, particularly since the death of Jamie Bulger, a two-year old killed in 1993 by two ten-year-old boys.

Part Two presents analyses of offending and offences as constructed by the mass media. 'Criminal Representations: Crimes and Criminals' deals with representations of bank jobs, sex crime, the Mafia, terrorism and serial killing. In Chapter 4, Jonathan Rayner discusses the often overlooked heist movie: a genre of crime films with a long lineage from the silent movies of train robberies to the recent glossy Hollywood remake of *Oceans 11.* In highlighting the work of director Michael Mann, Rayner argues that films such as *Heat* and *LA Takedown* offer an ambiguous construction of criminality. Chris Greer's work too, argues that the construction of, in this case, sex crime in the news is far from clear cut. In Chapter 5, Greer suggests that factors such as news-worthiness and financial pressures push reports towards the sensational rather than the discursive. This has been further borne out by the recent extensive media coverage of Operation Ore, implicating, among others, former Who guitarist Pete Townshend and television presenter Mathew Kelly in child pornography offences on the Internet. In Chapter 6, George Larke discusses constructions of the myths of organized crime in which she argues that, despite the divergence and intertextuality of media discourse, the cultural identity of the Mafia remains stable. Conventional notions of cultural pluralism are also discussed in Mark Hayes's timely piece on terrorism and the media in Chapter 7. Starting with the September 11th attacks in New York and Washington and moving to events in Northern Ireland, Hayes challenges the apparent symbiosis that is said to exist between political violence and the mass media. Part Two is concluded by Ian Conrich's interesting discussion of the development of seriality and wound culture in serial killer cinema. Exploring the notion of 'murderabilia', he argues that the blurring of factual and fictional representations of the serial killer create a narrative of horror based on both history and popular mythology, what Conrich terms 'a media repetition and exploitation of the violated body'.

Part Three, 'Criminal Decisions: Agencies and Agents', moves from

3

crimes and the criminal to mass-media representations of law enforcement, the courts and, finally, prison. Beginning with crime appeal programming in Chapter 9 , Deborah Jermyn discusses the spectacle of seeing criminal and victim in the television programme *Crimewatch UK*, arguing that the use of photographs in the programme significantly draws on, and contributes to, both criminal identification and notions of family. Michael McCahill too, is concerned with spectacle but shifts the argument in Chapter 10 to a discussion and analysis of surveillance technology reporting in three English newspapers. In considering media representations of the police, Rob Mawby in Chapter 11 explores the relationship between the mass-media construction of the police image and the consequent attitudes of the public. The subsequent two chapters move further along the criminal justice system to the courts, where mediated forms of adversarial justice are played out. Steve Greenfield and Guy Osborn, in Chapter 12, discuss the treatment of lawyers and justice in cinema. Drawing upon the dramatic facets of the legal process, they analyse the tension between law and justice, depicted as a battle between right and wrong in many law films. This, they argue, is a central theme, illustrating a fundamental tension in cinematic representations of lawyers. Television news coverage and factual representations of the English courtrooms have been brought closer recently following the recent moves by the Lord Chancellor to consider allowing cameras into appellate courts in England and Wales. In Chapter 13, Daniel Stepniak surveys the arguments and developments in putting real courtrooms on British television. He proposes that the 'morbid preoccupation' with high-profile American trials such as those of OJ Simpson and Louise Woodward have, in part, been to blame for the continuation of the ban on cameras and he considers why its continued existence may no longer be appropriate. The book ends where the criminal justice process, if not the criminal, often does – in prison. Here, the prison film and its role in public perceptions of imprisonment and penal populism are explored. In keeping with the rationale of *Criminal Visions*, the final chapter attempts to investigate the profound implications media representations of crime and justice may have on the public policy debate. This is also where we shall begin.

Representations and Perceptions: Why Crime and the Media Matter

As consumers of popular culture and news programming, we are surrounded by images of crime, law enforcement and the criminal justice system. In conjunction with the emergence of 'risk societies', public fascination with crime and justice continues to grow. In part, this is because most people have limited direct contact or experience with these matters and rely on media reports and representations of them for their knowledge. This mediation of the reality of crime and of audiences 'commuting' between the realms of factual news and entertainment programming has implications for public perceptions of law enforcement agencies, the courts and prisons as well as offenders and victims.

Criminological and sociological inquiry concerning the nature and role of the media in representing crime, what Ferrell and Websdale (1999) term 'cultural criminology', is relatively recent. Pivotal studies on deviancy amplification, moral panics and constructions of crime news were produced in the early 1970s. The work of Cohen (1971, 1972, 2002), Cohen and Young (1973), Young (1971, 1973), Chibnall (1977) and Hall *et al.* (1978) began to question, as Kidd-Hewitt observes, 'the media as purveyors of particular social constructions of social reality rather than as objective reporters' (Kidd-Hewitt, 1995: 13). Since then, an increasing number of sociologists, criminologists and media and cultural studies writers have concerned themselves with the effects of media representations of crime, surveillance technologies, crime and law enforcement in popular culture, news reportage of crime and discussion of the media as 'a subordinate role in all the major theoretical perspectives attempting to understand crime and criminal justice' (Reiner, 2002: 393). The growth in new media technologies has led to a marked increase in academic output on the media/crime nexus as well as increased concerns about the media's role in new challenges to security.

The established, and extensive, body of literature that explores the complex relationships between deviance, criminal justice, media and popular culture is dominated by arguments concerning 'effects'. Reiner (2002: 396) notes that wide-ranging literature reviews of effects research, such as Livingstone's (1996), suggest that output now runs into thousands of articles. These fall broadly into two categories: media causing deviant behaviour in society; and media as a form of social control cultivated by excessive consumption of crime coverage. Let us deal briefly with each in turn.

Slippery slopes and cultural dopes: copycatting and 'corrupting' effects of the media

The arrival of each new mass-media development has been accompanied by concerns about its potential criminogenic effects. Songs about criminals portrayed as heroes in the 16th century (Barker and Petley, 1997) have been replaced by Internet chat rooms and newsgroups as the latest in a long line of concerns about criminal activities and the media. The University of Michigan's 15-year study concluding that children who watch violent television programmes are at a greater risk of becoming aggressive, as reported in the *Daily Telegraph* (10 March 2003) is but the latest example of this effects research. In recent years, cases such as the murder of Jamie Bulger, the mass gun attacks at Columbine High School, Dunblane and Port Arthur have all prompted speculation of a connection with violent videos (Barker, 1997; Barker and Petley, 2001; Howitt, 1998; Leishman and Mason, 2003). However, despite an abundance of research over many years, the results are inconclusive. Julian Petley is more damning. In Chapter 2, he cites Cumberbatch's comments that:

> While tests of statistical significance are a vital tool of the social sciences, they seem to have been used in this field as instruments of torture on the data until it confesses something which could justify a publication in a scientific journal.

Cohen too notes:

> The crude model of 'media effects' has hardly been modified: exposure to violence on this or that medium causes, stimulates or triggers off violent behaviour. The continued fuzziness of the evidence for such links is overcompensated by confident appeals to common sense and intuition ... The prohibitionist model of the 'slippery slope' is common: if 'horror videos' are allowed, then why not 'video nasties?' Child pornography will be next and finally the legendary 'snuff movies'. (Cohen 2002: xvii)

These 'masterpieces of inconsequentiality' (Reiner, 2000: 53) are best illustrated by Schramm *et al.*'s conclusions on their research on the effect of television on children:

> ... for some children under some conditions, some television is harmful. For some children under the same conditions, or for the same children under other conditions, it may be beneficial. For most children, under most conditions, most television is probably neither particularly harmful nor beneficial. (Schramm *et al.*, 1961: 11)

Despite its inability to establish a causal link between media representations of violence and violent behaviour, and with an increasing critical mass decrying its usefulness, effects research continues to dominate popular debates about crime and the media. Perhaps more credible, and less methodologically suspect for sociologists and criminologists, are notions of media constructions of deviancy and their subsequent role as a form of social control.

Deviancy amplification and social control

What Kidd-Hewitt calls 'the rethinking of criminology' (1995: 11) in the early and mid-1970s challenged media representations of crime and deviance. Young (1971), Cohen (1972), Cohen and Young (1973), Chibnall (1977) and Hall *et al.* (1978) argued that 'amplification of deviance' by the media, caused 'moral panics', which in turn would lead to more state control in the form of increased criminal justice measures.

These 'folk devils' have been many and varied since Cohen's 'mods and rockers'. Indeed, Cohen himself, in his excellent reprise and reappraisal of moral panic theory (2002), identifies seven recent groups who have been objects of moral panics. From bullying and shootouts to refugees and asylum seekers, Cohen argues

> They are *new* (lying dormant perhaps, but hard to recognize; deceptively ordinary and routine, but invisibly creeping up the moral horizon) – but also *old* (camouflaged versions of traditional and well-known evils). (Cohen, 2002: viii)

In Chapter 3, Martin Innes discusses how the 'right story' ingredients can have 'a profound social reaction' and uses the recent murders of Damilola Taylor and events in Soham to illustrate what he terms, 'signal crimes', where the crime, as communicated by the mass media, acts as a 'warning signal that something is wrong in society'. Innes further suggests that mass media coverage of such crimes further engenders a fear of crime. In Chapter 1, Reiner *et al.*, in their discussion of crime reporting, refer to this selective reporting of crimes as what Surette has called the 'law of opposites'. Reiner *et al.* found in their survey of crime reporting since 1945 that the law of opposites continues to hold true, where two-thirds of crime news stories concerned violent or sex offences, which accounted for less than 10 per cent of crime recorded by the police.

A recent example of the moral crime tale's potential ability to manufacture social control was the reaction to the *News of the World*'s 'naming and shaming of paedophiles' campaign, instigated in July 2000, following the abduction and murder of eight-year-old Sarah Payne in Sussex. The paper launched a campaign to 'out' thousands of sex offenders throughout the UK, action that was supported by Sarah's parents, but condemned by senior police and probation officers as counterproductive. Street disturbances in the Paulsgrove housing estate outside Portsmouth were linked directly to the *News of the World's* campaign (Leishman and Mason, 2003). More recently, serious issues were raised about media coverage of asylum seekers and refugees following reports that the National Coalition of Anti-Deportation Campaigns, and in particular its leader, Lady Diana Brittan, had received hate mail. This followed the *Daily Mail's* campaign, which asked its readers to 'vent their anger' after the fund was granted £340,000 by the National Lottery (BBC Online).

Further fear-of-crime debates have focused on the crime appeals programme *Crimewatch UK*. Throughout its broadcast life, and despite presenter Nick Ross's 'don't have nightmares' message at the end of each show, *Crimewatch UK* has suffered from criticism that it dramatizes real crimes for entertainment purposes (Schlesinger and Tumber, 1993, 1994; Leishman and Mason, 2003, Jermyn; Chapter 9 of this volume). Despite *Crimewatch's* overt recognition, through Ross's homily that the pro-gramme is a compilation of the most serious crimes, Home Office ministers have been reported as blaming reconstructions in *Crimewatch* for 'stoking fear of crime' (Wintour, 2000).

While debates about fear of crime and effects of the media will continue in both academic and political arenas, the importance of representations of crime, deviance and justice in the media is unquestionable. *Criminal Visions* invites the reader to consider several questions about these representations: have traditional constructions of crime and law enforcement in the media now been reversed, where the criminal is celebrated and the criminal justice system villified? Do mass-media constructed images of the justice system show agents and agencies to be ineffective and crime as an ordinary occurrence? While there may well be diversity in the types of criminal visions in the media, is there increasing congruence in their focus? It is hoped that this book brings into focus a number of these issues and offers some new visions on this critical nexus.

Notes

1. Only a brief overview of this body of work is offered, rather than repeat the comprehensive reviews provided by, among others, Reiner (2002) and Kidd-Hewitt (1995).
2. The simplicity of this argument and the inherent problems in not testing it empirically are noted. For a discussion of the difficulties and assumptions made in claims about audience, see Martin Barker's perspective on film analysis (Barker, 2000).

References

Bailey, F. and Hale, D. (1998) *Popular Culture, Crime and Justice*, Belmont: Wadsworth.

Barker, M. (1997) 'The Newson Report: A Case Study in "Common Sense"', in M. Barker and J. Petley (eds) *Ill Effects*, 1st edn, London: Routledge.

Barker, M. (2000) *From Antz to Titanic: Reinventing Film Analysis*, London: Pluto.

Barker, M. and Petley, J. (1997) (eds) *Ill Effects*, 1st edn, London: Routledge.

Barker, M. and Petley, J. (2001) 'Introduction: From Bad Research to Good – A Guide for the Perplexed', in M. Barker and J. Petley (eds) *Ill Effects*, 2nd edn, London: Routledge.

Brown, S. (2003) *Crime and Law in Media Culture*, Milton Keynes: Open University Press.

Chibnall, S. (1977) *Law And Order News*, Tavistock: British Press.

Cohen, S. (ed.) (1971) *Images of Deviance*, Harmondsworth: Penguin.

Cohen, S. (1972) *Folk Devils and Moral Panics*, 1st edn, Harmondsworth: Penguin.

Cohen, S. (2002) *Folk Devils and Moral Panics*, 3rd edn, London: Routledge.

Cohen, S. and Young, J. (1973) *The Manufacture of News*, London: Constable.

Dyer, R. (1993) *The Matter of Images: Essays on Representations*, London: Routledge.

Ericson, R.V., Baranek, P. and Chan, J. (1987) *Visualising Deviance*, Milton Keynes: Open University Press.

Ericson, R.V., Baranek, P. and Chan, J. (1991) *Representing Order*, Milton Keynes: Open University Press.

Ferrell, J. and Websdale, N. (eds) (1999) *Making Trouble: Cultural Constructions of Crime, Deviance and Control*, New York: Aldine De Gruyter.

Hall, S., Critcher, C., Jefferson, T., Clarke, J. and Roberts, B. (1978) *Policing the Crisis: Mugging, the State and Law and Order*, London: Macmillan.

Howit, D. (1998) *Crime, the Media and the Law*, Chichester: Wiley.

Hurd, G. (1981) 'The Television Presentation Of The Police', in T. Bennett (ed.) *Popular Television and Film: a Reader*, London: British Film Institute.

Kidd-Hewitt, D. (1995) 'Crime and the Media: a Criminological Perspective', in D. Kidd-Hewitt and R. Osborne (1995) (eds) *Crime and the Media: the Postmodern Spectacle*, London: Pluto Press.

Innes, M. (2003) *Investigating Murder: Detective Work and the Police Response to Criminal Homicide*, Oxford: Oxford University Press.

Leishman, F. and Mason, P. (2003) *Police and the Media: Facts, Fictions and Factions*, Cullompton: Willan.

Levenson, J. (2001) 'Inside Information: Prisons and the Media', *Criminal Justice Matters*, 43, Spring, 14–15.

Livingstone, S. (1996) 'On The Continuing Problem of Media Effects', in J. Curran and M. Gurevitch (eds) *Mass Media and Society*, London: Arnold.

Mawby, R.C. (2002) *Policing Image: Policing Communication and Legitimacy in Modern Britain*, Cullompton: Willan.

O'Shaughnessy, M. (1999) *Media and Society: an Introduction*, Oxford: Oxford University Press.

Perlmutter, D. (2000) *Policing The Media: Street Cops and Public Perceptions of Law and Order,* London: Sage.

Rafter, N. (2000) *Shots in the Mirror*, Oxford: Oxford University Press.

Reiner, R. (2000) 'Romantic Realism: Policing and the Media', in F. Leishman, B. Loveday and S. Savage (eds) *Core Issues in Policing*, Harlow: Longman.

Reiner, R. (2002) 'Media Made Criminality', in M. Maguire, R. Morgan and R. Reiner (eds) *The Oxford Handbook of Criminology*, 3rd edn, Oxford: Oxford University Press.

Schlesinger, P. and Tumber, H. (1993) 'Fighting the War Against Crime – Television, Police, and Audience', *British Journal of Criminology* 33(1), 19–32.

Schlesinger, P. and Tumber, H. (1994) *Reporting Crime: the Media Politics of Criminal Justice*, Oxford: Clarendon Press.

Schramm, W., Lyle, J. and Parker, E.B. (1961) *Television in the Lives of Our Children*, Stanford, Cal.: Stanford University Press.

Sparks, R. (1992) *Television And The Drama Of Crime: Moral Tales and the Place of Crime in Public Life*, Milton Keynes: Open University Press.

Surette, R. (1998) *Media, Crime and Criminal Justice: Images and Realities*, 2nd edn, Belmont: Wadsworth.

Wintour, P. (2000) 'TV Series "Stoke Fear of Crime"', *The Guardian*, 7 November, 8.

Wykes, M. (2001) *News, Crime and Culture*, London: Pluto Press.

Young, J. (1971) *The Drug Takers*, London: Paladin.

Part 1
Criminal Visions in Context

Chapter 1

From law and order to lynch mobs: crime news since the Second World War

Robert Reiner, Sonia Livingstone and Jessica Allen

Introduction: Crime News Stories – Desubordination and Discipline

Deviance is the quintessential element of newsworthiness. Routine, predictable events – 'dog bites man', in the old cliche – are seldom reported (unless they involve major celebrities, as in the case of the Queen Mother's death). Events that appear to disrupt expectations, deviant occurrences, are the stuff of news, as all studies of news-gathering have confirmed (Ericson *et al.*, 1991). The news media parallel the entertainment industries in their focus on stories of crime and deviance, and this is even more true with the relatively new cross-breed of 'reality' television and other forms of 'infotainment' (Leishman and Mason, 2002, Chapter 7).

The prominence of crime stories in the media has been a focus of anxiety and debate (Reiner, 2002). The longest-running concern has been about the potentially criminogenic consequences of mass-media representations of crime, including crime news. Respectable fears about the glamorization of deviance and subversion of authority have accompanied each new form of mass medium, from cheap books and newspapers, through cinema and television, to video and the Internet, generating a huge research literature attempting to test the effects of media representations. This primarily conservative anxiety has been challenged by a polar opposite, radical perspective. This sees the media preoccupation with crime stories as a source of exaggerated public fear of crime fuelling support for authoritarian crime control policies. In this view the media, whether controlled by the state or by large corporations, are an ideological apparatus reproducing existing patterns of power and domination. Both of these polarized perspectives have been challenged to an extent by research on processes of production, which suggests overall a more complex set of influences generating news and other media content (e.g. Schlesinger and Tumber, 1994), supporting what Chris Greer's thorough analytic overview has described as a 'liberal pluralist' reading (Greer, 2001, Chapters 2–6).

Research Methods

The research reported in this chapter was part of a broader project charting the changing media representation of crime in various forms of media in the half-century after the Second World War. Its general aim was to examine whether the trends in the content of entertainment and news media crime stories supported either the view of the media as primarily a source of desubordination of authority or of social discipline. Specifically, it sought to ascertain whether the broadly agreed analysis of the features of media crime stories that had been developed by numerous studies held up over a long period of historical change. Almost all previous studies of media content focus on relatively short periods, and most have been conducted since the 1960s. However, the postwar period has witnessed profound transformations in patterns of crime and control (Taylor, 1999; Young, 1999; Garland, 2001). In what ways are these reflected in and influenced by changes in media representations? We set out to shed light on this through a historical content analysis, both quantitative and qualitative, of cinema, television series and newspapers, and of audience perceptions of the changes. The research was supported by a grant from the Economic and Social Research Council of Great Britain (no. L/210/25/2029), for which we thank them. The results for the entertainment media have been reported elsewhere, as has an analysis of audience reception (Allen *et al.*, 1998; Reiner *et al.*, 2000a, b; Livingstone *et al.*, 2001). This chapter looks at the implications of the newspaper material we collected (a briefer preliminary report was Reiner, 2001).

The press study we conducted analysed representative samples of stories from *The Times*, generally regarded as the British newspaper of record for most of the period, and the *Mirror*, a paper that contrasts with it in terms of market (tabloid versus 'quality') and politics (left rather than right-of-centre). Whilst this clearly is a limited base for generalization, and it would clearly be desirable to extend the analysis to more newspapers, it is a much larger sampling of stories across a broad period of time than has hitherto been assembled in the criminological literature. The quantitative analysis of the proportion of crime and criminal justice stories was based on a random 10 per cent sample of all 'home news' stories between 1945 and 1991 inclusive in the two papers. A more detailed quantitative and qualitative analysis of the way crime was represented was carried out for a smaller random sample of these stories. Ten days were selected randomly in both newspapers for every second year from 1945. In those issues all front-page stories, editorial pages and letters to the editor that primarily concerned crime were analysed, as were the crime news reports on the home news pages.

The Content of Crime News: the Established Model

As stated earlier, anxiety about the consequences of media representations of crime has generated a research industry examining the content of media crime stories. These have suggested certain recurring patterns, found in both entertainment and news stories. The basic finding of content analyses of media crime stories has been succinctly characterized as 'the law of opposites' (Surette, 1998: 47). The characteristics of crime, criminals and victims represented in the media are in most respects the polar opposite of the pattern suggested by official crime statistics or by crime and victim surveys. Content analyses often take the latter official measures as portraying the 'reality' of crime and thus regard the media picture as grossly distorted. However, given the problems and limitations of all official measures of crime, and even of independent research-based estimates, which have long been emphasized by criminologists (Maguire, 2002), it is necessary to be much more cautious about claims concerning the 'reality' of crime (Reiner, 2000). What is clear, however, is that there are certain distinctive features of media representations of crime that have been consistently demonstrated by content analyses of both entertainment and news stories. A recent overview of these studies suggests that the following characteristics of crime stories were regularly found by content analyses (Reiner, 2002: 378–93):

1. Stories about crime – both news and entertainment – are prominent in all media (the exact proportions varying according to different definitions of 'crime' stories).

2. News and fiction stories are overwhelmingly about serious violent crimes against individuals, primarily murder.

3. Offenders and victims portrayed by media stories are generally of higher status and older than those processed by criminal-justice agencies.

4. The risks of crime are presented as more serious quantitatively and qualitatively than the probabilities of victimization suggested by official statistics or victim surveys.

5. The effectiveness and the integrity of the police, and the criminal justice system more generally, are presented in an overwhelmingly favourable light. *Crime Does Not Pay*, as the title of a series of short films produced by MGM between 1935 and 1947 put it. Police deviance or failure tend to be presented within narrative frameworks that do not fundamentally impugn police legitimacy, for example by stressing that corrupt police officers are exceptional 'bad apples'.

6. Crime news focuses primarily on reports of specific cases, and there is little about wider trends, causes, or policy issues.

Although these features characterize crime stories, news and entertainment, in general, there are variations between different media and different markets (Ericson *et al.*, 1991). Television and print stories vary systematically in their presentation of crime, for example, as do newspapers and programmes aimed at elite, specialist or mass markets. The key question addressed in this chapter is whether there are also systematic variations over time, and if so, what these are. Specifically we consider how the media representation of crime and criminal justice has developed during the half-century after the end of the Second World War, a period of profound transformation in political economy and culture, and in patterns of crime and criminal justice policy. The next section will look at some of the quantitative aspects of change in crime news over this period.

Changing Patterns of Crime News

In many respects the quantitative analysis of the characteristics of crime news stories since the Second World War confirmed that the standard pattern outlined above applied throughout the period. However, within these broad features there are a number of significant changes of emphasis in the kind of crimes reported, the demography of offenders and victims, and the portrayal of the police and criminal justice.

The prevalence of crime stories

In line with the general conclusions from other studies, crime stories were a substantial proportion of all newspaper stories throughout the postwar decades. However, there was an increase in the prominence of crime news after the mid-1960s. Until then the overall percentage of home news stories that were primarily about crime averaged about 10 per cent in the two newspapers surveyed. Since the late 1960s this has doubled to around 20 per cent. For most of the period the percentage of crime stories was somewhat higher in the *Mirror* than in *The Times*, although by the 1990s the gap had closed. The proportion of stories about the criminal justice system also increased after the late 1960s in both papers (from around 3 per cent to 8 per cent), but remained a little higher in *The Times* than the *Mirror*.

The increasing proportion of crime stories itself suggests a growing concern with crime. This is underlined by the growing proportion of crime stories that feature multiple crimes. An increasing proportion of crime stories mention crimes other than the one that is the principal focus of the story. These secondary crimes (secondary not necessarily in seriousness but in their role in the narrative) can be of two distinct kinds. 'Consequential' crimes are ones linked to the principal crime, either as preliminary steps towards it or as results of it, for example stealing a car in order to commit a robbery, or to get away in afterwards. 'Contextual' crimes are ones not intrinsically connected to the principal crime in the story but mentioned as *obiter dicta*, for example remarks about the crime being part of a more general pattern of such offences. Table 1.1 shows the growth of such multiple crime stories.

There has clearly been a steady growth throughout the postwar period in the proportion of stories featuring consequential and contextual crimes. The latter in particular now feature in nearly half of all crime stories, indicating increasing attention to crime as a more general risk, beyond the specific cases focused on in particular stories.

Table 1.1   Multiple crime stories

Consequential crimes (as % of all principal crime reports)

1945–64	1965–79	1981–91
16	22	22

Contextual crimes (as % of all principal crime reports)

1945–64	1965–79	1981–91
19	32	44
N=211	*N=243*	*N=203*

What kinds of crime?

Homicide was by far the most frequent crime in news stories in both papers throughout the period, generating about one third of crime stories. However, there were significant shifts in the balance of crimes reported, as Table 1.2 shows.

The table shows the 'principal' crimes reported in newspaper crime stories, i.e. the crime that the story is constructed around. It confirms Surette's 'law of opposites'. The pattern of crimes reported in news stories is almost the obverse of the official statistics, throughout the decades since the Second World War. About two-thirds of crime news stories are primarily about violent or sex offences, but these account for

Table 1.2　Principal crimes in newspaper stories

Principal crimes in the *Mirror* (%)

	1945–64	1965–79	1980–91
Homicide	29	28	31
Violence	24	28	24
Property	16	8	9
Fraud	5	2	4
Against state	10	7	6
Public order	5	6	4
Drugs	–	4	8
Sex	7	4	8
Traffic	–	5	5
	N=112	*N=166*	*N=140*

Principal crimes in *The Times* (%)

	1945–64	1965–79	1980–91
Homicide	44	29	37
Violence	16	38	25
Property	21	5	5
Fraud	10	22	8
Against state	13	4	3
Public order	6	6	5
Drugs	–	3	3
Sex	3	1	6
Traffic	4	–	1
	N=99	*N=77*	*N=63*

less than 10 per cent of crimes recorded by the police (Barclay and Tavares, 1999: 4).

The emphasis on violent offences is as great in *The Times* as in the *Mirror*, although the proportion of sex offences reported is generally smaller. Within this pattern, however, there are some significant changes.

The proportion of stories about property crimes (such as burglary or car crime) in which no violence occurs has substantially declined. Property crime generated about one-fifth of all crime stories in the early part of the period, but now are hardly ever reported unless they involve celebrities or some highly quirky features, although they constitute over 90 per cent of crimes recorded by the police (Barclay and Tavares, 1999). An example of such a 'celebrity' angle making a property crime story prominent news was in the *Mirror* 6 July 1991. The Identikit picture issued by the police for a wanted handbag thief looked remarkably like the then Prime Minister John Major. This quirk led to the story of a very minor offence taking over the whole front page that day, complete with pictures of the prime minister and the Identikit of the thief under the headlines: 'This man is dangerous ... Wanted for stealing a handbag'.

Fraud cases are featured much more frequently in *The Times* than the *Mirror* (about 13 per cent of all crime stories compared with 4 per cent respectively). Drug offences (not linked to any violence) did not feature at all in the sample of stories before 1964. Since then they have come to account for 8 per cent of crime stories in the *Mirror* and 3 per cent in *The Times*.

Who are the offenders?

The characterization of offenders in newspaper stories also largely follows Surette's 'law of opposites'. All official statistics about offenders suffer from a major problem: the perpetrators of the overwhelming majority of offences are never identified. Less than 3 per cent of offences result in a conviction or caution (Barclay and Tavares, 1999: 29), so those who are officially labelled as offenders are a small, almost certainly unrepresentative sample of those who commit crimes. There is a similar 'dark figure' in relation to the data about newspaper stories about crime: many give no or only rudimentary information about perpetrators. However, the general pattern is that offenders who are portrayed in news stories tend to be older, and higher in social status, than their counterparts in official statistics. This is shown in Table 1.3.

The table shows that in one respect newspaper stories and official statistics concur in their portrayal of offenders: they are overwhelmingly male (84–91 per cent). The age of identified offenders is strikingly

Table 1.3   Offenders in newspaper crime stories 1945–91 (%)

	1945–64	1965–79	1981–91
Gender			
Male	84	90	91
Female	16	10	9
Age			
Under 18	1	1	–
18–20	16	25	7
20s	33	21	22
30s/40s	35	35	29
50s+	12	5	9
Age not indicated	2	9	34
Identified as minority ethnic group	1	2	6
Class			
Working class	17	8	12
Middle class	26	21	16
Upper class	6	2	1
Police	2	6	4
Military	9	1	11
Class not included	40	62	56
	N=245	*N=258*	*N=279*

different, however. The overwhelming majority of offenders described in news stories are aged between 20 and 40. About 40 per cent are aged over 30. Generally less than 20 per cent are under 20, and only a tiny handful under 18. However, more than 40 per cent of convicted or cautioned offenders are under 21 according to official statistics, and about one-quarter are under 18 (Barclay and Tavares, 1999: 24). In terms of social status, news stories disproportionately feature offenders who are higher on the social scale.

In more than half the news stories analysed no indication is given of the social status of offenders. However, offenders who are identified are much more likely to be middle or upper class (in occupational terms) than their counterparts in official statistics, although to a diminishing extent. Thus during 1945–64, 32 per cent of offenders who featured in news stories were at least middle class, whereas during 1981–91, 17 per cent were. Offenders who are dealt with by the criminal justice system, on the other hand, are disproportionately from the lowest socio-economic strata. The majority of prisoners, for example, were either unemployed or in unskilled or semi-skilled jobs. Few had middle or upper-class occupations (Walmsley *et al.*, 1992). News stories portray an increasing proportion of offenders as from ethnic minorities, although a much smaller percentage than are actually processed by the criminal justice system. Thus the proportion of news stories with ethnic-minority offenders increased from 1 per cent in 1945–64 to 6 per cent in 1981–91. But in 1992 the National Prison Survey found that 15 per cent of male and 23 per cent of female prisoners described themselves as black or Asian (Walmsley *et al.*, 1992). Thus, although in reality 'the rich get rich and the poor get prison' (Reiman, 2001), in news stories offenders are disproportionately characterized as higher up the social scale.

Who are the victims?

Victims have become increasingly prominent in newspaper crime stories. In the period 1945–64 the 112 *Mirror* crime stories we analysed gave details of 86 victims, but in 1981–91 the sample of 140 stories yielded accounts of 171 victims. In *The Times* the corresponding figures were 59 victims in 99 stories in 1945–64, and 56 in 63 stories in 1981–91. Whereas in the earlier period it was common for crime stories (most of which were about crimes against the person) to contain no account at all of the victims' characteristics, by the 1980s this was rare, and indeed in the *Mirror* in particular there were frequently portrayals of several victims in each story.

The characteristics of victims in newspaper crime stories follows the 'law of opposites' to a much smaller extent than the portrayal of crime types and offenders, as Table 1.4 shows. The table shows that the most commonly identified characteristic of victims in newspaper crime stories is their gender, which is nearly always indicated if the victim is portrayed at all. The victim's age is indicated in about two-thirds of cases, increasing from 30 per cent in 1945–64 to 38 per cent in 1981–91. Social class is discernible more rarely, and in a diminishing proportion of stories: 47 per cent in 1945–64, but only 29 per cent in 1981–91. Ethnicity is rarely stated: for only 3 per cent of identified victims throughout the period.

Although the portrait of victims in news stories is not a mirror of official crime surveys, the discrepancy is much less than for other aspects of crime. Table 1.4 suggests that the proportion of male victims identified in stories increases over the period, from 50 to 61 per cent. There are no official victim surveys before 1981, but the current statistics also suggest a male preponderance in victimization by violent crime (Barclay and Tavares, 1999: 15). The age of identified offenders in news stories parallels the results of crime surveys in indicating that more victims of violent crime are young rather than middle-aged or old, but the stories

Table 1.4   Victims in newspaper crime stories 1945–91 (%)

	1945–64	1965–79	1981–91
Gender			
Male	50	64	61
Female	50	36	39
Age			
Under 18	23	18	25
18–20	14	12	4
20s	6	16	13
30s/40s	14	12	16
50s+	12	8	5
Age not indicated	30	33	38
Identified as minority ethnic group	3	3	3
Class			
Working class	8	8	5
Middle class	22	19	16
Upper class	3	2	3
Police	11	14	0.5
Military	9	1	11
Class not included	53	56	71
	N=145	*N=185*	*N=227*

tend to exaggerate the risks of older groups. Whereas around 20–30 per cent of identified victims in stories are aged over 30, the overwhelming majority of victims of violent crime (especially male victims) are under 24 (Barclay and Tavares, 1999: 15). The preponderance of middle- (or higher-) class victims in news stories (about 20–30 per cent throughout the period) also exaggerates the risks of these groups. The British Crime Survey suggests that both property and violent crime risks are higher for the poor and socially marginal (Kershaw *et al.*, 2001 pp. 56–66).

The effectiveness and integrity of policing

The police are overwhelmingly the most frequently represented aspect of the criminal justice system in news stories. Although the police are primarily presented in a positive light throughout the period studied, as generally effective and honest guardians of the public, the portrayal of the police has become increasingly negative. Both the effectiveness and integrity of the police are challenged in a growing proportion of stories, as Table 1.5 shows.

Table 1.5   Police success and integrity in newspaper stories 1945–91

Clearing up crime
% of principal crimes reported as cleared-up

1945–64	1965–79	1981–91
73	63	51
N=211	N=243	N=203

Police deviance in newspapers 1945–91
% of all crime stories primarily concerning police deviance

10	12	19
N=270	N=289	N=254

Types of police deviance
% of police deviance stories

	1945–64	1965–79	1981–91
Corruption	21	9	14
Abuse of powers	42	59	45
Lifestyle	21	12	14
Discrimination	14	15	24

The table shows that between 1945–64 and 1981–91 the proportion of news stories featuring crimes cleared up by the police declined, from 73 per cent to 51 per cent. This still presents a more favourable picture of police effectiveness than official statistics do overall (clear-up rates had fallen below 30 per cent in the 1980s). But given that most news stories are about violent crime, they possibly underestimate police success: the clear-up rate for officially recorded violent crime was 68 per cent in 1997, and for murder, the most common crime in news stories, it was 91 per cent.

Stories about police malpractice have also increased since the Second World War. Table 1.5 shows that the proportion of crime stories about police deviance increased from 10 per cent to 19 per cent between 1945–64 and 1981–91. The most frequently reported type of malpractice throughout the period was abuse of powers, especially use of unjustified force. Personal corruption in the sense of the illicit use of their office for personal gain (usually pecuniary, but sometimes sexual favours) by officers was also frequently reported, as was a variety of 'lifestyle' offences against the discipline code but falling short of illegality, such as alcohol abuse. An increasing proportion of stories – the second largest category in the most recent period – concerned discrimination (usually racial, but increasingly gender) by police.

Conclusions: quantitative changes in the pattern of crime news

Overall, the results of the quantitative analysis suggest that the pattern of crime news found in previous studies holds for most of the half-century we studied – but ever more so. In general, Surette's 'law of opposites' sums up the relationship between news stories' representations of crime and the picture conveyed by official statistics. Crime in the news is overwhelmingly violent, most commonly homicide. Perpetrators and victims are typically older and higher in social status than their counterparts in the official statistics. The police are presented as honest and effective guardians of the public against crime.

However, there are quantitative trends in representations of crime in news stories in the half-century after the Second World War that are significant modifications in this overall picture (and these parallel the trends in entertainment stories; cf. Reiner *et al.*, 2000a, b). Stories about non-violent property crime – the bulk of offences recorded by the police or experienced by victims – were commonly reported in the first two postwar decades. However, they are now almost never reported unless they feature celebrities. The place of such stories has been taken by stories about drug offences, which did not feature at all in the earlier period. The now almost complete monopolization of crime news by stories about violence itself suggests that crime is represented as a more serious threat. This is confirmed by the trend to multiple crime stories, which conveys an image of a much more pervasive threat. The increasing representation of victims in crime stories implies more attention to the impact of crime. The overemphasis on older, higher-status offenders and victims also suggests an image of crime as more serious and calculated than the official statistical picture of crime as related to poverty and marginality, and involving primarily minor offending by socially deprived young men against other young men. The trends imply an increasingly threatening picture of crime in news stories. This is compounded by the more negative representation of the police, calling into question their effectiveness and integrity.

The Changing Discourse of Crime News Stories

Qualitative analysis of the shifts in crime news stories shows that these quantitative changes are indications of a deeper transformation in public discourse about crime (Young, 1999 and Garland, 2001 analyse this more generally). Crime news is inherently bad news. It reports the occurrence of activity that has been proscribed and sanctioned. However, its presentation in news stories during the first two decades of the postwar period was primarily as a series of unfortunate yet relatively isolated incidents. In so far as it was related to social causes, these were regarded as ones that were capable of resolution and were being dealt with by greater understanding and social reform. During the late 1960s and 1970s this was transformed into a representation of crime as increasingly threatening and out of control. It was presented as symptomatic of wider social crisis and ever more serious and pervasive in its impact on ordinary people. This changing representation of crime is indicated by a number of concrete thematic shifts in the reporting of crime news that was found in our sample of stories.

Accentuate the negative

There are many illustrations of how stories increasingly interpret occurrences in a negative way, emphasizing crime as an ever more menacing problem. One clear example is a pair of stories reporting essentially similar changes in the official crime statistics. Both are from the *Daily Mirror*, the first on 2 May 1961 (p. 7), the second on 26 August 1977 (p. 4). The 1961 story was the first report of the annual crime statistics that we found in our sample, though they now always attract much attention and concern. It was headlined 'Fewer sex crimes', and reported that there had been a 'slight' fall in the recorded number of sex crimes since 1959. This was contrasted with a rise of 10 per cent in indictable offences known to the police, including a 14 per cent increase in violence. What is remarkable is the emphasis on the good news, the 'slight' drop in sex offences, highlighted in the headline and the first paragraph, but the downplaying of the fairly large rise in violent and other offences. Throughout the story is written without any emotional or evaluative expressions, as a straightforward report of new information.

This is in stark contrast to the report in 1977. This is headlined 'Crime soars to new peak'. It is of course a story from a period in which law and order was beginning to be politicized and emerging as a leading issue with which the Conservatives under Margaret Thatcher were attacking the Labour government (Downes and Morgan, 2002). The changes in the crime figures reported are remarkably similar to the 1959 ones, but with every bit of bad news emphasized in detail. The overall rise in recorded crime was 1 per cent (by contrast with the 10 per cent of 1959). 'The grim Home Office figures show' a 10 per cent rise in violent crime, a 24 per cent increase in firearms offences, a 9 per cent rise in homicide, and a 15 per cent increase in muggings (mainly because of a 24 per cent increase in London – the rest of England and Wales reported an 11 per cent decline). Tucked away at the end, the story reports that 'there were 1,500 fewer sexual offences' according to the Home Office.

In short, the underlying statistical changes reported are very similar in the two stories. But whereas in 1961 the emphasis is on the good news, and the writing style is restrained and descriptive, the 1977 story spotlights the bad news in a tone of panic. The contrast illustrates a number of basic trends in the reporting of crime news. Above all, it indicates the construction of crime as a major problem posing an increasing threat both in extent and seriousness. It shows the news expressing and reinforcing the emergence of law and order as a public concern and a political issue. 'Bad news' and sensationalism have become core news values.

Victim culture: crime as a zero-sum game

The quantitative analysis has indicated the increasing attention given in news stories to victims of crime. The qualitative analysis indicates a profound change in the characterization of victims and their role within crime stories. Increasingly the harm done by crime is equated with the suffering and distress of victims, as well as the potential threat of victimization to readers, who are invited to identify with victims through portrayals of their ordinariness, innocence and vulnerability. Whereas in the earlier part of the period we studied there was also often a measure of concern for offenders, both to understand and if possible rehabilitate them, increasingly the victim–perpetrator relationship is presented as zero-sum: compassion for the offender is represented as callous and unjust to victims. This can be illustrated by many contrasting pairs of stories in our sample, of which I have selected two. The first pair of stories both concern violence against a child, the second pair both involve a marital triangle.

On 27 February 1945 the *Daily Mirror* front page prominently featured a photo of a two-year-old girl, looking sad and in pain, headlined 'Another cruelty victim'. Even in the murky photocopy I am looking at, even after more than half a century, the child's pitiful, anguished face cries out for comfort. The story is the main home news of the day. The rest of the front page is taken up by news of the war, and a brief note about the actor Cary Grant's separation from his wife. One paragraph in the leading story details the poor girl's injuries: black eye, bruises, 'red weal marks extended over her temple and across her cheeks'. Beyond this clinical detail there is no attempt to spell out the trauma and suffering of the victim, or the evil of the assault. Approximately two-thirds of the story focuses on the offender, a 26-year-old Birkenhead man who lived with the girl's mother, and who was sentenced to six months with hard labour. The last part of the story concentrates on his account of his own actions. The article reports that he claimed that 'the child's crying got on his nerves and that he "couldn't help himself" '. This was explained by the fact that 'he had been torpedoed three times and that his nerves were very bad'. What is noteworthy is the absence of demonization of the perpetrator, and the concern to understand how he could have carried out such an act from *his* point of view. Attempting to understand the offender is not seen as incompatible with the greatest concern for the victim, and condemnation of the act is taken for granted.

This can be contrasted with the way *The Times* reported a child murder case on 25 November 1989 (p. 3). This is a much more serious offence: murder rather than assault. Nonetheless, the presentation of the story suggests a fundamental transformation in discourse about serious crime since 1945. The story is the lead story on the main home news page. A banner headline reads 'Martial arts fanatic gets life for killing daughter aged five' and a smaller headline above it tells us that the 'Girl died from a combination of pain, shock and exhaustion after vengeful beating'. Half-way through the story a sub-headline says that 'Social workers held many case conferences but she slipped through the safety net'. Three pictures illustrate the story: a large one of the unfortunate victim, happy and smiling; her mother weeping; and her father, the killer, looking dishevelled and menacing in the style of mugshots. All are Afro-Caribbean. The most immediately noticeable contrast with the 1945 story is the use of much more emotionally charged language to emphasize the victim's suffering and the perpetrator's evil – not only in his actions but his essence. The assault leading to the girl's death is told in brutal detail, and the victim's pain and fear are stressed.

> Sukina had repeatedly pleaded, 'Daddy, don't beat me', but Hammond carried on … He turned up the hi-fi to drown the noise, beat her for 20 minutes with the flex, punched her in the stomach and then, when the girl could no longer stand, dragged her upstairs by her long, dark hair before throwing her fully clothed into the bath. Hammond … Subjected Sukina to a vengeful and sustained beating, using his fists, a ruler, and a piece of plastic tubing as well as the kettle flex.

Hammond is portrayed as essentially violent behind a façade of respectability and concern for his children. Outwardly he was a doting father, proud of his children and anxious that they should do well at school, but inwardly he was a 'moody fitness fanatic' and martial arts expert. His 'three children were placed on the at-risk register following incidents in which Sukina and her three year old sister were taken to hospital with broken limbs'.

The only glimpse at the defendant's perspective offered, reporting his admission that 'he lost control and did not realise what he was doing', is undercut by its placement in the middle of the detailed, gruesome account of his actions. The only comment showing any sympathy towards him comes from the mother: ' "Whatever they do to David will never bring my daughter back to me. I have got no feelings whatever towards him. But I cannot condemn him as he was a good father in a loving way. He just had a bad temper that he would not control." ' This is immediately countered by the detective superintendent in charge of the case telling us that the perpetrator had previous convictions. The killer is not the only character in the story who is blamed, however. Considerable attention is given to the failure of social services to protect the child adequately despite repeated warnings.

The presentation of these two stories is radically different in a number of ways. The 1945 *Mirror* story describes a tragic situation in which a child is assaulted by a man who is presented as himself a victim rather than an essentially evil person. The injury suffered is presented in detached, clinical language, and no emotional or evaluative adjectives are used to colour the report. The 1989 *Times* story, by contrast, is replete with adjectives stressing the victim's anguish and the perpetrator's pathologically violent character. It is noteworthy that by 1989 *The Times* is using more emotive styles of reporting than a tabloid had 45 years earlier. The stories illustrate a profound change in discourse about crime. By 1989 it has become a zero-sum game in which only the victim is represented as a suffering human being. Her plight is caused by two villains: a demonized brute who attacks her, and a negligent authority that fails to protect her. Instead of a complex human tragedy we have a one-dimensional battle of good versus evil.

This trend is illustrated further by the following two cases of violence in the context of a marital triangle. On 13 December 1945 the *Daily Mirror* published a story on its front page under the headline 'Three years for "savage" cripple who branded rival'. The story continued on the back page, under another headline, 'Cripple and branded woman "in a fervour" '. Some four months after the end of the Second World War the news agenda of the *Mirror* was returning to normal. Nearly all the front-

and back-page stories concerned crime, although the main news story was about the Bretton Woods agreement, which shaped the economic future of the postwar world. But this was the most prominent of several crime stories. It concerned a disabled woman who had branded another woman with whom her husband had 'associated' while his wife was in hospital. The story highlights the judge's comments while sentencing her to three years for the 'savage' offence. His emphasis is not so much on the brutality of her attack *per se* as that she took 'the law into her own hands' and used a punishment – branding – that 'our laws' now regarded as 'too revolting to the civilised mind to be inflicted for any offence whatsoever'. The bulk of the story concerns the anguished expressions of guilt by all three parties in this triangle. The husband pleads for mercy for his wife, while the victim is described as having accepted the branding as a deserved punishment after confessing to the 'association'. Both the victim and the husband seemed to accept the primary responsibility for what had occurred. Altogether this is presented as a tragic human situation, with no innocent parties, in which all are victims of their own wrongful actions and filled with remorse. The punishment is necessary to maintain the integrity of the law rather than to avenge harm done, to placate the victim's pain, or to incapacitate or deter an evil perpetrator.

On 6 July 1991 both the *Mirror* and *The Times* reported another case arising from a marital triangle. *The Times* covered it on the front page with a photo spread, and more fully on an inside home news page. The *Mirror* spread it over two full pages, with many photos. The case involved an armed man who held his ex-wife's lover hostage in a car for 29 hours, surrounded by armed police. The kidnapper had been alarmed that his children were to be taken into care – apparently a mistake as they were to stay with his ex-wife. The pictures in both papers exhibit much of the iconography of thriller movies: the surrounded car, police marksmen in bullet-proof vests, the hostage emerging with blood pouring from his left arm where he'd been shot, the handcuffed offender with face blacked out being led away. No doubt the prominence given to the story owed much to the availability of this dramatic visual material. The sharp contrast with the 1945 story is the construction of the narrative with a clear hero/victim and villain/perpetrator. Although the incident is referred to as tragic, the sympathies expressed are entirely one-sided. The violence is emphasized: the victim was threatened with a noose, the perpetrator was armed with a crossbow and gun, and shot the victim in the arm as police converged on the car (the story does not make it clear whether this was deliberate). The perpetrator is repeatedly described in one-dimensionally villainous terms as 'the gunman', and we are told that he had been involved in a 'tug of love drama' 20 years previously in Australia. His arsenal of weapons is described in detail. By contrast, the victim is described in heroic terms throughout: 'Hero is Mr Cool' reads a sub-headline, and the police credit him with 'remarkable resilience and patience'. What could be read as a tragic personal conflict in which everyone was a victim (as the 1945 story was constructed) has been transformed into a straightforward B-movie fight of good versus bad. This is achieved by representing the key protagonists as individuals rather than a reflection of respect for the law or any other overarching value system.

These pairs of stories illustrate the key change in the discourse of crime news reporting since the Second World War. The narratives have become personalized and sensationalized. What drives them is a battle against one-dimensionally evil villains who inflict dramatic and frightening suffering on individual victims, who frequently occupy the subject position of the narrative – a pattern we also found increasingly in crime fiction (Reiner *et al.*, 2000). The implications of this will be discussed below in the conclusion.

It's Not Business, It's Personal

In quantitative terms many aspects of the pattern of crime news stories remains constant in the half-century after the Second World War, and confirms the 'law of opposites'. In particular, there is disproportionate reporting of violent crime and of older and higher-status victims and offenders. Nonetheless, even in terms of the quantitative analysis much has changed. Property crime without violence has dropped out of the news picture, unless there is a celebrity angle, to be replaced by drug offences. Victims have increasingly been featured prominently, and often occupy the subject positions of crime stories. The police are represented in a much more negative way both in terms of effectiveness and integrity, although the predominant portrayal of them remains positive.

However, both the quantitative constancies and the changes must be seen as embedded in a fundamentally transformed discourse about crime and criminal justice, which is revealed in the qualitative readings. This transformation is paralleled by changes in entertainment crime stories (Reiner *et al.*, 2000 a, b). The most immediately obvious change was brought out by both the quantitative and the qualitative analyses reported above. Crime is now reported as a much greater risk than before, not just because it is more common, but because it is represented in much more highly charged, emotional terms as a serious threat to ordinary people that the reader is invited to identify with.

Related to this is the much greater individualism underlying the narratives. Crime is seen as problematic not because it violates the law or other moral reference points, but because it hurts individual victims with whom the reader is led to sympathize or empathize. Offenders are portrayed not as parts of social relations or structures that the victims or the public are also embedded in, but as pathologically evil. Any attempt to understand them, let alone any concern for their point of view or their rehabilitation, is seen as insensitive to the suffering of their victims. These features also testify to a decline of deference. Crime is seen as wrong not because of acceptance of legality as a benchmark of how people should behave but because it causes personal harm to individuals we identify with. The police and other authorities are portrayed as increasingly immoral or irrelevant.

All these developments have been paralleled in changes in the politics of crime and control more generally (Garland, 2001). Clearly they can only be understood as aspects of much broader transformations of political economy and culture, above all the combination of free market economics and increasing individualism since the 1970s. The result has been a shift in crime news from stories about the breaking and enforcement of a generally respected law, through the politicization of law and order, to an orchestration of hate and vengefulness against individual offenders supposedly on behalf of their victims in what sometimes amount to virtual lynch-mobs.

References

Allen, J., Livingstone, S. and Reiner, R. (1998) 'True Lies: Changing Images of Crime in British Postwar Cinema', *European Journal of Communication*, 47(4), 1–13.

Barclay, G. and Tavares, C. (1999) *Information on the Criminal Justice System in England and Wales: Digest 4*, London: Home Office.

Downes, D. and Morgan, R. (2002) 'The Skeletons in the Cupboard: The Politics of Law and Order at the Turn of the Millenium', in M. Maguire, R. Morgan and R. Reiner (eds) *The Oxford Handbook of Criminology*, 3rd edn, Oxford: Oxford University Press.

Ericson, R., Baranek, P. and Chan, J. (1987) *Visualising Deviance*, Milton Keynes: Open University Press.

Ericson, R., Baranek, P. and Chan, J. (1991) *Representing Order*, Milton Keynes: Open University Press.

Garland, D. (2001) *The Culture of Control*, Oxford: Oxford University Press.

Greer, C. (2001) *Crime in the Press: A Case Study of Sex Offending in Northern Ireland*, PhD thesis, Queen's University of Belfast.

Kershaw, C., Chivite-Matthews, N., Thomas, C. and Aust, R. (2001) *The 2001 British Crime Survey*, London: Home Office.

Leishman, F. and Mason, P. (2002) *Policing and the Media: Facts, Fictions and Factions*, Cullompton: Willan.

Livingstone, S., Allen, J. and Reiner, R. (2001) 'Audiences for Crime Media 1946-91: A Historical Approach to Reception Studies', *The Communication Review*, 4(2), 165–92.

Maguire, M. (2002) 'Crime Statistics: The "Data Explosion" and its Implications', in M. Maguire, R. Morgan, and R. Reiner (eds) *The Oxford Handbook of Criminology*, 3rd edn, Oxford: Oxford University Press.

Reiman, J. (2001) *The Rich Get Rich and the Poor Get Prison*, 6th edn, Needham Hts.: Allyn and Bacon.

Reiner, R. (2000) 'Crime and Control in Britain', *Sociology*, 34(1), 71–94.

Reiner, R. (2001) 'The Rise of Virtual Vigilantism: Crime Reporting Since World War II', *Criminal Justice Matters*, 43, 4–5.

Reiner, R. (2002) 'Media Made Criminality', in M. Maguire, R. Morgan and R. Reiner (eds) *The Oxford Handbook of Criminology*, 3rd edn, Oxford: Oxford University Press.

Reiner, R., Livingstone, S. and Allen, J. (2000a) 'Casino Culture: Media and Crime in a Winner-Loser Society', in K. Stenson and R. Sullivan (eds) *Crime, Risk and Justice*, Cullompton: Willan.

Reiner, R., Livingstone, S. and Allen, J. (2000b) 'No More Happy Endings? The Media and Popular Concern About Crime Since the Second World War', in T. Hope and R. Sparks (eds) *Crime, Risk and Insecurity*, London: Routledge.

Schlesinger, P. and Tumber, H. (1994) *Reporting Crime*, Oxford: Oxford University Press.

Surette, R. (1998) *Media, Crime and Criminal Justice: Images and Realities*, 2nd edn, Belmont: Wadsworth.

Taylor, I. (1999) *Crime in Context: A Critical Criminology of Market Societies*, Oxford: Polity Press.

Walmsley, R., Howard, L. and White, S. (1992) *The National Prison Survey 1991*, Home Office Research Study 128, London: HMSO.

Young, J. (1999) *The Exclusive Society*, London: Sage.

Chapter 2

Video violence: how far can you go?

Julian Petley

On 18 June 2001, Carl Daft of the film distributor Blue Underground angrily declaimed that: 'the right to free speech in the United Kingdom died today, and for that I have to say that I am ashamed to be British', and on 21 June Mark Kermode in the *Independent* bemoaned a decision that 'leaves British horror fans once again in the wilderness'. The cause of such fury and bemusement was the decision of the Video Appeals Committee (VAC) not only to uphold the British Board of Film Classification's (BBFC) decision to insist on 16 seconds of cuts in the video of Wes Craven's debut feature *Last House on the Left* (1972) before giving it an '18' certificate, but also effectively to criticize the Board for being too lenient to the film in the first place.

The grounds for both the Board's and the Committee's insistence that the film be cut before being distributed on video in the UK shed a good deal of light on the legal, regulatory and ethical reasons why it is still extremely difficult for films containing certain kinds of violent imagery to circulate legally on video in this country. In particular, the decision on *Last House on the Left* clearly illustrates the role played by the Obscene Publications Act 1959 (OPA), the Video Recordings Act 1984 (VRA) and the BBFC's *Classification Guidelines*. More generally, the decision demonstrates the BBFC's reading of both public opinion and clinical psychology on the matter of the alleged 'effects' of violent video imagery on both individual viewers and society in general. This particular case, then, also illustrates in more general terms the limits of the legally possible when it comes to the distribution in the UK today of videos containing images of violence.

Last House on the Left is loosely based on the Ingmar Bergman film

Jungfrukällan (*The Virgin Spring*, 1959). Craven's film tells the story of two country girls who, on a visit to New York, are abducted by a gang of drug peddlers, and, in the course of a journey towards the Canadian border, raped, tortured and finally killed. When their car subsequently breaks down in the country, the gang members ask for help at a nearby house, which turns out to be the home of the parents of one of their victims. Once they have discovered the truth of the situation, the parents wreak a terrible revenge.

The film was first submitted to the then British Board of Film Censors for cinema exhibition in 1974 and, unsurprisingly, given the strictness of the Board's policies at that time, rejected outright. It subsequently became available on video before the VRA came into force, but inevitably came to feature prominently on the Director of Public Prosecution's (DPP) infamous 'Top 60' list of 'video nasties', attracting no fewer than 113 convictions under the Obscene Publications Act between 1983 and 1987.

In 1999, in supposedly less hysterical times, *Last House* was submitted to the BBFC by the Feature Film Company for classification as a cinema release. On 19 May that year, BBFC Director Robin Duval wrote to the company explaining that the film 'contains a number of sequences involving gross violence committed against women, often in a context with clear sexual overtones. It invites the viewer to relish the detail of the violence and the killings.' The Board thus required cuts totalling some 85 seconds. However, although the first sentence is an uncontroversial statement of fact, the second is a highly questionable judgement and is a matter of opinion – one which, as we shall see, was continually to bedevil the film's progress through the hands of the BBFC and subsequently the VAC. Furthermore, it's one entirely at odds with the director's own assessment of his film, which he sees as: 'a protest against real violence in the world, and the downplaying of the reality of violence in films. We showed violence in its true ugliness, rather than taking the usual Hollywood path of making it glamorous and exciting and entertaining, which in essence is a lie' (quoted in Kermode, 2002a). Of course, it could be argued that directors are not best fitted to judge their own films, but no horror expert of whom I am aware disagrees with him on this matter, and most would readily concur with Kim Newman's argument that Craven uses his film 'forcefully to make the point that violence degrades everyone involved, victim and victimiser, just and unjust' and that it 'really communicates a powerful, intellectual revulsion that makes a far more effective anti-violence statement than Hooper's roller-coaster ride [*The Texas Chainsaw Massacre*, 1974]' (Newman, 1988: 55).

Receiving no reply from the distributor, the Board wrote to them again, asking if they were prepared to make the cuts. The company then signalled its unwillingness to do so, and thus, in February 2000, the BBFC formally rejected the work, explaining that it 'has concluded that the gross violence committed against women, often of a sexual nature, in *The Last House on the Left* is unacceptable both in terms of our published guidelines and in terms of public expectations'.

On 20 August 2001, Blue Underground submitted the film for video classification. It was viewed at every level of seniority in the Board, and finally by its president and two vice presidents. In the end, four cuts totalling some 16 seconds were requested, all of them concerning the scenes in which the two girls are tortured and killed. On 5 November, Blue Underground received a cuts list detailing the four excisions that the BBFC required in the film. These were described as follows: 'remove downward panning shot from woman's face to the front of her urine stained jeans. Resume on side shot of woman's face'; 'remove all sight of entrails being pulled out of woman's body'; 'remove all sight of young woman's chest being carved with knife'; and 'during nightmare sequence, remove all sight of young woman's chest being carved with knife'. On 14 November, Blue Underground informed the BBFC that they were unwilling to make the cuts required, and requested that the matter be referred to the Video Appeals Committee, a statutory body established under the VRA.

In the course of the following months, as the video proceeded through the appeals process, it soon became clear that the Board's concerns about sexual violence in the film were predicated on a number of different concerns, and I want now to explore each of these in turn as they arose at various points in the video's unhappy journey through the classification process, since it is these which so clearly illuminate the current limits beyond which violent imagery on video is considered legally impermissible in the UK.

The Obscene Publications Act

The letter detailing the cuts required before classification could take place cited the Obscene Publications Act 1959 as the ground for making these excisions. In other words, the BBFC, as a statutory body, could not pass a work which, uncut, might be liable to successful prosecution for obscenity. The Act lays down that a work shall be deemed obscene if its effect is: 'such as to tend to deprave and corrupt persons who are likely, in all circumstances, to read, see or hear the matter contained or embodied in it'. Until the early 1980s the Act had generally been invoked in order to prosecute material of a sexual nature, but in 1982, during the 'video nasty' furore, it was successfully cited in two test cases involving *Driller Killer* (1979), *I Spit on Your Grave* (1978), *Death Trap* (1976), *Cannibal Holocaust* (1979) and *S.S. Experiment Camp* (1976). These having established that the Act could indeed be used successfully to prosecute violent material, numerous prosecutions of these and other videos involving violence followed – including, as we have seen, *Last House on the Left*.

If the police seize material that they deem to be obscene, the Crown Prosecution Service (CPS) has to decide whether to prosecute for a criminal offence under Section 2 of the Act, or to go for a civil forfeiture hearing under Section 3. The former enables the defendant to mount – in theory, at least – a detailed defence of the material in question; for example, calling upon expert witnesses to pronounce on its literary or educational merits or other forms of 'public good' as laid down in Section 4 of the Act. However, very few can afford to mount a *Lady Chatterley*-style defence, and most defendants, terrified of being paraded as pornographers by a prurient press, simply want to get the case over and done with as quickly and quietly as possible. Section 2 cases also carry heavy penalties in the case of a successful prosecution: a maximum gaol term of three years and an unlimited fine if the defendant has elected to be tried by a judge and jury, or a maximum of six months in gaol and/or a fine of £5,000 if they have chosen to go before magistrates. On the other hand, a prosecution under Section 3 has its attractions to both sides: the distributor of the material runs no risk of being convicted as a criminal, as the action is taken solely against the material itself. He or she has the right to contest any forfeiture order, but in reality rarely does so, not least so as to avoid negative publicity; indeed, distributors in these cases do not have even to appear before the magistrates, and the matter can be dealt with by post, like a parking fine. From the point of view of a censorious local police force, Section 3 forfeitures present an unrivalled opportunity to dispose of large amounts of material of which they, or the local self-appointed guardians of morality, happen to disapprove, or even to put out of business a distributor to whom they have taken a dislike, as it is relatively easy to obtain a wide-ranging forfeiture order from magistrates, although just how easy this is will depend upon the make-up of the local magistracy. However, in certain parts of the country, matters will undoubtedly not have changed substantially since the days described by the Labour MP Leo Abse, when the fate of works prosecuted under the OPA were frequently determined by people:

Who often have been selected, quite deliberately, not because they enjoy a ribald story or have a Rabelaisian temperament, but precisely because they have a certain rigidity and rectitude about them which, although it may equip them in certain respects to deal with many laws, makes them, perhaps, peculiarly unsuitable and unacceptable to deal with the question of what is or is not likely to corrupt. (quoted in Robertson, 1979: 106)

All too often, therefore, cases brought under Section 3 of the OPA are little more than trawling operations, cheap and convenient forms of local censorship in which the merits and demerits of the actual works caught in the net are rarely if ever seriously considered, let alone debated in open court.

In its submission to the VAC, on 8 January 2002, the BBFC again brought up the matter of the OPA, stating that:

The Board considers that an overriding test of suitability for classification is that a video does not infringe the criminal law. The video work *The Last House on the Left* has been the subject of a number of convictions under the Obscene Publications Act 1959, the most recent being: 23 March 1994 – S3 forfeiture; 17 January 1994 – S2 conviction; 18 September 1991 – S2 conviction.

Both of the Section 2 cases were heard before magistrates; the defendants pleaded guilty and thus no sustained defence of the film was made in either case. It is thus quite reasonable to suppose that the video was dealt with in exactly the peremptory fashion described above. Indeed, David Pannick QC, in his submission on behalf of Blue Underground to the VAC, on 11 February 2002, stressed the fact that magistrates 'rarely hear informed submissions on the applicable legal standards'. Indeed, he could also have quoted the following: 'there is no doubt that Magistrates Courts reach inconsistent decisions on obscenity. It is unsurprising they should do so, given the widely subjective views held in respect of pornography' (quoted in Petley, 2000a: 100). The Committee members would have been bound to agree, since they themselves were the authors of the remark – in their landmark decision to grant an R18 certificate to the pornographic video *Makin' Whoopee!* in July 1998.

In the event, the VAC was not swayed by the argument that *Last House on the Left* might, if passed uncut, be found guilty under the OPA. As they put it in their final judgement:

We give some weight to the previous convictions but not very much. We do think that many, especially women, would find the video work to be contrary to section 2 of the OPA. A jury consisting entirely or substantially of women is, however, so unlikely as to be discounted. No jury so far has had the benefit of evidence in support of a section 4 defence. Taking into account all the circumstances we have our doubts whether a conviction would result, indeed we think it might be difficult to get a jury to agree upon a verdict.

However, this by no means renders irrelevant our discussion of the OPA in relation to videos containing violent imagery. Firstly, the *Last House on the Left* affair usefully clarified the role that consideration of the OPA had played in BBFC thinking about such videos up to this time. Secondly, and perhaps more importantly, it flushed into the open the so-called 'ten-year rule', to which we clearly owe a good deal of the cutting of violent scenes in many recently re-released 'nasties'.

According to Robin Duval's written statement to the VAC, on 13 May 2002: 'Recent evidence of a work's unacceptability in law must weigh heavily with the Board. The more recent the conviction, the more likely it is that cuts will be required or the work rejected.' However, he added: 'the Board has never operated any policy of automatic cuts or rejection for a work which has received an OPA conviction. Nor has the Board ever operated a time limit (Mr Daft has suggested 10 years) on convictions before they can be deemed to be spent.' The problem is, though, that this remark is extremely difficult to square with other statements made elsewhere by the BBFC. For example, this one from 10 September 2000:

> Our legal advice is that we cannot pass a DPP listed title uncut if it has any recent OPA convictions. We have been advised to take 'recent' convictions as meaning convictions within the last decade. When a 'video nasty' is submitted we first establish whether it has any 'recent' convictions and – if so – we know that it has to be cut, regardless of whether it would be acceptable under our guidelines. Examples include *Zombie Flesh Eaters*, *Tenebrae* and *Driller Killer*, all of which have been convicted within the last ten years (*Zombie Flesh Eaters* as recently as 1994 under Section 2) and so cannot be passed uncut even if we feel they are in line with our guidelines. (www.dtaylor.demon.co.uk/bpnasty.htm)

Then, apropos *Blood Feast* (1963), which was passed in June 2001, the BBFC itself noted: 'cautionary cuts required as a result of successful OPA prosecution in 1994' (www.bbfc.co.uk). Furthermore, a statement issued by the Board in April 2001, and quoted by Daft in his response to Duval's statement to the VAC, announced that:

> *House by the Cemetery* was last convicted under the Obscene Publications Act in 1994. It received this conviction as a result of its content, not simply because it was unclassified. In accordance with current BBFC policy, which is based on our latest legal advice, it was therefore necessary to make cuts to the video before classification. This is exactly the same situation as applies to *Zombie Flesh Eaters* and it is likely in the case of both films that no cuts would have been required had there been no recent convictions.

Daft also stated that he had been told by Mike Bor, former Chief Examiner of the Board, that the 'ten-year rule' had been forced upon the Board by the CPS, but when he, Daft, had spoken to the CPS about this, they had no idea that the Board was operating such a policy. Finally, in an interview with me, Duval stated that:

> If we look at a film now and we're clear that we would not ourselves have a problem with it if it didn't have an OPA record, and if we also discover that no jury has found it obscene for, let's say, ten years or more, then that's the point at which we can move towards a more liberal position, although very cautiously and carefully because we don't want to put up a challenge to the law. (Petley, 2001: 31).

The Video Recordings Act

If the OPA and the manner of its enforcement present one set of problems for videos containing violent imagery, then the Video Recordings Act 1984 poses an even tougher challenge.

Firstly, it is an exceedingly blunt instrument. As Robin Duval explained to the VAC:

> In recent years the police, with trading standards officers, have employed the Video Recordings Act as a more straightforward means than the OPA of getting a conviction, since all that has to be

proved is that a work has no BBFC classification. The penalties (fines, imprisonment) are similar to the OPA's. Indeed, the Home Office has specifically advised police forces to use the VRA instead of the OPA.

As Geoffrey Robertson and Andrew Nicol put it, in cases involving the distribution of unclassified videos:

> The issues for a court will generally be straightforward and uncluttered by any need for aesthetic judgement … Magistrates may issue warrants for search and seizure if satisfied that there are reasonable grounds for suspecting offences, and police may arrest persons suspected of offences under the Act if they refuse to give their names and addresses. The court may, as an additional punishment, order the videos to which the offence relates to be forfeited. (Robertson and Nicol, 2002: 750)

Thus, as the British courts have interpreted 'distribution' as including film fans swapping or trading tapes among themselves, terrified teenagers have had their homes forcibly entered by police and trading standards officers, their video recorders and video collections seized, and been put in a situation in which they face either an unlimited fine or imprisonment for up to two years, along with the inevitable campaign of vilification by their local papers. (For a full account of this frankly scandalous situation, see Petley, 2000.)

Secondly, the Act is predicated on the notion that certain videos may be actively 'harmful'. Thus when Blue Underground first approached the BBFC with the idea of submitting *Last House* for classification, Robin Duval, in a letter to Carl Daft on 30 April, stated that, in the Board's view: 'the disputed elements in *The Last House on the Left* are "potentially harmful to society" '. This was a reference to the extremely hasty and unwise amendment made to the Video Recordings Act in 1994 in the wake of the ludicrous idea put about by the press and other moral entrepreneurs that watching violent videos had directly 'caused' the murder of James Bulger. The reference was substantiated in a letter that the Board sent to Blue Underground in November, which pointed out that:

> All the cuts we have asked for in *The Last House on the Left* address the 'harm' concerns expressed in s4A of the VRA which directs the Board 'to have special regard (among the other relevant factors) to any harm which may be caused to potential viewers or, through

their behaviour, to society by the manner in which the work deals with (a) criminal behaviour ... (c) violent behaviour or incidents; (d) horrific behaviour or incidents; or (e) human sexual activity'.

Clearly, then, and perhaps hardly surprisingly given the febrile circumstances of its genesis, this is legislation predicated on the crudest possible notion of 'media effects', one that has increasingly been called seriously into question.[1] Indeed, in the course of the appeal, David Pannick reminded the BBFC that even its own *Annual Report 2000* had stated that, on the question of whether videos have an adverse effect on conduct: 'the evidence is, at best, inconclusive', and Robin Duval was forced to admit that: 'though the literature provides reason for concern about the possible social harms that may arise from portrayals of conventional violence in films, videos and on television, the ac-cumulated evidence is not – taken as a whole – conclusive'. This is indeed putting it mildly, and in this context it's perhaps worth quoting Guy Cumberbatch's most recent thoughts on the issue since he, as we shall see shortly, is an expert in whom the Board clearly places a good deal of faith. Thus, in a recent report for the Video Standards Council, he argues that:

The real puzzle is that anyone looking at the research evidence in this field could draw any conclusion about the pattern let alone argue with such confidence and even passion that it demonstrates the harm of violence on television, in film and in video games. While tests of statistical significance are a vital tool of the social sciences, they seem to have been used in this field as instruments of torture on the data until it confesses something which could justify a publication in a scientific journal. If one conclusion is possible, it is that *the jury is not still out. It's never been in.* Media violence has been subjected to lynch mob mentality with almost any evidence used to prove guilt. (Cumberbatch, 2001: 21; emphasis in original)

In the specific case of *Last House on the Left*, the Board argued that it was the way in which the film portrayed the violence inflicted on the two girls that made it so 'harmful' as to necessitate its cutting. In this respect it's important to note that, when Blue Underground first contacted the BBFC about a possible video release of the film, Robin Duval wrote to Carl Daft drawing particular attention to the press release concerning the cutting of the theatrical print of *Baise-Moi* (2000), which states that:

The Board's policy on sexual violence (published in its Classification Guidelines in September 2000) warns that where the portrayal eroticises sexual assault, cuts are likely to be required at any classification level. Additionally, any association of sex with non-consensual restraint, pain or humiliation may be cut. The policy is in part informed by the evidence of media effects research that violent pornography may excite aggressive responses from some male viewers. But the Board also recognises that the graphic presentation of violent non-consensual sex is unlikely to be acceptable to the British public at any level.

There are clearly two issues intertwined here. One is the Board's view that watching certain kinds of imagery involving violence in a sexual context may in itself be 'harmful'. The other is that such imagery may well not be acceptable to a significant number of people – quite probably because they too think it 'harmful'. Let's try to deal with these issues separately, as far as possible.

The Board's own view of the matter of 'harm' was made explicit in Duval's statement to the VAC, in which he quoted approvingly the latest edition of the Independent Television Code, published in Spring 2001, to the effect that:

> Research indicates that there is particular danger in representations of violence in a sexual context. Scenes of rape, or other non-consensual sex, especially where there is graphic physical detail or the action is to any degree prolonged, require great care. Graphic portrayal of violent sexual behaviour, or violence in a sexual context, is justifiable only very exceptionally.

After dealing with the controversy over the alleged effects of non-sexual images of violence, he continued:

> The situation with regard to violence *where there is a sexual or erotic element* is rather different. Here reservations fall away. There is a large and persuasive body of evidence over the years from respected and responsible researchers which shows that, where violence and sex are intermingled, the effects upon some people are likely to be harmful. The people concerned may only represent a small minority of the population (though some researchers would go further than that) but they themselves may be harmed and their actions may have a disproportionate and harmful effect upon society. In line with its specific duties under the VRA, the Board has

concluded that there is more than a sufficient basis in the evidence here for it to treat material of the kind represented by *The Last House on the Left* very cautiously indeed. (Emphasis in original)

Duval was clearly basing his arguments about research into the effects of viewing sexually violent material on an internal BBFC document written in 2002: *Sexual Violence. The Media Effects Research Evidence; a BBFC Review*. According to this, 'the strongest statements of concern come from American academics such as Donnerstein, Malamuth, Check and others'. However, this largely laboratory-based research by which the BBFC sets so much store (although, inevitably, others do not) concerns violent pornography, and is thus irrelevant in the case of *Last House on the Left*, which belongs firmly to a particular sub-genre of the horror film. It might, of course, be relevant if the BBFC were correct in arguing that the film 'eroticises sexual assault', but, as noted elsewhere in this piece, this is a highly questionable and contentious reading of the scenes featuring violence against the women. Indeed, the BBFC's reading and treatment of *Last House* seems to be based on a classic category error; as the feminist writer Avedon Carol has pointed out:

> Although 'video nasties' are often equated with, and mentioned together with, pornography, they are not in the same genre at all. Most genres these days have some sexual content in them, and some horror films use 'sexploitation' techniques, but they are not pornography and they are not sold as pornography. Buyers of pornography expect to see sex, not blood and gore. (Carol, 1994, 80)

It's interesting to note that, in a lecture to the Royal Society of Arts on 21 February 2001, Robin Duval stated that:

> ... our policy, which is clearly expressed in our old and new Guidelines and reiterated in regular public statements, is to take a strong line with material which suggests to younger *or* older viewers that there is pleasure in forcible sex. Most of all, we reject material which endorses the old male 'women like it really' rape myth. One of the reasons we do this is because of the research evidence that that is what turns some men on. And perhaps not just some. You may be aware of the North London and Glasgow Universities research about 18 months ago which found that one in two young British men thinks that raping a woman is acceptable in certain circumstances.

The report in question turns out to be *Young People's Attitudes Towards Violence, Sex and Relationships*, which was carried out for the Zero Tolerance charitable trust and published in 1998; the only problem is, however, that Duval's account of the report seems to have been based on a press caricature of the research findings. Admittedly these don't paint a particularly encouraging picture of the attitudes of *some* young people on these matters, but, without 'torturing the data', the nearest one can get to Duval's assertion is that one in five young men would consider it acceptable to force a woman to have sex were she his wife. After Duval's statement drew predictable gasps of shock from his audience, one of its more sceptical members, Dr Peter Woods, contacted Linda Regan, one of the researchers who worked on the report, who wrote back to the effect that:

> I do not agree with [Robin Duval's] statement – nowhere in the report do we say that one in two young British men thinks that raping a woman is acceptable in certain circumstances ... Robin Duval has chosen to interpret the report in a way that is not what was stated in the report. Unfortunately, as researchers we have no control over things like that!

In his statement to the VAC, Duval also argued that:

> It is important to be clear that the main significance of evidence of this nature from a regulatory point of view is that it identifies an essential area of policy concern. It does not tell us that any single work by itself will have a significant effect. But it does provide a clear warning about the harmfulness that would arise from the wider availability of similar abusive material. The concern is that ready accessibility would feed and stimulate individual pre-dispositions to abusive behaviour. As ever, the regulatory issue is one of precedent.

Thus *Last House on the Left* and, presumably, the 19 other videos that Duval revealed had been cut – one, *The House on the Edge of the Park* (1979), by nearly 12 minutes – in order to gain an '18' certificate, appear to have been judged not solely on their own merits and demerits but, to some extent, according to the well-worn 'finger in the dyke' principle. This may seem hardly fair to individual films, but this argument from quantity does, of course, enable the BBFC to get round the familiar criticism that snipping out little bits from one particular film does nothing to alleviate its allegedly 'harmful' qualities.

Turning to the allegedly 'harmful' qualities of *Last House* in particular, we find Robin Duval responding to David Pannick's remark that the violence in *Last House* was hardly exceptional in that 'humiliation, entrail-pulling and attacks with knives are all staples of the horror genre' by arguing that:

> Of course the BBFC has in the past allowed scenes of humiliation and attacks with knives. But, when assessing the suitability for classification of a sequence, the BBFC will always take into account the context within which the acts occur and the amount of detail, particularly of a violent and sexual character, which is shown. If the activity is unconvincingly portrayed, undetailed, comic, brief, or lacking in any elements which sexualize the violence, threat or humiliation, then the Board is less likely to require cuts. By contrast, in works in which such activities are portrayed with realistic brutality, graphically, at length and with elements that sexualize, the scenes will always be treated with great caution. They have been consistently cut by the BBFC.

Of *Last House* itself, he stated that: 'the technical and narrative crudeness of the film makes it difficult to justify except as an exploitative exercise in portraying extreme violence'. Noting that Wes Craven had gone on to direct the *Scream* series, he observed that: 'the parodic touch often apparent in that series is wholly absent from the presentation of the violence in *The Last House on the Left*, which is brutal and naturalistic with no possibly redeeming arguments of fantasy, comedy or social comment'.

The problem with this kind of approach is that, as already noted, it rests on a reading of *Last House* that runs completely counter to that of the experts on the film genre who have commented on the film. But there again, if censors accepted the full implications of the idea, now commonplace in media and cultural studies, that different readings of the same text are perfectly possible, they would simply be making themselves redundant. (For a useful summary of recent work on viewers' perceptions of violent imagery, see Firmstone (2002).) However, Duval's remarks about 'context' and *Scream* also suggest that things haven't progressed all that far beyond the days when, as Mark Kermode laments: 'horror cinema in Britain was hamstrung by the demands of a censor board which insisted that it could be anything but horrific' (Kermode, 2002b: 14–15).

'Public Opinion'

We turn now to the second issue involved in the Board's attitude to violent imagery, and especially violent imagery involving sexual elements: namely the acceptability to the public of such imagery.

In his statement to the VAC, Duval began by referring to some of the findings that arose from the BBFC's lengthy process of public consultation in 1999–2000, pointing out that:

> There was special concern about violence generally. 46 per cent of the national sample (base: 1249) were of the opinion that watching violence in films generally makes people more likely to be violent in real life. However, 51 per cent believed the BBFC violence guidelines were 'about right'. 42 per cent thought they were not strict enough. Most significantly, perhaps, only 5 per cent thought the guidelines were too strict.

With particular reference to the two Citizens' Juries that the Board organized (and before one of which, I should declare, I appeared as an expert witness), he noted that: 'their main concern was sexual violence, which they felt strongly should be handled with great care. One jury stipulated that it should not be allowed unless it was shown in a negative light'. Duval concluded that: 'the Board believes that it is reasonable to place some weight on the commonsense opinion of ordinary people in this area ... The reaction of ordinary people in general to what material may cause harm is of importance to the Board'.

He also drew attention to a survey conducted by the aforementioned Guy Cumberbatch for the Communications Research Group, which found that only 38 per cent of the 276 video-renting adults in the survey 'thought adults had the right to see graphic portrayals of sexual violence in videos and films' (with, it might be added, 34 per cent disagreeing and 27 per cent being unable to decide). The survey also included evidence culled from a viewing panel of 12 men and 13 women; these found *Last House* the most unacceptable of a group of films whose other members were *Straw Dogs* (1971), *A Clockwork Orange* (1971), *Death Wish II* (1982), *Baise-Moi* and *I Spit on Your Grave*. However, nine of the men on the panel decided that it should not be cut, whereas 11 of the women favoured either cuts or an outright ban. All but one of the panellists (i.e. 96 per cent) found the treatment of women sadistic, and 67 per cent agreed that the film invited the viewer to enjoy the spectacle of young women being stripped and killed. The panel concluded that: 'it was the absence of context or justification which made the unpleasant scenes in *Last House on the Left* so troublesome'. The fact that this is the whole point of the film, along with the revelation that the majority (67 per cent) of the panel read the film in a way with which horror experts clearly disagree, makes one wonder just how familiar were most of the panel members with the horror genre – or at least its more recent entrants. This in turn raises issues both about their competence to judge it – and similar horror films – and the weight that the BBFC ought to attach to their judgements. Equally, how much store should the Board set by 'public opinion', however diligently gathered, when the public has been subjected to more than 20 years of press stories about 'video nasties', stories which even the BBFC is now prepared to admit are largely prurient, sensationalist nonsense?

On 17 June 2002 the VAC delivered its verdict. The omens were not good. Early in its detailed judgement it warned that: 'at present, public opinion is greatly concerned at the violence prevailing in our society especially when weapons such as knives are used'. When it came to considering the evidence presented by Mark Kermode in the film's defence, the committee seemed to be holding its metaphorical nose, sniffily and peremptorily dismissing it as 'difficult to accept'. In the end, however, it was the matter of 'effects' that sank the appeal. On this question the Committee was adamant, stating that:

> We do not have any doubt that there is real concern among the public about the effects of showing violence, particularly upon children and vulnerable adults. Much of the violent crime com-mitted in this county is by young adults and the current level of knife related crime is high. There must also be a worry that a work such as the *Last House on the Left* will fuel this violence and cause susceptible viewers to imitate some of the scenes in it.

In this respect the film could indeed be harmful, and thus contravened the VRA. The Committee concluded its deliberations by stating that:

> We found it an unpleasant work with, we believe, the danger that parts may be imitated, especially the humiliating urination scene. We agree that there is a continual atmosphere of sexuality and violence and that the violence is sexual violence. The viewer is asked to relish the violence, the violence is relentless and the parts to be cut are the extreme end of that violence and humiliation. We are of the opinion that a significant number of viewers would be

fascinated by the violence and excited into amoral behaviour, in other words, harm may be caused ... We repeat, violence is greatly concerning the public especially the use of weapons, in particular knives which is a common denominator of this video. We need only rule upon 16 seconds of cuts but we are bound to say, using the words of Mr Duval in paragraph 36 of his statement, that we think the Board has been 'generous to the film-maker', indeed inappropriately so in our view, and we believe that this would be the view of the public.

The appeal was unanimously dismissed.

On 28 June Blue Underground received a Cuts Letter, which had been revised in the light both of the VAC's comments and Cumberbatch's research. The scenes that the Board required to be cut remained the same, but the total amount of time to be excised from one of these scenes (that involving the entrail-pulling) was increased from 3 to 18 seconds, making a total of 31 seconds in all to be removed. At first it appeared as if an outraged Daft would refuse to make the cuts and thus leave the video effectively banned from UK distribution. However, having purchased the video rights to the film, as well as entering into an extremely costly action with the BBFC and VAC, he had little option, ultimately, but to accede to their demands, and the video was passed on 17 July with the requisite 31 seconds of cuts. Subsequently a number of DVD extras were submitted and classified '18' without cuts, under the title *Celluloid Crime of the Century*.

What, then, does the sorry saga of *Last House on the Left* tell us about the regulation of violent images on video in Britain today – apart, that is, from the fact that horror video distributors would be well advised to steer clear of the VAC? The short answer is that these remain highly regulated – too highly for some, but, then again, not highly enough for others, as we have seen. Robin Duval's regime at the BBFC has undoubtedly been more open and liberal than that of his predecessor James Ferman – witness, for example, the passing without cuts on video and DVD of two notorious Ferman bugbears, *Straw Dogs* and *The Exorcist* (1973) – but, there again, less liberal than he sometimes likes to suggest (as in Petley, 2001: 30). On the other hand, openly to profess to liberal values when answerable to a liberal-baiting Home Secretary such as Jack Straw, and now a Minister for Culture, Media and Sport, Tessa Jowell, who appeared to be perfectly prepared, at the first howl of outrage from the *Daily Mail*, to condemn a television programme such as *Brass Eye* which she apparently had not even seen, is a protestation not to be taken lightly. Equally encouraging is the Board's apparent determination never again to allow itself to be bullied by the hypocritical humbug of Fleet Street's finest.

The real lesson of this piece, however, is that the Board is not, in many matters, its own master, and has constantly to be aware of not only the laws of the land – in particular the OPA and VRA – but also of how these are interpreted by the police, judges, magistrates and juries. If it is to retain public confidence it also needs to take into account public opinion, although how it should gauge this is an extremely difficult matter, given the populist ranting posing as 'public opinion' in much of the press, and the influence on many people's perceptions of the video industry of 20 years of ludicrous and distorted twaddle about 'video nasties'. If, as the Board's experiments with Citizens' Juries, 'Road Shows', published guidelines (BBFC, 2000) and various other forms of *glasnost* would seem to indicate, it is attempting seriously to inform and educate, as well as simply respond to, people's opinions, then this can only be thoroughly positive and welcome. Doubtless such a move will be condemned as 'liberal propaganda' by papers such as the *Mail*, which, rather than attempting to enlighten and inform people, would apparently rather whip up and exploit their fears for their own dubious and authoritarian ends; but if we are to have a serious debate about not simply video violence but the whole complex apparatus of film and video regulation in this country, then this is a very sensible and necessary first step.

Notes

1. See, for example, Cumberbatch and Howitt, 1989; Gauntlett, 1995; Cumberbatch, 2001; Barker and Petley, 1997/2001; Freedman, 2002. For an account of the woeful process whereby a piece of legislation premised on the sub-medieval idea of images actually 'harming' people made its way onto the statute book, see Petley (1994).

References

Barker, M. and Petley, J. (eds) (1997/2001) *Ill Effects: the Media/Violence Debate*, London: Routledge.

British Board of Film Classification (2000) *BBFC Classification Guidelines*, London: British Board of Film Classification.

Carol, A. (1994) *Nudes, Prudes and Attitudes: Pornography and Censorship*, Cheltenham: New Clarion Press.

Cumberbatch, G. (2001) *Video Violence: Villain or Victim?*, Borehamwood: Video Standards Council.

Cumberbatch, G. and Howitt D. (1989) *A Measure of Uncertainty: The Effects of the Mass Media*, London: John Libbey.

Firmstone, J. (2002) *Discerning Eyes: Viewers on Violence*, Luton: University of Luton Press.

Freedman, J.L. (2002) *Media Violence and its Effect on Aggression*, Toronto: University of Toronto Press.

Gauntlett, D. (1995) *Moving Experiences: Understanding Television's Influences and Effects*, London: John Libbey.

Kermode, M. (2002a) 'What Are They Scared Of?', *Independent*, 21 June.

Kermode, M. (2002b) 'The British Censors and Horror Cinema', in S. Chibnall and J. Petley (eds) *British Horror Cinema*, London: Routledge, 10–22.

Newman, K. (1988) *Nightmare Movies: A Critical History of the Horror Movie from 1968*, London: Bloomsbury.

Petley, J. (1994) 'In Defence of "Video Nasties"', *British Journalism Review*, 5(3), 52–7. Reprinted in T. O'Sullivan and Y. Jewkes (eds) (1997) *The Media Studies Reader*, London: Arnold, 188–95.

Petley, J. (2000a) 'The Censor and the State: Or Why *Horny Catbabe* Matters', *Journal of Popular British Cinema*, 3, 93–103.

Petley, J. (2000b) 'Snuffed Out: Nightmares in a Trading Standards Officer's Brain', in X. Mendik and G. Harper (eds) *Unruly Pleasures: the Cult Film and its Critics*, Guildford: FAB Press.

Petley, J. (2001) 'Raising the Bar', *Sight and Sound*, 11(12), December, 30–2.

Robertson, G. (1979) *Obscenity: An Account of Censorship Laws and Their Enforcement in England and Wales*, London: Weidenfeld and Nicolson.

Robertson, G. and Nicol, A. (2002) *Robertson and Nicol on Media Law*, London: Sweet and Maxwell.

Chapter 3

'Signal crimes': detective work, mass media and constructing collective memory

Martin Innes

Certain crimes seem to capture the mood of the times. In Britain, over the past decade, the killings of Holly Wells and Jessica Chapman, Amanda Dowler, Damilola Taylor, Sarah Payne, Stephen Lawrence and Jamie Bulger among others, have been the focus of extensive and extended media reporting. The mass-media coverage has been particularly important for its role in articulating and coordinating a social reaction to the individual cases that goes beyond the immediate concerns of the cases themselves. Each of these incidents has been accompanied by widespread popular concern that it signals that something is wrong with British society and its criminal justice process, which requires some form of corrective response. The murders of Holly Wells and Jessica Chapman, and of Damilola Taylor, led to concerns about the lifestyles and security of children in rural and urban communities respectively. These cases echoed concerns that had been expressed nearly a decade previously in respect of the Jamie Bulger case. The murder of Sarah Payne in Sussex resulted in a sustained media campaign and public demonstrations for greater control of known and suspected paedophiles. Perhaps the most influential case though was that concerning the murder of Stephen Lawrence, which evolved into a widespread examination of the presence of institutional racism in the criminal justice process. Even after the criminal justice process has concluded, traces of these crimes and their investigation remain in the public memory, as signifiers of some of the problems of manufacturing social control in late-modernity.

In these cases and others like them in both Britain and America, journalists have delved into the pasts of the victims, their families, potential suspects and the police investigation, to produce highly detailed accounts of the incident, its supposed precipitating causes and the outcomes of its occurrence. The mediated accounts and representations of these crimes have not simply reported the facts of the cases, they have functioned as dramatic articulations of popular fears about the seeming encroachment of the forces of disorder, drawing upon diffuse and inchoate existential anxieties about the state of contemporary society (Giddens, 1991).

In this chapter my aim is to deconstruct the process by which such 'signal crimes' are manufactured, in order to identify what are the sufficient and necessary conditions for their existence. I deploy the concept of 'signal crime' to capture how and why the social reaction to certain crimes by the media audience, based largely on the affective and informational content of mediated representations, may involve a change in their belief system and/or their taking some form of protective action. In effect then, the crime becomes important not just on its own account, but also as a signification. It is 'read' by the audience as a warning signal that something is wrong in society and some form of behavioural or cognitive adaptation is required.

In addressing this issue I am particularly concerned to show how the relationships that often exist or develop between police detectives investigating murders, and journalists reporting on their work, contribute to the creation of signal crimes in both intended and unintended ways.[1] The chapter starts by establishing a more refined definition of the concept of a signal crime. I then discuss how media use policing as both a topic and source for news, before looking at the benefits to police of such relations. I conclude by looking at the wider implications of the notion of signal crimes and what it tells us about the role of media in the politics of late-modern criminal justice.

Signal Crimes

Signal crimes can be defined as events that, in addition to affecting the immediate participants (i.e. victims, witnesses, offenders) and those known to them, impact in some way upon a wider audience. The nature of the impact upon this wider audience varies, but it will cause them to reconfigure their behaviours or beliefs in some way. The response to the signal may involve either an individual or collective decision to make changes to the environment through situational crime-prevention measures; modifications to routine activities to integrate risk-avoidance techniques; political demands for more policing, laws and social control;

and a less explicit, but equally important reframing of the cognitive maps that people use to locate potential dangers and threats in everyday life. Thus the initial reaction to the signal presented by the crime is fear about the risks posed by a source of danger, followed by some form of cognitive or behavioural adaptation.

This conceptual definition draws upon and seeks to integrate elements from several theoretical perspectives. Firstly, in stressing the semiotic properties of crime, the concept of signal crimes is informed by the evolving field of social semiotics (Hodge and Kress, 1988; Eco, 1983; Manning, 1996a). In particular, the definition blends elements of social semiotic theory with the perspective of symbolic interactionism, derived from the work of Mead (1962) and his followers. Interactionist sociology traditionally stresses the importance of signification, agentive inter-pretation and the functions of social reaction, thereby complementing the focus of social semiotics. The third theoretical influence is the developing area of cognitive sociology, which itself is informed by elements of symbolic interactionism and a number of associated perspectives, stressing the ways in which thinking styles and belief systems are always socially ordered (Cerulo, 2002; Vaughan, 2002).

Although the focus of this discussion is upon aspects of mediated communication, it should be noted that the definition of signal crimes provided above incorporates not just mediated processes of signifi-cation, but can also account for events and processes that take place at more parochial and local levels. For example, in their discussions of local community orders, both Skogan (1990) and Wilson and Kelling (1982) stress the impact of physical and social disorders in stimulating a process of 'community tipping' towards greater levels of disorder. In my terms, the presence of physical and social disorders are enacted as signal crimes by residents, indicative of the need for protective action. The course of action selected is likely to depend upon the social, political and economic resources available, but may include either a retreat from public space by members of the community, or alternatively, the insti-gation of informal or formal social controls to deal with the perceived causes of the deviance.[2] Failure to provide a quick response to a criminal or disorderly event by a community may also signal messages to potential deviants that this a suitable place to commit acts of de-linquency. However, for the purposes of this chapter, I am less concerned with such locally based problems. My focus is restricted to how the interventions of journalists in serious crime investigations, and their interactions with police investigators, contributes to the construction of signal crimes at a regional, national or international level.

In their seminal analyses of the processes of moral panic, both Cohen

(1972) and Hall *et al.* (1978) documented how journalistic techniques lead to certain key incidents becoming the focus of a symbolically loaded representation of a particular 'crime problem' that implicitly or explicitly references wider popular fears and concerns. Such symbolizations generate demands among the populace for solutions to the perceived problem, which results in growing pressure and demands for an expansion of the 'social control net' (Cohen, 1985). What Cohen's concept of moral panic thereby identifies is that there is a process of signification at work in the mediated processes of reporting of crime, which given the right story 'ingredients' and a particular set of social conditions, can be generative of a profound social reaction.

This focus upon the importance of processes of signification in constructing and defining public problems coheres with the findings of a wider research literature that has documented the role of mediated communication in the construction of a variety of popular fears and concerns. In particular, the growing literature on risk perception in relation to genetic, environmental and health hazards has started to provide greater understanding of how the arrangement of various signifiers shapes the fabrication of signified threats.

Studies of risk perception have shown that people do not respond to hazards or dangers in an objective, rational fashion; rather their threat assessments and reactions are moulded in accordance with an extant universe of cultural meanings and culturally legitimated explanations (Douglas, 1992). Furthermore, as Cutter (1993) has shown through studying health risks, people tend to worry more about high-profile, extra-ordinary, dramatic and visible risks than they do about the comparatively invisible hazards that they are routinely exposed to. In an effort to capture these cognitive processes, Slovic (1992) has sought to determine the 'signal value' of different hazards. By 'signal value' he means the 'significatory' properties that make people attend to some dangers rather than others. Confirming the findings of Cutter and other similar studies, Slovic identifies that popular fears tend to gravitate around dramatic, high-visibility risks that occur in poorly understood social systems. Although grounded in a social-psychological approach to risk perception, Slovic's approach to the dynamics and processes involved in apprehending threats and dangers can be usefully blended with the principles of social semiotics, thereby establishing an innovative conceptual framework through which to explore mediated representations of crime.

The usefulness of such a framework is illustrated by identifying the parallels between concerns about crime and other risks. The cases that tend to be routinely featured in media reportage and that become the focus for extended coverage tend to be the comparatively rare forms of serious violent crime (Soothill and Walby, 1991). In effect then, the cases that generate popular concern tend to be the extra-ordinary, dramatic, highly visible crimes, rather than those crimes that people are statistically most at risk of being a victim of. This directly mirrors Slovic's (1992) findings that certain incidents have a 'high' signal value, which establish them as focal points for popular concerns.

Media Using Policing

Analyses of crime in the media have repeatedly documented a pro-pensity for both fictional and factual coverage to focus upon serious crime and the role of police investigators in responding to such incidents (Reiner, 1997). As Sparks (1991) identifies, this orientation results in the communication of morality tales by journalists to their audiences, which convey the fundamental desirability of social order and the role of police as a 'thin blue line' acting to hold the forces of disorder at bay. This focus upon serious crime reflects the sense of drama that is inherent in these sorts of stories (Ericson *et al.*, 1987).

More pragmatically though, it has been identified that the pre-disposition of journalists towards crime stories also reflects the peculiar demands of their occupation. Just like any other bureaucratic organi-zation, the news office has to maintain a steady supply of product to meet the demands of their audience. Thus crime news is good news because it is almost guaranteed that there will be a steady supply of interesting, 'newsworthy' stories, which the journalist can draw upon as and when needed. As Rock (1973) explains, it is these bureaucratic demands that contribute to the 'eternal recurrence' of news through ritualized, cyclical and solipsistic routines of production.

Journalists work in accordance with particular medium, format and organizational constraints to produce stories that are attractive to their target audience. Most stories about crime are fairly simple narratives, where, as far as journalists and their audience are concerned, the details relayed about particular events in the world are merely part of the ongoing daily flow of news. A minority of these stories seem to have a bigger impact, though. For example, certain crime stories are covered for a long time by nearly every national and sometimes international media outlet (Innes, 1999). Almost invariably these stories relate to crimes of murder, often involving a 'good victim', that is a middle-class female, an attractive woman or a child. As a result of their high signal values, they can become akin to Manning's (1996b) notion of 'an axial political event' in the field of the criminal justice system: generating a considerable amount of popular fear and concern; stimulating popular and political debate about 'the crime problem'; sometimes leading to 'moral entrepreneurship' campaigns and reforms of the law or criminal justice practice. Thus they have a pivotal role in the production of what Altheide (1997: 648) dubs 'the problem frame':

> The problem frame promotes a discourse of fear that may be defined as the pervasive communication, symbolic awareness and expectation that danger and risk are a central feature of the effective environment.

But in order to explain what it is about these minority of cases that generates such a profound social reaction, we cannot look solely to characteristics of media organizations; we need to look also at the role of the police in this relationship.

Policing Using Media

The police constitute a key source for news organizations. For both national and local media outlets, the police and their investigations represent a staple ingredient of the daily diet of news. But as will become apparent, for the police too, there are advantages to be gleaned from cooperating with journalists.

As I have discussed elsewhere (Innes, 1999), the mass media constitute an important resource for detectives when investigating major crimes. Media interest in such cases can be harnessed by detectives in an effort to publicize the crime and thereby potentially generate new information from people who might have witnessed the incident, know the victim, or who might be able to identify possible suspects for the crime (Innes, 1999). This use and manipulation of media interest by police in the furtherance of their objectives reflects the fact that crime investigation is essentially a form of 'information work'. The role of the police investigation is to identify and interpret information about a past incident in order to construct an evidenced narrative account of what happened, thereby identifying who was responsible for committing the offence (Innes, 2003). As with other forms of investigative work though, detectives working on homicide enquiries are dependent to a significant extent on members of the public, cast as victims and witnesses, to provide them with the information they need to conduct their work (Hobbs, 1988; Greenwood et al., 1977).

Mediated communication is valuable to an investigation in this sense because it provides a mechanism for contacting a large number of people, quickly and over a wide area, for a comparatively small investment of resources. It thereby potentially enables detectives to acquire the information they need to identify a suspect or to understand how the crime happened. Such tactics are of particular consequence in late-modern societies where many people enjoy a significant amount of mobility in their everyday routines (Innes, 1999). Therefore, police have to be aware that the witnesses to a crime or those who might be in a position to nominate a suspect for a crime may not live locally, but may be dispersed over a wider geographic area. And although traditional investigative strategies such as house-to-house enquiries are often effective in identifying important information from the immediate vicinity of the crime, they have to be used in a geographically targeted manner, and consequently are less likely to be effective in locating anyone with relevant information from outside the local area.

The use of media as an investigative resource is based upon a number of interlocking strategies. Amongst the most commonly employed are:

- police appeals
- family appeals
- victim portraits
- reconstructions
- publicizing rewards.

I will now examine each of these in turn and, although for the purposes of analysis it is useful to separate these strategies, it is important to note that in practice they are frequently used in combination.

Police appeals

It is now commonplace for the Senior Investigating Officer (SIO) on a hard-to-solve murder to develop a media strategy for the purposes of assisting the progress of the ongoing enquiry. This is guided by two motivations. The first is to try to generate information from the public. The second, equally important consideration, is concerned with managing the interests of journalists. One thing that the police complain about regularly on high-profile investigations is that journalists, motivated by the possibility of getting a 'scoop', will interfere in the investigation by trying to identify and contact the victim's family and witnesses to get a story. But such actions can significantly impede the progress of the police investigation. As a consequence, it is now established policy for either the SIO, or their representative on an investigation, to provide regular updates to journalists in an effort to prevent them pursuing their own leads in a way that might harm the police's work.

Although for both police officers and journalists these appeals are often newsworthy events, in actuality they are fairly ritualized in terms of how they take place. Media communications made by investigating officers have been subject to increasing levels of governance in recent years, with detailed prescriptive guidance being issued on what to say and what not to say. Journalists are notified of the questions that the SIO or their representative will or will not be prepared to answer and the script used by officers is now fairly standardized.

Family appeals

An alternative to the SIO making an appeal is for members of the victim's family to perform this task. From the point of view of journalists this has advantages in that the higher emotional content of such appeals, when counterposed with the cool, detached professionalism of a police officer, makes for a better story. From the police's point of view it is important in that the visceral grief and emotion that is frequently displayed by family members in such circumstances, can be assumed to be more effective in persuading a member of the audience who thinks they know something about the crime to contact the police. But police are also aware that emotional displays of this kind make a good story for journalists and thus the case will receive more media coverage than it might otherwise do.

There are of course risks attached to encouraging family members to participate in staged appeals of this kind. The most obvious risk is that at a later stage of the investigation it may be revealed that one of the family members appealing for help from the public was involved in the commission of the crime. This has occurred in several now infamous cases. There are also problems in ensuring that the right message is communicated via the media. As will be discussed shortly, one problem of such strategies is that they can generate a vast amount of information, and just as too little information can impede an investigation, a rapid influx of information can also serve to limit the progress being made. Encouraging family members to participate in appeals also lays the police open to accusations of insensitivity and exploiting people who are in a difficult situation. However, it seems that some surviving family members often appreciate the opportunity to contribute to the investigation and to be doing something positive to assist in catching the killer (Rock, 1998).

Victim portraits

A particularly subtle way in which detectives seek to generate publicity for an investigation relates to the selection and publication of pictures of the victim. It is obvious that television is a visual medium, but this has manifest implications for which stories are covered on television news and how they are reported. The production values within contemporary television news organizations means that if a story is to be covered, some form of visual material will be required to ensure that the story can be presented in a sufficiently stimulating manner. Although visual material is less of a prerequisite for newspaper coverage of a major investigation, big stories certainly tend to be accompanied by visuals, and these often include photos of the victim released to the press by police. For both televised and newspaper stories, the presence of evocative visual materials increases the impact of the story concerned.

In making photographs or videos of victims available to the press, detectives are careful to try to control the image that is portrayed of the deceased. They know that particular types of photographs of particular types of victim are likely to be used by journalists covering a story. Even a cursory review of the national newspapers is sufficient to demonstrate that photographs of certain types of victims are more frequently used than others. Children and young, attractive women would be the archetypes of the victims whose pictures get used regularly in media crime stories.

Pictures of the victim are important to the police in generating publicity for a case, and detectives put a lot of effort into identifying a good photograph that can be used in a media campaign. Images are deliberately selected to convey the message to the media audience that the victim was a nice person and innocent of blame. Such symbolically loaded imagery is also felt to implicitly convey a sense that it is imperative that the perpetrator of the crime is caught, and the public should assist in this effort if they can. It is noticeable in a number of recent cases that this has been emphasized by police releasing pictures of the charged suspect taken in custody, thereby amplifying the 'demonization' of the perpetrator.

Reconstructions

Reconstructions are the most complex media strategies employed by police. They involve a considerable amount of effort to organize, require considerable resources to conduct, and hence are used comparatively rarely. The use of reconstructions tends to be restricted to especially high-profile cases where the police lines of enquiry are not progressing through more standard methods. The use of reconstructions is frequently justified by senior officers on the basis that it might help to jog someone's memory about something they witnessed potentially relating to the commission of the offence. However, there is as yet little evidence to support or contest the effectiveness of reconstructions in achieving this objective.

Publicizing rewards

Police appeals for information about a serious crime in the media are often accompanied by details of a reward on offer. Incentivizing the provision of information that may help to 'break' an otherwise hard-to-solve case is one way that police attempt to overcome any resistance that they feel there may be on the part of potential witnesses. But it is important to note that the announcement of a reward is itself a newsworthy event in the progress of an ongoing high-profile enquiry. As with some of the other strategies discussed previously, it is important to acknowledge that the publicizing of a reward is not necessarily one of the principal strategies associated with the investigative methodology used on homicide enquiries. Rather a reward may be publicized when the standard investigative strategies, such as house-to-house enquiries, tasking informants and researching family members and acquaintances, have been exhausted (Innes, 2003).

The use of the media as an investigative resource through deploying these strategies, either individually or in combination, can have a number of objectives for the police. Firstly, it is a way of seeking to increase the sense of psychological pressure felt by the offender, with the intention that it should encourage the person to turn him or herself in to the police, or to make an 'uncovering move' that will unwittingly reveal them to the investigation. Secondly, the strategy can be directed by a notion that it will encourage potential witnesses who may have seen something connected to the crime to come forward and tell the police about this. Thirdly, it may encourage people who have suspicions that someone known to them was involved in the commission of the crime, to forward their suspicions to the police. These three objectives are fairly instrumental. There is though a fourth, more expressive objective that underpins police cooperation with the media, reflecting the wider politics of criminal justice in contemporary society. This objective relates to the sense that managing public perceptions of policing through positive portrayals of police work is imperative to sustaining popular support for the police at a time when public trust in key institutions is increasingly fragile. Senior officers are aware of the fact that portrayals of police investigating serious crimes about which there is considerable public concern is a potentially important resource in 'the battle for the hearts and minds of the public' (Innes, 1999; Schlesinger and Tumber, 1994). They often seek to exploit these cases accordingly, allowing journalists 'on the inside' of high-profile investigations, in order to convey a positive message to the public. A similar approach is often attempted when an enquiry is facing mounting criticism about its seeming lack of progress.

From an SIO's point of view, generating a high public profile for an investigation can bring other advantages. It can be a useful device for securing or sustaining high levels of resource investment in an investigation. It is much harder for the management within the police organization to withdraw resources from an ongoing investigation if there is considerable media attention focused upon it. Therefore, it is possible to surmise that it can, in certain circumstances, be in the SIO's interests to ensure that the case receives widespread media attention, if he or she perceives a threat to the resourcing of their enquiry.

In his account of media–police relations Chibnall (1977) noted that the specialization of crime reporters in the major news organizations, together with a similar specialization among senior detectives, often contributed to the development of close relations between individuals as it led to the same small group of people investigating and reporting on the same cases. Changes in the news media and changes in the organization of policing and the role of detective work mean that these relationships are less likely to be present nowadays. The exception is the local media, where relationships between individual reporters and individual detectives may still be consequential. At a national level, cooperation between police and national news organizations is less likely to be based upon personal relations; rather it tends to be motivated by the sorts of structural pressures and mutual benefits that I have outlined above.

Overall then, the participation of police in media communications is frequently crucial to establishing a particular incident as a signal crime. Press conferences, reconstructions, distributing images and employing dramatic and emotional language are all ways in which the police, in seeking to advance their investigation, can contribute to an incident achieving a high public profile.

Communication Problems

Although there are potential benefits to be accrued by detectives in enlisting media organizations as investigative resources, there are attendant problems that accompany such an approach. The first problem is associated with a condition of 'information overload'. The second problem area relates to those circumstances where, for whatever reason, the investigation fails.

Using media to try to generate potentially relevant information from the public necessarily tends to produce a lot of irrelevant material for an investigation. If we consider the dynamics of the communicative process concerned, the nature of the problem is fairly self-evident. Mass-mediated communication is not targeted towards individual audience members; indeed the power of the respective media of communication is founded upon the ability to communicate the same information to many people (who may interpret it in different ways). However, when using media to try to track down potential witnesses, the police are effectively seeking to use them in a targeted fashion. Very few people out of the whole audience for a media appeal are likely to be in possession of information that is directly relevant to the police's interest. Therefore, in principle, it is in the investigators' interests to target their appeals as much as they can. This is particularly difficult to achieve, however, because it contradicts the primary pressure that in order to attract widespread media attention in the first place, the message to be communicated has to meet the journalistic criterion of 'newsworthiness' – that is, it should be interesting and accessible to a wide audience.

Therefore, because of the ways in which they work, media-based information-generating strategies designed to elicit information from the public frequently result in large amounts of data being forwarded to police from the public. Much of the material will prove to be irrelevant to the police interests. Nevertheless, detectives have to work through all of the information in an effort to identify whether there are any good leads in among all the misinformation and disinformation.

When media appeals are made by police as part of an investigation, they are aware that such a strategy is likely to generate a lot of ultimately useless information. Nevertheless, my research suggests that such aspects of major crime enquiries are frequently mis-handled. It is not unusual for communications to be insufficiently focused, overly speculative, or made too early in an enquiry before the issues of the case have been established, leading to a risk of swamping the investigation with information. This information overload can ultimately slow down the progress of the investigation, or in the most extreme cases, lead to a failure to identify the crucial lead or clue from the available information.

A second concern about the use of media as an investigative resource is that while there are advantages to using media to stimulate the provision of information from the public, it is important that investigative success follows from this. If detectives encourage media to participate and collaborate in an investigation by providing them with a high profile, the police will have created problems for themselves should the investigation subsequently fail to identify a suspect or to secure a prosecution. This represents an important point, in that for the viewing public, the signals that are associated with a crime can be as much about the failure of the police or the entire criminal justice process to respond effectively to the crime problem. For example, the Stephen Lawrence case was a signal crime for the problems it indicated in respect of the policing of minority-ethnic communities in Britain.

The Politics of Late-Modern Criminal Justice

According to a number of social theorists, we live in a historical era that is defined by the production and communication of information (Lash, 2001; Poster, 1991; Castells, 1996). Mediated communication is a central facet of this 'information age', relaying information between otherwise temporally and spatially separate actors, in the process blurring what were for former generations distinct public and private information systems (Meyrowitz, 1985). It can take what is an essentially private act, such as a murder, and rapidly make the details widely known. It is this dynamic that establishes media as potentially useful in the investigative process. Having identified both how and why detectives and media collaborate in publicizing individual cases, I now want to consider how such cooperation both reflects and is constitutive of wider social trends.

Culture and stories

In his discussion of the anthroplogy of culture, Geertz (1973) draws attention to the functions of what he dubs 'the stories a culture tells itself about itself'. For Geertz, culture is an ongoing accomplishment that is produced and reproduced via the content of the narratives that members tell to each other. In late-modernity, media play a key role in such processes, selecting stories about events and working up figurative representations about them, which will be collectively shared. In fact, media can be understood as a complex organizational system designed for the performance of this function. Crime, deviance and the response to such acts are one of the most common forms of story told via the mass media (Reiner, 1997). They are thus important to our culture inasmuch as they provide an institutionalized form of story-telling, wherein symbolic demarcations of the sacred from the profane, and the pure from the impure, are provided (Douglas, 1966).

These morality tales become particularly important in the context of a historical juncture, where as Garland (2001) describes, crime and the formulation of adaptive responses to it have become a defining concern for contemporary cultural formations. Within this 'late-modern crime complex' a number of previously inchoate and nebulous fears and concerns about social life and the potential dangers that assail us have become channelled and articulated through the crime problem, and its associated phenomenon of the fear of crime (Garland, 2001; Girling *et al.*, 2000). Detailed media coverage of a small number of particularly serious signal crimes has had a role to play in fostering the development of this complex. Such incidents have provided 'hyper-real' examples of the problems about which people are concerned, and as a result of the widespread media coverage that these signal crimes have received, citizens have shared knowledge of these events, thus allowing them to debate and consider them. Thus the media has played a key role not in defining what people think, but what issues they think about.

Crime Investigation and the Creation of 'Collective Memory'

Murder enquiries, as forms of 'reactive' crime investigation,[3] involve the interpretation of the physical detritus of the event, combined with accounts from victims, witnesses and suspects, in order to reconstruct the past incident and thereby establish a sense of what happened and who was responsible. In effect, the role of the police investigation is to construct a narrative account of who did what to whom, based upon the information and evidence available. Of course this account may be contested to a greater or lesser degree by various members of the audience, including the suspect, witnesses, or even victims (May, 2000; Rock, 1998). However, if the narrative that is manufactured via the police enquiry is accepted and legitimated by the decision of the court, then the police narrative becomes the accepted public definition of the event and how it took place.

When such narratives are reported by the mass media, particularly on the high-profile signal crime investigations that I have discussed, the products of the police investigation become something more than a way of publicly defining and classifying the nature of a particular incident. They provide the material for the construction of a 'collective memory'. In detailing how police have defined the situation and reporting who is the victim and who the perpetrator of the act, to a wider audience, the media contribute to establishing how this event is to be publicly remembered.

The concept of 'collective memory' was coined by Maurice Halbwachs (1992) to capture the ways in which social groups, communities and cultures manufacture shared understandings of their shared pasts according to present concerns. These memories held in common tend to gravitate around key events, becoming the focus for symbolically loaded forms of commemoration that reconfigure what is remembered in the light of current circumstances (Schwartz, 1997). Drawing upon Mead's (1932) theory of the past, it can be identified that the collective memory creation process symbolically reconstructs the past event as a reflection of the situated present, in an effort to legitimate a particular collective understanding. Memories of significant crimes, alongside other events, thus become mnemonics for reading the present (Fine, 2002).

In late-modernity, mass-media reporting of certain high-profile signal crimes, based as it is largely upon information provided by the police about the progress and findings of their investigations, has formed the basis for the fabrication of collective memories of numerous crimes. These recollections of crimes past exist for each generation at the transnational, national, community or parochial levels. Significant numbers of people hold collective remembrances about the details of particular offences, how they occurred, who was involved and the meanings it has for them.

As time passes, those who share the memories may not recall the precise details of the incident. Rather they hold in common a somewhat 'fuzzy' remembrance of what the police determine to have happened, and the dominant interpretation placed upon the events – their memory becomes more impressionistic. As such, the importance of this process of developing shared rememberings of signal crimes may lie in the way in which such collective memories provide key cognitive and affective reference points for people, in terms of how they understand the crime problem in their neighbourhoods, communities and society.

Conclusion

In this chapter I have proposed the concept of signal crimes in an effort to capture the ways in which certain acts seem to impact disproportionately upon how the crime problem in late-modernity is understood. Media of mass communication enable the sharing of knowledge about such events even though only a few people will have directly experienced them. But if we want to understand how and why certain incidents emerge as signal crimes, we cannot examine the role of journalists or media organizations in isolation. The active participation of detectives in seeking to encourage publicity for a case in order to assist in identifying the suspect or understanding how the crime occurred is often crucial to this process.

The nature and demands of modern major crime investigations, together with the bureaucratic demands of newsrooms, often coalesce to establish a situation where it is in the interests of both journalists and detectives to cooperate with each other on such cases. Journalists participate in such arrangements because of the opportunity of getting a 'newsworthy' story. From the point of view of detectives, publicity for a case allows for a large number of potential witnesses to be contacted comparatively easily, which might result in acquiring the 'lead' needed to 'crack' the case. Furthermore, such exposure is held to be potentially beneficial to policing overall.

There are, though, important consequences that flow from these collaborative interactions, in that they may amplify the signal value of a crime, and either intentionally or unintentionally transform it into a focal point for public concerns about crime and crime control. In such circumstances, the incident is constructed as a signal crime. Moreover, in the context of the 'late-modern crime complex', the prolonged and widespread attention paid by the public to these signal crimes forms the basis for the development of collective memories, such as has happened in cases like those of the Yorkshire Ripper, Soham, Sarah Payne, Stephen Lawrence and Jill Dando. In addition to these 'spectacle' cases that come to form part of the cultural landscape, each generation of a community and region will have other, more localized collective memories of crimes that have happened in their midst.

The collective memories that grow up around signal crimes function as mnemonics, subsequently framing the production of new signal crimes, which in turn reverberate with meaning for their audiences. Understanding how particular incidents are construed as signal crimes and form the basis for collective memories may then be particularly consequential in a cultural context where there is a pervasive feeling of malaise and a concern with the efficacy of traditional social ordering mechanisms. Under such conditions, the signals that incidents past and present convey may be vitally important in encouraging the expansion of social control.

Notes

1. A further detailed discussion of police–media relations in such circumstances is provided in Innes (1999), which also details the methods used to collect and analyse the data. Throughout the current discussion my focus is upon homicide enquiries, although it should be stressed that other offence types are also regularly construed as signal crimes.
2. This approach coheres with Sampson and Raudenbusch's (1999) recent discussion of 'collective efficacy'.
3. Reactive investigation refers to enquiries performed in response to a potentially criminal act. This differs from proactive forms of investigation, which essentially seek to anticipate some form of deviance in advance of it occurring.

References

Altheide, D. (1997) 'The News Media, the Problem Frame and the Production of Fear', *The Sociological Quarterly*, 38(4), 647–68.

Castells, M. (1996) *The Rise of the Network Society*, Oxford: Blackwell.

Cerulo, K. (ed.) (2002) *Culture in Mind: Toward a Sociology of Culture and Cognition*, London: Routledge.

Chibnall, S. (1977) *Law and Order News*, London: Tavistock.

Cohen, S. (1972) *Folk Devils and Moral Panics*, London: Palladin.

Cohen, S. (1985) *Visions of Social Control*, Cambridge: Polity Press.

Cutter, S. (1993) *Living With Risk*, London: Edward Arnold.

Douglas, M. (1966) *Purity and Danger*, London: Routledge.

Douglas, M. (1992) *Risk and Blame*, London: Routledge.

Eco, U. (1983) 'Horns, Hooves, Insteps: Some Hypotheses on Three Types of Induction', in U. Eco and T. Sebeok (eds) *The Sign of Three*, Bloomington: Indiana University Press.

Ericson, R., Baranek, J. and Chan, J. (1987) *Visualizing Deviance*, Milton Keynes: Open University Press.

Fine, G. (2002) 'Thinking About Evil: Adolf Hitler and the Dilemma of the Social Construction of Reputation', in K. Cerulo (ed.) *Culture in Mind: Toward a Sociology of Culture and Cognition*, London: Routledge.

Garland, D. (2001) *The Culture of Control: Crime and Social Order in Contemporary Society*, Oxford: Oxford University Press.

Geertz, C. (1973) *The Interpretation of Cultures*, New York: Basic Books.

Giddens, A. (1991) *Modernity and Self-Identity*, Cambridge: Polity Press.

Girling, E., Loader, I. and Sparks, R. (2000) *Crime and Social Change in Middle England*, London: Routledge.

Greenwood, P., Chaiken, J. and Petersilia, J. (1977) *The Criminal Investigation Process*, Lexington: D.C. Heath.

Halbwachs, M. (1992) *On Collective Memory*, Chicago: University of Chicago Press.

Hall, S., Critcher, C., Jefferson, T., Clarke, J. and Roberts, B. (1978) *Policing the Crisis: Mugging, the State, and Law and Order*, London: Macmillan.

Hobbs, D. (1988) *Doing the Business*, Oxford: Oxford University Press.

Hodge, R. and Kress, G. (1988) *Social Semiotics*, New York: Cornell University Press.

Innes, M. (1999) 'Media as an Investigative Resource in Police Murder Enquiries', *The British Journal of Criminology*, 39(2), 268–86.

Innes, M. (2003) *Investigating Murder: Detective Work and the Police Response to Criminal Homicide*, Oxford: Clarendon Press.

Lash, S. (2001) *Critique of Information*, London: Sage.

Manning, P. (1996a) *Semiotics and Fieldwork*, London: Sage.

Manning, P. (1996b) 'Dramaturgy, Politics and the Axial Media Event', *The Sociological Quarterly*, 37(2), 261–78.

May, H. (2000) 'Who Did What to Whom? Victimization and Culpability in the Social Construction of Murder', *British Journal of Sociology*, 50(3), 488–506.

Mead, G.H. (1932) *The Philosophy of the Present*, Chicago: University of Chicago Press.

Mead, G.H. (1962) *Mind, Self and Society From the Standpoint of a Social Behaviourist*, Chicago: University of Chicago Press.

Meyrowitz, J. (1985) *No Sense of Place: The Impact of Electronic Media on Social Behaviour*, New York: Oxford University Press.

Poster, M. (1991) *The Mode of Information*, Cambridge: Polity Press.

Reiner, R. (1997) 'Media Made Criminality', in M. Maguire, R. Morgan and R. Reiner (eds) *The Oxford Handbook of Criminology*, 2nd edn, Oxford: Oxford University Press.

Rock, P. (1973) 'News as Eternal Recurrence', in S. Cohen and J. Young (eds) *The Manufacture of News*, London: Constable.

Rock, P. (1998) *After Homicide: Practical and Political Responses to Bereavement*, Oxford: Clarendon Press.

Sampson, R. and Raudenbusch, S. (1999) 'Systematic Social Observation of Public Spaces: A New Look at Disorder in Urban Neighbourhoods', *American Journal of Sociology*, 105(3), 603–51.

Schlesinger, P. and Tumber, H. (1994) *Reporting Crime: The Media Politics of Criminal Justice*, Oxford: Clarendon Press.

Schwartz, B. (1997) 'Collective Memory and History: How Abraham Lincoln Became a Symbol of Racial Equality', *The Sociological Quarterly*, 38(3), 469–96.

Skogan, W. (1990) *Disorder and Decline: Crime and the Spiral of Decay in American Neighbourhoods*, New York: Free Press.

Slovic, P. (1992) 'Perceptions of Risk: Reflections on the Psychometric Paradigm', in S. Krimsky and D. Goulding (eds) *Social Theories of Risk*, Westport: Praeger.

Soothill, K. and Walby, S. (1991) *Sex Crime in the News*, London: Routledge.

Sparks, R. (1991) *Television and the Drama of Crime*, Milton Keynes: Open University Press.

Vaughan, D. (2002) 'Signals and Interpretation', in K. Cerulo (ed.) *Culture in Mind: Toward a Sociology of Culture and Cognition*, London: Routledge.

Wilson, J. and Kelling, G. (1982) 'Broken Windows', *The Atlantic Monthly* (March) 29–38.

Part 2
Criminal Representations:
Crimes and Criminals

Chapter 4

Masculinity, morality and action: Michael Mann and the heist movie

Jonathan Rayner

> Since the late 1980s representations of white males as domesticated, feminised or paternal have featured prominently in numerous films in a range of genres including comedies, romances, action movies and thrillers; so much so that the cultish but mainstream gangster movie as revitalised by Quentin Tarantino is about the only mode in which macho masculinity remains intact. (Davies and Smith, 1997: 19)

The above assertion of a restrictive and normative function in the representation of masculinity in contemporary Hollywood cinema suggests a marked retrenchment of conservative values. Recent entertainment films, such as *Mrs Doubtfire* (1993) and *Jumanji* (1995), which champion familial attachment, emotional articulacy and parental responsibility for the American male, promote a return to the social principles of classical, Hays Code Hollywood. (Introduced in the late 1920s, the code sought to prohibit or control the representation of controversial subjects.) In some cases, studio-era productions serve as clear generic and ideological precedents: *The Family Man* (2000) embodies a fantastic and comedic reaffirmation of domestic contentment reminiscent of *It's a Wonderful Life* (1946). Even the heroes of action movies have been defined in terms of the motivating and redemptive fatherly role (*Con Air*, 1997; *Collateral Damage*, 2002). The distinction of Tarantino's stylized thrillers from this trend emphasizes the role of the crime film in the exhibition of uncompromising and unaccommodating masculinity. However, where Tarantino's films offer an exaggerated and titillating portrayal of a violent and autonomous masculinity unrestrained by conventional moral or legal checks, the films of Michael Mann foreground rarefied, rather than simply stylized, forms of male endeavour that consciously reject paternal and domestic roles. Professional and perfectionist criminality is explored and venerated in Mann's work as a valid career choice, mutually exclusive with family life.

Mann has worked in both film and television as a producer, director and writer since the early 1970s, and most of the movies and series to which he has contributed have been concerned with crime. In both media, he has perpetuated and developed established genres and introduced innovation in texts that have influenced and defined their eras. His films *Thief* (1981), *LA Takedown* (1989) and *Heat* (1995) combine and extend the characteristics of gangster films and heist movies, while his series *Miami Vice* (1984–89), *Crime Story* (1986) and the film *Manhunter* (1986) represent the amalgamation of the director's emphasis on contemporary popular cultural forms and artefacts and the 1980s obsessions with surface style and consumerism. In the characterization of his protagonists and the exploration of their dilemmas, Mann foregrounds crises in and the erosion of conventional, societal values, as criminality emerges as a superior alternative to law-abiding, domestic existence. Mann's visual style, characterized by imbalanced widescreen compositions, location shooting in modern cityscapes and single, overriding colours dominating the *mise-en-scène*, articulates the isolation of his individualistic males and the incompatibility of the professional and domestic spheres. In Mann's oeuvre, the work of crime for criminals and police officers alike requires a professional and emotional detachment from societal standards of morality and conjugality. This alienation is at once sought, lauded, regretted and yet maintained, and leads to the subversion of the conservative ideology of law and order generally ascribed to the representation of crime in popular entertainment. For Mann's men, professionalism on either side of the law is preferable to deference to the values of conventional society, even where criminal activity is chosen as the route to the acquisition of a stable domesticity, and where law enforcement activity is putatively supportive of consensual social values:

> *Heat* is a film about work and its increasing personal costs. For the characters in *Heat*, work provides excitement and challenge, but it ultimately excludes any emotional life outside the demands of the job … their work – what it is, how they go about it, how they like it, what distracts them, and, especially, what they have to sacrifice to keep doing it – takes centre stage in the film and in the lives of the characters. (Lindstrom, 2000: 21–22)

The nature and implications of this choice in lifestyle are reflected in the characters' meticulously planned actions, and are verbalized in infrequent and idiosyncratic speech. Through the physical performance of individually determined roles (both the criminal 'act' and its attempted prevention), Mann's characters redefine, qualify and deny moral and behavioural norms, and evade domestication.

Genre Conventions, Character Traits

Thief, *LA Takedown* and *Heat* are heist movies, the sub-genre of crime films that concentrates on the planning, execution and repercussions of robberies or 'capers'. Although there are numerous discernible precedents and influences, *The Asphalt Jungle* (1950) and *The Killing* (1956) can be used for comparative purposes in order to highlight the vexed morality of Mann's films. The prominence of heist movies from the 1950s onwards reflects the decline of the Hays Code restrictions of the classical era, which hitherto had prohibited the detailed representation of criminal practices (Maltby, 1996: 239).

The Asphalt Jungle follows the preparation and undertaking of a safe-cracking operation, a project nurtured by a recently released and ageing criminal mastermind but financed by a gambling operator and a corrupt businessman. The gang assembled for the heist consists of a safe-cracker (who wishes to support his growing family with his take) and a gunman (who wishes to leave the urban environment and buy a farm in order to return to the rural idyll of his childhood). The film's narrative inspires compassion for the gang: the robbery is portrayed as an essentially victimless crime, and the individual goals stated by the gang are uncontroversial. Also the robbery represents a last offence and a last chance for escape and happiness for all its members. However, the gang's planning and expertise are undone by mischance during the heist and by treachery when the stolen goods are taken to their backers. The leader is recaptured, and both the safe-cracker and gunman are fatally wounded, the latter dying in a meadow after a futile attempt at escape into the country.

The apparent sympathy for the criminals in this narrative resides in their conventional motives for financial gain (the erasing of debts, support of family and escape from urban corruption to rural innocence). However, the tragic denial of these objectives in death and imprisonment is inseparable from an inherent judgement of criminality. By contrast, the corrupt businessman is allowed the dignity of suicide. In the words of the investigating police officer, the jungle of the title is not a corrupting environment responsible for the downfall of the gang, but a contested space, marked by minority antisocial behaviour which the police fight to contain. The conservatism of the police chief's closing speech, which punctuates the scenes of the gunman's death, justifies the gang's dissolution as both tragedy and punishment. A similar pattern (of scrupulous preparation overtaken by fate and individual weakness) is present in Stanley Kubrick's *The Killing*, albeit with a more dispassionate, observational stance towards the ignominious ends of the gang members. The latter film's complication of the plot's linear progression, in juxtaposing disparate but simultaneous events, can be seen as an influence on the self-conscious structuring of Tarantino's films, but Kubrick's clinical and impartial analysis of a crime differs from Tarantino's provocatively non-judgemental stance. The sense of tragedy alloyed with inevitable and justified punishment in the heist movie persists into later and non-American examples (e.g. *The Criminal*, 1960), but undergoes a gradual alteration in later decades. While expertise in crime remains paramount, it can be appropriated by non-criminals as a form of satire (*Fun With Dick and Jane*, 1976) or as a symbol of wealth and virility (*The Thomas Crown Affair*, 1968/1999). However, the representation of ineptitude in the heist movie also becomes associated with overt social and political commentary. Desperate protagonists are seen to be driven to criminal extremes by social and racial inequalities, but find these injustices reaffirmed by the punishments meted out by the establishment (e.g. Sidney Lumet's *Dog Day Afternoon*, 1975; the Hughes brothers' *Dead Presidents*, 1995). In such examples, sympathy and active support for the criminal are expressed within the text (by a vocal general public in Lumet's film), with the result that criminal activity assumes a revolutionary zeal.

The heist movie's abiding concentration on proficiency and unity of action in pursuit of a specified goal is central to Mann's crime films. The enhancement of professional expertise is foregrounded not as one characteristic but as the dominant and defining element of character. The realization of personal (masculine) identity is accomplished through vocational activity, and this refinement of action (in the protagonists' evaluation) peripheralizes or discounts moral and legal distinctions:

> The heist film frequently depicts ambition, work ethic, and the use of skills by the criminals that would be valued in the legal world of work, but these qualities are used instead in the service of crime. The effort to develop a detailed plan, gathering of workers with specific and diverse talents, search for financing, meticulous

preparation, trial runs, and concentration and precision-timing required for the heist itself – all these sound much like legitimate work. (Lindstrom, 2000: 25)

What distinguishes the criminal groups in Mann's films is their continuity. The crews are not assembled for specific tasks but work together routinely and repeatedly. These groups exist as focal points of association that outweigh the conventional family in importance. Prison experience, both as a common frame of reference and a collegiate base of acquaintance and loyalty (Letkemann, 1973: 38, 123–5) is stressed in *Heat*, where four of the gang members are identified as former inmates of Folsom State Prison. The character Neil McCauley's prison record, known and respected by policeman Vincent Hanna just as Neil is aware of the detective's career, is also the first topic of conversation during their meeting in the coffee shop.

Mann's protagonists seek personal goals that are similar in their idealism to those of the gang in *The Asphalt Jungle*. Frank, the 'self-employed' safe-cracker in *Thief*, operates with his own group of independent specialists in Chicago. He strives to assemble a fortune and a family in line with a plan laid out graphically in a collage of photos he carries in his wallet. This composite image contains a house, wife, child and his surrogate father and mentor, an ageing safe-cracker who is dying in prison. Frank's criminal activities are intended to facilitate rather than impede the rapid acquisition of a conventional and respectable middle-class life. The Chicago detectives who pursue Frank respect his professionalism, but only insofar as they expect and demand their own pay-off from his crimes in order to allow him to operate in peace. Appropriately, Frank's contempt for them arises from their indolence rather than their corruption: 'Did it ever occur to you to work for a living? Take down your own scores.' A more serious hindrance to Frank's life plan comes in the form of a crime 'family', an Italianate boss and his gang who seek to exploit Frank's expertise. The offer of speeding up his financial gain with robberies planned and financed by Leo and his gang is undercut by the loss of autonomy. Leo makes Frank a 'father', overcoming his problems in adopting a child by literally purchasing one for him, but as a result comes to see himself as Frank's father, and the owner of 'the paper' on his life.

Neil McCauley in *Heat* wishes to take his accumulated fortune to New Zealand, a specific pastoral idyll very distant from the urban environment of Los Angeles. Essentially he plans for an early retirement supported by the wealth amassed through his work. The motives for the other members of Neil's 'crew' vary subtly. Chris Shiherlis is a gambler who loses most of the earnings from their jobs, and who needs a big score on the last robbery to sustain his marriage. Michael Cheritto has a substantial fortune but continues with the gang's activities for the thrill rather than the financial gain involved. Trejo, the driver is relatively undeveloped, but Donald Breedan, his replacement on the crew's last venture, is characterized as the reformed recidivist unable to thrive in a vindictive society. His incautious return to crime on Neil's spontaneous offer appears at once tragic, inevitable and justifiably provoked. The singularity of this 'tight crew' is its multi-ethnic composition (encompassing Black, Italian, Hispanic and Anglo-Saxon American males), and its apparent commitment to domestic stability. All except Neil are connected to partners or spouses, and both Chris and Michael have children.

The group supporting Vincent Hanna, the leader of the Robbery Homicide squad, is superficially similar. The squad is variegated in racial and generational terms, including young, middle-aged, Black and Native American members. However, important distinctions emerge as both groups become more fully delineated. Where the film juxtaposes social outings by the two groups taking place on the same night, the apparent rowdiness of the cops in a bar contrasts with the restraint of the crew's behaviour in a restaurant with their families. Children are present at the crew's table, whereas it is obvious that some of the cops have 'dates' rather than long-term partners. In large measure, the two groups become defined in relation to their atypical leaders. Vincent's failed marriages are inseparable from his obsession with his work, but he coordinates the efforts of his subordinates, a group of similarly dedicated single men. Vincent's irascibility jars against Neil's self control, and yet Neil's solitariness alienates him from his companions. His rigorous, business-like approach hides a comparable desire for stability and a partner, which is potentially satisfied through his meeting with Eady. Ironically, both leaders assume a pastoral, counselling function in offering emotional support to others in the 'work' environment (Vincent gives solace to the victims of crime and Neil intervenes in Chris's and Charlene's marital problems) while their own emotional connections (to wives, partners and stepchildren) are compromised. Remarkably, Hanna upbraids his stepdaughter Lauren's unreliable father in the midst of an argument with his wife Justine about his own absences. Similarly, when Lauren chooses Vincent's hotel room for her suicide attempt, he is freed to respond to her professionally, as a victim rather than a relative.

In balancing the heist movie's analysis of criminal technique with the police procedural drama's exhaustive cataloguing of detective work,

Heat juxtaposes a film genre with an antithetical television narrative framework (Rubin, 1999: 244, 249). The connection and equation of each group's activities contribute to the film's erosion of legal and moral distinctions between them. However, the linkage of criminal and cop in Mann's work is at variance with the undercover investigator's pretence of kinship. In *T-Men* (1947) and *White Heat* (1949), the cop's infiltration of a gang never undermines his professional and moral identity. More recent films (*Deep Cover*, 1992; *Donnie Brasco*, 1997) have suggested the seductiveness of the criminal life, as much because of the apparent ineffectuality or corruption of the law-enforcement establishment as the conducive society of the gang. By comparison, Mann's elevation of the individualistic criminal above cops and gang bosses in *Thief*, and the equalization of legal and illegal professionalism in *Heat*, serve different and less conventional ends. Having suggested the motivations and goals for each elite group, both *Thief* and *Heat* lead inexorably towards a series of related losses and defeats. This nesting of comparable and concomitant tragedies within the principal, individual conflicts underlines the films' pervasive and subversive engagement with the ideology of crime genres in popular entertainment, and their questioning of the protagonists', antagonists' and audience's values.

Action and Execution

In Mann's films, the sequences that detail the robberies and burglaries receive emphasis as generic set pieces and as embodiments of the protagonists' codes and principles. The opening sequence of *Thief*, depicting Frank's drilling of a safe containing diamonds, is exemplary of this economy of characterization and narrative. The three group members (Joseph the driver scanning police radio frequencies, Barry disabling alarm systems, and Frank drilling the vault) are linked by cuts between their locations, but they work without need of verbal communication. The leaching of colour from the night shooting and the absence of establishing shots for this sequence (beyond a shot of the getaway car in an alley) act as a further isolation of their individual, albeit interdependent, action. The drilling of the safe is seen in a series of close-ups which centre on Frank's manipulation of the machinery and the painstaking movement of the bit into the door. An extreme close-up traces the drill's path through the door to reveal the exposed workings of the lock mechanism. Once the door is opened, Frank discards cash and jewels and selects only a collection of anonymous white paper packets from the safe's contents. The exit and escape, involving several exchanges of vehicle before the group disperses, are also accomplished wordlessly.

The definition of Frank's character through the enacting of this first heist is reinforced by the extended preparation and execution of the burglary which occupies the main plot. The identification of counter-measures to the next vault's alarm systems and the construction of a thermic lance to cut through its doors are shown in detail, as Frank assembles his team and equipment. However, this second heist, which is also completed perfectly and without incident, does not represent the climax or conclusion of the film's narrative. The climactic and des-tructive action of the film's conclusion centres instead on the incompatibility of Frank's professionalism with the demands of Mafia-based organized crime and with his domestic objective of home, wife and family.

The plot of *Heat* is also punctuated by the enactment of the crew's 'scores': an armoured car hold-up, a safe-breaking operation, and a bank robbery. In each case, pre-emptive and collaborative action is seen in preparation and execution. The anonymous purchase of explosives, the monitoring of the armoured car's progress and radio communication, the disabling of police pursuit vehicles and the crippling of alarm systems at the bank and precious-metals depository all serve to illustrate the crew's excellence and apparent unassailability. An additional action sequence follows a set-up and counter-ambush at a drive-in movie theatre, precipitated by a plan (suggested by Neil's fence Nate) to sell bearer bonds stolen during the armoured car raid back to their owner Roger Van Zant, a corrupt investment banker. This transaction, based on profiting from defrauded insurance, should be a logical move if Van Zant is the 'businessman' Nate assumes him to be, but Van Zant's pride provokes him to instigate the ambush by his henchmen. The crew's evasion of the trap is again marked by pre-planning and inter-dependence as Neil, Chris and Michael cooperate to wipe out their would-be assassins. However, despite the crew's apparent mastery of each criminal act and its repercussions, the consummation of each heist is interrupted by an irruption of chaos. The sudden ascendancy of disorder within the orderly conduct of crime threatens the completion of the individual score, but also previews the eventual dissolution and death of the crew and its members.

Although the criminal planning and execution progress perfectly for Frank, the project that his crimes are supposed to finance (the assemblage of home and family) actually proves deleterious to his career. Between the two pristine burglaries, Frank begins his association with Jessie. In outlining to her the delays imposed upon his objective by prison terms, he insists that nothing can prevent him from conjuring his dream family (depicted on his photo collage) into being. In a manner redolent of his aspiration, he does not accept her refusal to be part of his life, and counters her admission that she cannot have children with an instantaneous decision to adopt. Notably, Frank approaches Jessie after his meeting with Leo, and after his acceptance of assurances that with the crime family's scores he can amass his fortune and assemble *his* family more quickly. Unfortunately, Leo's motive for the procurement of Frank's house and son is restraint rather than reward. Once installed, Frank's wife and son function as instruments of control, since the 'family' boss assumes that threats to their safety will force Frank to conform. The irony of Leo's use of Frank's family in business is extended by Frank's businesslike response to Leo's fatherly equivocation ("Where is gratitude?" – "Where is my end? I see my money is still in your pocket, which is from the yield of my labour.") Illegality (the reclamation of the leased child and home, and the threatened prostitution of Jessie) endangers Frank's ersatz family. However, Frank's resolve to destroy the boss who seeks to control him also entails the ruin of the newly established family. He hands his savings to Jessie before expelling her from the house with their son. He then burns down his legitimate domestic and business premises (their home and his second-hand car lot) and throws away his 'life' picture. After his shoot-out with the crime family in which Leo and his henchmen are killed, Frank walks away into the night, now apparently bereft of all domestic and criminal attachments. His solitude, in professionalism and individualistic terms, is reaffirmed as a defeat for domestication, and a pyrrhic victory for personal principles. Without any other goal or association, he is again defined solely by vocation, delimited by the film's monosyllablic title. The perfection of Frank's work, his 'magic act', ultimately requires its and his removal from the criminal as well as the domestic milieu.

Where the forces that eventually destroy Frank's domestic project are connected to 'organized' crime, the chaos that threatens to overwhelm Neil's crew is characterized as an undisciplined and profitless form of criminality. Van Zant's preferment of reputation above business sense is matched, and later comes to be allied with, the uncontrolled violence of Waingro. Waingro is not part of the 'tight crew' before or after the armoured car hold-up, and the need for his inclusion is unspecified. That he is considered to be less experienced or reliable is suggested by his being armed with an inferior weapon during the hold-up: a pistol rather than the automatic weapons of the rest of the crew (Letkemann, 1973: 113). Aside from his disruption of the robbery, Waingro's other criminal acts (serial rape and murder) are portrayed as violently antisocial and pointlessly destructive. His unnecessary killing of one guard when the robbery has been completed dictates the execution of the others. Michael obeys Neil's logical command, interpreted by Vincent at the scene later, in order not to 'leave a living witness'. In similar fashion, the logic of self-preservation compels the crew to abandon the burglary at the precious-metals depository (where a lack of professionalism from the police reveals their planned ambush), to kill Van Zant's henchmen and to shoot their way out of the bank heist when the police are tipped off.

In each incident, when the chaos of the unplanned, the irrational or the motiveless intercedes, the crew strive to reimpose order. Although abandoning the precious-metals burglary represents a prudent avoidance of conflict, during the armoured car robbery, the ambush with Van Zant's men and the aftermath of the bank robbery, the attempt to reassert the crew's sense of order is based on an escalation of violence: the killing of the other guards and the ambushers and the extended gun battle in downtown Los Angeles, which envelopes police and pedestrians alike. A comparable but markedly unsympathetic escalation of violence characterizes the successive bank raids undertaken by the initially attractive, countercultural group of surfer-bank robbers in *Point Break* (1991). The effect of this shift is to emphasize, as in Mann's films, a personal bond between the FBI agent who infiltrates the gang and its enigmatic leader, while reinstating, unlike Mann, a conservative stance towards crime. Similarly, the actions and expertise of the gang assembled for a complex robbery in *Ronin* (1998) are codified as the preserve of an elite warrior caste. Set-piece sequences in Paris and Arles (at the Roman gladiatorial arena) emphasize the distinction of the group and their adversaries from the general populace, but in each case their activities result in an escalation of violence and its infliction on innocent bystanders. The portrayal of such disregard (when one of the gang members is in reality an under-cover or renegade CIA agent intent on foiling a terrorist plot) highlights the mismatch between disruptive violence and conservative ideology in action cinema, when compared with the ambivalent, self-conscious and self-destructive nature of violence in Mann's work.

The crew's reaction is in marked contrast to the premeditated, controlled and suppressive violence used at the outset of the armoured car and bank robberies (Letkemann, 1973: 100, 110). As the bank's occupants are herded together, Neil appeals to them rationally and emotionally in order to *avoid* the use of violence: 'We're here for the bank's money ... you're not going to lose a dime ... Think of your families'. Neil's entreaty is all the more ironic, given that the immediate repercussions of the robbery, including and provoked by the crew's violent response to the disordering of their plans, overwhelm and destroy several family units. Like other crime thrillers, such as *Bullitt* (1968) and *The French Connection* (1971), which can be defined by their controlled or chaotic chase sequences (Rubin, 1999: 250), the central theme of *Heat* is distilled by the reactive violence and endangerment of domesticity apparent in its heist sequences. The survival of the crew members' families and domestic environments is sacrificed to the professional cause, at the same time as their logical, professional but escalatory response to crises in action endangers the law-abiding public.

Action and Value

After the bank robbery, the deliberate decision to compromise the domestic sphere (previewed in Michael's admission of enjoyment of the 'juice' ahead of the financial reward) is marked by the actions of each member of the crew. The presence and influence of stable domestic and family environments have been recognized as significant checks upon the initiation of criminal behaviour (Felson, 1998: 23–26). By contrast, the intercutting between the crew members' homes or partners, which introduces the bank sequence (a shot of Eady packing to leave with Neil after the robbery, followed by one of Charlene Shiherlis at home with her son), underlines the lives and values placed in jeopardy. As a result, a similar pairing of shots (of Elaine Cheritto watching news of the gun battle at home, and of Breedan's partner Lily seeing a report of his death in a bar), emphasizes the pervasiveness and inevitability of loss. The juxtaposition of actions and environments articulates a choice rather than a competition of values. The most poignant and conclusive incident in the sequence, which encapsulates this choice, is Michael's instantaneous and pragmatic decision to take a child hostage to facilitate his escape. Any parental sentiment is secondary to the practical course of action. (As such, Michael's act prefigures Neil's abandonment of Eady.) Similarly, after his killing of Michael, Vincent's comforting of the child hostage (anticipating his rescue of Lauren) appears to be as much a professional as a pastoral response.

Michael's preference for action, as stated in the decisive meeting before the bank robbery, precipitates his subsequent actions and his death. By comparison, Chris's decision to undertake the bank raid is motivated by the desire to restore his domestic relationships. Chris is the first to open fire when the police appear outside the bank. After Chris is wounded, Neil instructs Nate to keep him safe until their escape route from the country is secured, but Chris decides instead to seek out Charlene, despite the risk of imprisonment. This sets in train a second series of pragmatic decisions, ironically antipathetic to the maintenance of domesticity. When she is brought to a safe house by the police in order to lure out Chris, Charlene is told by Sergeant Drucker that her only option to avoid imprisonment along with her husband, and the resultant institutionalization of her son Dominic, is to betray Chris and facilitate his capture. (Drucker's outline of Dominic's likely future after being raised by the state mirrors Frank's recollection of his own childhood in *Thief*, which he seeks to redress through his own adoption of a child in state care.) When Chris appears, her coded warning allows him to escape and her to avoid the repercussions for her own and her son's future, but the family unit is splintered irretrievably. Her action can be construed as equally selfless and self-serving (she protects her son and manages to maintain her own and her husband's freedom at the cost of their unity), but Chris's choice to leave embodies a final resignation from the family group.

Chris's dislocation from his family is compared with Neil's lack of similar commitments from the aftermath of the armoured car hold-up onwards. The argument between Chris and Charlene over his gambling debts results in his violent departure from their home and his spending the night on Neil's floor. The comparison of living spaces is indicative of the characters' status: Chris smashes various ornaments before he leaves his home, but in Neil's house the only articles on view are strictly functional (a telephone, his keys, his handgun and a coffeemaker). When he is seen alone in his house, Neil is isolated in extreme close-up at the farthest right edge of the frame, with the rest of the composition made up of the glass windows and the sea beyond. The single blue-grey colour and the racking of focus from the interior to the waves outside are indicative of Neil's alienation, and of the focus of his life existing beyond his dwelling. On waking up, Chris asks Neil two apparently long-standing and inseparable questions ('When are you going to get some furniture? … When are you going to get an old lady?'), to which Neil makes identical replies ('When I get round to it'). In one home, the irruption of violence is directed against the trappings of domesticity and illustrates the imperilled state of the family itself; in the other, there is no physical or material presence beyond the artefacts associated with work against which to react. It is noticeable that Neil's closest associates are also seen to be contained by work-oriented or neutral, social spaces. His meetings with Nate take place in cars and car parks, and he encounters Eady in the bookstore where she works and in a café. More revealingly, both Kelso (who gathers information electronically to set up the bank robbery) and Eady (who is pursuing her preferred career as a freelance graphic designer) are seen to work from home, converting the domestic space into a business premises. In addition to these compromised spaces, we see Van Zant's office being used as a living area when he fears Neil's revenge, but when he returns to his home it appears to be as under-furnished and unoccupied as Neil's. With the contamination of both Michael's and Trejo's home spaces (with the television report of the robbery watched by Elaine and the torture and death of Trejo and his wife at the hands of Waingro), no purely domestic environment remains unaffected by consequences of the crew's activities.

Of the policemen, only Vincent's domestic space is seen in the film, but this area is a site of unremitting conflict. Vincent is seen either rushing to leave, as on the morning of the armoured car hold-up, or returning late, on several evenings during his investigation. In any case, the house is not his but Justine's, forming part of her divorce settlement. The only possession Vincent seems to value in the house is his television, which he watches in preference to talking to Justine and which he insists on removing when he discovers her infidelity. This episode is remarkable in itself since it is the only occasion on which a meal is seen to be made in any of the homes, and yet even this food, prepared by Justine for her lover Ralph, is left uneaten. Vincent's withdrawal to the anonymity of a hotel room is succeeded by his discovery of Lauren in the bath tub. The suggestion of a familial bond between the policeman and his stepdaughter, intimated in her choice of his room for her suicide attempt, is undermined by the neutrality of this space and the professionalism of his response.

Vincent's preference for non-aligned or professional spaces is different from but comparable to Neil's desire for but failure to create his own home environment. The coffee shop scene, in which cop and criminal meet and converse for the first time, exemplifies their denial of attachments and considerations outside of professional commitments. The sequence is introduced by Vincent's return home to find a sink full of unwashed dishes and Justine dressed to go out. Unwilling to engage with marital or domestic concerns, he returns to work, and instigates the meeting with Neil on the freeway.[1] The seeking of this contact, immediately succeeding the avoidance of familial interaction, represents the crystallization of Vincent's choice, in line with Neil's, Michael's, Chris's and Charlene's. The resolution to meet Neil, prompted by their mutual, professional admiration, encapsulates the immersion of both characters in their intensive and exclusive activities, described by the director as a 'morphine groove of self-confidence and decisiveness' (Anon, 1996: 17).

The exchange between Vincent and Neil replaces the candid conversation between Frank and Jessie in *Thief*, in which a life plan financed by and eventually divorced from crime is mooted as an achievable goal. However, the earlier film ends with a loss, or more precisely a renunciation of this stated objective, and the hero's return to a solitary existence. In the coffee shop, Neil and Vincent note the similarity and, in their opinion, inevitability of their activities and choices, and consolidate the recognition and respect that their mutual surveillance has inspired up to this point. When police incompetence reveals the police stake-out at the precious-metals repository, Neil and Vincent appear to stare at each other via surveillance cameras. The centrality of their faces in the frame in inter-cut shots, and the appearance of Neil's face as a monochrome, negative image, illustrate graphically their equality in perception and judgement.

Their distance from a 'normal type life', which they recognize, nominally desire but ultimately abjure, is marked in the coffee shop by the presence of ordinary families around them: 'people living normal lives who have never used guns, never experienced physical violence, never been stolen from and never steal. Surrounded on all sides by this flow of normalcy' (Anon, 1996: 15). During the conversation, Neil repeats the maxim he stated earlier to Chris: 'Allow nothing to be in your life that you cannot walk out on in thirty seconds flat if you spot the heat around the corner.' When Neil asserts the primacy of this 'discipline' (which will eventually require his abandonment of Eady), Vincent describes this creed as 'pretty vacant', apparently unconscious of the irony in his own abandonment of Justine in order to establish contact with Neil. Neil's next remark, that 'it is what it is', encapsulates the unarguable, self-evidential nature of both men's professional principles. While the coffee shop scene notes visually and verbally an alternative to the paths the two characters have chosen, it ends with a recognition, and championing, of their difference and exclusivity. Each assures the other that their kinship will not prevent them from attempting to kill their adversary if their professional judgement demands it. Their final meeting confirms this necessity.

Conclusion: A Mutuality of Condition

Mann's heist films examine the intricacies of criminal activity and policing with an attention to detail that ultimately renders moral distinctions relative. The antisocial nature of criminal acts is defused by the promotion of expertise and discipline required for their successful enactment. The inclusion of comprehensible and sympathetic motivations for criminal behaviour (the constitution and support of families, the desire for self-realization and escape) might appear as an excuse for the crew's undertakings, and the loss of life and destruction of domesticity that attend the heists are certainly stressed in terms of tragedy and waste. However, these losses frequently appear ambiguous or one-sided. Michael's decision to go on the bank robbery, to take his hostage and his death are logical, albeit self-centred, selections which he does not survive to regret. Similarly, Eady's consternation at Neil's abandonment is based on her ignorance (compared with the viewer's knowledge) of his maxim. His earlier verbal commitment to her ('There's no point in me going anywhere any more if it's alone, without you') is, like Frank's contract with Jessie, ultimately incompatible with individual principles and professional conduct. Charlene's warning to Chris and Justine's resigned releasing of Vincent at the hospital before his final confrontation with Neil represent an informed female accession to the males' vocational demands.

Despite the inclusion of the domestic domain in Mann's films, as a fact, goal or ideal to be supported or defended by criminals and policemen alike, alternative systems of value, existential meaning and behaviour predominate for the male protagonists. Only in *Manhunter*, in which the FBI agent's investigations into the serial murder of families imperils his own household, is the hero allowed to complete his task, revoke his profession and return to the home. The annihilating 'givens' of adult life identified within existential psychotherapy – the inevitability of death, our inalienable free will, our fundamental solitude and the absence of meaning in life (Yalom, 1991: 4–5; Yalom, 1980) – are countered by personal strategies of comfort, containment and denial. Family connections at once represent a source of support and the potential for further stress, as separations and deaths reaffirm solitude and mortality. Although families, and by implication legal and conventional lives, exist in *Thief* and *Heat*, they do not represent the favoured repository of meaning for the male protagonists. Self-realization and meaning in life is achieved through the attainment of excellence and observance of self-imposed rules in work. The family is reduced to 'a tool, a defense against isolation' (Yalom, 1980: 362), which is discarded nonetheless, since it cannot defuse the crisis of meaning as effectively as the work of discipline, and the discipline of work. Criminal and police work are as equally invalid and anti-social in domestic terms as they become valid and admirable within their exclusive groups, and for the viewer.

The codification of dress, behaviour and expression in Mann's work goes beyond the simple elevation of visual style over narrative substance, as criticized in series like *Miami Vice*. It also assumes a greater significance in social and contextual terms, as it combines generic and moral debates with the discussion of pertinent, work-based 'lifestyle issues of the mid-1990s' (Lindstrom, 2000: 21). By comparison, the stylization of conduct and dress in contemporary Tarantino films such as *Reservoir Dogs* (1992) actually works to undermine their reverence for violent, individualistic manifestations of masculinity from within: 'the defining contradiction is between the symbolic signification of the sharp suits (conventional masculinity) and the frailty they expose, as for most of the film they are roughed up and drenched in blood' (Bruzzi, 1997: 89). Noticeably, Tarantino's emphasis on the compromised power of the criminal male rarely includes any representation of domesticity, even as a deselected alternative.

In *Heat*, Neil's spotless business suit is tarnished only by his own blood when he is fatally wounded by Vincent in their final shootout. The affluence and composure embodied in the suit mark his professionalism and become points of attraction for both Eady, when she watches him in the book store, and Vincent, whose own suit is frequently dishevelled. In a reversal of practice in mainstream cinema, *Heat* proposes Neil as an object for the gaze of both Vincent and Eady, instead of foregrounding the female as an erotic spectacle. In the bookstore scenes, Eady appears as a small and indistinct figure in the background as she watches Neil who, by contrast, dominates the foreground and centre of the frame. Consequently, she is not allowed to assume or retain the status of an erotic, desired object, as Neil's principles (the insistence on killing Waingro, and on abandoning her) remove her from the gaze and quash a conventional, heterosexual conclusion to the narrative. Instead, the two central males exchange narcissistic gazes derived from respect and desire, even as the film proposes them to the viewer as equals, adversaries and objects for admiration:

> Battles, fights and duels of all kinds are concerned with struggles of 'will and strength', 'victory and defeat', between individual men and/or groups of men. All of which implies that male figures on the screen are subject to voyeuristic looking, both on the part of the spectator and on the part of other male characters. (Neale, 1993: 16)

The reciprocal surveillance of the cop and the criminal, and their respective engineering and acceptance of the coffee shop meeting, articulate their literal and metaphorical regard for each other. They mirror and complement each other up to the point of death (Vincent only sees and shoots Neil when he is betrayed by his shadow), and in so doing provide the viewer with twinned points of voyeuristic identification, without a correspondingly secure moral, legal or conventional perspective. We are forced to confront the vagaries and ambiguities of social constructs of criminality, legality and domesticity, just as the law-breaking and law-enforcing protagonists are forced to acknowledge 'the mutuality of their condition' (Anon, 1996: 18). Mann's work within the crime genre stands as the apologia for the classical gangster film, and the apotheosis of the heist movie, in its articulation of insoluble social and moral ambiguities.

Note

1. In the previous incarnation of this narrative as *LA Takedown*, this encounter takes place by accident, lessening its impact as a conscious and enlightening meeting of kindred, solitary professionals.

References

Anon (1996) 'Bob and Al in the Coffee Shop: Michael Mann's Notes for the Coffee Shop Scene', *Sight and Sound*, 6(3), 14–19.

Bruzzi, S. (1997) *Undressing Cinema: Clothing and Identity in the Movies*, London: Routledge.

Davies, J. and Smith, C.R. (1997) *Gender, Ethnicity and Sexuality in Contemporary American Film*, Edinburgh: Keele University Press.

Letkemann, P. (1973) *Crime as Work*, Englewood Cliffs: Prentice-Hall.

Lindstrom, J.A. (2000) '*Heat*: Work and Genre', *Jump Cut*, 43, 21–30.

Maltby, R. (1996) 'Censorship and Self-Regulation', in G. Nowell-Smith (ed.) *The Oxford History of World Cinema*, Oxford: Oxford University Press, 235–48.

Neale, S (1993) 'Masculinity as Spectacle: Reflections on Men and Mainstream Cinema', in S. Cohan and I.R. Hark (eds) *Screening the Male: Exploring Masculinities in Hollywood Cinema*, London: Routledge, 9–20.

Rubin, M. (1999), *Thrillers*, Cambridge: Cambridge University Press.

Yalom, I.D. (1980) *Existential Psychotherapy*, New York: Basic Books.

Yalom, I.D. (1991) *Love's Executioner and Other Tales of Psychotherapy*, Harmondsworth: Penguin.

Chapter 5

Sex crime and the media: press representations in Northern Ireland

Chris Greer

Introduction

The relationship between media images and popular consciousness is complex and notoriously difficult to unpack (Reiner *et al.*, 2000a; Livingstone, 1996; Sparks, 1992; Cumberbatch, 1998; Young, 1981). Yet, as Miller and Philo (1999) point out, it would be absurd to suggest that there is no relationship at all. Indeed, it has become trite to suggest that the media do more than merely 'reflect' social reality. They can be instrumental in the orchestration of moral panics (Wilczynski, 1999; Thompson, 1998; Maguire, 1997; Goode and Ben-Yehuda, 1994; Jenkins, 1992; Cohen, 1980); they can be important symbolic mechanisms used in the construction of ideology (Schudson, 2000; Rolston and Miller, 1996; Herman and Chomsky, 1994; Fishman, 1978; Cohen and Young, 1981); and they can inform the political processes aimed at dealing with social crises (Beckett, 1994; Miller, 1993; Hall *et al.*, 1978). In short, how media represent social phenomena is central to how we, as media consumers with limited first-hand experience (Young, 1981), make sense of them and their 'place' in our everyday lives (Philo, 1999; Gamson *et al.*, 1992; Sparks, 1992; Ericson *et al.*, 1991; Entman, 1989).

In recent decades, sex crime, in all its myriad forms, has become a staple of media discourse (Thomas, 2000; Kitzinger, 1996; Marsh, 1991; Soothill and Walby, 1991; Smith, 1984; Ditton and Duffy, 1983). At the same time, the problem of sex crime – and especially the sexual abuse of children – has become a major source of fear and anxiety (West, 2000, 1996; Grubin, 1998; Hebington and Thomas, 1997). Media representations of sex crime give important indicators of the nature and extent of the problem, of how we should think and feel about it, of how we should respond to it, and of preventive measures that might be taken to reduce the risk of victimization. Yet without exception, research exploring the representation of sex crime in popular discourses has evidenced high levels of sensationalism, stereotyping and inaccuracy (see, *inter alia*, Kitzinger, 1999a, b; Howe, 1998; Meyers, 1997; Lees, 1995; Soothill, 1995; Skidmore, 1995; Benedict, 1992; Franklin and Parton, 1991; Soothill and Walby, 1991; Caputi, 1987; Nelson, 1984). In this chapter I want to present an overview of the research literature and then elaborate on some of the key findings of my own research, which explored the construction of sex crime in the Northern Ireland press.

Sex(ed) Crime in the Media

The vast majority of research on the representation of sex crime in the media has focused on the press, the reasons for which are quite straightforward. Press reports are easier to get hold of and to analyse in 'hard copy' format than film, television or radio programmes. There are some exceptions (Young, 1998; Kitzinger and Skidmore, 1995), but it is safe enough to say that the sociological analysis of sex crime in the media has, in practice, amounted largely to the sociological analysis of sex crime in the press.

Most studies have concentrated either on representations of sexual violence against women (Meyers, 1997; Grover and Soothill, 1995; Lees, 1995; Benedict, 1992; Soothill and Walby, 1991) or on the sexual abuse of children (for an overview see Goddard, 1996). Studies on the former have varied in scope, from the representation of specific offences like date rape (Lees, 1995), to rape, sexual assault and sex murder (Soothill, 1995; Jenkins, 1994, 1992; Benedict, 1992; Soothill and Walby, 1991; Cameron and Frazer, 1987), to violence (including sexual violence) against women more generally (Howe, 1999; Meyers, 1997). Images of child sex abuse have been explored in a context of offending in statutory care environments (Franklin and Parton, 1991; Campbell, 1988; Nava, 1988), by members of the clergy (Jenkins, 1996), by predatory strangers (Kitzinger, 1999b; Websdale, 1999; Best, 1990), or across a range of forms (Wilson and Silverman, 2002; Soothill *et al.*, 1998; Kitzinger and Skidmore, 1995; Jenkins, 1992). The sexual abuse of children in their own homes tends to be discussed in terms of its absence from, rather than prevalence in, media discourses (Greer, 2001; Kitzinger, 1996). The representation of the full spectrum of sex offences has also been investigated (Greer, 2003).

The theoretical and methodological approaches used in these studies have varied considerably. Not unexpectedly, there is a leaning toward feminist scholarship. But analyses have been informed by a diversity of perspectives (see below). Like the literature on crime and the media more generally (Reiner *et al.*, 2000a, b), much of the research on representations of sex crime has looked at all the coverage in a single, relatively short time period, or focused on specific cases (Howe, 1998; Meyers, 1997; Benedict, 1992). A good few studies, though, have considered representations over longer periods, in some cases several decades, facilitating the investigation of changes and continuities over time (Greer, 2003; Kitzinger and Skidmore, 1995; Jenkins, 1992; Soothill and Walby, 1991).

The first systematic analysis of sex crime in the media combined both of these approaches. In *Sex Crime in the News*, Soothill and Walby (1991) conducted a longitudinal analysis of press reports (primarily of rapes and sexual assaults) in the postwar period and then focused in more detail on the final year examined in their fieldwork, 1985. The questions asked in the study have resurfaced in media analyses of sex crime ever since: What is the image of sex crime portrayed in the press? Why does coverage focus on the very few disturbed serial rapists, rather than typical rape? Why is the overall media picture so distorted and inaccurate? Though serious consideration of the news production process is lacking in Soothill and Walby's (1991) study, their analysis highlights the selective, sensational and misleading way in which sex crimes are reported. The authors observe, for example, that 'sex crime for the media is essentially when a women or girl is sexually assaulted by a total stranger. In contrast, the importance of other kinds of sexual assaults is subtly undermined in various ways by the focused reporting of the media.' (1991: 148). They also note that 'serious academic work in the general area of sexual violence is poorly reported in the media', and that 'there is a lack of analysis beyond the most simple observations' (1991: 148–49). This study remains one of the most frequently cited in the academic literature.

Howe (1998), in the edited collection *Sexed Crime in the News*, approaches the issue of sex crime somewhat differently. She argues that 'there is a problem with the whole idea of "sex crime"' (1998: 1) and is critical of Soothill and Walby (1991) because in their research 'what counts as sex crime is taken as given' (1991: 2). Though Soothill and Walby draw attention to some important policy issues, it is suggested that 'the sex of these apparently obvious sex crimes is never interrogated' (1991: 2). Here it is argued that 'sexed' crime is a preferable term because, as one contributor explains, it 'refers to the simultaneous relevance of both gender and sexuality' (Atmore, 1998: 124–25). Howe's book is thus structured around a critical framework concerned to explore popular discourses about crime, violence, gender and sexuality but also, and more interestingly, to call into question the hegemonic white Anglo-feminism that has informed so many critiques of those discourses (see also Paglia, 1992). The contributions in *Sexed Crime in the News* seek to problematize conventional notions of sex crime by broadening the horizons of analysis to include a wider range of topics. These include press reporting of anti-gay laws (Morgan, 1998) and the construction of gendered and sexualized discourses around HIV/AIDS as a means of containing women and feminine sexuality (Grimwade, 1998), as well as more obvious issues like child sexual abuse (Atmore, 1998) and rape (Young, 1998).

In *Intimate Enemies: Moral Panics in Contemporary Great Britain* (1992) and *Pedophiles and Priests: Anatomy of a Contemporary Crisis* (1996), Jenkins focuses on child sex abuse (in the UK and the US respectively). These studies are located within the constructionist paradigm for social problems research, which places a primary emphasis not on the objective nature of putative social problems, but on the processes through which they come into public view in the first place (Loseke, 1999; Best, 1995; Sasson, 1995; Spector and Kitsuse, 1977; Kitsuse and Spector, 1973). They seek to establish how sex crimes and related issues come to be defined or 'framed' in popular consciousness (see also Pfohl, 1977; Best, 1990). Jenkins rightly insists that the construction of sex crimes, including their representation in the media, 'must be understood in their broader social and economic context' (1996: 14). Hence, the social construction of child sex abuse is explored systematically from a range of different perspectives (social, cultural, economic and political), although, as in Soothill and Walby's (1991) work, the consideration of influences within media newsrooms is notable by its absence. Perhaps most significantly, Jenkins highlights the complex and highly ideological nature of the processes through which sex crimes come to prominence in popular consciousness, and the centrality of mass media in the struggle for definitional ownership and political power (see also Thomas, 2000).

The influences within newsrooms – structure, culture, hierarchy, working habits – are taken up by Benedict (1992). In *Virgin or Vamp: How the Press Covers Sex Crimes*, Benedict explores the press reporting of four major cases in the US during the 1970s and 1980s. The extent to which this small number of cases can be said to represent the 'norm' is questionable (Soothill, 1995), but some important arguments are advanced that have found support elsewhere (Meyers, 1997). The central theme – as the title suggests – is the tendency of the press (and the public) to polarize women in sex crime cases into either 'virgins' or 'whores'. Journalists, Benedict argues, do this 'through their choice of vocabulary, the slant of their leads, the material they choose to put in or leave out, and they often do it unconsciously' (Benedict, 1992). It is suggested that the press's insensitive and sometimes cruel treatment of women in sex crime cases is seldom due to individual malice. Rather, it results from characteristics of society that are deeply embedded within the culture, namely the gender-biased nature of language and prevailing myths about women, sex and rape. These myths guide how news is both produced and processed, but do so implicitly in a way that can influence even the most well-meaning commentators. Thus, 'a myth-saturated woman will be just as insensitive to rape cases as a myth-saturated man, especially given the conditions and habits of newsroom behaviour' (Benedict, 1992: 6).

More recently, Meyers (1997) has drawn similar, though in places more radical, conclusions. In her study *News Coverage of Violence Against Women*, Meyers argues that sex crime narratives are informed by 'traditional notions of appropriate gender roles' (p. 3), which in turn are rooted in the patriarchal structures of society that institutionalise women's inequality and subjugation. While Benedict (1992) examines a few high-profile sex crimes that received sustained national coverage, Meyers prefers to concentrate on local news that 'focuses more on common, noncelebrity violence that many women experience' (Myers, 1997: 4). In particular, objection is made to the representation of male abuse as discrete incidents because this 'denies the social roots of violence against women and that individual incidents of abuse are part of a larger social problem' (1997: 118). News coverage is found to be influenced heavily by the 'virgin–whore' dichotomy, and notions of race, class and age that result from the convergence of 'male and white supremacist ideologies' (1997: 119). The answer for Benedict (1992) and Meyers (1997) is media reform at the individual and institutional levels. Both acknowledge that this is a highly ambitious project, but both insist that reform is not beyond the realms of possibility.

Kitzinger and Skidmore's (1995) research on the construction of child sex abuse combines content analysis and interviews with journalists, professionals and survivors with focus group research to assess 'the potential and limits of people's ability to deconstruct and 'resist' media accounts' (1995: 12). The findings of their media analysis echo many of those mentioned above. With respect to audience reception, the authors observe that while most participants 'knew' abuse happened more often in domestic or institutional settings, 'their fear often focused on external sites such as woodland or wasteland' (p. 9). And though many 'knew' that abuse is most often committed by someone the child knows, 'their fear focused on strangers' (p. 9). In fact, they argue, 'audience understandings of how they might detect child abuse, the sources of danger and their ideas about intervention were often in conflict with the information which children's charities and social work agencies are trying to promote' (p. 8). The incorporation of audience research demonstrates an increasingly sophisticated approach that seeks to account for the production, transmission and reception of representations of sex crime, and begins to unpack how media images, personal experience and other forms of cultural knowledge interact (see also Reiner *et al.*, 2000b).

These few examples should give some idea of the diverse methodological and theoretical approaches informing investigations of the construction of sex crime in popular discourses. They should also highlight the considerable variance in the breadth of analysis undertaken by different scholars. One common characteristic of much of this research has been its partiality; in particular, the tendency to focus on the end product of news journalism, often at the expense of considering the processes through which images of sex crime are actually produced. Yet despite their clear differences, all of the studies find that although sensitive, restrained and informative representations of sex crime do exist, they are generally stereotypical, frequently sensational, and sometimes wholly inaccurate. These and other issues can be illustrated by turning now to my own research on the construction of sex crime in the Northern Ireland press. The points made in the following sections are drawn from a wider research project completed in 2001, and are developed and discussed in greater detail in Greer (2003).

Sex Crime and the Northern Ireland Press

In conducting this research I wanted to address the partiality of many previous studies by considering not only the representations of sex crime consumed by news readers, but also the complex (and at times highly competitive) processes through which sex crimes are constructed in press discourse. The aim was to understand and explain press representations of sex crime in their wider context. To this end, the analysis considered: key influences on news production (cultural, political, organizational, economic); the nature and significance of relationships between journalists and their sources; the resultant images of sex crime that feature in press discourse; and the relevance of wider change in late modernity. Determining what counts as 'sex crime', as we have seen, has been the subject of some debate (Thomas, 2000; Howe, 1998). For this study, legal definitions were used to classify offences into the following categories; Rape, Sexual Assault, Sexual Abuse of Children and Young Persons, Incest, Sexual Offences against the Mentally Impaired, (Consensual) Homosexual Offences, Indecency Offences, Pornography Offences, and Sexual Harassment.

The regional press in Northern Ireland comprise five main newspapers; three regional dailies (the *Belfast Telegraph*, the *Irish News* and the *News Letter*) and two Sunday regionals (the *Sunday World* and the *Sunday Life*). One further newspaper (the *Irish Times*, a daily produced in Dublin but with offices and a substantial readership in Northern Ireland) was also considered. All sex crime reports appearing in these newspapers were collected and collated over four one-month periods between 1985 and 1997 (January of 1985, 1990, 1995 and 1997). This timeframe facilitated the investigation of shifts in the nature and extent of coverage over time. Data from the resultant archive, totalling just over 500 press items, were supplemented with semi-structured interviews with key players in the news production process, including journalists and editors, police and probation officers, legal practitioners, counsellors and, crucially, survivors of sexual abuse. Before discussing some of the findings, it is useful to comment briefly on the political context of news production in Northern Ireland.

News production in Northern Ireland

The political division in Northern Ireland is reflected to varying degrees in the editorial 'lines' of the regional press in so far as each newspaper subscribes to a more or less unionist or nationalist agenda (Rolston, 1991).[1]

In a small jurisdiction like Northern Ireland, where political culture is at the forefront of everyday life, a newspaper's position on the constitutional issue can define almost entirely the audience it attracts. More importantly, a newspaper's politics can influence profoundly its representation of the British state and its apparatuses of control. The issue of law and order in Northern Ireland is a highly contested terrain and is prone to generate deeply partisan coverage (Bromley, 1997). But whereas matters of crime and control are wrenched routinely into a unionist or nationalist groove, some issues are so emotionally charged that they resonate with equal intensity across cultures and transcend party politics. One such issue is the problem of sex crime (Greer, 2001).

The increasing prevalence of sex crime in the press

Between 1985 and 1997, the number of sex offences recorded by the police grew by 328 per cent (from 47 to 201 in January of those years), while the number of regionally committed offences reported in the press grew by 206 per cent (from 18 to 55 in January of those years). If sex crimes committed outside Northern Ireland are included, the increase rises to 216 per cent (from 31 to 98). While the number of recorded sex offences quadrupled, the number reported in the press trebled. This is not unexpected, since only a tiny fraction of criminal events, sexual or otherwise, are deemed sufficiently newsworthy to merit press attention (Surette, 1998; Schlesinger and Tumber, 1994; Soothill and Walby, 1991; Hall *et al.*, 1978; MacDougall, 1968). Though sexual violence is generally considered more newsworthy than other types of criminality (Marsh, 1991), seemingly to an increasing degree (Reiner *et al.*, 2000a), a rise in the number of recorded offences does not necessarily equate to a rise in the number that make good copy. More significant is the rate of increase.

Figure 5.1 illustrates the rate of change in the number of sex offences recorded by the police (the then Royal Ulster Constabulary, or RUC) and the number reported in the press between 1985 and 1997. It indicates that press attention to sex crime (and it is worth noting that journalists receive the majority of sex crime news from the police) has increased at a much greater rate than offences recorded by the police. This trend is significant. Reports of child sex abuse dominated throughout,

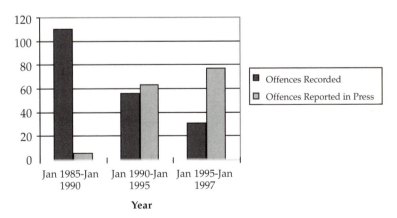

Figure 5.1 Percentage increase in number of sexual offences recorded by RUC and number reported in the press.

accounting for almost half of all items in the archive (48 per cent).[2] The next most frequently reported offences were rape and sexual assault, which accounted for 21 per cent and 9 per cent of items respectively. There was little change in the prevalence of these offence types over time.

The dramatic and disproportionate growth in press attention to sex crime in Northern Ireland has both reflected and contributed to growing awareness about sexual victimization. To explain this increase requires consideration of a variety of influences: the changing nature of media markets; the impact of high-profile cases; political change in Northern Ireland; wider cultural change in late modernity; and the activities of organizations both as news sources and in the wider public sphere. There is insufficient space to develop such a discussion here, although each of these factors and their collective impact are discussed elsewhere (Greer, 2003). Having illustrated the extent of the increase in press attention to sex crime in Northern Ireland, thus locating what follows in some sort of context, the remainder of the chapter raises some qualitative issues relating to how sex crimes are constructed.

The Context of Coverage: Causes, Risks and Prevention

The vast majority of sex crime coverage (90 per cent) in the archive was case-based. That is, most items described a particular incident or series of incidents, rather than discussing wider issues such as risks, prevention, resources for survivors or debates around legal issues. This is a common finding (Kitzinger, 1996; Skidmore, 1995; more generally, see McNair, 1999; Rock, 1973). The event-based nature of reporting can be understood as a consequence of the organizational constraints on news production and the various criteria that determine the newsworthiness of press stories.

First, the need to produce reports according to tight deadlines contributes to their event orientation because journalists seldom have time to 'dig deeper' in order to develop wider debates (Schudson, 2000; McNair, 1999; Galtung and Ruge, 1970). As one Belfast journalist commented: 'We're a daily news operation and it's bang, bang, get a story out, and it doesn't necessarily get the reflection it would deserve'. Second, events – including sex crimes – are more newsworthy if they are dramatic, with some element of human interest, preferably containing a novel twist, such as the involvement of persons of high status (Cavender and Mulcahy, 1998; Chibnall, 1977). These characteristics are best constituted through the portrayal of specific acts and individuals

(Surette, 1998; Ericson *et al.*, 1987). This combination of influences leads to the consistent prioritization of events over issues.

What is most striking, however, is the extent to which the discussion of wider issues diminished over time, from one in six articles in 1985 to one in fifteen in 1997 (see also Kitzinger and Skidmore, 1995). Generally, journalists do not consider the discussion of causes, risk and prevention to be particularly newsworthy. For this reason, advice on these issues was nearly always located within the context of an ongoing investigation in which an actual offender was committing actual offences against actual victims, invariably dominated by the suggestion that the attacker could strike again. In this way, the relatively mundane discussion of general issues could be imbued with a sense of urgency and drama. The following example illustrates this point.

A series of assaults on women perpetrated by a man posing as a taxi driver received sustained coverage in the three Belfast dailies in 1995. In each report the details of the offences were described, along with a description of the attacker. The suggestion that the attacker might strike again was the dominant theme throughout and advice to women was couched in these terms. The *Belfast Telegraph* report, 'Warning Over Bogus Taxis' (4 January 1995: 8), issued the investigating officer's caution that 'we don't know how dangerous this man could be', while the *News Letter*'s 'Bogus Taxi Driver Sparks Rape Alert' (4 January 1995; p. 13) urged women 'to be on their guard'. Advice was thus presented as a specific and urgent 'warning' (rather than a general discussion) and formed part of a wider, highly dramatic – and highly newsworthy – narrative of a serial sex offender at large (see also Soothill and Walby, 1991).

Advice from police officers and counsellors urged women to 'phone for a taxi, ask who the driver is, and make sure it carries the Department of the Environment registered licence' (*News Letter*, 4 January 1995: 13); 'only use clearly marked legal taxis' (*Belfast Telegraph*, 4 January 1995: 8); and 'check taxi driver's credentials' (*Belfast Telegraph*, 3 January 1995: 3). This form of direct address by accredited sources was undoubtedly helpful within the specific context of the case. Any information that might lead to a reduction in victimization is worthwhile. But there is a wider issue here, related to the type of offending to which advice on crime avoidance and personal safety most often related.

The vast majority of sex offences are not committed by strangers. In most cases, whether the rape or sexual assault of women and men or the sexual abuse of children, the victim knows the offender (Grubin, 1998; Mirrlees-Black *et al.*, 1996, 1998; West, 1996; Stanko and Hobdell, 1993; Stanko, 1990; Smart, 1989; Campbell, 1988; Gordon, 1988; Finkelhor and

Yllo, 1985; Hall, 1985; Dobash and Dobash, 1979). Yet the discussion of risks and prevention – on the few occasions it featured – focused on offences by seemingly random predators. The association of advice on personal safety almost exclusively with these types of offence sends the clear, but deeply inaccurate, message that it is strangers who pose the greatest threat.

The Stages of Coverage

Press reports were categorized into five main stages of coverage; the initial offence and investigation; court proceedings; the prison experience; post-release from prison; and other (reports not relating to any one case specifically). The most common stages were the initial offence and investigation and the court stage, which together accounted for around three-quarters of the archive. It is these two stages that will form the basis of the discussion here.

The initial offence and investigation

Coverage of the initial offence and the ensuing police investigation accounted for around one-quarter of news items in the archive. Offences reported at this stage were frequently violent in nature and, further reinforcing the message that strangers pose the greatest threat, almost two-thirds of these reports (61 per cent) described assaults committed by unknown assailants. The emphasis on stranger-assaults has been identified as a prevalent feature of media discourses in a range of sex crime studies (Kitzinger, 1996, 1999b; Websdale, 1999; Kidd-Hewitt, 1995; Kitzinger and Skidmore, 1995; Soothill and Walby, 1991). Soothill and Walby (1991: 34) observed a decade ago that the 'manifestation of the sex beast in florid form does not happen very often in the media, but the coverage is consistently geared up toward sponsoring the arrival of the sex fiend on the national scene'. The disproportionate focus on cases of 'stranger-danger' at this stage of coverage, combined with the selective issuing of advice on personal safety and crime prevention, suggests that this is also true of coverage in Northern Ireland. Moreover, the image of the predatory sex attacker, I would argue, has become even more resonant in recent years.

In late modernity, when high crime rates have become an accepted social fact (Garland, 2000), fears about crime and personal safety focus most sharply on images of outsiders and strangers (Bauman, 2000; Hale, 1996). Press narratives tap into widespread fears and anxieties, feeding off prevailing associations of risk and dangerousness with the unknown 'other' while at the same time giving them substance in an ongoing dialectical interplay. One need only consider the volatile and, at times, extremely violent reaction to the re-housing of sex offenders in the community – in Belfast and elsewhere – to gain some insight into just how deeply embedded the stereotype of the sexual predator has become, especially when the potential victims are children (MacVean, 2000; Thomas, 2000; Kitzinger, 1999b).

The common perception that sex offenders are markedly different from 'normal people' (Kitzinger and Skidmore, 1995) derives undoubtedly in part from their stereotypical representation in the media (Websdale, 1999). But also, and more subtly, it is reflective of the social and psychological processes through which distinctions are established between the normal and the deviant, the good and the evil, the 'safe' and the 'unsafe'. The suggestion in media discourses that 'the real dangers to women and children come from freakish strangers rather than intimates or companions' (Websdale, 1999: 111) is in many ways easier to sustain (Smart, 1989). It is more practical in terms of day-to-day routines and, where children are concerned, more conducive to communicating where dangers may lurk (Kitzinger, 1999a).

The extent to which people's knowledge about risk and dangerousness can conflict with their fear is demonstrated in Kitzinger and Skidmore's (1995) focus-group research on child sex abuse. In light of the above, it is perhaps not surprising that 'images of suspicious strangers' are found to be more potent than images of 'dangerous uncles or threats from within the family home' (Kitzinger, 1999a: 9). Faced with the ontological insecurities of everyday life (Giddens, 1990), a place of safety from the perceived dangers 'outside' is a crucial part of social existence (Bauman, 1998) – and what safer place than the home (see also Loader *et al.*, 2000). Suspicious strangers constitute a threat that, although fearsome, is more practicable than the reality; that most sexual assaults are committed by acquaintances, friends and relatives, frequently in the home.[3] The Northern Ireland press's overemphasis of stranger-assaults, most concentrated in this stage of coverage, helps to reinforce the notion of 'otherness' associated with sex offenders, even though this might not tally with what people know, intellectually, to be true.

Court proceedings

Court reporting constituted the largest single category of items, accounting for 47 per cent of the overall archive. When broken down into the different stages of the judicial process, most court reports related to the committal or open prosecution (29 per cent of the archive). The judge's summing-up and sentencing of offenders accounted for slightly less than one-fifth (18 per cent) of the archive. The types of offence reported at this stage varied greatly, but one conspicuous feature was the much smaller proportion of reports relating to stranger-assaults (18 per cent of court reports).[4] The general orientation towards court coverage can be understood in both organizational and cultural terms.

Organizationally, the accepted wisdom is that the 'tendency to report cases at the stage of the trial derives partly from the economy of concentrating resources at institutional settings like courts, where newsworthy events can be expected to occur regularly' (Reiner, 2000: 142). The Northern Irish regionals each 'take a service' from freelance journalists (or 'stringers') who attend court sessions daily and sell on the 'best' stories to whoever is interested. High levels of court reporting, then, cannot be explained by the high concentration of journalists at institutional settings. That said, resources are tight, and taking a service frees up journalists for other tasks. Editors will, of course, send in-house reporters to cover cases that are especially important. But in terms of maximizing the numbers of available staff, ensuring that deadlines are met and routinizing the manufacture of the news product, the organizational advantages of receiving a regular and reliable flow of pre-packaged daily court reports are clear.

In cultural terms, the emphasis on court proceedings represents an appeal to the authority of the judiciary, who are recognized as the guardians of law and order, the administrators of justice and the definers of 'deviance' and 'normality' (Ericson *et al.*, 1991). The 'official' condemnation of deviants – especially those as publicly reviled as sex offenders – is nowhere more effectively (or dramatically) played out than in the courtroom (Carlen, 1976; Garfinkel, 1956). It is here that the rule of law is brought publicly to bear on those who would contravene the legal order and, in so doing, pose a threat to the wider social and moral constitution of 'respectable' society. Like crime more generally, individual sex crimes are seldom reported from start to finish. But the cumulative content of press representations first indicates how order is breached, and then – through the dramatization of the investigation, trial, sentencing and judge's admonition – how it is restored.

In the courtroom the normative boundaries of acceptable and legitimate behaviour are re-established and a sense of moral closure is found in the 'reassertion of the values of society and the limits of its tolerance' (Hall *et al.*, 1978: 66). This final point is of special significance in the context of political flux in Northern Ireland, where significant sections of the community reject the legitimacy and authority of the

British state. As noted, though the regional press may espouse conflicting views on other issues of law and order, the construction of sex crime is based on the assumption of a moral consensus in which party politics holds little currency. The most important differences between regional representations of sex crime relate to style and market rather than culture and ideology. Key among these is the use of language.

The Language of Sex Crime Narratives

Journalists are frequently criticized for their use of sensationalist labels like 'beast', 'monster' and 'fiend', which further reinforce the image of sex offenders as aliens and outcasts, rather than friends, relatives and members of the community (Thomas, 2000; Websdale, 1999; Soothill *et al.*, 1998; Kitzinger, 1996; Soothill and Walby, 1991). Certainly, this was a key complaint among practitioners – and some journalists – who participated in this research. But an important distinction needs to be made here between the daily and Sunday press in Northern Ireland. The three main dailies produce news coverage that is, in large part, broadsheet in nature. The Sundays, by contrast, are tabloids in both form and flavour.

Stereotypical terms like 'beast', 'monster' and 'fiend' were virtually absent from daily press reporting. They appeared with much greater frequency in the Sunday tabloids, and were virtually ubiquitous in one newspaper – the *Sunday World*.[5] Consideration of the representations in this newspaper is most instructive here. One story, headlined 'Don't Dump Sicko Here', began 'Evil sex beast [named offender] has been re-housed back in Ulster in a street where children play' (*Sunday World*, 5 January 1997: 7). In another, which made the front page, the headline 'Child Pervert Cheat Caged at Last' was followed by 'This is the sick child sex beast convicted of shock new sex offences …' (*Sunday World*, 26 January 1997, front page). The editor had clear views on the use of these labels: 'Survivors of sex crime call them fucking monsters, and … we are the newspaper that these people come to. And if they call them monsters, we'll call them monsters, it's dead simple.'

Jennifer (not her real name) is a survivor of child sex abuse whose story was reported in the Northern Ireland press. She supported fully the use of these terms, and explained why:

One of the great things that … they do is they actually call them 'monsters' and all sorts of horrible words, and I think that's great because that's exactly what these people are. I had never thought about [my abuser] like that before. He wasn't a monster, he was my uncle ... I hadn't felt any anger before then. I hadn't been able to feel any anger. And that was the first time that I thought, 'Yes, he is a fucking bastard, he is a fucking monster'. I felt vindicated by the fact that someone had actually acknowledged that what he had done to me was horrific ... I thought that that was absolutely brilliant.

A spokesperson for the Belfast Rape Crisis Centre described the cathartic release that media coverage can offer survivors, providing 'a sense of power and control over their lives to be able to speak out about the injustices they have suffered and also to help others'. The therapeutic benefits of having one's abuser publicly denounced should not be underestimated, still less overlooked. Yet on the issue of identifying the correct areas of risk, and thereby trying to reduce further victimization, the message from practitioners and survivors interviewed for this research was clear. As Peter (not his real name), a survivor of child sex abuse, put it:

The media need to let the public know an abuser can be the most innocent looking person in creation. They range from the man next door to your uncle, to a brother or a sister. Priests, of course, lawyers, doctors, anyone ... A sexual abuser has no sign to tell of his intent, none whatsoever. And that needs to come across.

The use of stereotypical labels, as many have noted (Thomas, 2000; Grubin, 1998; Soothill *et al.*, 1998), gives the clear indication that offenders are somehow visually distinguishable from 'normal' people.

There is a further issue regarding the use of language in the *Sunday World*. These terms were not used solely to describe child sex abusers, but all perpetrators of sex crime. The headline 'Y-Front Affront', for example, introduced a tongue-in-cheek report beginning 'An Ulster sex fiend – who gets his kicks from stealing underwear from clotheslines – leaves a trademark behind ...' (*Sunday World*, 29 January 1995: 21). Another story headlined 'Gays Ignore Cameras to Have Sex in Toilets' began 'Gay sex fiends are hopping off buses and having it off in a public loo' (*Sunday World*, 26 January 1997: 13). Virtually identical terminology was used in each case to describe behaviours that differed enormously in terms of deviance, dangerousness and harm done. The indiscriminate use of these terms makes explicit the reductionist sentiment that predatory child sex abusers, people who steal underwear from clotheslines, and consenting adult homosexuals who engage in sexual acts in a public place are the same – they are all 'sex beasts', 'sex fiends' and 'sickos'.

This practice conflates the vast diversity of 'criminal' sexual behaviours into one problem (see also West, 2000). The distinction between those behaviours is blurred and, by consequence, so too is the distinction between the perpetrators, who are increasingly grouped into one homogenous criminal 'type'. In this way, the view is promoted that all sex offenders are equally dangerous and threatening, and that they are all to be reviled with the same emotional intensity. The former coordinator of the police service's Child Abuse and Rape Enquiry (CARE) unit[6] suggested that communities make little distinction between different types of sex offender:

> It's the paedophile bandwagon, everybody goes on about paedophiles but in actual fact they are talking about anybody, any sex offender ... Those people who are looking those people out of their area, they don't see the difference between a sex offender and a paedophile. It's all one group.

And the director of the Northern Ireland Probation Service remarked that 'sex offenders are seen as this group of people who are all the same'. The homogenization of sex offenders in sections of the print media through the indiscriminate use of stereotypical labels contributes to both generating and sustaining this perception by implicitly reinforcing its validity in the public imagination.

The Aim of Sex Crime Narratives

The use of sensational and stereotypical labels is deeply problematic, though restricted largely to the Northern Irish Sunday tabloids.[7] A further characteristic of press coverage, concerning the constraints on news production in a transforming marketplace, is experienced by reporters universally. With the proliferation of media in recent decades, competition in the press market has become especially fierce (Sparks, 2000; Thompson, 2000; Barwise and Gordon, 1998). The result has been the 'tabloidization' of the media, and widespread claims that outlets are 'dumbing down' in an effort to win greater market popularity (Bourdieu, 1998; Bromley, 1998; Franklin, 1997). In this climate, where, in the words of one Belfast journalist, 'newspapers have to fight to get their attention', the primary aim of sex crime narratives is not to inform; it is to shock.

As one Sunday editor explained, 'We normally do shock first of all. After you have shocked, you then have to offer advice, and all the do's and don'ts ... But first of all you have to shock, otherwise they'll not be interested in reading it.' A daily broadsheet news editor described the key element as 'the "F me" factor, and you can imagine what the 'F' is for'. Echoing the determinants of newsworthiness described above, he went on to explain that sex crime stories should ideally contain 'violence, the warning factor, you know, the idea that this could happen to anybody' and the sense that sex crimes are being committed 'on your doorstep'. Another broadsheet journalist noted:

> I mean all journalists are in the business of shocking, and the only time I am going to get on the front page is with a story that will shock you. As a journalist I want to be on the front page and I want to find the kind of angle that will get me on the front page, and that's just the nature of the business.

By definition, 'shock' suggests 'novelty' – it conjures images of an event or situation that is 'deviant, equivocal and unpredictable' (Ericson *et al.*, 1991: 4). The 'nature of the business', then, dictates that those sex crimes that are more typical will be considered less newsworthy and, as a result, be less likely to receive even modest press coverage, still less front-page prioritization (Meyers, 1997; Benedict, 1992). What this means is that journalists are under constant pressure to seek out new angles, better 'spins', the exceptions to the rule, in order to maintain a strong presence in the journalistic arena and, whenever possible, secure their by-lines on front-page stories. This pressure, in turn, militates against reporting the social reality of sex crime and, therefore, impedes the construction of narratives that promote greater understanding of the phenomenon.

Conclusions

There are clear problems with the representation of sex crimes in the press. I have highlighted just a few, namely the implicit and explicit suggestion that strangers pose the greatest threat, the homogenization of sex crime and its perpetrators through the indiscriminate use of highly emotive and stereotypical language, and the decline in discussions on wider issues such as causes, risk and prevention. These characteristics are concentrated in, but by no means restricted to, the tabloid press in Northern Ireland, and have been widely evidenced by studies examining representations of sex crime elsewhere. Any analysis of press representations of sex crime, however, would be incomplete if it failed to acknowledge the clear benefits that have resulted from the increased prevalence of the issue in newsprint media discourse (Gough, 1996).

Press attention to sex crime has been central in creating a climate in which survivors feel less inhibited about coming forward and disclosing their abuse, whether to counselling organizations or to the police. The Belfast Rape Crisis spokesperson commented that 'the media has been part of raising public awareness. [There is] more awareness and slightly less feeling ashamed than there would have been ten years ago ... That doesn't change how they feel inside, but it might change whether they are prepared to come forward.' Newspapers in Northern Ireland, including the tabloids, have produced informative accounts that contain all the elements of drama and human interest that make for compelling reportage, without the sensationalism and stereotyping that character-izes so much coverage. The same is true for the press in other jurisdictions (Gough, 1996; Skidmore, 1995; Benedict, 1992). But the problems are still profound.

My research in Northern Ireland thus far has sought to develop an understanding and explanation of press representations of sex crime in their wider context. In the process, as noted above, I have tried to address the partiality of many earlier studies by investigating both the news product and the processes through which that product comes to be formed, framed and textured. The findings highlight a wide range of influences that militate against portraying the social reality of sex crime. Market pressures, structural-organizational constraints, the deter-minants of newsworthiness, and the career aspirations of individual journalists in an increasingly competitive industry all orient representa-tions of sex crime toward the sensational and the shocking, usually at the expense of any serious discussion of issues that might actually help to reduce victimization. Some of those interviewed for this study went so far as to suggest that press representations may actually increase the chances of victimization by identifying the wrong areas of risk and misdirecting efforts at prevention and protection (Greer, 2003). Those who would seek to reform the way in which the newsprint media portray sex crimes must engage seriously with each of those issues outlined above. And that challenge will not easily be overcome.

Notes

1. Broadly speaking, unionists support the maintenance of the union between Northern Ireland and the rest of the UK, and nationalists advocate the establishment of a united Ireland, comprising both north and south, subject to the executive powers of an all-Ireland government. For detailed accounts of the conflict, see Bew *et al.* (1996); Ruane and Todd (1996); McGarry and O'Leary (1995); Bowyer Bell (1993); Bew and Gillespie (1993); O'Dowd *et al.* (1980). With respect to the press, the *Belfast Telegraph* and *News Letter* are openly unionist, and the *Irish News* is openly nationalist. The *Irish Times* claims to be a 'paper of record' with a non-partisan stance on the constitutional issue, but is widely acknowledged as maintaining a pro-nationalist line. The Sunday papers are less overtly political. The *Belfast Telegraph*'s sister publication, the *Sunday Life*, was described by a number of journalists as 'fairly neutral'. In the words of the editor, 'we are obviously a "law and order" newspaper. We are supportive of the security forces, but we don't write them a blank cheque.' The *Sunday World* claims political neutrality. In practice, however, it leans toward nationalism.
2. Media attention to the issue of child sex abuse has been such that examinations of press coverage elsewhere have evidenced a phenomenon generically referred as 'social problem fatigue' (Finkelhor, 1984), but in the present context more specifically known as 'child abuse fatigue' (Goddard, 1996; Skidmore, 1995; Kitzinger and Skidmore, 1995). It describes a level of journalistic 'overkill' on child sex abuse stories, where editors and reporters become frustrated with continually producing reports on the same phenomenon, and at the same time concerned that readers will grow weary of reading them. There was no evidence of 'child abuse fatigue' in the Northern Ireland press (see also Goddard, 1996).
3. This would appear to be a type of displacement. For a discussion from a psychoanalytic perspective of the role of anxiety and, in particular, its displacement in fear of crime, see Jefferson and Hollway (2000).
4. Establishing the proportion of court reports addressing stranger-assaults raises the issue of what constitutes a 'stranger'. Although no pre-existing relationship may be stated explicitly in a press report, if 'consent' is cited as the key issue (which it frequently is) the victim and offender must have been known to each other, if only in the most casual sense. If a woman is walked home and then assaulted by someone she has met in a bar that night, for example, there is some sort of pre-existing relationship, but they may reasonably still be thought of as relative strangers. In this analysis, stranger-assaults were taken to be those cases in which the victims were – or so it seemed from the report – sexually assaulted by individuals with whom they had no apparent previous relationship or contact.
5. This type of language would appear to be used with much greater frequency in the English national press, and not just in the tabloids (Soothill *et al.* 1998).

6. The Child Abuse and Rape Enquiry (CARE) unit was established in 1985 to deal exclusively with sex crime cases. Police reforms – and the CARE unit especially – were widely praised by practitioners and survivors interviewed for this research.

7. Though it should be noted that all of the national English newspapers are readily available in Northern Ireland, including those tabloids which, as Soothill *et al*. (1998) show, use these terms regularly.

References

Atmore, C. (1998) 'Towards 2000: Child Sexual Abuse and the Media', in A. Howe (ed.) *Sexed Crime in the News*, Sydney: The Federation Press.

Barwise, P. and Gordon, D. (1998) 'The Economics of the Media', in A. Briggs and P. Cobley (eds) *The Media: An Introduction*, London: Longman.

Bauman, Z. (1998) *Globalization: the Human Consequences*, Cambridge: Polity Press.

Bauman, Z. (2000) 'Social Uses of Law and Order', in D. Garland and R. Sparks (eds) *Criminology and Social Theory*, Oxford: Oxford University Press.

Beckett, K. (1994) 'Setting the Public Agenda: "Street Crime" and Drug use in American Politics', *Social Problems*, 41(3), 425–47.

Benedict, H. (1992) *Virgin or Vamp*, Oxford: Oxford University Press.

Best, J. (1990) *Threatened Children*, Chicago: University of Chicago Press.

Best, J. (1995) *Images of Issues: Typifying Contemporary Social Problems*, 2nd edn, Hawthorne, NY: Aldine de Gruyter.

Bew, P. and Gillespie, G. (1993) *Northern Ireland: A Chronology of the Troubles, 1968–1993*, Dublin: Gill and Macmillan.

Bew, P., Gibbon, P. and Patterson, H. (1996) *Northern Ireland 1921–1996: Political Forces and Social Classes*, London: Serif.

Bourdieu, P. (1998) *On Television and Journalism*, London: Pluto.

Bowyer Bell, J. (1993) *The Irish Troubles: A Generation of Violence 1967–1992*, Dublin: Gill and Macmillan Ltd.

Briggs, A. and Cobley, P. (eds) (1998) *The Media: An Introduction*, London: Longman.

Bromley, M. (1997) 'Writing Terrorism Out of the Story', in A. O'Day (ed.) *Political Violence in Northern Ireland: Conflict and Conflict Resolution*, London: Praeger.

Bromley, M. (1998) 'The "Tabloiding" of Britain: "Quality" Newspapers in the 1990s', in H. Stephenson and M. Bromley (eds) *Sex Lies and Democracy: The Press and the Public*, London: Longman.

Cameron, D. and Frazer, E. (1987) *The Lust to Kill: A Feminist Investigation of Sexual Murder*, Cambridge: Polity Press.

Campbell, B. (1988) *Unofficial Secrets: Child Sexual Abuse – The Cleveland Case*, London: Virago Press.

Caputi, J. (1987) *The Age of the Sex Crime*, London: The Women's Press.

Carlen, P. (1976) *Magistrates' Justice*, London: Martin Robinson.

Cavender, G. and Mulcahy, A. (1998) 'Trial by Fire: Media Constructions of Corporate Deviance', *Justice Quarterly*, 15(4), 697–719.

Chibnall, S. (1977) *Law and Order News*, London: Tavistock.

Cohen, S. (1980) *Folk Devils and Moral Panics: The Creation of the Mods and Rockers*, Oxford: Oxford University Press.

Cohen, S. and Young, J. (1981) *The Manufacture of News*, London: Constable.

Cumberbatch, G. (1998) 'Media Effects: The Continuing Controversy', in A. Briggs and P. Cobley (eds) *The Media: An Introduction*, London: Longman.

Curran, J. and Gurevitch, M. (eds) (2000) *Mass Media and Society*, 3rd edn, London: Arnold.

Ditton, J. and Duffy, J. (1983) 'Bias in the Newspaper Reporting of Crime', in *British Journal of Criminology*, 23(2), 159–65.

Dobash, R.E. and Dobash, R. (1979) *Violence Against Wives*, New York: Free Press.

Entman, R. (1989) 'How the Media Affect What People Think: An Information Processing Approach', *Journal of Politics*, 51(2), 347–70.

Ericson, R., Baranek, P. and Chan, J. (1987) *Visualising Deviance: A Study of News Organisation*, Milton Keynes: Open University Press.

Ericson, R., Baranek, P. and Chan, J. (1989) *Negotiating Control: A Study of News Sources*, Milton Keynes: Open University Press.

Ericson, R., Baranek, P. and Chan, J. (1991) *Representing Order: Crime, Law and Justice in the News Media*, Milton Keynes: Open University Press.

Ferrell, J. and Websdale, N. (eds) (1999) *Making Trouble: Cultural Constructions of Crime, Deviance, and Control*, Hawthorne, NY: Aldine de Gruyter.

Finkelhor, D. (1984) *Child Sexual Abuse: New Theory and Research*, New York: Free Press.

Finkelhor, D. and Yllo, K. (1985) *License to Rape: Sexual Abuse of Wives*, New York: Holt, Rinehart and Winston.

Fishman, M. (1978) 'Crime Waves as Ideology', *Social Problems*, 25, 531–43.

Franklin, B. (1997) *Newszak and News Media*, London: Arnold.

Franklin, B. (ed.) (1999) *Social Policy, the Media and Misrepresentation*, London: Routledge.

Franklin, B. and Parton, N. (eds) (1991) *Social Work, The Media and Public Relations*, London: Routledge.

Galtung, J. and Ruge, M. (1970) 'The Structure of Foreign News', in J. Tunstall (ed.) *Media Sociology*, London: Constable.

Gamson, W., Croteau, D., Hoynes, W., and Sasson, T. (1992) 'Media Images and the Social Construction of Reality', *Annual Review of Sociology*, 18, 373–93.

Garfinkel, H. (1956) 'Conditions of Successful Degradation Ceremonies', in *American Sociological Review*, 61, 420–24.

Garland, D. (2000) 'The Culture of High Crime Societies: Some Preconditions of Recent "Law and Order" Politics', *British Journal of Criminology*, 40, 347–75.

Garland, D. and Sparks, R. (eds) (2000) *Criminology and Social Theory*, Oxford: Oxford University Press.

Giddens, A. (1990) *The Consequences of Modernity*, Cambridge: Polity Press.

Goddard, C. (1996) 'Read All About it: The News About Child Abuse', *Child Abuse Review*, 5(5), 301–09.

Goode, E. and Ben-Yehuda, N. (1994) *Moral Panics: The Social Construction of Deviance*, Oxford: Blackwell.

Gordon, L. (1988) *Heroes of Their Own Lives: The Politics and History of Family Violence*, New York: Penguin.

Gough, D. (1996) 'The Literature on Child Abuse and the Media', *Child Abuse Review*, 5(5), 363–73.

Greer, C. (2001) 'Risky Business', *Criminal Justice Matters*, 43, 28–9.

Greer, C. (2003) *Sex Crime and the Media: Sex Offending and the Press in a Divided Society*, Cullompton: Willan.

Grimwade, C. (1998) 'Reckless Sex: The Discursive Containment of Gender, Sexuality and HIV/AIDS', in A. Howe (ed.) *Sexed Crime in the News*, Sydney: The Federation Press.

Grover, C. and Soothill, K. (1995) 'The Social Construction of Sex Offenders', *Sociology Review'*, 4, 29–33.

Grubin, D. (1998) *Sex Offending Against Children: Understanding the Risk*, Police Research Series, Paper 99, Policing and Reducing Crime Unit, London: Home Office.

Hale, C. (1996) 'Fear of Crime: A Review of the Literature', *International Review of Victimology*, 4, 79–150.

Hall, R.E. (1985) *Ask Any Woman*, Bristol: Falling Wall Press.

Hall, S., Critcher, C., Jefferson, T., Clarke, J. and Roberts, B. (1978) *Policing the Crisis: Mugging, the State and Law and Order*, London: Macmillan.

Hebington, B. and Thomas, T. (1997) 'Keeping Track: Observations on Sex Offender Registers in the US', *Crime Detection and Prevention Series*, Paper 83, Police Research Group, London: Home Office.

Herman, E. and Chomsky, N. (1994) *Manufacturing Consent: The Political Economy of the Mass Media*, New York: Pantheon.

Hope, T. and Sparks, R. (eds) (2000) *Crime, Risk and Insecurity*, London: Routledge.

Howe, A. (ed.) (1998) *Sexed Crime in the News*, Sydney: The Federation Press.

Howe, A. (1999) '"The War Against Women": Media Representations of Men's Violence Against Women in Australia', in J. Ferrell and N. Websdale (eds) *Making Trouble: Cultural Constructions of Crime, Deviance, and Control*, Hawthorne, NY: Aldine de Gruyter.

Jefferson, T. and Hollway, W. (2000) 'The Role of Anxiety in Fear of Crime', in T. Hope and R. Sparks (eds) *Crime, Risk and Insecurity*, London: Routledge.

Jenkins, P. (1992) *Intimate Enemies: Moral Panics in Contemporary Great Britain*, Hawthorne, NY: Aldine de Gruyter.

Jenkins, P. (1994) *Using Murder: The Social Construction of Serial Homicide*, Hawthorne, NY: Aldine de Gruyter.

Jenkins, P. (1996) *Pedophiles and Priests: Anatomy of a Contemporary Crisis*, New York: Oxford University Press.

Kidd-Hewitt, D. (1995) 'Crime and the Media: A Criminological Perspective', in D. Kidd-Hewitt and R. Osborne (eds) *Crime and the Media: The Post-Modern Spectacle*, London: Pluto Press.

Kitsuse, J. and Spector, M. (1973) 'Toward a Sociology of Social Problems: Social Conditions, Value Judgements and Social Problems', in *Social Problems*, 20, 407–19.

Kitzinger, J. (1996) 'Media Constructions of Sexual Abuse Risks', *Child Abuse Review*, 5(5), 319–33.

Kitzinger, J. (1999a) 'A Sociology of Media Power: Key Issues in Audience Reception Research', in Philo, G. (ed.) *Message Received*, London: Longman.

Kitzinger, J. (1999b) 'The Ultimate Neighbour from Hell? Stranger Danger and the Media Framing of Paedophiles', in B. Franklin (ed.) *Social Policy, the Media and Misrepresentation*, London: Routledge.

Kitzinger, J. and Skidmore, P. (1995) 'Child Sexual Abuse and the Media', Summary Report to ESRC. Award no. R000233675. Report available from Glasgow Media Group.

Lees, S. (1995) 'The Media Reporting of Rape; The 1993 British "Date Rape" Controversy', in D. Kidd-Hewitt and R. Osborne (eds) *Crime and the Media: The Post-Modern Spectacle*, London: Pluto Press.

Livingstone, S. (1996) 'On the Continuing Problem of Media Effects', in J. Curran and M. Gurevitch (eds) *Mass Media and Society*, London: Arnold.

Loader, I., Girling, E. and Sparks, R. (2000) 'After Success? Anxieties of Affluence in an English Village', in T. Hope and R. Sparks (eds) *Crime, Risk and Insecurity*, London: Routledge.

Loseke, D. (1999) *Thinking About Social Problems: An Introduction to Constructionist Perspectives*, Hawthorne, NY: Aldine de Gruyter.

MacDougall, C. (1968) *Interpretative Reporting*, New York: Macmillan.

MacVean, A. (2000) 'Risk, Policing and the Management of Sex Offenders', *Crime Prevention and Community Safety: An International Journal*, 2(4), 7–18.

Maguire, M. (1997) 'Crime Statistics, Patterns and Trends: Changing Perceptions and their Implications', in M. Maguire, R. Morgan and R. Reiner (eds) *The Oxford Handbook of Criminology*, 2nd edn, Oxford: Oxford University Press.

Marsh, H. L. (1991) 'A Comparative Analysis of Crime Coverage in Newspapers in the United States and Other Countries From 1960–1989: A Review of the Literature', *Journal of Criminal Justice*, 19(1), 67–80.

McGarry, J. and O'Leary, B. (1995) *Explaining Northern Ireland: Broken Images*, Oxford: Blackwell.

McNair, B. (1998) *The Sociology of Journalism*, London: Arnold.

McNair, B. (1999) *News and Journalism in the UK: A Text Book*, 3rd edn, London: Routledge.

Meyers, M. (1997) *News Coverage of Violence Against Women: Engendering Blame*, Thousand Oaks, London: Sage.

Miller, D. (1993) 'Official Sources and "Primary Definition": The Case of Northern Ireland', *Media, Culture and Society*, 15, 385–406.

Miller, D. and Philo, G. (1999) 'The Effective Media', in G. Philo (ed.) *Message Received*, London: Longman.

Mirrlees-Black, C., Budd, T., Partridge, S. and Mayhew, P. (1998) *The 1998 British Crime Survey*, Home Office Statistical Bulletin, Issue 21/98, London: Home Office.

Mirrlees-Black, C., Mayhew, P. and Percy, A. (1996) *The 1996 British Crime Survey*, Home Office Statistical Bulletin, Issue 19/96, London: Home Office.

Moore, C. (1995) *Betrayal of Trust: The Father Brendan Smyth Affair and the Catholic Church*, Dublin: Marino.

Moore, C. (1996) *The Kincora Scandal: Political Cover-up and Intrigue in Ulster*, Dublin: Marino.

Morgan, W. (1998) '"Damned in the Eyes of the World": The Media, Sexed Crime and Tasmania's Anti-Gay Laws', in A. Howe (ed.) *Sexed Crime in the News*, Sydney: The Federation Press.

Nava, M. (1988) 'Cleveland and the Press: Outrage and Anxiety in the Reporting of Child Sexual Abuse', in *Feminist Review*, 28, 103–21.

Nelson, B.J. (1984) *Making an Issue out of Child Sex Abuse: Political Agenda Setting for Social Problems*, Chicago: University of Chicago Press.

O'Day, A. (ed.) (1997) *Political Violence in Northern Ireland: Conflict and Conflict Resolution*, London: Praeger.

O'Dowd, L., Rolston, B. and Tomlinson, M. (1980) *Northern Ireland: Between Civil Rights and Civil War*, London: CSE Books.

Paglia, C. (1992) *Sex, Art, and American Culture*, London: Penguin.

Pfohl, S. (1977) 'The "Discovery" of Child Abuse', in *Social Problems*, 24, 310–23.

Philo, G. (1999) *Message Received*, London: Longman.

Reiner, R. (2000) *The Politics of the Police*, 3rd edn, Oxford: Oxford University Press.

Reiner, R., Livingstone, S. and Allen, J. (2000a) 'Casino Culture: Media and Crime in a Winner-Loser Society', in K. Stenson and D. Cowell (eds) *Crime, Risk and Justice*, Cullompton: Willan.

Reiner, R., Livingstone, S. and Allen, J. (2000b) 'No More Happy Endings? The Media and Popular Concern About Crime Since the Second World War', in T. Hope and R. Sparks (eds) *Crime, Risk and Insecurity*, London: Routledge.

Rock, P. (1973) 'News as Eternal Recurrence', in S. Cohen and J. Young (eds) *The Manufacture of News: Social Problems, Deviance and the Mass Media*, London: Constable.

Rolston, B. (1991) 'News Fit to Print: Belfast's Daily Newspapers', in B. Rolston (ed.) *The Media and Northern Ireland: Covering the Troubles*, Basingstoke: Macmillan.

Rolston, B. and Miller, D. (eds) (1996) *War and Words: The Northern Ireland Media Reader*, Belfast: Beyond the Pale.

Ruane, J. and Todd, J. (1996) *The Dynamics of Conflict in Northern Ireland: Power, Conflict and Emancipation*, Cambridge: Cambridge University Press.

Sampson, A. (1994) *Act of Abuse: Sex Offenders and the Criminal Justice System*, London: Routledge.

Sasson, T. (1995) *Crime Talk: How Citizens Construct Social Problems*, Hawthorne, NY: Aldine de Gruyter.

Schlesinger, P. and Tumber, H. (1994) *Reporting Crime: The Media Politics of Criminal Justice*, Oxford: Clarendon Press.

Schudson, M. (2000) 'The Sociology of News Production Revisited (Again)', in J. Curran and M. Gurevitch (eds) *Media, Culture and Society*, 3rd edn, London: Arnold.

Skidmore, P. (1995) 'Telling Tales; Media Power, Ideology and the Reporting of Child Sexual Abuse in Britain', in D. Kidd-Hewitt and R. Osborne (eds) *Crime and the Media: The Post-Modern Spectacle*, London: Pluto Press.

Smart, C. (1989) *Feminism and the Power of Law*, London: Routledge.

Smith, S. (1984) 'Crime in the News', in *British Journal of Criminology*, 24(3), 289–95.

Soothill, K. (1995) 'Sex Crime News From Abroad', in R. Dobash, R. Dobash, and L. Noaks (eds) *Gender and Crime*, Cardiff: University of Wales.

Soothill, K., Francis, B. and Ackereley, E. (1998) 'Paedophilia and Paedophiles', in *New Law Journal*, 12 (June), 882–3.

Soothill, K. and Walby, S. (1991) *Sex Crime in the News*, London: Routledge.

Sparks, C. (2000) 'From Dead Trees to Live Wires: The Internet's Challenge to Traditional Newspapers', in J. Curran and M. Gurevitch (eds) *Mass Media and Society*, 3rd edn, London: Arnold.

Sparks, R. (1992) *Television and the Drama of Crime: Moral Tales and the Place of Crime in Public Life*, Buckingham: Open University Press.

Spector, M. and Kitsuse, J. (1987) *Constructing Social Problems*, Hawthorne, NY: Aldine de Gruyter.

Stanko, E. (1990) *Everyday Violence*, London: Unwin Hyman.

Stanko, E. and Hobdell, K. (1993) 'Assault on Men: Masculinity and Male Victimisation', in *British Journal of Criminology*, 33(3), 400–15.

Stephenson, H. and Bromley, M. (eds) (1998) *Sex Lies and Democracy: The Press and the Public*, London: Longman.

Surette, R. (1998) *Media, Crime and Criminal Justice: Images and Realities*, 2nd edn, Belmont: Wadsworth.

Thomas, T. (2000) *Sex Crime: Sex Offenders and Society*, Cullompton: Willan.

Thompson, J.B. (2000) *Political Scandal: Power and Visibility in the Media Age*, Cambridge: Polity Press.

Thompson, K. (1998) *Moral Panics*, London: New York: Routledge.

Walker, N. (ed.) (1996) *Dangerous People*, London: Blackstone Press Limited.

Websdale, N. (1999) 'The Social Construction of "Stranger-Danger" in Washington State as a Form of Patriarchal Ideology', in J. Ferrell and N. Websdale (eds) *Making Trouble: Cultural Constructions of Crime, Deviance, and Control*, Hawthorne, NY: Aldine de Gruyter.

West, D. (1996) 'Sexual Molesters', in N. Walker (ed.) *Dangerous People*, London: Blackstone Press Limited.

West, D. (2000) 'The Sex Crime Situation: Deterioration More Apparent Than Real', *European Journal on Criminal Policy and Research*, 8, 399–422.

Wilczynski, A. (1999) 'Moral Panics and the Reporting of Child Sex Abuse', in *The Australian and New Zealand Journal of Criminology*, 32(3), 262–83.

Wilson, D. and Silverman, J. (2002) *Innocence Betrayed: Paedophilia, the Media and Society*, Cambridge: Polity Press.

Young, A. (1998) 'Violence as Seduction: Enduring Genres of Rape', in A. Howe (ed.) *Sexed Crime in the News*, Sydney: The Federation Press.

Young, J. (1981) 'Beyond the Consensual Paradigm: A Critique of Left Functionalism in Media Theory', in S. Cohen and J. Young (eds) *The Manufacture of News: Social Problems, Deviance and Mass Media*, London: Constable.

Chapter 6

Organized crime: Mafia myths in film and television

George S. Larke

Introduction

Hollywood gangster films, like many other genres, have referred to other media for narrative and thematic inspiration. Since the 1970s such inter-textual negotiations are no less prevalent. In fact, with the increased critical acclaim encouraged by 'New Hollywood' films such as *The Godfather Parts I, II and III* (1972, 1974, 1990) and *Goodfellas* (1990), cultural myths surrounding the Mafia have attracted huge interest from all media. However, it is no longer the lone gangster that dominates cultural discourses, but concepts of collectivity involving Mafia families, loyalty and respect.

Film has never operated in isolation from other cultural events. However, the televised Senate Hearings on Organized Crime in the 1950s have had a profound influence on subsequent film and television representations of the Mafia. Since then, the continuing dominance of Mafia in the media through the biographies of, *inter alia*, Bill Bonnano, Sammy Gravano and John Gotti, and television (HBO's *The Sopranos*) means that mythologies surrounding the existence, operating practices and ethnicity of organized crime are still developing and popular. Myths and film (*Little Caesar*, 1930; *Public Enemy*, 1931; *Scarface*, 1932) concerning the gangsters of the 1930s tended to focus on individual outlaws rather than criminal groups. Myths of the postwar period and beyond have concentrated on criminal organizations, or Mafia, and this has had a profound effect upon the structure and development of the later gangster films. This chapter will examine the ways in which post-1960s Hollywood gangster films and television employ very similar narratives that are constructed from the main elements of Mafia myths: Sicilian/Italian heritage, *compareggio*[1] and family hierarchies, crime as business and the influence of *omerta*.[2] Mafia myths also thrive on the precept that Italian-American identity remains separate from White American identity; a concept that Steinberg (1989), among others, has called 'white ethnicity'. This precept also maintains the notion that Mafia crime remains prevalent, but essentially separated from law-abiding mainstream American society.

Mafia Myths: Sources and Origins

Any explanation of the evolution of Mafia myths in Western culture is hampered by the various myths that have been circulating in varied domains. These include the American political perspective of publicized concerns and beliefs of Congress. There is also the sociological con-sideration of immigrant assimilation in American society since the early twentieth century, which has included ethnographic studies of immigrant poverty in urban areas. The cultural histories of some European homelands are also used in immigrant biographies and ethnographic studies to explain behaviour and beliefs. Furthermore, there is the law-enforcement perspective that is concerned with specific crime waves in America's recent history. And finally, there is the all-encompassing domain of the media text that has not only reported on all these perspectives, but has also provided commercial and cultural products featuring criminals in organized groups in literature, film and television.

In the 1950s and 1960s interest in the Mafia was given three very influential boosts. Firstly, the Kefauver Senate Hearings of 1951–52 cate-gorically expressed a belief in a nationwide criminal organization called the Mafia. Secondly, Joe Valachi's testimony to the McClellan Committee in 1963 included details about many top-level meetings, business dealings and killings in the Mafia. More importantly, Valachi described the structure and named all the titles and ranks, as well as names of many top-level Mafia bosses. The publicity that his testimony received, shown on live television, coupled with the publication of his story by Maas (1968) and even a film of the events (*The Valachi Papers*, 1972), made his testimony influential across a wide spectrum of popular media.

In consequence of the first two events, Mario Puzo's 1969 book, *The Godfather*, was published at a time when the fascination with Mafia myths was still prominent in news stories and government initiatives. Puzo's *The Godfather,* although primarily a work of fiction, unashamedly takes its form from Valachi's testimony and many of the events that he described, and makes indirect references to the Kefauver Senate Hearings. The immense popularity of book and subsequent film[3] means that it has possibly become one of the most influential descriptions of the American Mafia family in the twentieth century. Although the work is fictional, Puzo's story recapitulated Kefauver's and Valachi's statements and thus appeared to confirm them.

A desire to unveil the secret workings of Mafia life through clues provided in fiction, journalism and biographies has dominated discussions of the subject since the 1950s. Such unveiling has made the rules and traditions of the Mafia seem part of mainstream American culture. Commenting on fictional mob boss Tony Soprano (played by James Gandolfini), in HBO's immensely successful television series, *The Sopranos,* Holden describes Soprano as 'a harried forty-something middle-class Joe who, except for his occupation, is not all that different from the rest of us' (Holden, 2001: xiv). His occupation, head of a Mafia family, is incorporated into the broader structure of television comedy and soap opera. This occurs in a way that suggests not only that Mafia business is still alive, if not exactly well, in American culture, but also that it is easily understood in terms of its structure and traditions by a mass audience. The reasons behind such knowledge can be partly found in Hollywood gangster films since the 1960s.

Goodfellas (1990) has been viewed as a relatively realistic portrayal of Mafia life (*The Guardian* 25 October 1990; *Daily Mail,* 26 October 1990, *Western Mail,* 27 October 1990), although the realism, it could be argued, owes as much to generic verisimilitude as historical fact. Films such as *Goodfellas,* as well as, *Mean Streets* (1973), *State of Grace* (1990) and *Donnie Brasco* (1997) that are deemed 'realistic' by critics and audiences tend to assert the brutal self-serving nature of the Mafia, while those dubbed 'romantic', such as *The Godfather* trilogy, *Carlito's Way* (1993) and *Analyze This* (1999) focus on family loyalties and traditions. Under this rubric, *Goodfellas* has been viewed by some critics as a condemnation of Mafia mythologies, while in comparison, *The Godfather* trilogy romanticizes them. It is evident that, although the films are different, it is problematic to simply contrast them in this way. *The Godfather* was condemned for its brutality at the time of its release. For example, Donald Zec writing in the *Daily Mirror* stated, 'it is vicious, it is brutal and I doubt whether such casual and unremitting slaughter has ever been matched in a single motion picture' (22 August 1972). Similarly, both the *Sun* (22 August 1972) and *The Scotsman* (23 August 1972) compared the film to 'Nazi propaganda'. The film was, however, applauded by other critics: *New Society* suggested it was an arena where 'heroes act out large and noble destinies' (21 September 1972). *The Guardian* is not alone in regarding the film a 'one of the best gangster films of all time' (20 June 1996).

What is particularly interesting is the ways in which the complexities of gangster narratives, especially with regard to mythologies, are reflected in the differing responses of reviewers and critics. However, films reflect elements from mythologies that may appear contradictory, but the very structure of myth, as stated earlier, allows for such discrepancies. *Gotti* (1996) reflects *The Godfather's* mythical version of the Mafia ideal, but is mingled with *Goodfellas*-style brutality. This is epitomized in a conversation between John Gotti (Armand Assante) and Neil Dellacroce (Anthony Quinn). Gotti has killed a 'made man' (a full member of the Mafia) from a rival family. The bosses call for Gotti to be killed in return, according to the rules, or ethics, of Sicilian Mafia. Neil successfully pleads for Gotti's life by identifying him as like a son to him, thus reflecting the family element of Mafia myths by implicitly suggesting that Gotti's life is saved by such loyalties. However, Neil warns Gotti that if the bosses had said 'you gotta go, I would have come here today with these two zips and you would go […] You break the rules and this whole goddam thing of ours cracks and crumbles'. Unlike *Goodfellas* or *Casino*, but in a similar way to *The Godfather Trilogy*, *Gotti* suggests that the rules are there for protection, rather than constriction. Therefore Mafia mythologies can deflect any inconsistencies and contradictions within gangster films by encompassing very different representations of characters and activities and encouraging very different audience responses.

Compareggio *and Hierarchies*

Casino (1995) develops Scorsese's earlier representations of bosses,[4] by portraying the Mafia old guard as financial leeches upon the working guys, and as out-of-touch, overly controlling patriarchs, who would kill a man for adultery or verbally disrespecting a made man. This develops earlier narratives, such as *Mean Streets,* where Charlie is advised by Uncle Giovanni (played by Cesare Danova) to choose his friends wisely: 'an honourable man has honourable friends'. The narrative then focuses on Charlie's conflict between loyalty to his 'dishonourable' friends and aspirations for Mafia membership. In *Goodfellas*, Pauly Cicero (Paul Sorvino) explains that he cannot allow Henry (Ray Liotta) to get divorced, as family is sacrosanct in Mafia life: 'You gotta go back, it's the only way. You gotta keep up appearance'. Similarly, in *Casino*, Remo

Gaggi (Pasquale Cajano) asks Frank Marino (Frank Vincent) about Nicky Santoro's (Joe Pesci) affair with Ginger (Sharon Stone) as he is warned of its effect on business. Frankie's narration tells us:

What could I say? I knew if I gave them the wrong answer, I mean, Nicky, Ginger, Ace, all of 'em could wind up getting killed. Because there's one thing about these old timers, they don't like to see any fucking around with other guy's wives. It's bad for business.

In this case, Sicilian Mafia ideals are shown to be profit-orientated, emphasizing the business element of the Mafia myths, rather than the purely ethical, and suggesting that they are often used to bully the lower ranks into toeing the line. However, neither Nicky, nor Ace Rothstein's (Robert DeNiro) actions encourage audience sympathies, in that they are callously self-serving. Therefore, the bosses' fear of disorderly conduct can be viewed as a justified reaction to the younger generation's inability to abide by traditional Mafia ideals.

In short, Scorsese's films often focus on the Mafia as a patriarchal construct simultaneously protecting, but also constraining, a younger generation of Italian-Americans, or gangster 'wannabes'. As stated, reviews have suggested that his films provide an 'antidote to *The Godfather*'s mythic version of the Mafia' (Smith, 1990: 68). It is also important to remember, however, that myths are always developing and so *Goodfellas* simply offers a new version of older myths. This does not mean to say that Scorsese's antidote eclipses previous myths. In fact, the individualism portrayed in his characters not only destroys the Mafia families, but in doing so justifies the bosses' seemingly old-fashioned rules and thus reinforces the myths found in *The Godfather*. Therefore, it is far more productive to understand the films as part of a wider continuous narrative of Mafia myths that is constantly evolving.

The Sopranos links references to *The Godfather* (especially through its characters' occasional references and idolatry of the films) with suburban family soap opera and some clever reworkings of old Mafia clichés. The result is a highly enjoyable parody of the Mafia. This is a clear indication of the prevalence and popularity of Mafia myths. *The Sopranos'* success as a mainstream television series (albeit only on a subscription channel in the USA) shows the extent to which the Mafia is now a part of mainstream culture. It is essential that audiences must feel they know and understand this society enough in order to be able to easily understand and enjoy how it is being parodied.

Sicilian heritage

The secrets of the Mafia have become widely known through some of the most commercially successful gangster films since the 1960s, such as *The Godfather* trilogy and *Goodfellas*. These films fulfil the criteria identified earlier as the primary elements of Mafia myths. Both prioritize the importance of Sicilian heritage and thus, at first glance, appear to consider Mafia as determined by race. For instance, the Corleone family hail from Sicily and the narrative often makes allusions to Tom Hagen (Robert Duvall) as an outsider, due to his Irish-German identity. He is the family's *consigliare* (legal adviser) and adopted brother to Sonny (James Caan), Michael (Al Pacino), Connie (Talia Shire) and Fredo Corleone (John Cazale), but is rejected by Michael, in Part One of *The Godfather* trilogy, when Michael wants to build the family's strength. In Part Two, Michael reverses this and picks Tom to be his deputy, rather than Fredo. This is a significant factor in signalling the breakdown of family loyalties. Fredo has betrayed Michael, but Michael also betrays the family unity by ignoring his brother and, thus, the Sicilian heritage: 'I was passed over' explains Fredo later, 'I shouldda had respect'. Part Three focuses on Michael's desperate attempts to rekindle connections with his Sicilian roots and his family, but to no avail.[5] Similarly, in *Goodfellas*, it is explained that only those with an unblemished heritage, 'whose Sicilian blood can be traced right back to the home country' (Henry Hill's narration), can become 'made men' (complete Mafia members). Henry Hill is half-Sicilian, half-Irish, Jimmy Conway (Robert DeNiro) is Irish, and Tommy DeVito (Joe Pesci) is Sicilian. Thus, even though Tommy is the least competent, with an unpredictable and dangerous temper and with little respect for fellow Mafiosi, he is the only candidate for full Mafia membership. In short, he is an exaggerated version of Sonny Corleone, heir to the Corleone family by birth, but someone who Vito always maintained was a 'bad Don'. This makes Sicilian heritage akin to royal lineages, wherein birthrights determine future rulers. *The Godfather* and *Goodfellas* identify two flaws in this system. Firstly, in a system based on Sicilian or Italian heritage, the inclusion of outsiders weakens the traditions on which unity is based. Outsiders Jimmy Conway and Henry Hill corrupt and eventually destroy the Mafia family in *Goodfellas*, first by their involvement in drug business and, second, through Henry's testimony. Secondly, an insistence on ethnic purity and birthrights means that, occasionally, bad men will rise to be leaders.

In *The Sopranos* the Mafia is again shown to be a common element in an Italian/Sicilian heritage. When Tony confesses his involvement to his daughter he explains that it is so much part of his family heritage that 'maybe being a rebel in my family would have been selling patio furniture on Route 22'. In other words, Mafia is an unavoidable part of his identity. Thus, whether it is condemned or romanticized it remains a constant presence.

While individual enterprise is applauded in American society (Webster, 1998) and often associated with the classic gangster films (Warshow, 1948; McArthur, 1972; Cawelti, 1976), it is less easily defined in later films. It could be argued that individual enterprise is stifled in films such as *The Godfather, Goodfellas* and *Donnie Brasco*. The emphasis is on individual sacrifice in favour of firstly the criminal family and secondly the national network: Michael Corleone sacrifices his legitimate career, Henry Hill's individual enterprise brings about his downfall and Lefty Ruggiero (Al Pacino) in *Donnie Brasco* identifies himself as merely a cog in the criminal system, rather than a key player. Allusions to a wider criminal network are also prevalent, especially through Hyman Roth (Lee Strasburg) in *The Godfather Part II* (1974), and trips to Florida to negotiate with other families in both *Goodfellas* and *Donnie Brasco*. It could be argued that these films lament the loss of individual freedom against the increasingly corporate nature of modern business practices. This is one of the reasons given for Tony Soprano's anxiety attacks in the television series. The 'business' of Mafia is taking over from the 'value system', through which he learned his trade. He cannot control events to the extent he feels he should be able to. Just like Michael Corleone, Tony is unsure whether it is his failing as a boss, or modern society's disregard for Mafia tradition that is causing his stress. The notion of corporate identity that permeates these narratives alienates individuality, in that an individual's criminal ambition is stifled within the corporate style of Mafia business. Individual enterprise is still romanticized, for instance Chris Moltisano (Michael Imperioli, in *The Sopranos*) constantly searches for his own 'arc' (a reference to the rise-and-fall trajectory of classic Hollywood gangster narratives) that importantly involves moments of individual success. However, his nostalgia for a traditional gangster role is represented in comedy in the face of the modern Mafia's emphasis on corporate styles of business.

However, corporate styles can also be viewed favourably. Cressey (1969) maintains that the Mafia operates as a business, with coherent national networks of associates. *The Godfather* trilogy and *Goodfellas* perpetuate that mythology. Furthermore, the corporate nature of criminal activity combines notions of extended family loyalties with business tactics. Albert Fried, who chronicled the rise and fall of the Jewish gangster in American culture, notes that:

Italian-Americans have tended to keep their vocation going inside their families, often marrying into similar families, thus perpetuating the institution generation after generation, much as skilled craftsmen once did through guilds. (Fried, 1993: xiv)

Fried suggests that Jewish gangsters during Prohibition were as powerful as the Italians, but had no notable successors to carry on the business. Thus, an attention to Sicilian heritage and family ties bound within corporate-style operations is held to account for the success and longevity of Italian Mafia culture, rather than individual enterprise. This also accounts for its seeming superiority during the late twentieth century as the oldest Mafia tribe in terms of ethnic identity. Therefore, in each of these films the Italian Mafia ideal is presented through Italian ethnic identity and the acceptance of patriarchal Mafia rules and traditions are portrayed as essential for a family's continued existence. The fact that all of these narratives question, disrupt or endanger those same traditions does not alter the fact that it is Mafia traditions that bind the family together.

The Italian Mafia is presented as the pinnacle of the Italian community, the significance of which is twofold. It emphasizes the fusion between Italian-American identity and the Mafia, but it also focuses on the extent to which the community element of Mafia myths is founded in Italian ethnic identity. The fusion between the two suggests that as long as an Italian-American community exists, the Mafia will also exist in one form or another. This is evident in all the films and television series discussed so far, but it is also evident in films that do not focus directly on Mafia business, such as *A Brooklyn State of Mind* (1996). Marketed as a gangster film, the narrative focuses on a young man's discovery of the true nature of his father's death 20 years earlier. Set in New York's Little Italy, the patronage of Danny Parente (Danny Aiello) as a Mafia man is accepted without question. He is also the leading voice in the assertion of traditional family and community ideals. As part of the Mafia myths, this character embodies the contradictory nature of such ideals. He is one of the few people who cares about family loyalty and his cultural heritage, but he is also unveiled as the murderer of the boy's father and a leading extortionist of local businessmen. Thus, this one character represents both the romance and the brutality of Mafia myths.

The Italian Mafia ideal has dominated gangster films since the 1960s.[6] The Sicilian heritage is both romanticized and condemned, but it is nevertheless promoted as the original and most powerful. The importance of family is maintained by focusing on the disastrous results of any lapses in unity. Ethnic identity is highlighted as the dominant signifier of heritage and unity. Italian ethnicity has become the Mafia ideal, against which all others are measured. This is partly due to the commercial success of *The Godfather* trilogy and Scorsese's films, but it is also due to the focus on Italian communities in Senate hearings and biographies since the 1950s. Thus the Italian Mafia now represents the mainstream in gangster films, yet remains Other to law-abiding society. Here, then, is yet another persistent contradiction. The exclusivity of the Italian Mafia family keeps them as Other in relation to mainstream society, but this aspect is also romanticized to the point of cliché. Exclusivity and romanticizing ethnic heritage form part of the allure of the Mafia.

Fact and Fiction

As already stated, Mario Puzo's novel *The Godfather* draws some of its detail from Joe Valachi's testimony to the McClellan Committee. The Capo regime structure of the Corleone family is a replica of Valachi's description of Mafia hierachies, which in turn is based on the Roman Empire's military structure. On a more anecdotal level, in *The Godfather Part I*, Clemenza (Richard Castellano) explains to Michael that after he kills Police Chief McClusky (Sterling Hayden) and Sollozo (Al Lettieri), the family will 'hit the mattresses', as there will be a gang war. The phrase 'going on the mattress' is explained in Valachi's testimony:

> You see, during the Catellammarese trouble [a Mafia war] we had to take mattresses with us as we were moving from one apartment to another. Sometimes we only had a minute's notice, and so you needed a mattress to sleep on. This is our meaning of going on the mattress. (Maas,1968: 110)

Films after *The Godfather* that are based on biographies, testimonies or autobiographies also concentrate on the intricacies of Mafia life. For example, we learn about the selection process and power of 'made men' in *Goodfellas*, based on Henry Hill's testimony and Nicholas Pileggi's biography, *Wiseguy* (1984). Various modes of torture and execution appropriate to certain crimes are explained in *The Godfather Part II* and *Casino*. We discover the fatal meaning of being 'sent for' in *Donnie Brasco*, based on the published experiences of FBI agent Joe Pistone, *Donnie Brasco: My Undercover Life in the Mafia* (1989), where execution is most often dealt out by the closest associates of the victim. Films such as *Honor*

Thy Father, based on Guy Talese's biography of Joe Bonanno, or *Gotti*, based on contemporary headlines, provide details on the bosses of high-profile Mafia families, the Bonannos and the Gambinos, their heritage, their rules and business operations. The extent to which these biographies and films fashion popular concepts of the Mafia also appear in the firest series of *The Sopranos*. Tony's invitation to join a golf club results in an uncomfortable interrogation from other members. They ask how well he knows John Gotti, how close to truth is *The Godfather* story? While on the one hand these scenes are designed to make audiences sympathize with Tony against the ignorance of those that pre-judge him and his heritage, by referring to both reality and fiction it serves to perpetuate the strength of these Mafia myths. Such dialogue, set sequences and references operate not only as signifiers of genre convention, but also as signifiers of Mafia myths, which operate as a continuous discourse across different films. It is not so much the allusion to fact that underscores the films, but rather allusions to mythologies that interact between notions of ethnic identity, historical events, biographies, fictional literature, television, even advertising, as well as cinema. Popular concepts of the Mafia are so prevalent in recent American cultural history that their validity defies scrutiny. It is impossible to ascertain the truth; what remains and is perpetuated is myth.

Allusions to factual events and the structure and workings of the Mafia are so common that films that do not advertise a specific recourse to factual events can also add to the ever-developing network of Mafia mythologies. The narrative of *The Funeral* (1995) is woven around popular Italian superstitions, for example that a dead man's wounds will bleed if his killer enters the room where the coffin sits. This, according to Ray Tempio (Christopher Walken), is why rival gangsters do not attend each other's funerals. This premise provides both the tension and the naïve motivation for revenge killings in the film. However, it also functions as a reminder of the interaction between Mafia identity and Italian historical culture. The parodies *Analyze This* and *Mickey Blue Eyes* (1999) rely on popular understandings of Mafia myths, and also make allusions to such popularity in two ways. In *Analyze This*, Dr Ben Sobel (Billy Crystal) has enough understanding of Mafia mythologies to know how to behave when forced to take Paul Vitti's (Robert De Niro) place at a 'sit down' between Mafia bosses. His use of stereotypical Italian phrases and gestures is clearly used for comic effect and to reflect his preconceptions of Mafia dialogue, but he knows the importance of the event and the need to negotiate peace with the fellow families. It is also assumed that audiences possess this knowledge since this set scene, reminiscent of the meeting of the five families in *The Godfather*, is not overtly explained. Similarly, in *Mickey Blue Eyes*, Davenport's (Hugh Grant) attraction to and understanding of his fianceé's Mafia relatives are fuelled by knowledge of previous Hollywood films. Davenport learns enough to be able to pass himself off convincingly as a 'wise guy', thus suggesting, albeit through parody, that real Mafiosi are just like their Hollywood counterparts.

Omerta

Gangster films are fuelled by mythologies of the Mafia, but in turn such films influence the continuing development of those mythologies. Thus, the distinction between fact and fiction is blurred to the extent that both romanticize the Mafia. One of the most important examples of how allusions to factual events are used to romanticize the Mafia and its power appears in *The Godfather Part II*. This example also foregrounds the importance of *omerta* as one of the ultimate displays of loyalty in Mafia mythologies. Michael Corleone is indicted to appear before a Senate Committee hearing on charges of organized criminal activity. His old associate Frankie Pentangeli (Michael V. Gazzo) has provided testimony against him that will almost certainly guarantee a conviction. The film version of the hearings resembles newsreel footage of the original Kefauver and McClellan hearings. The layout of the courtroom, the crowds, the inclusion of journalists, the constant noise and the charts of Mafia family hierarchies, are based on actual events. The inclusion of such scenes also echoes the previous year's *Lucky Luciano* (1974), which employed realist film-making techniques and included the re-creation of discussions from the International Conference on Drug Traffic (1952) at the United Nations Headquarters. However, the cinematography used in *The Godfather Part II* Senate hearings is in line with the rest of the film. The lighting is colder than the rich sepia tones used in *Part I* and the flashback sequences in *Part II*, but still richly defined and employing deep focus to emphasize the crowded arena and the centrality of Michael's presence. The film makes use of realist techniques, but combines them with the choreographed *mise-en-scène* associated with *The Godfather* films, thus emphasizing the interaction of fact with mythology.

The scenes that cover the day of Pentangeli's testimony show Michael arriving in the courtroom with Pentangeli's brother (Salvatore Po), who has flown in from Sicily. This man is shown in traditional Sicilian rural costume and he speaks no English. Thus, we are encouraged to assume that he represents both Michael's and Pentangeli's heritage. Upon seeing his brother, Pentangeli retracts his statement and the case against

Michael instantly collapses. Further information is provided in a subsequent conversation between Michael and his wife Kay (Diane Keaton). Kay finds it incredible that Pentangeli's brother simply being there could alter his testimony. She asks how it was that 'all he had to do was show up'. Michael explains that the brother was there to help Pentangeli: 'it was between the brothers Kay, I had nothing to do with it'. Kay's questions are there for the purpose of expressing possible audience concerns: was Pentangeli's brother a hostage, who would be killed if Pentangeli went ahead and testified? The more ethical reason, in line with Mafia mythologies, is suggested later by Pentangeli's conversation with Tom Hagen. Pentangeli's brother was a Don in Sicily and lived by the old traditions of Mafia. One of the oldest and most powerful forces in Mafia mythologies is *omerta*. Pentangeli's brother was there to remind him of his oath of 'silence till death'. To break the code meant dishonouring his family name, thus dishonouring his brother, their wives and all their children. These scenes express the strength of honour and loyalty that are thought to exist in Mafia traditions.

The function of these scenes in *The Godfather Part II*, as part of the development of Mafia mythologies in gangster films, is to suggest the Mafia as a powerful force that evades scrutiny and destruction through its code of *omerta*. Allusions to the Kefauver Committee Hearings, which were held during the same years in which the narrative is set, work on two levels. Firstly, they suggest that Puzo's scripted events are based on fact, which in turn gives credence to other featured events, such as the bribing of a senator for a gambling licence and pre-revolution Cuban business deals. The outcome of such a narrative is mythology. Secondly, the inclusion of such scenes in the film adds credence to the notion that the Mafia exists and that it beat the Kefauver Committee by upholding its code of *omerta*, as suggested in Moore's account of the hearings. Pentangeli's instant retraction and subsequent suicide, in order to restore his family's honour, offer a romantic insight into the power of Mafia heritage and loyalties. These scenes use allusions to factual events to promote the romance of Mafia honour as real and workable codes. Thus, the Mafia is promoted as an organization that can really exist, and whose moral standards remain superior to American democracy and law-enforcement agencies, who cannot comprehend or undermine such loyalties. In turn, such mythologies underscore a romanticized and homogenous view of ethnicity, which through the upholding of traditional values, is an effective weapon against white, Anglo-Saxon Protestant (WASP) imperialist values.

Ethnicity

In one sense, the Italian Mafia is the ideal against which all cultures in America are measured. Consequently, and compared with all other ethnic crime, it is arguable that the Italian Mafia is so much a part of American culture that it represents normality, or it has been assimilated into the mainstream so much that it is indistinguishable from WASP male ideals. This is the argument made by Vera Dika (2000), who suggests that *The Godfather* is essentially a white male fantasy. She argues that *The Godfather* promotes white male identity as tribal, or identifiable as an homogenous entity, at least on a fantasy level. This is achieved because, she argues, Italianicity in the film is submerged beneath the universal themes of male bonding and business. When added to the possibility of the Italian Mafia as assimilated into mainstream culture, it would appear that Dika has a valid argument. However, it is not true to say that ethnicity is submerged. While *The Godfather*, or more recently, *The Sopranos* can be read as a white male fantasy, such a reading ignores the very foregrounding of Italian identity that makes it possible for the films and television series to function as 'safe' white male fantasies.

The fantasy of a secret society with masculine rituals, not dominant but under threat can be traced back to Warshow's original assessment of the popularity of the gangster film (Warshow, 1946). Audiences identify with the freedom, while simultaneously separating themselves from the actions. However, this separation relies on the identification of difference between the audience and the criminal. The iconography and conventions of the films have been circulated in popular culture to the extent that the Mafia are no longer unique, or distinct from mainstream identity, in the same way as they were in the early 1970s. However, the gangster narrative structure still focuses on the exclusivity of this world in opposition to mainstream society. It is still a convention in film and television that gestures, dialogue and costume isolate Mafia identity from mainstream society, to the extent that dialogue or actions often still require explanation within the text. Thus, the Mafia remains a unique and exclusive society to a multi-ethnic audience.

Conclusion

Mafia myths appear to be confused by the conflicting interaction of many contributors. The political and law-enforcement agenda seems often to be at odds with images shown in popular entertainment. Even though the Kefauver Committee and other agencies failed to provide conclusive evidence one way or another about the Mafia, no one seems to have been 'really' listening anyway. The media loved Valachi's testimony in 1962 and the public loved Puzo's story in 1969. The myths remain consistently flexible to provide meanings across different decades and cultural domains. They provide feasible evidence of a counterculture, an underworld that exists within society that defies, and maybe even influences, national politics and law enforcement. This, in turn, suggests that no matter how wealthy, powerful or respectable the face of America becomes, it still may provide an environment for outlaws to exist under the surface. Furthermore, these outlaws, or networks, are not threatening to the ordinary citizen. The films both acknowledge a social climate of inexplicable and random violence while also offering safe explanations. The violence is shown to be the work of others, and we cannot be victims of it unless we become involved, probably through our own actions, within this world. No matter how tenuous or romantic these assumptions may appear, they provide the backbone for countless film and television productions, novels, biographies and true crime testimonies published in America.

Myths also give particular film narratives credibility as authentic portrayals. For instance, myths of Sicilian culture and heritage mean that films such as *The Godfather, Mean Streets, Goodfellas, Casino, The Funeral* and *Donnie Brasco*, and the television series *The Sopranos*, appear as credible examples of how the Mafia has developed in American society through the Sicilian or Italian-American community. As stated, the fact that Mario Puzo credits Joe Valachi's testimony as a primary influence for the book *The Godfather*, or the fact that *Goodfellas* was based on the testimony of Henry Hill, and *Donnie Brasco* on the memoirs of FBI agent Joe Pistone (Johnny Depp), gives the resulting films a credibility as realistic portrayals of Mafia life, even though they refer to myths rather than proven facts.

Mafia myths also operate to define boundaries between the criminal and ordinary society. Whether the Mafia is romanticized or condemned in its actions, it is always defined as different or separate from ordinary society through its exclusivity, secrecy and ethnic heritage. The cultural imperative of Mafia myths is similar in post-1960s films, just as it was in earlier examples, defining boundaries between the criminal world and the rest of society. According to Roland Barthe's (1973) assessment of myth in discourse, the function of myth is to make sense of an unstable concept within more stable narratives. This, however, is an illusory practice, as myths within discourse are constantly subject to change. However, the cultural problems that Mafia myths address and temporarily resolve are the boundaries between criminality and the law, but also notions of individual enterprise and the increasing corporate nature of American business, assimilation and anti-assimilationist ideals. It is not the case that one side is always prioritized over the other. In *The Godfather* and *The Sopranos*, law-abiding society is suggested to be as corrupt and based on similar ideals to the family's criminal activities. In contrast, *The Funeral* shows the criminal community to be a brutal, unpredictable arena, which encourages the feeling that, in comparison, the world outside this community must be safer and more stable. The loss of individual enterprise is lamented in *Goodfellas*, but Mafia unity as corporate strength is also romanticized. Sicilian culture and heritage are shown to be oppressive and brutal in *The Godfather*, *Mean Streets*, *Goodfellas*, *Casino*, *The Funeral* and *Donnie Brasco* and these films thus encourage the notion that assimilation would rid communities of such archaic practices and superstitions. However, these same films and especially the television series also show Sicilian heritage and culture as nurturing and offering individuals a sense of identity and belonging in comparison to the alienating, false homogeneity of assimilationist society that offers no security for anyone.

Notes

1. *Compareggio* is the Italian word for non-blood family relationships, especially relevant to the godfather–godson relationship.
2. Roughly translated, *omerta* denotes the code of silence by which all *Mafiosi* abide. It also translates as a suspicion of all government and law. Both of these can be traced back to the distrust that exists, according to popular conception, within the Sicilian psyche towards the government and official law enforcement agencies over many centuries.
3. Cowie (1997) notes that the book had sold over 1 million copies in hardback alone. The film *The Godfather* (1972) earned more than a billion dollars in worldwide sales and also, 'in critics' and audience polls would consistently rank in the top half-dozen motion pictures ever made' (Cowie, 1997: xxii).
4. For example, the powerful and dapper Uncle Giovanni (Cesare Danova) in *Mean Streets* (1973) and the stoic and traditional Pauly Cicero (Paul Sorvino) in *Goodfellas* (1990).
5. An example of Michael's disconnection from his cultural heritage is evidenced when he struggles to pronounce the title of the most famous of Sicilian Operas, Mascagni's *Cavelleria Rusticana*. He apologizes for this by explaining 'I've lived in New York too long'.
6. For examples of films that challenge this ideal see *Miller's Crossing* (1990), or *King of New York* (1990). While these films acknowledge the power of the Italians, they focus mainly on their brutality and corruption.

References

Albanese, J. (1989) *Organised Crime in America*, Cincinnati: Anderson Publishing Co.

Albini, J.L. (1971) *The American Mafia: Genesis of a Legend*, New York: Meredith Corporation.

Barthes, R. (1973) *Mythologies*, London: Paladin/Grafton.

Bell, D. (1953) 'Crime as an American Way of Life: a Queer Ladder of Social Mobility', *The Antioch Review*, 13 (June); reprinted in D. Bell (1988) *The End of Ideology: On the Exhaustion of Political Ideas in the Fifties*, Cambridge, Mass.: Harvard University Press, 127–50.

Browne, N. (2000) (ed.) *Francis Ford Coppola's The Godfather Trilogy*, Cambridge: Cambridge University Press.

Cawelti, J.C. (1976) 'The Mythology of Crime and Its Formulaic Embodiments', in *Adventure, Mystery & Romance*, Chicago: University of Chicago Press, 51–79.

Cowie, P. (1997) *The Godfather Book*, London: Faber and Faber.

Cressey, D.R. (1969a) 'The National and Local Structures of Organized Crime', in D.R. Cressey and D.A. Ward (eds) *Delinquency, Crime and Social Process*, London: Harper and Row, 867–83.

Cressey, D.R. (1969b) *Theft of a Nation: The Structure and Operations of Organized Crime in America*, New York: Harper and Row.

Dika, V. (2000) 'The Representation of Ethnicity in *The Godfather*', in N. Browne (ed.) *Francis Ford Coppola's The Godfather Trilogy*, Cambridge: Cambridge University Press, 76–108.

Fried, A. (1993) *The Rise and Fall of the Jewish Gangster in American* (revised edn), New York: Columbia University Press.

Gambino, R. (1974) *Blood of My Blood: The Dilemma of the Italian Americans*, New York: Doubleday.

Hess, H. (1998) *Mafia and Mafioso: Origin, Power, Myth*, 2nd edn, London: C. Hurst & Co.

Holden, S. (ed.) (2001) *The New York Times on The Sopranos*, New York: ibooks.

Ianni, F.A.J. (1972) *A Family Business: Kinship and Social Control in Organized Crime*, New York: Russell Sage Foundation.

Levi-Strauss, C. (1968) *Structural Anthropology* (trans. C. Jacobson and B.G. Schoepf), London: Allen Lane.

McArthur, C. (1972) *Underworld USA*, London: British Film Institute.

McClellan, J.L. (1963) *Crime Without Punishment*, New York: Duell, Sloan & Pearce.

Maas, P. (1968) *The Valachi Papers*, New York: G.P. Putnam.

Moore, W.H. (1974) *The Kefauver Committee and the Politics of Crime 1950–1952*, Columbia: University of Missouri Press.

Smith, D.C., Jr. (1975) *Mafia Mystique*, New York: Basic Books.

Smith, G. (1990) 'Street Smart: Martin Scorsese Interviewed', *Film Comment*, 26(5), 68–74.

Sobchack, V. (1977) 'Film Genre, Myth, Ritual and Sociodrama', in T. Sari (ed.) (1982) *Film/Culture: Explorations of Cinema in its Social Context*, New Jersey: Scarecrow Press, 147–65.

Steinberg, S. (1989) *The Ethnic Myth: Race, Ethnicity and Class in America*, Boston: Beacon Press.

Warshow, R. (1946) 'The Gangster as Tragic Hero', in *The Immediate Experience: Movies, Comics, Theatre and Other Aspects of Popular Culture*, New York: Anchor Books, 83–8.

Webster, D. (1988) *Looka Yonder! The Imaginary America of Populist Culture*, London: Routledge.

Chapter 7

Political violence, Irish Republicanism and the British media: semantics, symbiosis and the state

Mark Hayes

As media images of the attack on the World Trade Center in New York were transmitted instantaneously across the globe, it appeared to underscore the notion that 'international terrorism' was the greatest single threat to democracy and civilization. The ensuing 'war' against what George W. Bush referred to as 'the axis of evil' would constitute a 'global crusade' against 'terrorism'. In the USA and Britain, policy-makers argued that a military response was not only a moral imperative but could, as Vice-President Dick Cheney cautioned, last indefinitely (Milne, 2001). Given the magnitude of what had immediately preceded these comments, it was widely assumed, not only that such a response was legitimate, but that everyone knew precisely what 'terrorism' amounted to. Indeed, in the context of the vivid images of destruction in New York, it appeared insensitive (if not absurd) to request any kind of definitional clarification. As Conor Gearty pointed out (prior to the tragic events of September 2001):

> the description of certain violence as 'terrorist' is now something that we take so much for granted that the word has rooted itself in our psyche, bringing with it all those intense anxieties about sudden and arbitrary violence with which as a society we have become pre-occupied (Gearty, 1997: 2).

In fact, for many years prior to the attack on New York, there has been an implicit assumption in Western liberal democracies that most sensible people were aware of precisely what constituted 'terrorism'. According to Richard Schaffert, former Director of Policy Studies at NATO, terrorism is 'a unique form of violence unacceptable to civilised societies' (Schaffert, 1992: 20). Terrorism 'expert' Paul Wilkinson is marginally more expansive, asserting that 'terrorism' can be 'briefly defined as coercive intimidation, or more fully as the systematic use of murder, injury, and destruction or threat of same to create a climate of terror, to publicise a cause, and to coerce a wider target into submitting to its aims' (Wilkinson, 1990: 27). Moreover, Wilkinson has argued that terrorists engage in 'cowardly acts', 'lack the heroic qualities of humanity and magnanimity', and operate on the basis of 'an idiosyncratic code of rules and values' (Wilkinson 1997: 64, 1990: 28–29). According to Wilkinson, terrorism is characterized by its 'unpredictability', 'arbitrariness', 'amorality' and its willingness 'to sacrifice all moral and humanitarian consideration for the sake of some political end' (Wilkinson, 1990: 28–29). In essence, terrorists are 'murderers who seek to destroy the democratic rights of their fellow citizens' (Wilkinson, 1990: 33). The venal nature and purpose of 'terrorism' is, apparently, axiomatic.

One of the primary reasons for the prevalent preoccupation with terrorist activity is the ubiquity of coverage in the media. Of course the media play a critical role in conveying political information to large, undifferentiated audiences. As Negrine points out, 'empirical research has long confirmed that for most people the mass media are the major source of information about world events and political affairs' (Negrine, 1996: 1). In short, the media (broadly conceived) gather, interpret and disseminate information, thereby helping to set the political agenda and, in some respects, helping to construct the parameters of our political knowledge. However, this general observation becomes far more significant when the subject of coverage is political violence, since many commentators have identified a 'symbiotic' relationship between terrorism and the media (see for example Wardlaw, 1989; Wilkinson, 1990, 1997).

This symbiosis is said to stem from the critical and complex interrelationship between the tactics utilized by terrorists and the overriding priorities of the media. Terrorism has been clearly identified as a communicative strategy that relies primarily upon the media as a channel to convey particular political messages. As Laqueur puts it, 'classic terrorism is propaganda by deed, and propaganda is impossible without the media' (Laqueur, 2001: 43). Moreover, Western political systems are viewed as particularly susceptible because, 'in liberal democratic societies, the major terrorist organisations can make maximum use of the freedoms of speech and press that prevail' (Wilkinson, 1990: 26). As McNair reiterates, 'terrorism can only have significance as a communicative act if it is transmitted through the mass media to an audience. Unless it is reported, the terrorist act has no social meaning' (McNair, 1999: 173).

Given the extent of this apparent 'symbiosis', attention has inevitably been focused upon the precise role of the media and, more controversially, the extent to which media output might facilitate terrorist objectives. For instance, some analysts have argued that journalists sometimes appear to be eager collaborators, providing carefully choreographed coverage for an audience captivated by the images of terror. Laqeuer elucidates:

It has been said that journalists are terrorists' best friends because they are willing to give terrorist operations maximum exposure. This is not to say that journalists as a group are sympathetic to terrorists, although it may appear so. It simply means that violence is news … and the media find in terrorism all the ingredients of an exciting story. (Laqueur, 2001: 44; see Hoffman, 1998: 142)

Wilkinson is less sanguine, and has berated 'trendy journalists', arguing that 'the terrorists can readily find useful idiots to latch on to crypto-terrorist propaganda and parrot its slogans in the name of radical and critical comment' (Wilkinson, 1990: 31). Indeed, Hoffman suggests that infatuation with terrorism via the media has become a particular feature of contemporary British experience: 'in Britain the media (and public) fascination with terrorists is second perhaps only to that with the country's royal family' (Hoffman, 1998: 154). According to Hoffman, terrorism has become a 'perverted form of show business' (Hoffman 1998: 134).

Certainly some observers believe that the media in the West have magnified the political importance of various terrorist groups who successfully exploit the linkages between media, public opinion and decision makers (Laqueur, 2001; Nacos, 1994; Wilkinson, 1990). Indeed, Schaffert argues that the mere act of media coverage confers a kind of spurious status and legitimacy by portraying such groups as politically motivated rather than 'criminals' and 'murderers' (Schaffert, 1992: 64, 68). In this sense the media may, albeit unwittingly, contribute to terrorist success and even precipitate a contagion effect. Consequently some have argued for increased censorship, voluntary codes of conduct and/or closer cooperation between government officials and journalists, in order to forestall the malignant media–terror nexus (Wilkinson, 1990; Clawson, 1987). As Kingston explains, 'it is essential to the anti-terrorist effort that the media not succumb to pressure from terrorist organisations for coverage of their criminal exploits' (Kingston, 1995: 226).

Schaffert's analysis is particularly interesting and instructive because he suggests that the relationship between terrorism and the media is not 'symbiotic' as such, but 'parasitic' (Schaffert, 1992). The mutual benefit implied in the term 'symbiosis' is misleading, he argues, because in the long run terrorists want to destroy the society upon which a free press depends. As Schaffert confirms, 'political terrorists targeting the governments and citizens of liberal democratic societies seek the destruction of those societies' (Schaffert, 1992: 75). Here Schaffert is simply reflecting the contemporary consensus that terrorism is an absolute evil, perpetrated by deluded fanatics who are motivated principally by ideological obsession or basic criminality. Although they seek to exploit the media, the terrorists are, according to Wilkinson and others, contemptuous of the values that underpin democratic society (Wilkinson, 1997: 64). This is the kernel of conventional wisdom – the aim of the terrorist is to destroy democracy, and in this heinous task they have, to an extent, been abetted by a naïve and complicitous media.

The Provisional IRA and the Media

For obvious reasons the recent focus of attention has been upon Osama Bin Laden and the al Qaida network. However, in terms of proximity the most pertinent example for the British public is the Provisional IRA (PIRA). The PIRA on the face of it, provides a classic example of a 'terrorist' organization. However, if we focus more closely upon the Provisional IRA, and media coverage of its activities, we can tease out and identify critical weaknesses in the conventional consensus on terrorism. Not only is the relationship between the media and the PIRA far more complex than orthodox interpretations might suggest, but a more considered analysis indicates that some of the more prevalent conclusions about the nature of 'terrorism' have been constructed upon erroneous assumptions.

In terms of the media coverage of PIRA activity, the material evidence indicates unambiguously that it has not facilitated Republican objectives at all. Indeed, the British state has made a concerted effort to intervene in order to ensure that the media did not in any way assist Republican aims (Curtis 1998; Miller, 1994; Rolston and Miller, 1996). Rather than acting as a passive conduit for 'Provo' propaganda, the media have been the (at times willing) accomplice of state power in the struggle against the Republican movement. After the civil rights marches in the late 1960s, when civil resistance turned to armed rebellion and Northern Ireland became more 'newsworthy' (Taylor, 1999), the British state became acutely aware of the importance of manipulating media output. The overall objective was to construct a particular perception of the conflict and, more specifically, to manufacture a negative image of its political adversaries. The aim was to portray the British state as essentially benign, acting as a neutral arbiter between irreconcilable communities, and the PIRA as a malevolent criminal conspiracy and primary cause of the violence. This was achieved in a number of ways, some of which can be outlined very briefly here.[1]

Throughout the period of what was euphemistically referred to as 'the troubles', successive British administrations used the legal system (or the threat of law) to restrict access to relevant information. Legislation, not specifically designed to control the media, was nevertheless deployed by state authorities to constrain their activities. For example, the Prevention of Terrorism Act (1974) Section 11 (which was added in 1976) made it an offence not to pass on information that might lead to the capture of a terrorist, and the 1981 Contempt of Court Act could force journalists to declare sources in the interests of national security or to prevent crime and disorder. The Official Secrets Acts of 1911 and 1989 (Section 2) and the Public Records Act (1958) not only reflected a culture of secrecy at the heart of governance in Britain but also restricted access to relevant documentation on Ireland. Disclosure of 'sensitive' security information could also be prevented via the use of Public Interest Immunity Certificates and the (voluntary) 'D Notice' system. The subsidiary effect of this 'security' legislation was to control the output of relevant official information, inhibit the utilization of 'unofficial sources' and thereby impede genuine investigative journalism.

There is also ample evidence of more informal pressure applied by government upon the media. Here the complex personal inter-relationships between government officials and appropriate broad-casters and editors proved critical. As Carruthers points out:

> shortly after the emergence of the PIRA in 1970 the government made it clear that British broadcasters, whatever the BBC's Charter commitment to impartiality, were not in fact expected to be impartial as between the IRA and the British Army, or between the IRA and the government (Carruthers, 2000: 180).

As Lord Hill confirmed as Chairman of the BBC Governors (in a letter to Home Secretary Reginald Maudling in November 1971) 'the BBC and its staff abhor the terrorism of the IRA and report their campaign of murder with revulsion' (quoted in Carruthers, 2000: 180). Indeed, Roy Mason, during his tenure as Secretary of State for Northern Ireland (after 'special category status' for Republican prisoners had been withdrawn) put relentless pressure on the BBC to endorse the process of 'criminalisation' (Taylor, 1996: 70). Of course the BBC is an organization particularly susceptible to pressure because of its mode of governance and public funding and there are numerous specific examples of government influence, informally applied. For instance, in 1979 when a BBC film crew covered IRA units manning roadblocks in Carrickmore, the government reacted furiously because the images conveyed implied both a security failure and local support for the PIRA (Curtis, 1998: 165). Scotland Yard subsequently raided the BBC under the terms of the Prevention of Terrorism Act in order to confiscate untransmitted footage, and the reaction of Margaret Thatcher, who 'went scatty' (Carruthers, 2000: 182), was not lost on BBC executives (Curtis, 1998: 167). Also, the 'Real Lives' ('At the Edge of the Union') documentary made in 1985, which focused on Republican leader Martin McGuinness and, among other things, showed him with his children, was banned initially by BBC governors. Although shown subsequently with judicious editing, the government evidently felt that the image of McGuinness as a family man (rather than 'terrorist') was entirely inappropriate (Miller, 1994: 38; Carruthers, 2000: 183).

Perhaps the most controversial example of a programme subjected to official pressure was 'Death on the Rock' (1988), which examined the circumstances surrounding the killing of three IRA volunteers on Gibraltar by the SAS (specifically eye-witness accounts that indicated that unarmed IRA members were shot after surrendering). Thames Television and programme-maker Roger Bolton were put under enormous pressure by the Thatcher administration (Bolton, 1996: 118; Carruthers, 2000). The documentary was eventually broadcast but the government set up an investigation by Lord Windlesham, which reported in January 1989. Although the report concluded that the programme was generally accurate, Thatcher rejected the findings and Thames did not get its franchise renewed. As Peter Taylor has noted:

> when it comes to Northern Ireland the pressure is constant. It consists of not just the standard letter of protest from government and opposition to the IBA and the offending contracting company, but personal meetings between the Chairman of the Authority and the Secretary of State and Chief Constable of the RUC (Taylor quoted in Coogan, 1995: 304).

In a sense 'Death on the Rock' was an exception because it was eventually broadcast, but many other programmes were banned, delayed or re-edited as a result of informal interference by government (see Curtis, 1998; Pilger, 1993).

It is also the case that, with regard to coverage of the PIRA, the so-called 'reference upwards' system within media structures amounted to an insidious form of self-censorship (Curtis, 1998: 173). Such a system was introduced into the BBC in 1971 and guidelines were revised after the Carrickmore episode. The imposition of various guidelines, for instance the BBC's News and Current Affairs Index, Guidelines for Factual Programmes and Style Guide (Rolston and Miller, 1996: 142) meant that BBC reporters had to seek permission from senior executives, including the Director General, before interviewing members of the IRA (Curtis, 1998: 6). A similar system evolved at ITV, where the Independent Television Authority and the Independent Broadcasting Authority had wide-ranging powers to exercise control over programming. The effect of such restrictions can be seen in the meagre number of interviews actually conducted with Republican activists during the conflict, and the fact that when interviewed they were treated as 'hostile witnesses' (Carruthers, 2000: 181). Journalists were expected to behave 'responsibly' in order to pre-empt government intervention, and this effectively distorted professional practice and undermined the critical autonomy of programme-makers (Elliot, *et al.*, 1996: 346). Output was therefore often amended or cancelled because of rigorous internal scrutiny, and the concomitant institutionalized caution amounted to a subtle and efficient form of censorship.

In fact Thatcher, in attempting to deny terrorists the 'oxygen of publicity', imposed direct censorship in 1988, which lasted until after the PIRA ceasefire in 1994 (Taylor, 1999: 250). The broadcasting ban amounted to 'the most direct and extensive interference with freedom of expression in the history of British broadcasting' (Miller, 1994: 66). The government, fearful of an electoral breakthrough by Republicans, argued that the political party Sinn Fein was simply a front for a murder gang, and a Home Office notice prohibited the broadcasting of any words spoken by a person who represented a listed organization. The terms of the ban, as Carruthers points out, were deliberately vague in order to precipitate maximum self-restraint among broadcasters (Carruthers, 2000). The nervousness of the regulatory authorities was such that the IBA even banned the song 'Streets of Sorrow' by The Pogues, which made reference to the innocence of the 'Birmingham Six' and 'Guildford Four'! In practice, official requirements on interviews were circumvented to some extent by the use of subtitles or dubbing, but the ban was nevertheless an extraordinary tactic during peacetime. The aim was to further marginalize the PIRA, delegitimize Republicanism and even dehumanize Sinn Fein. As Stan Cohen has pointed out, 'Gerry Adams was kept off British television not because of the unlikely prospect that he would convert anyone to the IRA cause, but because there was a possibility that he would seem more human' (Cohen, 2000: 38). In short, 'the government was searching for a means to stigmatise the IRA's political wing without resorting to such a measure of dubious profit (and legality) as internment without trial' (Carruthers, 2000: 184).

It is also evident that the state used extensive disinformation strategies, 'black propaganda' and 'psychological operations' (Curtis, 1998: 229; Rolston and Miller, 1996) in order to manufacture particular images of the 'enemy' and thereby reinforce the British perspective of the conflict. The British Army Information Policy Unit (IPU) was set up in 1971 with the explicit aim of discrediting the Provisionals and enhancing the image of the security forces. The IPU distributed public-relations literature, forged posters, and provided journalists with non-attributable information about the IRA which was designed to disorientate and confuse Republican activists and convince the public of PIRA malevolence. For instance, 'black propaganda' accused the PIRA leadership of embezzling funds, deploying children in military operations, using unstable or cancer-forming ingredients in bomb-making and even using dogs as target practice! (Curtis, 1998: 119). The PIRA were thereby portrayed as criminally motivated or psychotic, while soldiers were eulogized as neutral peacekeepers in an ancient and irrational tribal conflict. Such counter-insurgency strategies were in fact common colonial practice, as Brigadier Frank Kitson has explained: 'wars of subversion and counter-subversion are fought, in the last resort, in the minds of the people' (Kitson, quoted in Troops Out Movement, 1991: 21). In fact the IPU became known as the 'Lisburn Lie Machine' in journalistic circles, and was subsequently disbanded. The role of manufacturing images, though less explicit, was taken over by other agencies such as the RUC press office and the Northern Ireland Information Service. As Miller states, 'the presentation of Britain as neutral in the conflict is part of a deliberate counter-insurgency strategy in which the Northern Ireland Information Service plays a key role' (Miller, 1993: 98). In short, state propaganda was designed to discredit the PIRA and undermine support for the insurgents, thereby margin-alizing Republicanism, sustaining British morale and winning over international opinion.

Of course, in addition to all of this 'official' interference and pressure, media outlets were subject to the inevitable constraints imposed by the requirements of a capitalist economic framework. Business values pre-dominated and the interests of proprietors and advertisers invariably set ideological boundaries. Editorial values therefore reflected a distinct political disposition, and newspapers and broadcasting organizations were never likely to view sympathetically the activities of the PIRA. Lord Aylestone, Chair of the Independent Television Authority, set the tone in 1972, saying 'Britain is at war with the IRA in Ulster and the IRA will get no more coverage than the Nazis would have done in the last war' (quoted in Coogan, 1995: 298). As the *Daily Express* put it in November 1971:

> while British troops are involved in fighting a terrorist-anarchist organisation ... there is no room for impartiality ... people who bomb, kill and maim in order to smash the fabric of society put themselves outside the normal conventions, which include freedom of speech ... the soldier or policeman who never knows where the next shot will come from deserves support in a hazardous and desperately difficult task. The snide remark which undermines his morale is almost as bad as the sniper's bullet (quoted in Curtis, 1998: 9).

As Curtis says 'the media's identification with the troops was instant and total' (Curtis, 1998: 24; McCann, 1972).

Conversely, Republicans were routinely blamed for the violence, even when the material evidence was exceedingly thin. For example, after Bloody Sunday in January 1972 the *Daily Mail* asked rhetorically, 'who is really responsible for the 13 deaths in Ulster yesterday? ... the blood is on the consciences of irresponsible political leaders and the fanatical IRA' (quoted in Curtis, 1998: 45). Newspapers, especially the tabloids, concentrated on the effects of violence, while venting their collective spleen after high-profile attacks: 'murdering bastards' (*Daily Star*), 'wicked assassins' (*Sun*), 'evil men' (*Daily Mail*), 'psychopathic thugs' (*Daily Express*) – serious analysis was meagre, with little or no attempt to explain or contextualize the violence (Curtis, 1998: 114). Individual Republicans were derided and demonized; for instance, Maire Drumm (Vice-President of Sinn Fein, who was assassinated in hospital) became 'grandmother of hate', and Mairead Farrell (assassinated in Gibraltar) was called 'the angel of death' (Rolston, 1996: 416). The press regularly used the rhetoric of 'godfather' and 'mafia' to underscore the image of gangsterism and criminality. Often journalists would rely on un-corroborated 'official' information and, as Fr Des Wilson has pointed out, many did not venture far beyond the Europa Hotel in Belfast

(Wilson, 1997: 153). Consequently, critical and controversial subjects, such as the 'shoot to kill' policy by security services, the use of plastic baton rounds, torture techniques utilized to extract confessions, collusion between the state and loyalist paramilitaries and so on, were underexamined.

The net effect of all of this was what Tim Pat Coogan called the 'capped telescope syndrome' (Coogan, 1995). In essence, manipulation of media coverage had three overriding objectives: the reluctance to allow anything that was broadly supportive of the Nationalist position; an extreme sensitivity to information that might place the security services in a negative light; and 'an abhorrence of anything which depicted the IRA in situations which indicated a degree of community support or a human face' (Coogan, 1995: 306). In effect the media 'largely functioned as a public relations arm of the British government in its efforts to contain terrorism' (Spencer, 2000: 177). As Miller says, 'the media operate within a set of constraints in which power is clearly skewed towards the state. The major constraints on the media are those imposed by the economic context of media production, the use of the law, government intimidation, direct censorship and self-censorship' (Miller, 1994: 277).

Given that the aim of this 'propaganda war' was to criminalize the PIRA, it is also worth pointing out that in articulating this particular 'vision' of its adversary, the British state has been assisted by the crudely sculptured popular images of Republican activists portrayed in popular fiction. In many ways the images conveyed here are more powerful for not having been explicitly inspired by official intervention (Magee, 2001). Attitudes and opinions disseminated via the fictional narrative of the novel, play or film have sustained shared cultural assumptions, perpetuated prejudice and reinforced the predominant 'official' view of the PIRA 'terrorist'. In fact fictional accounts of the 'troubles' have consistently represented the PIRA as the cause of the conflict (Rolston and Miller, 1996: 403), and Republican activists as manipulative, cowardly and motivated by a toxic combination of power, bloodlust and revenge. In effect, as Magee has indicated, 'troubles fiction' illustrates the primacy of one discursive position, providing 'testament to the ubiquitous cultural penetration of Britain's point of view in regard to the conflict' (Magee, 2001: 2). This 'generic bias', Magee argues, has meant that fiction writers have acted as a 'para-literary' wing of the British state, providing a secondary means of manufacturing hegemony and reinforcing dominant values (Magee 2001).

This prescient observation is thrown into a much sharper light if we consider television drama (Curtis, 1998: 132) or Hollywood's even narrower frame of reference. The most cursory acquaintance with rogue Republican Sean Miller in the film *Patriot Games* (based on Tom Clancy's novel and directed by Phillip Noyce, 1992), or Brad Pitt's portrayal of misguided Frankie 'the Angel' McGuire in *The Devil's Own* (directed by Alan Pakula, 1997), reflect a particular value structure that reinforces the rectitude of state authority. At its crudest, a simplistic vision is constructed around the dichotomy between (state) good and (terrorist) evil, and emphasis is placed upon individual psychology and personal motivations which are abstracted from the social and political environment. This is not to suggest that thoughtful, nuanced and contextualized representations do not exist, since the work of Ken Loach (*Hidden Agenda*, 1990), Terry George (*Some Mother's Son*, 1996) and Ronan Bennet's novel *The Second Prison* (1992) are evidence of such. However, the predominant focus in film and fiction is very much upon individual pathology and the irrationality of the violent terrorist, which is often contrasted to the positive values of liberty, justice and democracy, usually reflected in the agents of the state. Although Elliot *et al.* (1996) make the important observation that certain modes of programming are more 'open' to providing a challenge to orthodox assumptions, such as 'authored' documentaries and single plays, the majority operate primarily within the terms of reference set by official discourse (Elliot *et al.*, 1996: 344). Thus the PIRA, as the incarnation of evil, has been well established in popular culture.

This prevailing attitude has even on occasion been reflected in certain 'scholarly' accounts of the Provisional IRA where the language is hardly less emotive than in the pages of popular tabloids and paperbacks. For instance, Wilkinson (1994a) has referred to the 'petty tyrants', 'quasi-fascist godfathers' and 'mafia racketeering' of the PIRA, and Kingston, emblematic of this febrile tendency, asserts unequivocally that 'there are no limits by which IRA depravity and inhumanity are bounded' (Kingston, 1995: 217). In short, some academic literature has tended to generate far more heat than light.

Irish Republicanism and the Critical Importance of Context

At this juncture it is necessary to return to the factual context by making some brief observations about the reality of Provisional Republicanism in Ireland. In Northern Ireland, when the attempt to secure civil rights for the Catholic minority by conventional 'democratic' methods was effectively repressed by the Unionist regime, elements within the Nationalist community began to question the legitimacy of the state. The

Provisional IRA emerged toward the end of 1969, during the civil rights disturbances, and was set up with the immediate defensive task of protecting Catholic areas from Loyalist attacks. The initial aim of community defence was subsequently supplanted by the more traditional Republican aspiration of national self-determination. Thus the central hypothesis of Provisional Irish Republicanism was that the Stormont regime, which governed Northern Ireland until 1972 and which had systematically discriminated against Catholics, was irreformable. Moreover, Stormont, which had been constructed upon notions of Protestant supremacy, was effectively sponsored by a British state that, Republicans argued, had no right to rule in Ireland. Causal responsibility for the conflict, from a Provisional perspective, lay with a sectarian administration underpinned by British authority.

Drawing upon a tradition of Republican resistance dating back at least to Wolfe Tone's United Irishmen in 1798, and reflected most graphically in the Easter Rising of 1916, the Provisionals deployed armed resistance against the state. The idea of precipitating a national catharsis via armed rebellion has a long tradition in Ireland and as the Provisionals themselves put it:

> the mandate for armed struggle stems from the British government's denial of the Irish people's inalienable right to the free exercise of sovereignty and national self-determination ... armed struggle is not a dogma, it is a form of struggle dictated by the absence of any viable democratic alternative for the realisation of Irish national rights and justice. (spokesman for Oglaigh na hEireann quoted in *An Phoblact/Republican News*, 7 March 1996).

The strategy deployed by the PIRA included targeting British soldiers and the RUC, and a campaign of commercial bombing. There were several high-profile attacks on the representatives of the British state such as the assassination of Earl Mountbatten in 1979, the bombing of the Grand Hotel in Brighton in 1984, and the mortar attack on Downing Street in 1991; as well as attacks on the economic infrastructure such as the Baltic Exchange and Bishopsgate bombs in London in 1992 and 1993. Moreover, the PIRA has also been responsible for some of the most brutal acts of violence perpetrated during the conflict, such as the Enniskillen (1987) and Shankill Road (1992) bombs.

The point here is not to defend the Republican position as such, but rather to acknowledge the existence of an alternative perspective that has been relatively unexplored in the mainstream media, and to suggest that there were other, much deeper socio-political forces at work in precipitating armed rebellion. More disconcertingly perhaps, contrary to the popular myth manufactured by the British media, most IRA volunteers were perfectly ordinary, usually working-class people, indigenous to the Nationalist community. Indeed, evidence would suggest that Provisional IRA volunteers considered quite carefully the functional utility of violence and the moral consequences of armed resistance, which was seen as a transient tactic rather than a sacrosanct principle.[2] Contrary to the stereotypical image of the religiously inspired monosyllabic moron, PIRA volunteers were generally articulate, non-egoistic, mission-committed and politically motivated (Bean and Hayes, 2001; Magee, 1997, 2001). That politics provided the primary dynamic for Republican activists was most clearly evident during the no-wash protests against 'criminalization', which culminated in the Hunger Strikes of 1980 and 1981 when ten Republican prisoners died in pursuance of political status. Political motivations were also clearly articulated in magazines like *An Glor Gafa* ('The Captive Voice') set up in 1993 by Republican prisoners, and in internal documentation, such as the 'Historical Analysis of the Struggle' (IRA/Long Kesh, received 1993). Thus Republican violence was (for the most part) neither an inexplicable emotional spasm nor a private criminal act for personal gain, but rather a public expression of political purpose. As former Hunger Striker Laurence McKeown has said, the prison authorities and British government 'found it impossible to impose upon Republican prisoners the construct of "criminal" ' (McKeown, 2001: 236). Interestingly, certain elements in the British intelligence services and armed forces have effectively acknowledged this. For example, General Sir James Glover (former Commander-in-Chief UK Land Forces and Intelligence Officer in Northern Ireland), in a secret intelligence report leaked to the press, commented upon the political motivation of activists and the fact that a military resolution to the conflict was unlikely (Miller, 1994: 9, 299; McKeown, 2001: 236).

The uncomfortable fact is that the Provisional IRA did not cause the 'troubles' in Ireland, but were a symptomatic manifestation of political misrule. Moreover, in some respects the Republican movement was animated by themes that are conventionally assumed to embody the very antithesis of terrorism. Emerging from a community that was denied basic civil rights, Republicans sought liberty, democracy and national self-determination. Individual PIRA activists adhered to values that were not at variance with prevailing moral codes, and their claim to have been ethically motivated is certainly not without foundation. As some of the more considered accounts of political violence have conceded, so-called 'terrorist' activity can be the product of logical strategic analysis and choice, rather than psychotic blood-lust or irrational fanaticism. As Gilbert has indicated, 'so long as there is no obvious and readily available way of translating popular wishes into changed state structures there is no good argument to the conclusion that support for terrorism aimed at changing them is not a "legitimate" political opinion' (Gilbert, 1992: 148; see Crenshaw, 1998). In short, the immorality of engaging in armed resistance in pursuit of political objectives cannot simply be assumed.

Yet as we have seen, the media contributed significantly to the misrepresentation of reality since 'the media created representations which criminalised rather than politicised the conflict' (Spencer, 2000: 19). As Curtis says, 'the media have always endeavoured to depict the IRA as external to, and unrepresentative of, the nationalist community … the books were (being) cooked in order to establish the IRA not as a product of the conflict, but as the cause' (Curtis, 1998: 128, 90). As Miller argues, 'counterinsurgency theorists misconceptualise the power of the media. The media in Britain do not and have not supported the Provisional republican movement. Indeed both Sinn Fein and the IRA have been consistently excoriated in the mainstream media' (Miller, 1994: 281). Attempts by the Republican movement to get its own message across, via a proactive publicity department, *An Phoblact/ Republican News* and even Internet technology singularly failed to alter the 'reality' constructed by the culture industry (Curtis, 1998: 262). As Cohen has observed, the creation of political monsters and 'folk devils' is a calculated strategy in totalitarian regimes, but has also been used selectively in modern democracies (Cohen, 2000: 39), and the PIRA would appear to be a case in point. Yet the emphasis on criminality, despite its resonance in popular consciousness and culture, constituted a complacent fiction which, it might be argued, has impeded the current peace process.

In many respects the space for a peaceful resolution to the conflict in Ireland was created as a consequence of the evolving political strategy of the Republican movement. The reorientation toward more conventional participatory politics via Sinn Fein after the Hunger Strikes highlighted the possibility of electoral progress (Hayes, 1998). As Sinn Fein made electoral headway and moved towards constitutional politics, the Republican leadership convinced the PIRA of the possibility of political progress and the need to move away from armed resistance. Indeed the prospect of a post-military political scenario emerged as a result of the dialogue between Gerry Adams and John Hume, which formed the background to the Downing Street Declaration and the subsequent Good Friday Agreement (1998). Sinn Fein signed the Mitchell Principles, which included an absolute commitment to 'democratic and exclusively peaceful means of resolving political issues', and prioritized a diplomatic strategy that focused upon a configuration of forces sympathetic to Irish nationalism. Brokerage politics prefigured a far more pragmatic approach, and a new agenda was articulated in Republican discourse which emphasised the need for compromise, consensus and an agreed Ireland (Hayes, 1998).

Perhaps not surprisingly, the media was very slow in coming to terms with this new direction and was persistently sceptical of Republican intentions. Despite an ongoing ceasefire and weapons decommissioning, the infatuation of the media with the vulgarized vision of 'PIRA terrorist' has meant that in some ways the politics of negotiation has been more difficult to control, posing communicative problems for policymakers (Spencer, 2000). As Ronan Bennet put it, 'many British commentators and editors simply loathed Adams and the IRA' (Bennet, 2002: 137) and were far more comfortable dealing with the simplistic stereotypical images. For example, as Spencer indicates:

> a tendency to read an IRA ceasefire in terms of how it could make the situation worse rather than better not only ran counter to political efforts … but maintained the stereotypical view of the IRA as a pathological organisation which had not changed. Clearly an inaccurate assessment and one which reflected the media's difficulty in breaking free from the terrorism paradigm (Spencer, 2000: 179; see Spencer, 1997)[3].

The rhetoric of criminality may have resonated with the British public, given propaganda images conveyed by the media, but the government was forced to deal with the reality of political context and Sinn Fein's electoral mandate. As Miller and McLaughlin have asserted, this dramatic transformation made 'all mainstream media reporting over the last 25 years seem seriously threadbare … The emergence of the "peace process" in Ireland caught journalists on the hop' (Miller and McLaughlin, 1996: 423, 436).

Definitional Disputes and the Construction of Meaning

In some ways the reluctance to acknowledge the new reality in Ireland not only reflected deeply rooted and erroneous preconceptions in the media, but also highlighted the more general underlying questions concerning the nature of 'terrorism'. As Milne says, referring to the current crusade against global terrorism, 'for all the square jawed resolution on display in western capitals about the prosecution of the war, there is little agreement even within the heart of the coalition, about what terrorism actually means' (Milne 2001). Indeed, the definition of terrorism has been extended in recent years to include 'eco-terrorism', 'narco-terrorism', 'cyber-terrorism' and broader individual acts of extortion, rape and even currency speculation (Guelke, 1998: 7). In fact Gearty has identified no less than 109 different definitions and 22 'defining' characteristics, and concludes that:

> the concept of terrorism has never been a useful or intelligent way of describing political violence and the term is itself now more or less entirely meaningless ... terrorism as a subject has thrived precisely as a result of this intellectual vacuity, which governments have long recognised and cleverly exploited for their own ends (Gearty, 1997: 3, 17).[4]

The debate over 'terrorism' is usefully encapsulated in the oft-quoted aphorism about one person's 'terrorist' being another's 'freedom fighter' (Whittaker, 2001: 3–13); and the definitional difficulty is clearly illustrated by well documented individual examples, such as the transformation of Nelson Mandela from 'terrorist' to international statesman (the ANC was included in the US State Department publication *Patterns of Global Terrorism*, 1987) (Gearty, 1997: 33). Conversely, the Mujihadeen, once 'freedom fighters' sponsored by the USA in Afghanistan against Soviet forces, are now 'terrorists' to be ruthlessly eliminated. Moreover, as Chomsky points out, the military response to terrorism is likely to take a much greater toll on innocent lives (Chomsky, 2002: 26); and the USA, self-proclaimed leader of the free West, has sponsored its share of corrupt and authoritarian regimes, and indeed has backed campaigns of terror against political opponents (Herman, 1982).

In essence, labelling organizations and individuals as 'terrorist' is little more than self-serving semantic sophistry. Yet terminology is extremely important because labels signify images, and political battles are fought on a linguistic terrain. Use of the term 'terrorist', although facile, has a definite semiotic and ideological function in emphasizing notions of legitimacy and power. Once the label of 'terrorist' is fixed, subsequent discourse is severely circumscribed and encoded with meaning, so there is little space to generate alternative explanations. As Crenshaw puts it:

> it is clear from studying the literature on terrorism, as well as the

public debate, that what one calls things matters. There are few neutral terms in politics, because political language affects the perceptions of protagonists and audiences, and such affect acquires a greater urgency in the drama of terrorism (Crenshaw, 1995: 7).

The use of the word 'terrorism' is not a neutral descriptive term but a crude pejorative epithet designed to delegitimize an adversary, and is usually reserved for enemies of the state. Therefore, despite its seductive simplicity, the concept of terrorism is tendentious and potentially dangerous.

In response to the 'terrorist threat', political authorities in Britain and the US have introduced legislation which, according to Amnesty International, threatens the liberties that differentiate liberal democracies from more authoritarian regimes.[5] Using the rhetoric and imagery of criminality, and the discourse of policing and law enforcement, Western governments are effectively eroding civil liberties. Indeed, in the post-Cold War era of US global supremacy, 'terrorism' is replacing the 'Communist threat' as the mechanism by which governments mobilize support for enhancing the coercive capability of the state (Pilger 2002: 14). There is a grave danger that terrorism is becoming, as Davis puts it, the 'steroid of empire' (Davis, 2001: 50). Indeed, Wardlaw has made the telling point that:

> it is an old and well-tried trick to divert attention from economic and social problems to focus attention on an ill-defined and frightening 'enemy'. In many parts of the world today, terrorism is such a diversion. In fact it is possible to imagine governmental officials doing more to destroy democracy in the name of counter-terrorism than is presently likely to be achieved by terrorists themselves (Wardlaw, 1989: 78; Carruthers, 2000: 192).

Yet the repressive reflex of the state has precipitated minimal discussion in the mainstream media (Knightly, 2002; Lawler, 2002). As Hackett says 'journalists as well as their audiences are tempted to "rally round the flag" in a time of national crisis, and the political and military leadership on which the media depend for information is not about to encourage critical questioning' (Hackett, 2001–2: 52). It may be that, as Gearty has argued, 'the loose language of terrorism has become too dangerous to be acceptable in any healthy democracy' (Gearty, 1997: 56).

When it comes to 'terrorism' there needs to be more emphasis on aetiology and analysis that transcends rudimentary descriptive discourse. Even the most grotesque acts, inspired by an apocalyptic fundamentalism, have their roots embedded deeply in poverty, oppression and geo-politics. As Howard Zinn (2000) has argued, 'to try to explain and understand terrorism is not to justify terrorism. But if you don't try to explain anything, you will never learn anything'.[6] The multifarious manifestations of political violence need to be related more explicitly to social, political and cultural context. Here the Irish example is instructive because the orthodoxy that demonized PIRA 'terrorists' as the immoral alchemists of anarchy was based on fundamental misconceptions.

Moreover, rather than terrorists successfully exploiting a symbiotic relationship with the media, the Irish experience clearly indicates that the media obfuscated reality by creating crude decontextualized images of a political adversary. Yet such incomplete and distorted images continue to be channelled, to a large extent, through an unreflective media that is prone to lurid sensationalism. As McNair has pointed out with regard to the news media, coverage:

> tends to eschew explanations and analysis of the events reported, a generalisation which is no less true of terrorism. The audience sees the bomb exploding or the hijacker waving his gun from the cockpit of an aircraft, but will not very often be provided with the historical background or political context to the events taking place (McNair, 1999: 175).

In fact, 'devoid of the necessary historical and political context which would make sense of violent actions, terrorism often appears to the public as little more than psychotic behaviour' (Carruthers, 2000: 192). As Carruthers confirms, 'it is quite possible for public awareness of a terrorist group's existence to be raised by media attention, without that audience being any better informed as to the organisation's objectives' (Carruthers, 2000: 191).

There is no doubt that in mediating reality, 'the media' help to create meaning, thereby facilitating the construction of cultural and ideological categories. In classifying certain politically motivated violence as 'terrorist', the media are, for the most part, reflecting the dominant political dispositions of those who wield power. Of course the media are not a monolithic mouthpiece for government propaganda, but when it comes to 'terrorism' (despite a few very honourable exceptions) most media outlets are content to regurgitate superficial and simplistic story lines in which high-profile villains dominate a 'master frame' that focuses upon the struggle against 'absolute evil' (Hackett, 2001–2).

Despite the compelling attraction of pluralism as a normative theory, the appearance of diversity and a multiplicity of productive units, the media have generally exercised considerable discursive power in support of the state. This is particularly true in relation to so-called 'terrorism' where the media help to 'manufacture consent' for state policies (Herman and Chomsky, 1994; Nineham, 1995; Curran and Seaton, 1997; Reiner, 2002).[7] Here questions concerning ideological hegemony and the need to control the cognitive contours of political knowledge and the parameters of dissent in a democracy are thrown into a much sharper light. As Chomsky has argued, 'the fact that the voice of the people is heard in democratic societies is considered a problem to be overcome by ensuring that the public voice speaks the right words' (Chomsky, 1993: 19). Similarly, Pilger states unequivocally that 'thought control in capitalist democracies is by necessity more thorough than in tyrannies. You can't enforce it with tanks' (Pilger, 1993a: 14). Certainly, in terms of the coverage of 'terrorism' the media have created visions and images that misinform and mystify reality. In so doing the media, by perpetuating patterns of ignorance and facilitating punitive state countermeasures, continue to degrade the quality of democracy.

Notes

1. See Curtis (1998), Miller (1994) and Rolston and Miller (1996) for greater depth and detail.
2. During the course of related research the author has conducted many interviews with Republican volunteers, some of which have been archived in the Linenhall Library Belfast; see also Bean and Hayes (2001).
3. In many respects the rigidity of the media position has let the Republican leadership off the hook by asking the wrong questions. Instead of persistently attacking Sinn Fein's integrity and democratic credentials, the most controversial question was whether Adams and the Republican leadership had effectively abandoned traditional Republican objectives. These really awkward questions have been left to ex-IRA activists like Tommy McKearney, Brendan Hughes, Tommy Gorman and Anthony McIntyre.

   Spencer (2000) argues that the media posed significant difficulties for policymakers trying to make peace. This is true to an extent, but Spencer underestimates the extent to which the British state had already secured its overriding objective, which was to incorporate Republicans (minus Republicanism) into an ongoing peace process and stabilize the Northern Ireland state (a telling point made to the author on numerous occasions by ex-PIRA activist Dr Anthony McIntyre).

4. Wilkinson disagrees, stating unequivocally that 'the problems of establishing a degree of common understanding of the concept of terrorism have been vastly exaggerated. Indeed, I suspect that some have tried to deny that any common usage exists as a device for obstructing co-operation in policies to combat terrorism' (Wilkinson, 1990: 27; Wilkinson, 1994b).

5. The Terrorism Act 2001 introduced by the New Labour government describes 'terrorism' as 'the use or threat, for the purpose of advancing a political, religious or ideological cause, of action which involves serious violence against a person or property' (Terrorism Act, quoted in Whittaker, 2001: 3). In the USA, the inelegantly titled 'Uniting and Strengthening America by Providing Appropriate Tools Required to Interrupt and Obstruct Terrorism' or 'Patriot Act' came into force on 26 October 2001.

6. Academics bear a heavy responsibility here. In the field of 'terrorism' it is entirely possible to be considered an 'expert' without ever actually having any contact with them. Indeed, as Zulaika points out, 'such complete lack of contact with the subjects under study is not only usual but even appears inevitable and desirable in the study of terrorism. The source of this anomaly is that we, too, abide by the general view that terrorists are by their very nature "untouchables", highly dangerous people whose contact should be avoided under any circumstances. Terrorist researchers follow the perception fostered by the media that, whatever else they are, terrorists are best categorised as "people wholly unlike us" ' (Zulaika 1991: 44–45).

7. Although designed and deployed with reference to the US media, and of more limited utility with reference to Britain (not least because of the residual existence of a public service tradition), the 'propaganda model' still yields useful insights. See Herman (2000), who rejects criticisms and argues for the continuing relevance of the 'propaganda model' as a 'guided system' rather than a deterministic conspiracy theory.

Further analysis is evidently required here because, 'the bulk of the literature on the relationship between the media and terrorism is dismaying. Some of it is blatantly propagandistic, consisting of shrill jeremiads, exhortations, tendentious examples and undocumented assertions. Un-examined assumptions abound, terms go undefined, and arguments are untested' (Paletz and Schmid, 1992: 23).

References

Bean, K. and Hayes, M. (eds) (2001) *Republican Voices*, Monaghan: Seeysu Press.

Bennet, R. (2002) 'None So Blind', *Index on Censorship*, 31(2), issue 203 (April), 134–40.

Bolton, R. (1996) 'Death on the Rock', in B. Rolston and D. Miller (eds) *War and Words: The Northern Ireland Media Reader*, Belfast: Beyond the Pale.

Carruthers, S. (2000) *The Media at War: Communication and Conflict in the Twentieth Century*, London: Macmillan.

Clawson, P. (1987) 'Why We Need More but Better Coverage of Terrorism', *Orbis*, 30(4) (winter), 701–10.

Chomsky, N. (1993) *Necessary Illusions: Thought Control in Democratic Societies*, London: Pluto Press.

Chomsky, N. (2002) 'Confronting the Monster', *Index on Censorship*, 31(1), issue 202 (Jan), 24–9.

Cohen, S. (2000) 'Some Thoroughly Modern Monsters', *Index on Censorship*, 29(5), issue 196 (Sept–Oct), 36–43.

Coogan, T.P. (1995) *The Troubles: Ireland's Ordeal 1966–1995 and the Search for Peace*, London: Hutchinson.

Crenshaw, M. (1995) 'Thoughts on Relating Terrorism to Historical Contexts', in M. Crenshaw (ed.) *Terrorism in Context*, Pennsylvania: Pennsylvania State Press, 3–24.

Crenshaw, M. (1998) 'The Logic of Terrorism: Terrorist Behaviour as a Product of Strategic Choice', in W. Reich (ed.) *Origins of Terrorism*, Washington: Woodrow Wilson Press, 7–24.

Curran, J. and Seaton, J. (1997) *Power Without Responsibility: The Press and Broadcasting in Britain*, London: Routledge.

Curtis, L. (1998) *Ireland: The Propaganda War*, Belfast: Sasta.

Davis, M. (2001) 'The Flames of New York', *New Left Review*, 12, (Nov–Dec), 34–50.

Elliot, P., Murdock, G. and Schlesinger, P. (1996) 'The State and "Terrorism" on British Television', in B. Rolston and D. Miller (eds) *War and Words: The Northern Ireland Media Reader*, Belfast: Beyond the Pale.

Gearty, C. (1997) *The Future of Terrorism*, London: Phoenix Press.

Gilbert, P. (1992) 'The Oxygen of Publicity: Terrorism and Reporting Restrictions', in A. Belsey and R. Chadwick (eds) *Ethical Issues in Journalism and the Media*, London: Routledge, 137–53.

Guelke, A. (1998) *The Age of Terrorism and the International Political System*, London: Tauris.

Hackett, B. (2001-2) 'Covering (up) the "War on Terrorism": The Master Frame and the Media Chill', *Soundings*, issue 19 (winter), 46–53.

Hayes, M. (1998) 'The Evolution of Republican Strategy and the "Peace Process" in Ireland', *Race and Class*, 39(3) (Jan–March), 21–39.

Herman, E. (1982) *The Real Terror Network*, Boston: South End Press.

Herman, E. (2000) 'The Propaganda Model: A Retrospective', *Journalism Studies*, 1(1) (Feb), 101–12.

Herman, E. and Chomsky, N. (1994) *Manufacturing Consent: The Political Economy of the Mass Media*, London: Vintage.

Hoffman, B. (1998) *Inside Terrorism*, London: Victor Gollancz.

Howitt, D. (1998) *Crime, Media and the Law*, Chichester: John Wiley.

Keene, F. (2001) 'The Mind of a Terrorist', in J. Baxter and M. Downing (eds) *The Day That Shook The World*, London: BBC Worldwide.

Kieran, M. (ed.) (1998) *Media Ethics*, London: Routledge.

Kingston, S. (1995) 'Terrorism, the Media, and the Northern Ireland Conflict', *Studies in Conflict and Terrorism*, 18(3), 203–31.

Knightly, P. (2002) 'Losing Friends and Influencing People', *Index on Censorship*, 31(1), issue 202 (Jan), 146–55.

Laqueur, W. (2001) *The New Terrorism*, London: Phoenix Press.

Lawler, P. (2002) 'The "Good War" after September 11', *Government and Opposition*, 37(2), (Spring), 151–72.

Magee, P. (1997) 'Do They Mean Us?' *Guardian*, 3 September.

Magee, P. (2001) *Gangsters or Guerrillas? Representations of Irish Republicans in 'Troubles Fiction'*, Belfast: Beyond the Pale.

McCann, E. (1972) *The British Press and Northern Ireland*, Northern Ireland Socialist Research Centre, www.cain.ulst.ac.uk

McCann, E. (1994) 'Mad Dogs or Good Terrorists?', *New Statesman and Society*, 18, (March), 16–18.

McKeown, L. (2001) *Out of Time: Irish Republican Prisoners Long Kesh 1972–2000*, Belfast: Beyond the Pale.

McNair, B. (1999) *An Introduction to Political Communication*, London: Routledge.

Miller, D. (1993) 'The Northern Ireland Information Service and the Media: Aims, Strategy, Tactics', in J. Eldridge (ed.) *Getting the Message: News, Truth and Power*, London: Routledge, 73–103.

Miller, D. (1994) *Don't Mention the War: Northern Ireland, Propaganda and the Media*, London: Pluto.

Miller, D. and McLaughlin, G. (1996) 'Reporting the Peace in Ireland', in B. Rolston and D. Miller (eds) *War and Words: The Northern Ireland Media Reader*, Belfast: Beyond the Pale.

Milne, S. (2001) 'Terror and Tyranny', *Guardian*, 25 October.

Nacos, B. (1994) *Terrorism and the Media*, New York: Columbia University Press.

Negrine, R. (1996) *Politics and the Mass Media in Britain*, London: Routledge.

Nineham, C. (1995) 'Is the Media All Powerful?', *International Socialism*, issue 67 (Summer), 109–51.

Paletz, D. and Schmid, A. (eds) (1992) *Terrorism and the Media*, London: Sage.

Pilger, J. (1993a) 'The Brave New Media World', *New Statesman and Society*, 11 June, 14–15.

Pilger, J. (1993b) 'Silence of the Lambs', *New Statesman and Society*, 20 August.

Pilger, J. (2002) *The New Rulers of the World*, London: Verso.

Reiner, R. (2002) 'Media Made Criminality: The Representation of Crime in the Mass Media', in M. Maguire, R. Morgan and R. Reiner (eds) *The Oxford Handbook of Criminology*, Oxford: Oxford University Press.

Rolston, B. and Miller, D. (eds) (1996) *War and Words: The Northern Ireland Media Reader*, Belfast: Beyond the Pale.

Sarraj, E. (2001) 'Bombs and Madness: Understanding Terror', *Index on Censorship*, 30(4), issue 201 (Oct), 7–13.

Schaffert, R. (1992) *Media Coverage and Political Terrorists: A Quantitative Analysis*, New York: Praeger.

Schmid, A. and de Graaf, J. (1982) *Violence as Communication*, London: Sage.

Schapiro, S. (2002) 'Conflict Media Strategies and the Politics of Counter-Terrorism', *Politics*, 22(20), (May), 76–85.

Spencer, G. (1997) 'Talking Peace: Political Communication Through the Television News Media and the Northern Ireland Peace Process', *Contemporary Politics*, 3(3), 267–76.

Spencer, G. (2000) *Disturbing the Peace? Politics, Television News and the Northern Ireland Peace Process*, Aldershot: Ashgate.

Street, J. (2001) *Mass Media, Politics and Democracy*, Basingstoke: Palgrave.

Tangen Page, M. von (1996) 'The Inter-relationship of the Press and Politicians during the 1981 Hunger Strike at the Maze Prison', in P. Catterall and S. McDougall (eds) *The Northern Ireland Question in British Politics*, London: Macmillan, 162–73.

Taylor, P. (1996) 'The Semantics of Political Violence', in B. Rolston and D. Miller (eds) *War and Words: The Northern Ireland Media Reader*, Belfast: Beyond the Pale, 329–39.

Taylor, P. (1999) *British Propaganda in the Twentieth Century: Selling Democracy*, Edinburgh: Edinburgh University Press.

Thomas, M. (2001) 'An Assault on Freedom', *Guardian*, 26 November.

Troops Out Movement (1991) *In Whose Name? Britain's Denial of Peace in Ireland*, London: Blackrose Press.

Wardlaw, G. (1989) *Political Terrorism: Theory, Tactics, Counter-Measures*, Cambridge: Cambridge University Press.

Whittaker, D. (ed.) (2001) *The Terrorism Reader*, London: Routledge.

Wilkinson, P. (1990) 'Terrorism and Propaganda', in Y. Alexander and R. Latter (eds) *Terrorism and the Media: Dilemmas for Government, Journalists and the Public*, London: Brassey.

Wilkinson, P. (ed.) (1993) *Terrorism: British Perspectives*, Aldershot; Dartmouth.

Wilkinson, P. (1994a) 'Bringing the IRA to Justice', *Parliamentary Brief*, 2(7) (April/May), 5–7.

Wilkinson, P. (1994b) 'Terrorism', in M. Foley (ed.) *Ideas that Shape Politics*, Manchester: Manchester University Press.

Wilkinson, P. (1997) 'The Media and Terrorism: A Reassessment', *Terrorism and Political Violence*, 9(2), (Summer), 51–64.

Wilson, D. (1997) *Democracy Denied*, Dublin: Mercier.

Zinn, H. (2002) *Terrorism and War*, London: Seven Stories Press.

Zulaika, J. (1991) 'Terror, Totem and Taboo: Reporting on a Report', in C. McCauley (ed.) *Terrorism Research and Public Policy*, London: Cass, 34–49.

Chapter 8

Mass media/mass murder: serial killer cinema and the modern violated body

Ian Conrich

The serial killer film is a prevailing mode of contemporary cinema. Conjoining elements of the horror film, for instance, the stalker narratives of the 1980s, and the psychological investigative thriller, a popular and commercial modern Gothic has emerged. These films may explore police procedures and the commitment of the detective, forensic scientist or psychological profiler, but it is the serial killer that is arguably the attraction. Not too far removed from the modern horror film's mythical monsters of Jason Voorhees, Michael Myers, Leatherface and Freddy Krueger, these screen imaginations of the body violator imitate aspects of true crime and connect with society's most infamous serial killers: from Jack the Ripper and Ed Gein to Ted Bundy and Jeffrey Dahmer.[2]

The fictional Norman Bates and Hannibal Lecter are perhaps the screen's most mythical serial killers. Both have inspired a consumer trade in related products, with 'Bates Motel' labelled accessories such as towels, soap dishes and shower curtains available for bathrooms, and plastic replicas of Lecter's facial guard, intended as both party gear and a children's plaything, on sale at toy stores such as Hamley's.[3] There is a discernible serial killer cult in contemporary Western culture, and it has elevated such extreme human behaviour not only to the point at which it may hold a popular fascination but where, for some, it has lead to obsession and idolatry. As a cultural product, cinema is perhaps responding to society's morbid interests. Although the wave of serial killer films that has flooded mainstream cinema since the early 1990s (the term 'serial killer' introduced by the FBI in the mid-1970s, was quickly popularized by the media during the 1980s), can also be understood through a recognition of issues of exploitation and repetition. Film production, as an example of the mass media, is driven by commercial gains and is aware of the potential profitability of engaging with stories of a contemporary social value or with those in high circulation; the success of one production almost inevitably inspiring copies. Key serial killer films such as *Manhunter* (1986), *Henry: Portrait of a Serial Killer* (1986), *The Silence of the Lambs* (1991), *C'est arrivé près de chez vous* (1992) *Man Bites Dog*, *Natural Born Killers* (1994), *Se7en* (1995), and, of course, the earlier classics *Psycho* (1960) and *Peeping Tom* (1960), mark significant periods of development and/or popular reception for the sub-genre. These productions have been considered in detail elsewhere (for example, Halberstam 1992; Sconce 1993; Adams 1996; Dyer 1999; Simpson 2000), though at the loss of other examples, for instance, *Body Parts* (1991), *Ghost in the Machine* (1993), *Copycat* (1995), *Virtuosity* (1995), *Fallen* (1998), *Resurrection* (1998), *The Bone Collector* (2000) and *The Cell* (2000). Such films may be less stylish, accomplished or revered but are, I would argue, equally revealing of some of the extreme concepts and boundaries of serial killer fiction.

The existence of these 'lesser' movies outside of what would appear to be a pantheon of serial killer films should not prohibit a consideration of what are, here, the more exploitative forms of the sub-genre. On the contrary, although these films are frequently imitative, they offer a view on the subject of the copy. Forming part of this discussion, these American films will be regarded as aestheticized exhibitions of torture and violence that combine ingenious new methods of murder, with re-enactments of infamous patterns of death. Further consideration will be given to their depiction of what will be argued is a series of modern violations of the body, as films that dramatically visualize the rupturing of domestic and private space, the effect of the mass media and a reliance on technology. This discussion will begin by exploring the Internet, where serial killer culture is distinctly advanced.

'Murderabilia' and the Internet

In the fantasy of the films *Ghost in the Machine* and *Brainscan* (1994) the imagined serial killers operate via cyberspace; the digital medium of the computer enabling an omnipotent murderer to transport between and penetrate a seemingly endless possibility of private and domestic environments.[4] In addition, in *Cyberstalker* (1996), the killer uses the Internet to select his victims, and in the film *Copycat*, the Internet serves as a key link for the serial killer to contact and threaten the apartment-bound criminal psychologist Helen Hudson (Sigourney Weaver). Hudson's initial reaction to her situation is to close down her computer – 'I'm unplugging this. It's an open window he can crawl in anytime he likes.' Within the reality of a contemporary consumerist society, these ideas may not appear so far-fetched. The quantity of Internet sites exploring and celebrating real-life serial killers reveals the extent to which this is a subject of cultural interest. Here, the Internet has been operating as a marketplace for serial killer-related products, which fetishize a murderer or allow for a particular private association. In accessing any of the many sites devoted to serial killers, the user opens up their personal or domestic environment to the possibilities of cyber-space, with its endless scope for image and information retrieval. Furthermore, items for sale on the Internet belonging to or associated with the serial killer are focal objects that can extend a convicted murderer's presence beyond the computer screen and, through purchase, into the home.[5]

Famously, the Internet auction site ebay, once the centre of such cultural exchange, banned among its users, on 17 May 2001, the sale of what has become known as 'murderabilia'.[6] In an Internet report written before ebay banned murderabilia, Andy Kahan noted that on a daily basis there were on average over 100 items available under the search word 'serial killer', and at its peak there were 'as many as 189 listed auction items'. Kahan noted items available such as autographed socks, the fingernail clippings and handprints of serial killer Roy Norris, '[c]lumps of hair' of the infamous murderers Charles Manson and Arthur Shawcross, letters from Henry Lee Lucas and Richard Davis, the death certificate for Manson victim Sharon Tate, and dirt from John Wayne Gacy's crawlspace. Kahan also discovered a 'hard-to-find board game titled Serial Killer [that] was marketed in a body bag for $50. The object [of which] is to kill the most babies (game pieces) and become the king of serial killers'.[7]

Following ebay's ban, the web pages offering murderabilia migrated, diversified and developed Internet commercial autonomy. A search of what is currently being offered reveals the continuing extent of such trade and, here, I would propose a division of items. Murderabilia can be separated into the historical (kept over time) and the 'fresh' (recently obtained and, commonly, directly from the incarcerated murderer); the donation (presented by the killer) and the acquisition (received by an individual without the killer's knowledge or perhaps consent); the crime-specific, or what Mark Pizzato (1999: 91) terms 'sacred relics' (belonging to a murder) and the celebration (commemorating murder);[8] the mass-produced, the hand-created and the ephemeral; the toy (almost always for adults), the plaque (including wall clocks and calendars) and the display (T-shirts, baseball caps, badges); and personalized memorabilia (with the killer's signature, and sometimes an address to a recipient), the souvenir, and the corporal object (from the killer's own body).

Of course, an item can belong to more than one category. For instance, available from Spectre Studios, a small independent business in Denver, Colorado, are a series of six-inch tall hand-made figurines, sculptured by David Johnson and individually painted in the image of the serial killers Dahmer, Gein, Gacy and Bundy.[9] Unsurprisingly, the figurines, which are commemorative adult toys being produced without the murderers' (or victims' family's) consent, have attracted criticism, and Spectre Studios was the subject of a story from ABC News.[10] In contrast, there are a variety of sketches, doodlings and paintings by serial killers on sale at Internet sites, unique creations that can be either historical or 'fresh', donated or acquired, hand-crafted or ephemeral and perhaps signed.[11] At another site, for LordSpider, a handwritten note by Manson can be bought. There is also available a 'Charlie's Angels' snowglobe that contains the glass-encased photos of three female members of Manson's gang; a barbecue apron featuring the cannibalistic Ed Gein; a fridge magnet of the cannibalistic Dahmer (who kept the body parts of victims in his fridge); and a 'Dahmer's Diner' wall clock displaying severed arms for the clock's hands, and in the middle a picture of the serial killer wearing a chef's hat. Most disturbingly, the site promotes a two-foot-tall Dahmer doll with a zipped front, inside of which can be revealed a recently consumed victim that can be pulled apart, as the advertising declares 'Open me up for a sure delight and see who I ate for dinner last night', 'Unzip Jeff's jumpsuit and inside is a fully dismemberable Dahmer victim'.[12]

The Dahmer doll consumer can manipulate both killer and victim; beyond this the dismemberable insert of the eaten man is just one example of what is essentially the composite nature of murderabilia and serial killer culture. The Dahmer victim, forever a detachment of a larger body, can be taken apart, but then there is also the feeling that a serial killer can be reconstructed in part through the various purchasable corporal objects: hair, fingernails, handprints and personal belongings such as original clothing and the tools associated with the criminal acts. Clearly, the manipulation of this image of a killer, although it is in-complete, carries greater accuracy and realism. However, taking the idea even further there is also the composite killer constructed from the identities and belongings of different murderers, in extreme, a 'super-killer', combining dislocated yet definite parts. The popularity of both the Spectre Studios figurines and several series of collectable trading cards featuring different serial killers and 'seasonal statistics' (Grant, 1999: 23) illustrates a consumer desire to assemble a common parade of extreme human behaviour. It is an idea that has been explored by several Hollywood films (*Copycat*, *Virtuosity* and *The Bone Collector*) in which the killer's identity is either constructed from other killers, or their crimes imitate a collection of previously documented accounts.

Seriality and the Killer Assembled

The serial killer is a social aberrant, yet also a cultural construct. It is a figure of popular myth, with the actions of a notorious few creating the source for the manufacturing of a line of simulacra, imagined identical copies for which no original exists. As Denis Duclos notes, 'fiction writers are fascinated by the unbelievable examples they find in real-life crime' (1998: 3). Duclos later observes that 'Dahmer, Bundy, and many other "mass production" killers talk about an orderly, repetitive multitude of identical acts' (1998: 164). The very serial nature of the killer, the ritualistic behaviour in a sequence of murders identified by numbered victims, establishes a classification and a compartmentalization of the crime. Interestingly, the production of serial killer trading cards, featuring a consistent collection of individuals, shares some similarities with the ordered acts of murder or the arranged series of uniform snapshots regularly printed by the media to record the list of victims. Media interest and consumer appetite are perhaps sustained by the knowledge of a sequence. As Keith Soothill and Sylvia Walby noted in their 1991 study on the reporting of sex crime, 'there seems to be an increasing focus in television on sexual cases where there are thought to be many victims' (1991: 43). But there is also a possessiveness in aiming to complete a set of cards; a fascinating consumerist variation on the killer's desire to create the never-to-be-achieved completeness in amassing victims, those who will be eternally 'owned', in notoriety, by the murderer.

Seriality is, for Elizabeth Young, an explanation for the chilling effect of serial killer cinema since its 'repeatability [of the act of murder] suggests that there is ... an endless stream of such crimes spilling not only from film to film but beyond the borders of all film, to the non-film "real world" itself' (1992: 5–6). There is certainly a point of seriality in the production line of serial killer films, though identifying such movies reveals a number of issues. There is significant diversity in the range of serial killer fictions: from realism to fantasy, true crime to the mythical, the psychological thriller to the horror film. It is easy to register the screen accounts of real-life serial killers, which have all been packaged on video – for instance, *10 Rillington Place* (1971, based on John Christie), *Zärtlichkeit Der Wölfe* (1973; *Tenderness of the Wolves*, based on Fritz Haarman), the television mini-series *Helter Skelter* (1976, based on Manson), the television movie *The Hunt for the Night Stalker* (1991, based on Richard Ramirez), *Cold Light of Day* (1991, based on Dennis Nilsen), the television mini-series *To Catch a Killer* (1992, based on Gacy), the cable television movie *Citizen X* (1995, based on Andrei Chikatilo), *From Hell* (2001, based on Jack the Ripper) and Tartan Films' planned trilogy of productions that so far has yielded *Ed Gein* (2000) and *Bundy* (2002). Even here, however, there are fictionalizations and fantasizations with the story of the Wisconsin cannibal Ed Gein inspiring films such as *Psycho* and *The Texas Chainsaw Massacre* (1974), and Jack the Ripper as the subject of *Hands of the Ripper* (1971; in which the Ripper's daughter continues his work), *Time After Time* (1979; H.G. Wells, using his time machine, chases Jack the Ripper to modern-day San Francisco), and *Terror at London Bridge* (1985; in which the spirit of the Ripper is transported to Arizona, as London Bridge is dismantled and re-erected in the US).[13]

Fantasy scenarios become common at the point at which the serial killer film converges with the horror genre. The extreme behaviour of the serial killer is often justified here as stories engage, unrestrained, with concepts of the supernatural, the occult, revivification, reanimation, virtuality, transplantation and transformation. In *Child's Play* (1988), a film that has inspired three sequels, the Lakeside Strangler transfers his soul, with the help of witchcraft, into a toy shop doll which is subsequently animated by the killer;[14] executed (often electrocuted) serial killers live again through possession, body-hopping, shape-shifting, body-part transplants, dreams and electricity in *Destroyer* (1988), *Shocker* (1989), *The Horror Show* (1989), *The Exorcist III* (1990), *The First Power* (1990), *Body Parts* (1991), *Sleepstalker: The Sandman's Last Rites* (1994) and *Fallen* (1998); they can continue killing despite death or incarceration through invisibility in *The Invisible Strangler* (1976), spectrality in *The Frighteners* (1996) or mutation in *Jack Frost* (1997), where the convicted murderer transforms into a killer snowman after exposure to an experimental liquid DNA. These movies borrow from the realm of the post-slashers which I have noted elsewhere. In the films in the *Nightmare on Elm Street*, *Hellraiser*, *Puppetmaster* and *Candyman* series, which began in the mid-1980s, the killer continues to live after extermination through transference, alternative dimensions, the imaginary, the hyperreal, and freakish and bizarre twists of science and nature (Conrich, 2003: 110).

In opposition to such mythical and sensational creations, there is the 'intelligence', and the stark (though stylized) realism of *Henry: Portrait of a Serial Killer* (see Sconce, 1993: 104–106), and the art house horror of the foreign films *Nattevagten* (1994, *Nightwatch*) and *Funny Games* (1997). The killers in these films appear on the surface quite normal, and perhaps bland and non-threatening. As Steffen Hantke writes, in consideration of Buffalo Bill in *The Silence of the Lambs*, John Doe in *Se7en*, and Richard Thompson in *The Bone Collector*, 'the killer's body tends to be inconspicuous, average, and thus distinctly unspectacular' (2003: 35). It is an argument which is, for instance, shared by Mark Seltzer (1998: 10) who, like Hantke, observes the connection to the profile of the true crime serial killer. Yet, this does overlook the line of fictional murderers who populate the many horror hybrids and films such as *Body Parts*, *Virtuosity*, *Ghost in the Machine*, *Sleepstalker* and *The Cell*, in which the serial killer appears, on the contrary, quite spectacular either on the surface or within their alternative realm.

It is perhaps wrong to isolate a serial killer type within popular fiction, when the number of relevant films and therefore the range of imaginary characterizations are so vast. Evidently, there is a history of screen psychopaths, and Andrew Tudor observes within the horror film a dominant trend for the representation of psychotics in the 1978–83 period. 'Rarely has any single category so dominated a period' (1989: 67–68), Tudor writes, with 38 per cent of films during this time presenting psychosis as the source of the movie threat, and the figure passing 50 per cent for the early 1980s. Such a growth can be explained by the recognition of a rush of slasher films following the commercial success of *Halloween* (1978) and *Friday the 13th* (1980) (see Conrich, 1995). The slasher film characteristically concentrates on a group of teenagers who are murdered in turn by a malevolent force. Here, the threat is from a certain serial killer, particularly if the FBI's definition is employed of 'an offender associated with the killing of at least four victims, over a period greater than seventy-two hours' (Seltzer, 1998: 9) , yet these productions are treated as a separate sub-genre of the horror film.

Crucially, there are differences, with Annalee Newitz writing that:

> serial killers' psychopathology allows them to function 'normally' in most situations; many are able to hide their periodic moments of homicidal psychosis. Most are drifters who commit similar crimes in a number of regions over a period of time. The most noteworthy and characteristic aspect of serial killing is the relative randomness of the victims. (Newitz, 1999: 68)

These serial killers can be contrasted with slasher film creations such as Voorhees, Myers and Leatherface, and even post-slashers such as Krueger and Candyman (though not neo-slashers such as the murderers in the *Scream* trilogy of films [1996–99]), screen characters who are permanently abnormal, their psychosis all-encompassing, and their killing spree, although seemingly random, localized and within a specific film largely contained within a short period of time. A further difference is that slasher films promise a spectacle of death in process, whereas the serial killer film often displays the body *post-mortis*. But what marks out the two sub-genres even more is the process of criminal investigation. Whereas within the slasher film the police are either absent, incompetent, ineffectual, or unwilling to accept there is a threat, in the serial killer movies, which are very much detective fiction, the individuals tracking the murderer are committed, skilled and prepared to make sacrifices. There are, however, frequent exchanges and cross-overs between the investigator and the killer. The films *Tightrope* (1984), *Striking Distance* (1993) and *Stranger by Night* (1994) establish the central protagonist of the policeman as a key suspect in the serial killings; the policemen in *Virtuosity* and *Se7en* are shown to be clearly guilty of murder; and the policemen in *The Eyes of Laura Mars* (1978), *Kiss the Girls* (1997) and *Nightwatch* are revealed to be the killers; while the killers in *The Silence of the Lambs* and *Copycat* become police consultants. The prison psychologist in *Body Parts* acquires as a transplant the arm of an excecuted strangler, which maintains some of its previous owner's rage (as Bill Crushank [played by Jeff Fahey] declares 'I now have a murderer's blood in my blood'), while in *The Cell*, the detective is placed deep within the mindscape of a serial killer, with the aid of a neurological transfer system.[15] In the latter film, sharing the space of the psychotic creates obvious apprehension and tension; fear which is to a degree experienced in *The Silence of the Lambs*, by Clarice Starling (Jodie Foster) on her prison visits to Hannibal Lecter (Anthony Hopkins), and by *Copycat*'s Helen Hudson during her Internet link to incarcerated serial killer Daryll Lee Cullum (Harry Connick Jnr). It is, though, the actual presence of the serial killer within the home of the protagonist that generates arguably the greatest threat and is one example of a modern violation of the body, which will be the subject of the discussion that follows.

Violation/Technology/Imitation

The value of domestic comfort and security is emphasized continually throughout serial killer fiction and is certainly a key theme in the group of 'lesser' films listed above. Within these films, the protagonist is presented as retreating to the safety and shelter of the home, a space which is sometimes associated with a partner or family unit. There are clear narrative passages that establish the domestic space of the protagonists in *Virtuosity* and *Fallen* and, in particular, in *Body Parts*, *Ghost in the Machine*, *Copycat*, *Resurrection* and *The Bone Collector*. But, interestingly, all these films establish the protagonist's home or family unit as one of absence or loss: from the brutal death of a mother and child at the hands of a serial killer (shown in flashback) in *Virtuosity*, and the accidental death of a child (shown in flashback) in *Resurrection*, to the absence of any family members in *Copycat* or *The Bone Collector* (bar the film's awkward postscript). The domestic space is special and is a sacrosanct refuge from the troubles of the outside world. Where there is an absence or the loss of a family member, the domestic space is marked as one of a previous violation or incompleteness that places importance on remaining loved-ones and new relationships, to which the serial killer presents a frightening threat. The murderer makes multiple visits to the apartment of the psychologist in *Copycat*; a violation of the investigator's private space which is repeated in *Resurrection*, in which the detective's home is the site at which a family associate is slaughtered by the serial killer. In *Virtuosity* a psychologist's child is kidnapped and, in *Fallen*, family members of Detective John Hobbes (Denzel Washington) are marked while asleep with letters that are part of the word 'Apocalypse'.

In *Copycat* and *The Bone Collector*, the investigator is house-bound, incapacitated from venturing into the public spaces of the city outside – as a result of agoraphobia, with Helen Hudson in the former, and quadriplegia, with Lincoln Rhyme (Denzel Washington) in the latter; disabilities caused by exposure to extreme situations in the course of their profession. While isolation may suggest vulnerability, the home appears as a supportive expanse for the individual with Hudson's and Rhyme's apartments built around a central open-plan living space, suitable for opposing Hudson's fear of the hidden and Rhyme's feelings of suppression. Placed around Rhyme and Hudson, within this central space, is a group of monitors and computer screens upon which, in their confinement, each is dependent; a technology base with which the home-bound can interact to assist with external communication, knowledge acquisition and physical and mental well-being.

Within their enclosures, Hudson and Rhyme are initially shown to reject further investigative work and they are unwilling to engage at first with the visiting detectives who bring with them crime scene photographs. Indeed, such is the impact of the introduction of serial killer crime within their private space that Hudson hyperventilates and Ryhme experiences a seizure. But the lure of the investigation is too strong and it inhibits their complete extrication from the profession, as they open up their previously cleansed environment, requesting access to crucial documentation, storing, enhancing or manipulating received images and, in the case of Rhyme, allowing a team of mobile investigators and forensics to import an array of specialist equipment and establish a base within his home.

Hudson's and Rhyme's home-based investigations both utilize the power of the Internet for locating important information. It is a portal through which the outside world can be reached, though it is also one through which the crimes, and with Hudson, the killer, can enter virtually into the home. Technology is extremely important to Hudson and Rhyme as a crucial part of their daily existence and as an extension of the self. For Rhyme, in particular, the technology is life-supporting, his total dependence on the machinery to which he seems permanently conjoined exemplified by the computer mouse button which is ever-present at the end of his index finger. At the start of the serial killer's attack on Rhyme, his index finger is broken and the technology is closed down. Like the email messages sent by the serial killer to Hudson, corruption of such vital technology is a violation of the private body and its space of security.

The power of technology and its centrality to modern society is exploited in both *Virtuosity* and *Ghost in the Machine*, two films in which broadcast and new media sustain the activities of the serial killer. *Virtuosity*'s killer, Sid 6.7 (Russell Crowe), is a virtual-reality composite of the identities of 200 notorious murderers (created for law-enforcement training) who manages to break free of his digital world of captivity and as a 'nandroid' (a synthetic organism) wreaks havoc on a future society. As an artificial creation this modern Frankenstein has the power of regeneration (if it is shot or cut it can repair through silicon absorption when in contact with glass) and combined with its astounding composite identity is offered as an ultimate serial killer threat. Attracted to media attention and seeing his image on television, this murderer (imitating the media-seeking behaviour of true crime serial killers) switches all the television channels in an electronics shop to the news broadcast in which he is featured. Seduced by television stardom (as are the serial killers in the films *Star Time* 1992 and *Crimetime* 1996), he later commandeers a television station where he introduces the start of 'Death TV', a new programme in which viewers request the manner in which captives should die. 'You will not be able to take your eyes off the screen', Sid 6.7 advises his audience as viewing figures surge. Here, serial killer performance, live and interactive, is broadcast direct into homes and, as in today's society where murderabilia and detailed web pages are available on the Internet catering for the demands of a serial killer cult, the public is attracted to images of death so long as they are relayed from a distance.

Such distance is removed in *Ghost in the Machine* in which the modern world's endless computer databanks and network systems come under the frightening control of the Address Book Killer. Digitally entering a hospital's computer mainstream, during an electrical disturbance while his brain activity is being scanned, this serial killer, whose trademark is to systematically enter the homes of people listed in personal address books, presents arguably the greatest violation of the individual's private space. Not only can the home be targeted via the very technology which is there to provide comfort and security (the domestic space can be penetrated by the killer travelling along electricity cables) but all computer-stored personal records can be accessed, altered or removed.

The Internet is not the only mass-media form through which the private space is threatened or contaminated. The body-hopping serial killer in *Fallen* communicates its presence by singing through its host body an extract from the Rolling Stones' song 'Time is on my Side', perverting the original meaning of the lyrics to suggest an omnipotent and indomitable force. The manner in which the lyrics are sung in the same style and by such a variety of previously unconnected people creates an effective uncanny experience, particularly in the police station where surrounded by strange-behaving colleagues Hobbes sees a familiar workspace transformed into the incomprehensible and the unknown.

Similarly, in *Copycat*, Hudson receives a letter from the serial killer that communicates her fate through the lyrics of the song 'Murder by Numbers', written by the pop group The Police.[16] This is far from being the only threat, with the private space of Hudson's bedroom violated by the discovery, while she is in bed, of a plague of ants and, under her mattress, a copy of a paperback with a severed finger bookmarking a page. The book, *My Life with a Knife*, 'The intimate story of a mass murderer', written by *Copycat*'s fictional serial killer Daryll Lee Cullum, is signed by Cullum and addressed to Hudson: 'Hey Doc. Hope you like the book. Love and sloppy kisses'. This donated and personalized item of murderabilia is, within Hudson's private space, distinctly unwanted, not only for the way in which it contaminates an inner room of the apartment, and in which it signifies intrusion, but the gift is from the incarcerated Cullum, of whom Hudson is definitely no fan. In fact,

Hudson is herself a celebrity of crime, as she declares 'a damn pin-up girl' for serial killers, and in a moment of trading she agrees to exchange for information from Cullum a signed pair of her used 'undies'. In the film's postscript these are repackaged by Cullum, who despatches them, Charles Manson-like, to a new disciple.

There is a perpetuality here in the crime of serial killing, where the capture of one sows the seeds for another to begin. If the trading of Hudson's panties among serial killers is perversely ironic, then there is seemingly humour too in Cullum's confessed sale of his 'spirit', or semen, for $500 on the Internet – a comment perhaps on the absurd extremes of murderabilia, but a device that allows the incarcerated Cullum to extend his influence through the potential fathering of a brood of Cullum copies.

The idea of the copy is strong not only in the film *Copycat*, a movie which is explicit in its referencing of true crime, but it is a recurring theme across serial killer fiction. In their study of sex crime, Soothill and Walby observe that occasionally a new offender will copycat a previous murder, but they argue that evidence 'suggests that the copycat phenomenon is a danger to which the media [print journalism and television news] may be contributing' (1991: 42). The mythologization of notorious crimes is a factor too within the film production of serial killer fiction. Casual references to Gacy, Bundy, Dahmer and Jack the Ripper are made in *Resurrection*; while in *Virtuosity*, the programmable identities of infamous mass murderers (Peter Sutcliffe, Gacy and, even, Saddam Hussein and Emperor Hirohito) that were employed in the creation of Sid 6.7 flash up on screen as a computer document is searched. True crime serial killers supposedly crave media fame (see Newitz, 1999: 77); if so they would be satisfied with their immortalization in Hollywood films, though reciprocally Hollywood is able to 'authenticate' its fiction by referencing or imitating the known extreme human behaviour of the few.

In *Copycat*, the serial killer who, in using new victims, recreates the infamous murders of the Boston Strangler, the Hillside Strangler, David Berkowitz and Dahmer is, within the film's diegesis, imitating fact. The precision in replicating the crimes aestheticizes the murders, with detail carefully captured in a series of grisly though composed still-lifes. Here, ingenious methods for murder are not just the obsession of the serial killer, but also for the film-makers who push the boundaries of the fiction in creating spectacular and dramatic crime scenes. *Resurrection*'s concept is perhaps the most grim, with the serial killer collecting in turn seven body parts: two arms, two legs, a head, a torso, and (unsuccessfully) a new-born baby's heart. These are then combined and mounted on to a cross to resemble Christ, in preparation for his supposed Easter resurrection. As a detective states, the killer has a 'chopping list' and this requires that he find victims sharing names and similar occupations with the Apostles: for instance, a shipping magnate called Peter representing Peter the fisherman. The victims' bodies, once mutilated, are marked with Roman numerals indicating a specific chapter and verse from the Bible.

The surgical precision with which the body parts are removed is echoed in *The Bone Collector*, where a serial killer is also inspired by passages in a book – this time an early twentieth-century collection of crime stories, *The Bone Collector: True Accounts of a Murderer*.[17] The medical knowledge exhibited by the killer, the design of the book of crime stories from which he receives inspiration, the choice of the locations selected and the antiquity of the objects left at the murder scene belong to another period that resonates with the crimes of Jack the Ripper. As with so many serial killer fictions, there is an imitation of aspects of true crime. These 'mass production' killers seemingly serve as a catalogue of movie design with film-makers combining different elements for commercial effect. Murderabilia, in a way, demonstrates the composite nature of the culture with serial killer cinema not unlike *The Bone Collector's* surgeon drawing on true crime and removing parts of different bodies in the creation of a narrative of horror. Reliant not just on history but popular mythology, the mass production of serial killer films also borrows and imitates from itself (*Resurrection* copying from *Se7en*, *The Bone Collector* copying from *Se7en* and *Copyca*t), creating a media repetition and exploitation of the violated body.

Notes

1. I would like to thank Frank Lafond, Caroline Hardy and Roy Smith for their helpful comments and suggestions.
2. Voorhees appears in the ten films in the *Friday the 13th* series (1980–2002); Myers appears in seven of the eight films in the *Halloween* series (1978–2002); Leatherface appears in the four films in *The Texas Chainsaw Massacre* series (1974–95); and Krueger appears in the seven films in the *A Nightmare on Elm Street* series (1984–94).
3. Norman Bates, the subject of Robert Bloch's novel *Psycho*, first appeared on screen in Alfred Hitchcock's adaptation *Psycho* (1960). The film spawned three sequels: *Psycho II* (1983), *Psycho III* (1986), and *Psycho 4: The Beginning* (1990), a remake, *Psycho* (1998), and a telefeature, *Bates Motel* (1987), a pilot for a planned television series. Hannibal Lecter, created by the novelist Thomas Harris, has been the subject of four movies *Manhunter* (1986), *The*

Silence of the Lambs (1991), *Hannibal* (2001), and *Red Dragon* (2002). The Bates and Lecter films were spoofed in *The Silence of the Hams* (1993).

4. Similarly, in the film *Shocker* (1989), executed serial killer and television repairman, Horace Pinker, is able to move across spaces via broadcast signals.

5. See
http://www.geocities.com/SunsetStrip/Birdland/4524/vommerch.html and
http://www.members.tripod.com/~SerialKillr/SerialKillersExposed/fanclubs.html (accessed 14 November 2002).

6. ebay banned the sale of murderabilia from crimes committed within the last 10 years.

7. Andy Kahan, 'Kill Culture. The Marketing of Murderabilia', http://www.apt213.com/culture/marketing.html (accessed 14 November 2002). Kahan is the Director, Crime Victims Division, to the Mayor of Houston, Texas.

8. The items sold in auction that once belonged to Dahmer are a good example of the crime-specific. In order to raise funds for the families of Dahmer's victims, in May 1996, items (312 in total) were sold including the hypodermic needles, tools, vat and fridge that were used to kill, dismember, dispose of and store bodies. See http://www.cnn.com/US/9605/08/dahmer.auction (accessed 14 November 2002).

9. http://stores.yahoo.com/spectrestudios (accessed 14 November 2002).

10. http://www.abcnews.go.com/sections/us/DailyNews/serialkillers-figures020325.html (accessed 14 November 2002).

11. See, for instance, http://www.angelfire.com/oh/yodaspage/art.html (accessed 12 November 2002). The Internet also contains portraits of serial killers by their admirers – see http://www.sandralondon.com/nico/killer/paintings.htm (accessed 12 November 2002).

12. http://www.angelfire.com/celeb/lordspiderskillers/toys.html (accessed 14 November 2002).

13. For further discussion of Gein and Jack the Ripper films, see Sullivan (2000) and Coniam (1998), respectively. For a discussion of the endurance of the Ripper myth on screen and in literature see Caputi (1987: 26). Later, she writes that '[t]he puzzle of the Ripper's identity, his melodramatic name, the way the crimes so suddenly and inexplicably ceased, the unprecedented brutality of their execution, the symbolic character of the victims: all these are said to explain what Nigel Morland has called "the imaginative folk lore that has always surrounded him"' (Caputi, 1987: 30).

14. The *Child's Play* sequels are *Child's Play 2* (1990), *Child's Play 3* (1991), and *The Bride of Chucky* (1999).

15. A similar fiction is constructed in the single-plot drama *Eye*, one of three short films in the anthology *Body Bags* (1993). In this story, a successful baseball player loses his right eye in a car accident and is given a replacement from a recently executed serial killer, who had slaughtered seven young women. The player subsequently experiences ghastly visions

of childhood cruelty and murder and resolves to destroy the eye that offends.

16. See also the overt use of popular music in *American Psycho* (2000), where the killer offers critical reviews of 'the bland, ephemeral pop icons' (Black, 2002: 113) Huey Lewis and the News, Whitney Houston and Phil Collins.

17. See also the film *Writer's Block* (1991), in which a copycat serial killer imitates the murders in a series of crime novels.

References

Adams, P. (1996) *The Emptiness of the Image*, London: Routledge.

Black, J. (2002) *The Reality Effect: Film Culture and the Graphic Imperative*, London: Routledge.

Caputi, J. (1987) *The Age of Sex Crime*, London: The Women's Press.

Coniam, M. (1998) 'Jack the Ripper on Video: a Miscellany of Mad Doctors, Implausible Theories and Dodgy Looking Experts', in H. Fenton (ed.) *Flesh and Blood Book One*, Guildford: FAB Press.

Conrich, I. (1995) 'How To Make A "Slasher" Film', *Invasion*, 11, 48–9.

Conrich, I. (2003) 'The *Friday the 13th* Films and the Cultural Function of a Modern Grand Guignol', in F. Lafond (ed.) *Cauchemars Americains: Fantastique et Horreur dans le Cinema Moderne*, Liège: Les Editions du CEFAL.

Duclos, D. (1998) *The Werewolf Complex: America's Fascination with Violence*, Oxford: Berg.

Dyer, R. (1997) 'Kill and Kill Again', *Sight and Sound*, 7(9), 14–17.

Dyer, R. (1999) *Seven*, London: British Film Institute.

Grant, B.K. (1999), 'American Psycho/sis: The Pure Products of America Go Crazy', in C. Sharrett (ed.) *Mythologies of Violence in Postmodern Media*, Detroit: Wayne State University Press, 23–40.

Halberstam, J. (1992) 'Skinflick: Posthuman Gender in Jonathan Demme's *The Silence of the Lambs*', *Camera Obscura*, 27, 36–53.

Hantke, S. (2003) 'Monstrosity Without A Body: Representational Strategies in the Popular Serial Killer Film', *Post Script*, 22(1), 32–50.

Newitz, A. (1999) 'Serial Killers, True Crime, and Economic Performance Anxiety', in C. Sharrett (ed.) *Mythologies of Violence in Postmodern Media*, Detroit: Wayne State University Press.

Pizzato, M. (1999) 'Jeffrey Dahmer and Media Cannibalism: The Lure and Failure of Sacrifice', in C. Sharrett (ed.) *Mythologies of Violence in Postmodern Media*, Detroit: Wayne State University Press.

Sconce, J. (1993) 'Spectacles of Death: Identification, Reflexivity, and Contemporary Horror', in J. Collins, H. Radner, and A.P. Collins (eds) *Film Theory Goes to the Movies*, London: Routledge.

Seltzer, M. (1998) *Serial Killers: Death and Life in America's Wound Culture*, London: Routledge.

Simpson, P.L. (2000) *Psychopaths: Tracking the Serial Killer Through Contemporary American Film and Fiction*, Carbondale and Edwardsville: Southern Illinois University Press.

Soothill, K. and S. Walby (1991) *Sex Crime in the News*, London: Routledge.

Sullivan, K.E. (2000) 'Ed Gein and the Figure of the Transgendered Serial Killer', *Jump Cut*, 43, 38–47.

Tudor, A. (1989) *Monsters and Mad Scientists: A Cultural History of the Horror Movie*, Oxford: Basil Blackwell.

Young, E. (1992) '*The Silence of the Lambs* and the Flaying of Feminist Theory', *Camera Obscura*, 27, 4–35.

Websites

http://stores.yahoo.com/spectrestudios
http://www.abcnews.go.com/sections/us/DailyNews/serialkillers-figures020325.html
http://www.angelfire.com/celeb/lordspiderskillers/toys.html
http://www.angelfire.com/oh/yodaspage/art.html
http://www.apt213.com/culture/marketing.html
http://www.cnn.com/US/9605/08/dahmer.auction
http://www.geocities.com/SunsetStrip/Birdland/4524/vommerch.html
http://www.members.tripod.com/~SerialKillr/SerialKillersExposed/fanclubs.html
http://www.sandralondon.com/nico/killer/paintings.htm

Part 3
Criminal Decisions:
Agencies and Agents

Chapter 9

Photo stories and family albums: imaging criminals and victims on *Crimewatch UK*

Deborah Jermyn

Since it first appeared on British television screens in 1984, *Crimewatch UK* has established itself as the country's leading television crime-appeal programme, outliving its intermittent rivals, consistently winning impressive audience figures, securing itself a highly visible and perhaps surprisingly comfortable position among the BBC's stable of regular, reliable and popular programming. Its format of reconstructions of serious crimes; interviews with police and victims' families; photos, videos and CCTV footage of suspects – all underpinned by an entreaty to the audience to phone the studio, live, with information – has attracted much criticism (Jermyn, (forthcoming) 2004). Nevertheless, in this essay I want to reflect on the programme's popularity and argue that much of *Crimewatch*'s enduring success lies in the way it responds to and perpetuates our culture's perennial fascination with identifying and seeing both criminals and victims. While in pragmatic terms, images of criminals are clearly necessary requisites to the programme's aim of identification and/or apprehension, their potency in the public imagination goes far beyond this. I contextualize *Crimewatch*'s use of images of criminals by situating it within the historical association that has long existed between photography and criminal apprehension, a relationship particularly borne out by the relatively contemporaneous development in the mid-nineteenth Century of photography and increasingly more sophisticated police-detection practices. Images of victims fulfil a rather different set of curiosities and cultural uses than those of the criminal. Here I examine how video footage and photographs of victims are often used to underline victims' familial ties, be that through the familial voice-overs and testimonies that accompany them or through the inclusion of photographs that place the victim with family members and at family events. In this way I suggest that *Crimewatch*'s use of visual evidence draws on two key photographic traditions: the 'photo story' and the 'family album'.

In fact, just as the development of photography has been entwined with that of criminal identification, so too has it been entwined with Western culture's representation and construction of the family. For photographic technology to maximize its market potential, it had to be consumed on a mass scale as a leisure activity, shaped as a domestic product; thus 'cameras and films have been developed with the family in mind' (Holland, 1991: 4). In *Crimewatch*, these twin components of photography's evolution – that is, its foundations in criminal identification and domestic photography – are both returned to and evocatively drawn on. While the notion of a 'photo story' underlines how even in a multi- and new-media age still-photography retains powerful narrative capabilities, the evoking of the 'family album' is evidence of how *Crimewatch* generally retains, adheres to and promotes conventional and conservative ideological structures. The insistence on placing victims within familial formations, as a means of emphasizing their worth and the significance of their loss, perpetuates the notion that it is primarily through their roles within the conventional family unit that individuals can be positioned, identified and legitimized, thus endorsing the hegemonic institution of the family. The ramifications of this, as Michele Barrett and Mary McIntosh observe, is that 'The overvaluation of the family devalues other lives' (cited in Holland, 1991: 7). Furthermore, as Carter's work (1998) has shown, this focusing on familial ties has particular ramifications for women victims in the media's representation of sex crimes, since their positioning as within or outside of the conventional structures of the family is used as a means of indicating their relative 'blameworthiness'. My analysis of *Crimewatch*'s use of photography, drawing on a sample of the programme taken from January to June 2000, engages methodologically with the approach that John Hartley (1992) has called 'forensic analysis': photos – artefacts that Hartley describes as 'mute witnesses' – become subjects 'coaxed into telling a story' (1992: 30). Thus, while I conceptualize the family album and the photo story as core structures in *Crimewatch*'s use of photography, these are both more broadly underwritten by Hartley's conceptualization of photos as 'talking pictures'. In his words:

No picture is pure image; *all of them, still and moving, graphic and photographic, are 'talking pictures'*, either literally, or in association with contextual speech, writing or discourse. (Hartley, 1992: 28) (italics added)

Investigating Faces – Picturing the Criminal

Although CCTV and video may mark the zenith of the crime appeal's access to 'reality' (Jermyn, 2003), the still photo is also enduringly very much evident as a staple and fundamental component of its structure. In fact, it can be argued that the history or development of photography takes place in tandem with that of modern policing and detection and that almost from their inception, both were bound up in the functions of each other. Hamilton and Hargreaves suggest that 'The invention of photography was finally announced in 1839' (2001: 57), while 'The use of photography to record the likeness of criminals can be dated back to at least 1841' (2001: 101).[1] This suggests that virtually as soon as photographic technology became marketable, its potential as a tool of surveillance and social control was exploited. Indeed, Tagg draws out this link: 'At the very time of photography's technical development, the functions of the state were expanding and diversifying in forms that were both more visible and more rigorous' (1988: 61). I want to argue, then, that *Crimewatch* perpetuates the operation of a long association between photography and criminal apprehension, one arguably already in place by the mid-nineteenth century when photography became a means of making the criminal 'visible'.

The mid-nineteenth century was an era that was already preoccupied with attempting to develop systems of classification and order. Partly, this is seen in the scientific endeavours of the age and their subsequent use of photography; the drive to produce taxonomies of race, social deviance and insanity where photography was used to identify distinguishing 'characteristics' and thus predictable and recognizable 'types' (Henning, 1997: 220–21). The massive expansion of British cities and population mobility in the 1830s had led to burgeoning fears of disease and crime. With the breakdown of traditional rural communities came an era where for the first time, *en masse*, one might not know or recognize one's 'neighbours' or the man passing on the street. One could not be sure, then, of who/where disease and crime were emanating from. Police forces expanded, as did the desire to develop more accurate and effective means of fixing the identities of suspects. The use of anthropometry at this time – an elaborate system of measuring parts of the human body – was a laborious means of distinguishing one individual from another. With the heralding of photography, the development of the police 'mug-shot' was a massive technological advance that made it far more manageable to keep people observed, fixing their image in a transportable and reproducible form (*History of Surveillance*, Channel 4, 5 August 2001). It is difficult not to draw parallels between the development and adoption of photography as a means of surveillance by police at a time of social malaise in the 1840s, and the harnessing of CCTV and video technology to criminal identification in the 1980s; a shift which was absolutely instrumental in and evidenced by the emergence of *Crimewatch* in 1984. This was a time when once again there was something of a moral panic ensuing in relation to crime, policing and the breakdown of community in Britain, crystallized in the contentious 'fear-of-crime' debates that preoccupied the media of the time (Gunter, 1987). And there are similarly unresolved questions about determinism in both instances: to what extent did the development of the technology enable the expansion of surveillance – or did the desire for surveillance drive the development of the technology? (McCahill, this volume).

As the Victorian era went on, photography was used increasingly for criminal identification purposes, not just in terms of identifying the individual suspect, but in being able to identify criminal 'types'. The sciences of physiognomy and physical anthropology aimed to demonstrate that particular physical attributes indicated the propensity for criminality or other degeneracy and deviance such as mental illness. In Britain, Francis Galton pioneered composite photography – rephotographing portraits on the same plate by successive multiple exposures to create a composite image of a 'type' – in order to try to devise 'a new system of physiognomic record which would show the features common to three types of criminal; violent criminals, felons and sexual offenders' (Hamilton and Hargreaves, 2001: 96). The Victorians became fascinated with identifying criminals, not just in terms of locking up the deviant, but in the sense of being able to 'tell' what someone's physical attributes indicated about their moral fibre; in being able to distinguish 'them' from 'us'. It is this compulsion to look at criminals, to try to 'read' them, to try to spot the signs of their 'difference' that constitutes the fundamental allure of *Crimewatch*'s photo-montages of wanted criminals. Just as this fascination with 'seeing' fuelled the Victorian preoccupation with the classification and identification of criminals, it fuels the enduring popularity of *Crimewatch*. As guides to physiognomy, detection and crime novels grew in popularity, the Victorian era apparently introduced a trend where many ordinary people fancied themselves as amateur detectives and pursued such knowledge as a way of alleviating uncertainty in an era marked by social and technological shifts; a *zeitgeist* that might equally be evoked to describe the *Crimewatch* viewer and the audience for 'real-crime' programming more broadly since the mid-1980s.

But what if we invert our dominant ways of reading mug-shot imagery? What if we try to understand its construction and circulation from the point of view of the criminal? Looking at Victorian mug-shot records, Ronald Thomas of Trinity College has commented that:

> Some cultures believe that having your photo taken takes your soul. Looking through some mug-shot files one can understand that belief. There is a kind of haunting quality to those photographs. A person has been trapped within the frame of the camera, imprinted for all time in a single gesture, with a single expression, defined by a technology which is entirely beyond one's control.
> (*The History of Surveillance*, Channel 4, 8 April 2001)

Thomas goes on to explain the frightening circumstances in which such photos were taken: the suspect would have been arrested, restrained and faced with unfamiliar and imposing equipment. The photographer would have been an eerie figure hidden under a hood, the camera could have been mistaken for some kind of weapon; 'It look(ed) like a scene of execution' (ibid.). Thomas is referring here to the period of the mid-19th century, an age when photography was still a novelty, where the capabilities of its technology were still beyond the imagination. He demands that we reconfigure the way we understand historical mug-shot imagery here; not seeing it, as the preoccupations of the day would have had us do, as a fascinating insight into the physiognomy of the criminal, nor even only analysing it today as an instance of the Victorian preoccupation with classification, but instead to reflect on it from the perspective of the *photographed*. Specifically, he asks us to consider how the context of its taking may have affected its apparent content, the demeanour and expression of the photographed. Criminal photography clearly, like any form of photography, was never capable of capturing an objective image; as a means of surveillance it would never be entirely 'scientific' in that human agency dictated its gaze. If as Thomas calls for, we reimagine the meaning of the criminal mug-shot by reflecting on it from the perspective of the photographed, an entirely new way of reading the image emerges, one that *Crimewatch* and popular culture's use of mug-shot imagery generally never attempts to reflect on or open up. Indeed, John Tagg calls for similar awareness of the significance of the context of the photo's making, and for caution about its relationship to the 'real', when he writes:

We have to see that every photograph is the result of specific and, in every sense, significant distortions which render its relation to any prior reality deeply problematic and raise the question of the determining level of the material apparatus and of the social practices within which photography takes place. (1988: 2)

The way our culture has predominantly read photography of the criminal, our search for the signs of 'difference', the very fact of our fascination with such imagery, arguably tells us more about ourselves than about the photographed.

Telling Photo Stories

Crimewatch, then, like all appeal programmes, makes significant use of surveillance 'evidence' of criminals in its appeals. But this material is combined with other visual traditions surrounding the image of the *victim*. This is another kind of visual 'evidence', which is crucial to the programme but which has gone neglected in existing analyses of the programme such as Schlesinger and Tumber (1993). In fact no critical work on *Crimewatch* to date has reflected on the extent to which the programme incorporates and is structured around visual records of the victims. This is a significant omission, since it is not just photos and videos of criminals that *Crimewatch* pivots on, but the images of their dead victims. Susan Sontag has written:

All photographs are *memento mori*. To take a photograph is to participate in another person's (or thing's) mortality, vulnerability, mutability. Precisely by slicing out this moment and freezing it, all photographs testify to time's relentless melt. (1977: 15)

If all photographs are 'touched with pathos' (ibid.) and the movement of time, if they all prefigure death and the fragility of life, then the photograph of the murder victim is doubly charged with the emotive power of the medium. For Barthes also, photography is inextricably bound up with death, with 'that terrible thing which is there in every photograph: the return of the dead' (1993: 9). He too suggests all photos are inscribed with the promise of the individual's inevitable death and with photography's characteristic sensibility of 'what-has-been'. The photograph of an already dead person, then, is marked by 'the defeat of Time'; their photo speaks to the fact of both '*that* is dead and *that* is going to die' simultaneously (1993: 96). It is for all these affective reasons that photos of the murder victim compel and resonate so acutely in *Crimewatch,* and across culture more widely.

Real pictures of the victims, the stuff of family albums everywhere, pervade *Crimewatch*. In fact, one of the core aesthetic structures that recurs in *Crimewatch* is its use of a particular pattern of visual triangulation. In this structure, interviews with police officers or bereaved family members are commonly conducted so that a monitor featuring a close-up of the victim lies prominently behind them, between the presenter and the interviewee. Their picture thus forms a third point in the 'two-shot', which clearly seeks to underline the victim's resonance in this exchange. In comparison with the panopticist material of criminals, most often shown photographed unawares in public spaces by an impersonal surveillance camera or by a police photographer in the anonymous setting of a custody room, pictures of the victims are personal and private, taken from family functions, celebrations, in homes and on holidays. Sometimes photos of criminals are also drawn from such scenes; and this in a way makes them more fascinating, more shocking, than the mug-shot, since it places the 'deviant' in the realm of the ordinary. As we've seen, the primary or defensible function of criminal photos is clear – they are shown to aid identification/ apprehension. Beyond this, as the development of photography in the 19th century in tandem with the Victorian fascination with anthropological and physiognomical classification demonstrated, they also fulfil our inquisitive need to see what 'deviants' look like, as if they might look different from other 'ordinary' people. Photos of the victims fulfil similar desires while also satisfying an entirely different set of cultural needs.

These images seek to inscribe victims as ordinary individuals in the midst of extraordinary crimes, as members of families and communities. As with criminal photography, they provide evidence that satisfies our curiosity and almost rather primal need to see what these victims, these identifiably real people, were 'like' – that is, were they like 'us'? The familiar images drawn from family albums confirm that they were. Just as photography was virtually immediately harnessed to a surveillance function in the mid-19th century, so too was it quickly drawn on to become the pre-eminent means of documenting the domestic. One could say, in fact, that the family album is another form of surveillance, 'tracking' one's history, origins and movement over years, through generations.

All the narrative forms at work in *Crimewatch,* from 'Your Call Counts' (where the audience is updated on the results of previous appeals and congratulated for helping secure convictions) to the appeals and

reconstructions, might be called 'photo stories', since their accompanying voice-overs unfold around images of either the victim or
criminal. Photos 'anchor' these stories and make them 'real'. The power
of the photographic *'punctum'*, as Barthes named it, is consciously
employed and manipulated by the crime-appeal genre. He adopts the
term *punctum* in *Camera Lucida* to express the capability of some photos
to move the spectator, found in those photos where an element:

> Rises from the scene, shoots out of it like an arrow, and pierces me.
> A Latin word exists to designate this wound, this prick, this mark
> made by a pointed instrument: the word suits me all the better in
> that it also refers to the notion of punctuation, and because the
> photographs I am speaking of are in effect punctuated, sometimes
> even speckled with these sensitive points: precisely these wounds
> are so many *points ... punctum* is also: sting, speck, cut, little
> hole ... (Barthes, 1993: 26–7)

The programme's continual return to photographs of the victim in
appeals and juxtaposition of images of life with stories of death seek to
employ the 'punctum' of every image. Even the reconstructions are
'framed' by pictures of the victim, providing an expressive way into
their story and a poignant (quasi-)closure. In *Crimewatch* the victim's
image is recurrently used to open the reconstruction – where typically
the presenter introduces the case next to a monitor with the victim's
picture on-screen before we cut to a close-up of that picture – and to close
the reconstruction, where we cut back to the studio after pausing for a
moment on a still of the victim. The fascination with and implied stories
that lie behind photos of victims make them a fundamental part of the
way the programme is constructed. In just a handful of images the
programme-makers need to communicate enough about the victim to
make the viewer respond on some kind of emotional level, be that guilt,
empathy, sympathy or outrage. Interestingly, though the photographic
traditions at stake here may seem far removed from one another – that is,
criminal identification/the 'mug-shot' versus family photography –
they are very much historically interlinked. Throughout the 19th
century there was a burgeoning drive to employ the camera and photographic technology for the services of surveillance and classification,
and this occurred in parallel with a growing demand for domestic
photography and social portraiture. The Victorian fascination, then,
with social classification was evident in the way photography was
harnessed to cataloguing *the family* as much as criminals and 'deviants'.
In Hamilton and Hargreaves' words:

There is a distinct sense in which nineteenth-century family albums can be seen as forms of the 'domestic museum', and the obsessive concern with their compilation is part of the nineteenth-century fascination with using photography to establish a complete, objective and comprehensive social inventory in a period obsessed with taxonomy and social order. (Hamilton and Hargreaves, 2001: 57)

Just as the composite photography technique pioneered by Francis Galton was used to identify the distinguishing characteristics of particular criminal types, so too was it used within families to produces an 'ideal family likeness' (Hamilton and Hargreaves, 2001: 97–98). Our fascination with photos, with using photography to be able to know, see and recognize, is as equally borne out by the traditions of the family album as it is by criminal identification. The particularly compelling aspect of *Crimewatch*'s use of photography, then, is that it brings these two traditions together again.

'Family Albums' – Picturing the Victim

In a personal interview, I asked *Crimewatch* Series Producer Katie Thomson why victims' photos were drawn on so recurrently in the programme. In a response worth quoting at length here, she replied:

> We're always trying to say these are real lives we're talking about, this isn't an interesting reconstruction, this is a real person or family that's been destroyed. And home video helps a lot with that, because I think that has a real impact. It makes people feel this person was moving and walking and talking and enjoying a birthday party six months ago and now they're dead. And the same with their photos. I think if you had no image of the real person you start thinking the whole thing isn't real. (personal interview, 2002)

This response points on a number of levels to the way in which *individual* victims are typically constructed by the programme as *family* members; Thomson notes how it is not just 'a real person' who has been 'destroyed' but by extension a family; she registers how 'home video', i.e. film shot in *domestic* contexts, dramatically underlines this context of loss; she specifically invokes 'a birthday party', the quintessential familial celebration, to illustrate her point. Victims do not exist in isolation in *Crimewatch*, but in numerous ways are very much grounded within family units. They are constructed not as individuals in and of themselves but as spouses, children, siblings and parents.

This is seen, firstly, in the reconstructions that tell the story of their murders but which also often provide 'back-story' by placing them within familial contexts; in the interviews in which bereaved relatives recall them; and in the photos and videos we see of them often taken from 'family albums'. In some ways this entails the movement of 'private' media into the public realm, involving a kind of voyeurism where moments from other people's lives that were captured for the eyes of their familiars and intimates are laid bare for all to see. Yet before critiquing *Crimewatch* for indulging this voyeuristic tendency, one should note the curious relation the family album holds to notions of the private and public. On the one hand, family albums are consumed within relatively restricted circles; yet they are very often made up of events and spaces that are public, which involve a certain degree of 'performance' from the photographed; weddings, parties, holidays, graduations.

What is more certain is that the privileging of the family seen in *Crimewatch*'s evocation of the family album is another way in which the programme adheres to a largely conservative ideological framework. Kuhn argues that 'In the process of using – producing, selecting, ordering, displaying – photographs, the family is actually in the process of making itself', largely adhering to culturally circumscribed conventions in the process (1995: 17). Though there may be room to 'read' these images in more oppositional ways, as Kuhn discovers in her subsequent deconstruction of her own family album, by drawing on the family album *Crimewatch* contributes to the cycle she describes. It perpetuates the way in which certain kinds of imagery constitute appropriate material for the family album and, by extension, certain kinds of relationships, events and aspirations constitute the family itself. It is through their family ties that the victim in *Crimewatch* is primarily defined and, implicitly, valued, a disheartening sentiment for those who do not hold or preserve such ties.

For example, two of the most openly emotional interviews featured in the sample used here were both with the bereaved partner of a young parent. In April 2000 Bill Johnson is interviewed by Fiona Bruce about the death of his wife on Grand National day in Liverpool four years earlier. Walking towards a monitor featuring a large image of a young woman holding a tiny baby, Bruce explains that Pauline Johnson was knocked down by a hit-and-run driver just five minutes from Aintree and that she later died from her injuries. This image (the 'third point' in the triangle) remains between/behind Bruce and the bereaved husband throughout the interview. Bruce commences, 'Bill, thanks for coming in. You can see a picture of Pauline here behind us. Your son was just six months old when she was killed' – at which point we cut to a close-up of the monitor – 'How's he coping with it all?' Much of the interview that follows then primarily inscribes the dead woman as a wife and mother, cutting to focus on Bill as he explains how he has told their son that his mother is an angel who lives on a cloud in heaven. The tragedy of her loss is entirely grounded in her being the mother of a young child. There seems to be little space for any other angle or way of understanding who Pauline Johnson was and what she did in her life. Similarly, in the case of Jay Abberton, murdered during an argument outside a Brighton night-club (May 2000), his partner Tania Haynes painfully describes how his death has left her to bring up two children alone. In the familiar triangulation structure again, the monitor between/behind her and Fiona Bruce carries a smiling picture of her and Jay together in happier times as she explains:

> It's been devastating for my family. We were a very happy family, we were a thriving family, life was good. The bottom line is Jay went out that night to celebrate a friend's birthday promising to take our two children for a bike ride the next day ... [at this point we cut to a c/u of Tania speaking] ... and he never came home. And for me, as I would imagine for Jay, the greatest pain is the fact that my children have been deprived of his life, his care, his guidance throughout their years.

As the interview goes on, the monitor cuts from the still photo of the couple together to what appears to be a holiday video. This pictures Jay sitting outside in the sunshine at a table, i.e. moving and animated, just as his partner talks about coming to terms with his death. In short, ways of defining or remembering victims outside of the family are very largely tangential to *Crimewatch*. The testimonies of colleagues, friends, tutors or neighbours are all largely negligible and always secondary to the family. It is difficult to imagine a *Crimewatch* victim outside of the parameters of the family: to not be in a family would be to not be a proper victim.

In *Family Snaps* (1991) Holland argues that the enduring conventions of the family album operate as a means of disavowing the increasing fragmentation of the traditional family unit in contemporary Western culture. That *Crimewatch* places such evident stock by these kinds of images demonstrates its endorsement of this tradition. Paraphrasing work by Barrett and McIntosh again, Holland writes:

Contemporary British society gives priority to an institution that is at best only partial and exists chiefly in what they call a 'familial' ideology which exerts pressure on public policy and social life. Family albums echo that ideology as childhood and leisure times are obsessively recorded. The camera is part of a lifestyle based on house, garden and car which moulds the aspirations of the suburban nations of the prosperous West. (1991: 5)

This description is potently borne out by the reconstruction of the murder of schoolboy Keith Lyon in the March 2000 programme, a reconstruction which is interesting also in that it is an old case (from 1967) being reopened due to advances in forensics. The foregrounding of time, memory, nostalgia, loss and historical authenticity that this entails make the absence/presence of the image even more acutely affective in this instance. Paraphernalia of the 1960s such as clothes, buses and cars all remind the viewer that this is a historical reconstruction, as do the extracts from TV news footage of the time, old newspaper headlines and the disjunction in the representation of Keith's family then and now. The reconstruction is largely 'narrated' by Keith's younger brother, a sibling who is barely more than a toddler in the photos and cine-camera footage that are woven through the reconstruction, but a grown man in the 'now' of the appeal. Similarly too, the young mother to two small children in 1967 is transformed into an elderly woman interviewed in the present, while their father, the celebrity band leader Ken Lyon, is now absent and not accounted for at all. Keith's brother's voice-over opens with his observation that 'I don't remember anything before', but he recalls his father coming home unexpectedly on the night that Keith was found stabbed to death. As their mother explains how she was told that his body had been found, we cut to a black-and-white still of Keith as a little boy and zoom in as she notes, 'And that was the beginning of the rest of our lives'. His brother explains, 'This was a time when my parents had everything they wanted really. A nice home, two children. They were very happy at the time.' Accompanying this description of the idealized family unit is a montage of cine-footage that evocatively condenses a handful of choice moments and images. Their mother climbs out of a car smiling with Keith; the two children play in the sea with an inflatable; their dad cuddles the dog on the grass. These images do not foreground Keith so much as the whole family. They are images of the aspirational family, with as much currency in 2000 as they would have had in 1967; they condense the notions of domesticity, leisure and accomplishment with that of material abundance: cars, holidays, gardens, pets, even the fact of having had a cine-camera. The camera here has indeed been used as Holland describes, preserving 'familial ideology' in its 'obsessive recording' of childhood, leisure and affluence.

Like a real family album (as Kuhn's *Family Secrets* (1995) has vividly testified), *Crimewatch*'s photo stories are incomplete and fragmented, in that they cannot depict every aspect of a life; they require the viewer to order and make sense of them, to fill in the gaps, which with 'our longing for narratives' (Holland, 1991: 1) we willingly do. The January 2000 edition of the show features a short appeal on the murder of Joe Bazra, a shopkeeper shot and killed in his corner shop in Glasgow, which succinctly illustrates the drive to make sense of a 'photo story' since there is no reconstruction, but rather a series of still images and video footage with a voice-over from presenter Fiona Bruce. It demonstrates how the programme must simultaneously personalize the victim, ground them within a family and appeal to a community ethos. As we see Bazra in a snapshot standing alone on the pavement outside his shop, Bruce tells us: 'He was the sort of man we'd all like to have running our local corner shop. For pensioners who couldn't get out he'd deliver their groceries personally and he'd never let anyone go hungry if they couldn't pay the bill.' Both the ideal citizen (selfless, considerate, giving) and ideal community (supportive and close, frequenting local corner shops rather than depersonalized supermarkets) are evoked here. Bazra stands with his arms by his sides, upright and looking straight ahead, almost standing to attention, framed in the doorway of his shop. The picture connotes his pride in having this shop, his own business; it had been a significant enough part of his identity for him to be photographed outside it. But there is also a terrible poignancy and irony in our knowing now as he could not have, that this shop, the source of his pride in this photo, would one day go on to become his murder-scene.[2] Indeed, the next shot brings us full circle, as we cut to news footage of the shop again, but this time masked off by police tape, adorned with flowers and with Joe absent.

While Bruce tells us that 'Everyone knew and liked Joe Bazra. They *really* feel his loss', the accompanying image is a formal portrait of him with two women, one of them dressed in a graduation gown; we assume that they are his wife and daughter. The graduation photo, that quintessential image of parental pride, individual industry and familial bonding, is a staple of countless family albums and living-room walls, and many of the audience will have their own (virtually identical) versions. Indeed, Jeremy Seabrook found in his ethnographic research into family albums that 'Although the photographs evoke personal memories, it is interesting to observe how many of these are shared by countless others. What seems to individuals a unique and, indeed, private destiny is in fact part of a wider social pattern' (1991: 178–9). The documenting of certain key images/events in our culture is so pervasive that such photographs cannot be thought of only as personal records, so much of their meaning and significance is ingrained and shared throughout that culture. The use of such images again ties the victim to familiar kinds of roles, spaces and values that the audience will, presumably, largely understand and share. It is interesting, then, that though the image of the graduation ceremony at this point shows Bazra as a family man, the voice-over refers to the bigger social context of his loss. We end finally with a picture of him smiling, in close-up. Joe Bazra has been shown both as an individual, whose loss has very personal ramifications for those close to him, and paradoxically as a kind of 'everyman', whose murder was a random act the like of which could impact on any of us. Joe Bazra's narrative, communicated in just a few words and images, is one of nostalgia but also family, hard work, community, drive and altruism – a narrative that is so pervasive and revered in our culture that it can be counted on to strike a familiar chord with viewers.

(Tele-)Visions of Domesticity

This contextualization of victims within families, then, is crucial for numerous reasons. Firstly, as Series Producer Katie Thomson indicated in interview above, it is a key component in how the programme perceives itself as being 'real'. Secondly, and related to this, it is of course crucial to the programme's audience address; our sympathy and empathy are very much sought by the inscription of bereaved families. It is also particularly significant to the representation of women victims, since existing work on female victims of sexual crime has shown how their place as 'deserving' or 'undeserving' victims is recurrently constructed by the British press in terms of whether they adhere to conventional familial structures or not (Carter, 1998). Finally, Thomson's attention to 'family' is also significant in the way that it bears out one of the key conceptualizations of TV within television studies, promoted by Corner (1999), Hartley (1992) and Ellis (1994) among others, of TV as a 'profoundly domestic phenomenon' (Ellis, 1994: 113). In this conceptualization, the notion of 'the family' is absolutely central to television's operation, both in terms of who it perceives to be its predominant audience and in the preoccupations of its programming (Ellis, 1994: 113). Although it might be inappropriate to describe *Crimewatch* as family viewing (though it would be fascinating to ascertain the extent to which it is watched in this way), it is clear that it does approach the institution and sanctity of the family with the kind of reverence that Ellis describes as symptomatic of television broadly:

> 'The home' and 'the family' are terms which have become tangled together in the commercial culture of the twentieth century. They both point to a powerful cultural construct, a set of deeply held assumptions about the nature of 'normal' human existence. (1994: 113)

In *Crimewatch,* the recurrent placing of victims within families affirms this 'normality'. We should note, of course, that just as Ellis decries the archaic inappropriateness surrounding television's privileging of the conventional nuclear family unit in the latter half of the twentieth century, television has had to diversify its conception of the audience since the era in which Ellis was originally writing, i.e. 1982. Nevertheless, the dominance of 'the ideological notion of the nuclear family' (1994: 115) that he speaks of prevails in the way *Crimewatch* operates.

In an evocative image of television's intimate place in the home, Ellis describes how 'The TV set is another domestic object, often the place where family photos are put: the direction of the glance towards the personalities on the TV screen being supplemented by the presence of "loved ones" immediately above' (1994: 113). Indeed, Hartley's 'empirical but textual reading of the presentation of TV sets, and of the viewing environment, in the early days of Australian TV' (1992: 100) identifies exactly the same phenomenon. In his sample of photos and stories from people recalling their use and 'dressing' of their televisions in the 1950s and 1960s, the tops of television sets became 'shrines of family remembrance', adorned with photos of children, weddings and portraits (1992: 108). If Ellis's imagined viewer, and the descendants of Hartley's historical viewers, still style their home in this way, imagine the potency, then, of *Crimewatch*'s 'family albums' unfolding in this context. In this vision of the *Crimewatch* viewer watching at home, their own 'loved ones' in picture frames *above* the television are dramatically juxtaposed with the grief and loss now written into others' family pictures seen *within* the television frame on-screen. The domestic comfort or stability suggested by the idealized family album is rendered acutely unsettled, the family photos above- and on-screen contrasting in a conjunction where Barthes' notion of the photographic 'punctum' reaches its zenith.

Picture This – Snapshots of Crime

In *Camera Lucida*, Barthes speculates that the fascination of photography must decline; 'And no doubt, the astonishment of *"that-has-been"* will also disappear. It has already disappeared: I am, I don't know why, one of its last witnesses' (1993: 94). The continuing success of *Crimewatch* would seem to suggest otherwise. In short, *Crimewatch* pivots on the structures, meanings and pleasures afforded by visual records of victims and criminals. The ideological and social frameworks contained within these are largely conventional and familiar: the fascination with looking for the signs of 'difference' in the deviant criminal; the spectacle of criminal identification and apprehension; the containment and definition of the individual within the structures of the family; the pre-eminence and privileging of membership of the traditional family as a legitimate and revered norm. While we should not presume that viewers do not engage in multiple and/or oppositional ways with the programme, nevertheless in these themes *Crimewatch* works to marginalize other ways of thinking about criminals and victims that would prove problematic to its representations and would risk rupturing its generally uncomplicated vision. The fact of the increasing fragmentation of the traditional family unit is absented, as victims are enduringly 'pigeon-holed' into easy and identifiable familial roles, a kind of shorthand for legitimizing both them (as innocent and undeserving victims) and the hegemonic institution of the family itself. Equally, the perspective of the criminal is absent in these 'snapshots' of crime, another way in which the programme steadfastly evades opening up diverse or oppositional discourses around criminality, to fall back instead on the age-old fascination of the singular, defining image of the criminal deviant.

Notes

1. There is some difference of opinion here with Tagg, however, who notes, 'In Britain, local police forces had been using photography since the 1860s' (1988: 7).
2. This is a particular potency drawn on again in the widely published picture of the murdered *Crimewatch UK* presenter Jill Dando, circulated just after her murder, where she is captured standing on her doorstep in a photo taken a few weeks before she was to be shot there. For a detailed discussion of the media's representation of Dando's murder, see Jermyn (2001).

References

Barthes, R. (1993) *Camera Lucida*, London: Vintage.

Carter, C. (1998) *News of Sexual Violence against Women and Girls in the British Daily National Press*, PhD thesis, Cardiff University.

Corner, J. (1999) *Critical Ideas in Television Studies*, Oxford: Oxford University Press.

Ellis, J. (1994) *Visible Fictions*, 2nd edn, London and New York: Routledge.

Gunter, B. (1987) *Television and the Fear of Crime*, London: John Libbey and Company Ltd.

Hamilton, P. and Hargreaves, R. (2001) *The Beautiful and the Damned: The Creation of Identity in Nineteenth Century Photography*, Aldershot: Lund Humphries.

Hartley, J. (1992) *The Politics of Pictures*, London: Routledge.

Henning, M. (1997) 'The Subject as Object: Photography and the Human Body', in L. Wells (ed.) *Photography: A Critical Introduction*, London: Routledge, 217–48.

Holland, P. (1991) 'History, Memory and the Family Album', in P. Holland and J. Spence (eds) *Family Snaps: The Meanings of Domestic Photography*, London: Virago, 1–14.

Jermyn, D. (2001) 'Death of the Girl Next Door: Celebrity, Femininity and Tragedy in the Murder of Jill Dando', *Feminist Media Studies*, 1(3), November, 343–59.

Jermyn, D. (2003) '"This *Is* About Real People!" – Video Technologies, Actuality and Affect in the Television Crime Appeal', in S. Holmes and D. Jermyn (eds) *Understanding Reality Television*, London: Routledge.

Jermyn, D. (2004) 'Fact, Fiction and Everything in Between: Negotiating Boundaries in *Crimewatch UK*', in J. Furby and K. Randell (eds) *Screen Method: Comparative Readings in Screen Studies*, London: Wallflower Press.

Kuhn, A. (1995) *Family Secrets: Acts of Memory and Imagination*, London: Verso.

Schlesinger, P. and Tumber, H. (1993) 'Fighting The War Against Crime: Television, Police and Audience', *British Journal of Criminology*, 33(1), 19–32.

Seabrook, J. (1991) 'My Life is in That Box', in P. Holland and J. Spence (eds) *Family Snaps: The Meanings of Domestic Photography*, London: Virago, 171–85.

Sontag, S. (1977) *On Photography*, London: Penguin.

Tagg, J. (1988) *The Burden of Representation: Essays on Photographies and Histories*, Basingstoke and London: Macmillan.

Chapter 10

Media representations of visual surveillance

Michael McCahill[1]

As a number of writers have pointed out, the mass media and criminal justice systems have begun to penetrate each other to such an extent that it is increasingly difficult to make a distinction between 'fact' and 'fiction' (Surrete, 1998; Reiner, 2002; Leishman and Mason, 2003). Over the last decade, entertainment programming based on real police officers in action has proliferated (e.g. ITV's *Crime Fighters*), and video recordings of criminal events in process are frequently used in news broadcasts, like the terrorist bomb explosion in Ealing and James Bulger being led by the hand from a Bootle shopping mall. Meanwhile, in the United States the OJ Simpson car chase was broadcast live to the watching millions, and the subsequent trial became a national news event in which the media co-opted 'the criminal justice system as a source of high drama and entertainment' (Surette, 1998: 72) (Stepniak, this volume). More recently, in a reversal of the 'civilizing process' identified by cultural historians (Elias, 1978), the Oklahoma City bomber, Timothy McVeigh, urged all Americans to watch his execution (*Observer*, 8 April 2001). It is estimated that 1,500 media people turned up to report on the event, and 300 victims, relatives and witnesses were allocated tickets for a CCTV showing of the execution (*Guardian*, 11 June 2001).

In an attempt to come to terms with these developments many writers have drawn upon Foucaultian notions of 'panopticism' and 'synopticism'. For instance, some have suggested that the advent of CCTV and telecommunications systems means that panopticism (where the few observe the many) is no longer confined to enclosed and controlled settings such as the prison or the factory. In this respect, the power of the panopticon has been dramatically enhanced by technological developments that have allowed the disciplinary gaze to extend further and further across the entire social fabric (McCahill and Norris, 2002). However, for other writers the development of the mass media has meant that the Benthamite project of the panopticon has been replaced by the synopticon (where the many observe the few) (Mathiesen, 1997; Boyne, 2000). The emergence of synopticism is also said to have transformed 'hierarchies of surveillance' by allowing the wider society to scrutinize the activities of the powerful (Mathiesen, 1997; Haggerty and Ericson, 2000). While accepting that trends towards synopticism are taking place, this chapter argues that the most recent developments in systems of punishment and social control have been towards the intensification of panopticism (where the few see the many) rather than synopticism. Moreover, where trends towards synopticism are evident, they usually involve the many watching the deviant 'other' rather than the powerful. The chapter begins with a general discussion of some of the theoretical issues, before going on to provide an analysis of CCTV reporting in three English newspapers.

Surveillance and the Mass Media – Some Theoretical Issues

Thomas Mathiesen (1997) has suggested that today we live in a 'viewer society' where the mass media allow the many to see and admire the few. A perfect example of this trend is the 'reality television' boom, which has led one commentator to suggest that 'the British have come to stand alone as a people obsessed with watching the daily lives of their country-men on television' (*Observer*, 19 December 1999: 2). The most recent development in 'factual entertainment' came with the birth of the 'formatted documentary' (*Together Again, Hotel Getaway, The Tourist Trap, Castaway 2000, Shipwrecked, Survivor* and *Big Brother*), which places members of the public in artificial situations in which social experiments are conducted for the benefit of the camera and the watching millions (Brunsdon *et al.*, 2001). In some respects, these programmes illustrate how panopticism and synopticism *'have developed in intimate interaction, even fusion, with each other'* (Mathiesen, 1997: 223; emphasis in original). While many of these programmes are based on the use of panoptic systems (designed to allow the few to see the many), they function synoptically by allowing millions of TV viewers to watch those who have had their actions monitored and recorded by visual surveillance systems.

The interaction or fusion between panopticism and synopticism is also evident in news reporting. Today, for example, many of the crime stories that appear on the news and in the press are accompanied by a visual representation of events captured by the millions of CCTV cameras operating in public and semi-public space. The omnipresence of surveillance cameras in the UK provided the mass media with visual obituaries of James Bulger being led to his death from a shopping mall, Jill Dando shopping in Hammersmith, and Damilola Taylor skipping across a paved square in Peckham. The emergence of visual surveillance systems has also penetrated the workings of the criminal justice system. For instance, the recent introduction of CCTV systems into custody suites and police cells means that potentially the activities of custody officers could come under just as much scrutiny as those of the inmates (Newburn and Hayman, 2002).

The monitoring of the powerful has also been facilitated by the proliferation of video cameras that allow the general public to tape instances of police brutality (Haggerty and Ericson, 2000: 618). The most infamous case took place on 3 March 1991, when George Holliday used a video camera to film the video of Black motorist Rodney King being battered by four White police officers of the Los Angeles Police Department. The resulting two-minute footage showed that King 'was hit 56 times with a baton, leaving him with 11 skull fractures, brain damage and kidney damage' (Wazir, 2002: 26). Meanwhile, in the UK a number of CCTV systems operating in public space have recorded examples of police brutality which have been widely reported in the press (*Guardian*, 24 August 1999; *Hull Daily Mail*, 20 February 1998; *Guardian*, 7 August 1999; *Guardian*, 22 February 2000).

However, despite these trends towards synopticism, the most recent developments in strategies of surveillance and social control involve an intensification of panopticism (where the few see the many). For instance, the last decade or so has witnessed a dramatic increase in the use of new surveillance technologies that facilitate the surveillance of entire populations. Feeley and Simon (1994: 173), for example, have argued that justice is becoming 'actuarial', and its interventions increasingly based on risk assessment, rather than on the identification of specific criminal behaviour. This paradigm shift has given rise to a whole new range of strategies of 'risk management'. These include the testing of employees for the use of drugs (Gilliom, 1994), the blanket DNA testing of entire communities (Nelkin and Andrews, 1999), and the use of city-centre CCTV surveillance systems that seek to regulate groups as part of a strategy of managing danger (Norris and Armstrong, 1999).

Of course, not everyone is equally subject to the regime of these systems of social control. For example, in the context of drugs testing, newspaper reports suggest that managers of the London Underground are using drug tests 'as a disciplinary weapon, and picking on ethnic minorities' (*Independent on Sunday*, 22 November 1998). Also, in some parts of the United States welfare applicants who refuse to submit to drug testing will have their application for assistance denied (American Civil Liberties Union, 18 April 2000). Similarly, the question of whether genetic testing falls equally on different social groups has arisen in the context of employment and insurance. In the early 1970s, for example, some insurance companies in the United States 'denied coverage and charged higher rates to African Americans who were carriers of the gene for sickle cell anemia' (Colonna, 1998: 4). The disproportionate targeting of the deviant 'other' is also found in the context of visual surveillance. For instance, in their study of three open-street CCTV surveillance systems, Norris and Armstrong (1999) have shown how the CCTV operators disproportionately target particular social groups. In short, the operation of these systems leads 'to the over-representation of men, particularly if they are young or black' (1999: 196).

In this respect panopticism has not disappeared; rather its impact has become socially differentiated. Zygmunt Bauman (1992, 1997), for example, draws a distinction between the 'seduced', who become socially integrated by means of market dependency, and the 'repressed', who are controlled by the old disciplinary techniques of surveillance. These developments are most clearly pronounced at the urban level where public space is being reconstituted, not as an arena for democratic interaction, but as the site of mass consumption (Davis, 1990). In the United States, for example, Davis has shown how the development of secured 'skyway' systems and 'gated communities' are eliminating 'the democratic admixture on the pavements' (1990: 231). In some cities 'overstreet malls' have 'created a virtual spatial apartheid in the city, with middle-class whites above, and blacks and poor people below' (Boddy, 1992: 141). Urban geographers have identified similar trends in the UK where the development of gated residential communities, the private policing of semi-public space and the deployment of CCTV systems 'should also be seen as part of the fortress impulse' (Bannister *et al.*, 1998: 27). The evacuation of public space can in turn engender increasing reliance on mass-media images and perceptions of crime to the extent that anxiety and the 'fear of crime' have become an institutionalized feature of modern society (Sparks, 1992: 12). Thus while the introduction of CCTV systems is cited by many politicians as an effective way of reducing the widespread 'fear of crime', it may be that such strategies are adding to the fear and insecurity already brought about by wider processes of 'deregulation' and 'privatization' (Bauman, 1997: 204).

As a number of writers have pointed out, many of the programmes of practical action that flow from contemporary strategies of crime control increasingly are addressed not to central-state agencies such as the police, 'but *beyond* the state apparatus, to the organisations, institutions and individuals in civil society' (Garland, 1996: 451; O'Malley, 1992; Fyfe, 1995). In some respects, these developments could be seen as a form of synopticism (where the majority of 'law-abiding citizens' are encouraged to watch the few). Once again, however, it is not the powerful that are subject to this scrutiny, but the deviant 'other' and the 'outcast'. While politicians have suggested that there are limits to what the state can achieve in the context of crime control, there is at the same time a 'growing demand on the central state to show that the machine is still working' (Pratt, 2002: 176). This involves attempts by the state to reclaim the power of sovereign command by the use of phrases like 'zero tolerance', 'prison works', 'tough on crime' and 'three strikes' (Garland, 1996). Against this background we see an increase in emotive and ostentatious forms of punishment directed at the 'outcast' and deviant 'other' (Pratt, 2000). In the United States, for example, the return of the chain gang and community work sanctions that compel the offender to wear stigmatic clothing are designed to make the deviant 'other' advertise his or her criminality to the world at large (Pratt, 2000).

In the UK, television and newspapers have played a major role in these developments by attempting to encourage citizen involvement in the area of crime control. For instance, television programmes like *Crimewatch UK* and *Crimestoppers* contain Photocalls asking viewers to identify suspects from CCTV footage (Jermyn, this volume). In some areas, local newspapers have teamed up with *Crimestoppers* in an attempt to encourage citizen involvement in crime prevention activity. One local newspaper, for example, published the following headlines accompanying 'mug shots' from video surveillance footage designed to encourage 'active citizens' to phone in with information as to the whereabouts of local villains (McCahill, 2002: 64):

'Do You Know Them?' (20 June 1996)
'Plea to Readers to Identify 12 Men' (11 July 1996)
'Do You Know Man on B&Q Camera?' (19 August 1996)
'Wanted: Do You Know These People?' (17 January 1997)
'Police Want to Trace This Woman' (4 August 1997)

In one article, a local newspaper printed pictures taken from CCTV footage of a young mother and her two children with the headline: 'Mother Fagin's Young Helpers'. The newspaper reported that a mother and her two young children had been captured by a local supermarket's CCTV system 'carrying out a Fagin-style raid' in a local market town on the outskirts of a northern city. The article encouraged people to phone in with the names of the suspects who, as the newspaper put it, 'spoke in a rough Northern City accent'. The description of the woman as Mother Fagin also depicted her as 'other' and conjured up Dickensian images of the 'dangerous classes' (McCahill, 2002: 64–5).

While most strategies of 'responsibilization' have stemmed from official state-sanctioned policy, it is also possible to identify trends towards similarly expressive extra-legal sanctions (Pratt, 2000, 2002). These may be the work of local vigilante groups targeting and inflicting punishment on known or suspected offenders. Once again, the media have encouraged these developments with campaigns against paedophiles – 'Does a Monster Live Near You?' (*News of the World*, 23 July 2000: 2, cited in Pratt, 2002: 177). More recently, in an ironic twist to the Bulger case, pictures of Robert Thompson (one of the killers of James Bulger) taken from a shopping mall CCTV system were posted on the Internet, leading some to worry about an increase in the likelihood of misdirected attacks (BBC News, 25 June 2001).

It was the abduction and murder of James Bulger that 'dramatically launched CCTV into the public debate surrounding the control of crime as the fuzzy [CCTV] pictures of the little boy being led from the shopping centre were replayed night after night on television' (Norris and Armstrong, 1999). The case also received enormous attention in the press ('For Goodness Sake Hold Tight to Your Kids', *Sun*, 16 February 1993) and gave an almost irresistible impetus to the introduction of CCTV. Following the Bulger case CCTV was presented as the latest 'silver bullet' in strategies of crime control (Marx, 1992). The dominant political and media discourse surrounding CCTV fitted neatly with this idea of a 'technical fix' and became a common feature of the language of politicians who claimed that CCTV was a 'friendly eye in the sky' that will 'put criminals on the run'. In the early 1990s, these statements were supported by a number of dramatic success stories that were in turn 'transmitted by television and newspapers keen to report on this "wonderful new" technology' (Norris and Armstrong, 1999: 63–4). Today, of course, citizens of the UK have become the most surveilled population in the world (Muncie, 2001: 298), which means that 'selling the silver bullet' is no longer an issue. In order to examine how the debate on CCTV has changed ten years after the Bulger case, the next section will examine news reporting on visual surveillance systems in three English newspapers.

CCTV in Three English Newspapers

This section analyses newspaper coverage of CCTV in the *Daily Telegraph* (a 'right'-of-centre newspaper with a readership of just over 1 million), *The Guardian* (a 'left'-of-centre newspaper with a readership of 387,000) and the *Evening Standard* (a London daily newspaper). As we will see shortly, over the last couple of years the introduction of speed cameras has become a major issue in news reporting on visual surveillance systems. This is interesting in relation to our earlier discussion on synopticism and panopticism because it allows us to compare news reporting on speed cameras, which target the 'powerful' or 'respectable' (i.e. the motorist), and open-street cameras, which target the deviant 'other'. All CCTV stories (i.e. stories that included the word CCTV or a related keyword) that appeared between 1 November 2000 and 1 November 2001 have been selected. This search produced a total of 626 stories. However, 37 per cent of these were 'peripheral' CCTV stories (i.e. stories where CCTV or a related key word was mentioned but was totally unrelated to the general theme of the article). The analysis is, therefore, confined to the remaining 63 per cent (392) of CCTV stories. However, before presenting the analysis of these stories, this section begins by saying something about what makes CCTV such a good story.

News values and sources

Over the last decade the rapid growth in the use of CCTV surveillance systems has provided the mass media with a seemingly never-ending supply of crime stories. For example, in 1993 *The Guardian* had 15 stories mentioning CCTV. This increased to 46 in 1994 and 50 in 1995 (Norris and Armstrong, 1999: 71). By the year 2000, however, a keyword search on CCTV and related terms in the same newspaper produced a total of 275 stories. But what is it about CCTV that makes it such a good story? To answer this question we need to consider the selection criteria used by journalists to identify newsworthy items. A number of writers have identified some of these key 'professional imperatives'. These include stories that tend to prioritize the present over the past (immediacy); the unusual over the normal (novelty); the dramatic over the mundane (dramatization); the simplistic over the complex (simplification); and personalities rather than structures (personalization) (Chibnall, 1977).

Many of the issues surrounding the introduction and use of visual surveillance systems fit very neatly with the professional and cultural assumptions that underlie a journalist's judgement about what is news and what is not. The introduction of CCTV systems automatically succeeds on the first two criteria of newsworthiness (immediacy and novelty). They are about the immediate present rather than the distant past. For example, one newspaper reported how 'A chief constable ... came under fire yesterday after disclosing that his own forces cameras were to be re-painted dark blue' (*Daily Telegraph*, 19 October 2001). Other stories stressed the imminent arrival of 'new' CCTV systems:

'London Buses to Get Spy Cameras' (Headline: *Evening Standard*, 15 December 2000)
'New Cameras Focus on Fuel Bandits' (Headline: *Evening Standard*, 2 January 2001)
'Bus Lane Drivers Face 700 Hundred More Cameras' (Headline: *Evening Standard*, 27 March 2001)
'6,000 More Speed Cameras on the Way' (Headline: *Daily Telegraph*, 14 August 2001)

CCTV news stories also lend themselves to dramatization. By placing them in the context of the 'battle against crime', certain aspects of CCTV's operation and effects can be highlighted for dramatic effect:

'Policing London's War Zone' (Headline: *Evening Standard*, 16 January 2001)
'West End War on "Ibiza-style" Yobs' (Headline: *Evening Standard*, 8 March 2001)
'People Rejoice at War on Yobs and Thieves' (Headline: *Evening Standard*, 23 May 2001)
'More CCTV in Crime War' (Headline: *Guardian*, 22 August 2001)

Reportage on CCTV also has little difficulty in reducing complex issues to common-sense simplicity such as 'spy cameras to catch vandals' (*Evening Standard*, 18 May 2001) or 'CCTV cuts crime on estate by 45 per cent' (*Daily Telegraph*, 27 December 2000). The personalization of the stories can also be achieved with minimum effort. At the beginning of the 1990s, for example, local newspapers used victim accounts ('Shopkeeper's Camera Plea' after a spate of robberies at his shop) to call for the introduction of CCTV systems to prevent future victimization (Norris and Armstrong, 1999: 73). In the current sample of national newspapers, however, the call for cameras was not such an important issue. In these newspapers the personalization of stories was achieved by reporting accounts of victimization where the suspect may have been caught on camera. For instance, 'WPC hit me with baton' (*Evening Standard*, 30 August 2001) or 'Hindu girl tells of school hall hammer attack' (*Daily Telegraph*, 18 October 2001). In this way, stories of 'everyday crime', which would probably warrant little news space, are reshaped in the light of CCTV to give them news value.

The news value of a story is enhanced further if it can be presented as part of an ongoing 'newsworthy theme'. For instance, following a suspected terrorist bomb explosion in central London the Evening Standard released the following articles:

'Bomb Suspect Caught on Camera' (Headline: *Evening Standard*, 6 August 2001)

'Yard Sifts CCTV Calls Over Bomber' (Headline: *Evening Standard*, 7 August 2001)

'New Plea in Search for Bomber' (Headline: *Evening Standard*, 8 August 2001)

'Ealing Blast to be Re-enacted' (Headline: *Evening Standard*, 9 August 2001)

'We Will Catch the Bombers' (Headline: *Evening Standard*, 9 August 2001)

As a number of studies have shown, CCTV stories in the regional press tend to be dominated by local elites who use the press to emphasize the positive aspects of CCTV (Norris and Armstrong, 1999; McCahill, 2002). Thus in their analysis of three local newspapers, Norris and Armstrong (1999) found that 86 per cent of voices cited in 60 CCTV stories belonged to those who were involved in a partnership set up to promote the CCTV system (i.e. local councillors, police, council officials and business leaders). Similarly, in his study of CCTV reportage in a recession-hit northern town, McCahill (2002) found that 71 per cent of voices cited in 186 CCTV stories belonged to those who were promoting the system (i.e. members of the Chamber of Trade, police and councillors). The same studies also found that the vast majority of voices cited in stories were supportive of the use of CCTV. One study, for example, found that only two (out of a total of 272) 'voices' were critical of the introduction of CCTV (McCahill, 2002).

The findings from our analysis of the current sample of CCTV stories are very different to those found in studies of local newspapers. As Table 10.1 shows, in the CCTV stories that contained quoted sources (i.e. those talking about CCTV), almost half (47 per cent) were critical of surveillance cameras. If we look at each newspaper individually we can see that in the *Evening Standard* half (50 per cent) of the quoted sources were 'supportive' of cameras, whereas in *The Guardian* slightly less than half (44 per cent) of voices were 'supportive'. Perhaps most surprising

Table 10.1 Orientation of 'voices' in CCTV stories

Orientation of voices	All papers	Evening Standard	Daily Telegraph	Guardian
Supportive (%)	37	50	25	44
Critical (%)	47	34	59	39
Neutral (%)	16	16	16	17
N =	260	70	119	71

are the figures for the *Daily Telegraph*, which show that almost six out of ten (59 per cent) quoted sources were critical of the introduction of CCTV. How can we account for these findings? Have newspapers in the UK suddenly become critical of CCTV? To answer this question we need to look in more detail at the stories themselves.

Good Cameras and Bad Cameras

As a number of studies of crime and the mass media have shown, ideological strategies in news reporting are often developed in order to legitimate relationships of power and dominance (van Dijk, 1998). Van Dijk, for example, argues that the structure of ideologies will very often involve 'positive self-presentation and negative other-presentation' (1998: 61). In other words, ideological discourse is often polarised – 'we are good, they are bad'. In the current sample of newspapers, media representations of visual surveillance systems are based on a similar strategy of ideological polarization. Generally speaking, cameras that monitor 'Them' (e.g. thieves, robbers, muggers) are good, while cameras that monitor 'Us' (e.g. motorists, workers) are bad.

As Norris and Armstrong (1999) have shown in their analysis of the regional press, the dominant discourses in news reporting in the early 1990s were 'emphasising effectiveness', 'downplaying displacement', and 'your liberties are safe with us' (1999: 79). These writers report that almost every single one of the 60 stories in their study made some reference to the efficacy of CCTV. In the current sample, there has been a shift from 'selling the silver bullet' to the 'silver bullet in action'.

As Table 10.2 shows, the top four news themes are 'caught on camera', 'speed cameras', 'fighting crime' and 'searching tapes'. The dominant news theme was 'caught on camera' which made up over a quarter (26 per cent) of CCTV stories. The ubiquity of surveillance cameras in the

Table 10.2 CCTV stories in three English newspapers (1 November 2000 – 1 November 2001)

News stories	All papers (top four)	Evening Standard	Daily Telegraph	Guardian
Caught on camera	26%	29%	12%	30%
Speed cameras	27%	13%	63%	21%
Fighting crime	15%	22%	13%	8%
Searching tapes	8%	13%	0%	7%
Crowd control		9%	0%	4%
Cameras are coming		4%	3%	5%
Traffic management		3%	0%	0.7%
CCTV doesn't work		2%	1%	1%
Civil liberties		1%	6%	7%
Resistance		1%	0%	3%
Protectional		1%	0%	3%
Watching execution		0%	1%	4%
Security risk (no CCTV)		0%	0%	4%
Others		2%	1%	3%
N =	392	164	86	142

UK means that today many crime stories that appear in the press can be accompanied by a visual representation of events captured by the millions of CCTV cameras operating in public and semi-public space:

'Dando Verdict: Lost Clues that Led Police to the Killer' (Headline: *Guardian*, 3 July 2001)
'Caught on Camera: The Last Journey of Damilola Taylor' (Headline: *Guardian*, 15 December 2000)

The 'fighting crime' news theme claimed that CCTV had either 'cracked crime' (headline: 'CCTV Cuts Crime on Estate by 45 per cent', *Daily Telegraph*, 27 December 2000), or was about to 'crack crime' (headline: 'New Cameras Focus on Fuel Bandits', *Evening Standard*, 2 January 2001). The 'searching tapes' news theme described how CCTV was used as an investigative tool in some of the widely publicized crime stories that appeared in the newspapers. For instance, following the Ealing bomb explosion in August 2001, the *Evening Standard* reported that 'Anti-terrorist squad detectives are today scouring through hundreds of hours of CCTV film taken from businesses in the Ealing area in a bid to find the face of the bomber' (*Evening Standard*, 6 August 2001).

The news themes described above ('caught on camera', 'fighting crime' and 'searching tapes') focused mainly on the use of open-street CCTV systems that target the deviant 'other' (murderers, thieves, terrorists, etc.). The vast majority of these stories tended to portray visual surveillance systems in a positive light. However, in other CCTV stories it was the 'powerful' or 'respectable' (e.g. motorists, workers, etc.) who were subject to the cameras gaze. In these stories a critical discourse begins to emerge. The majority of stories guided by a 'civil liberties' discourse, for example, were critical of the use of cameras that monitor 'Us' (i.e. workers):

'How to Tell if Big Brother is Watching You' (*Observer*, 13 May 2001)
'Every Move You Make: Be Afraid, Big Brother is Getting Even Bigger' (*Observer*, 24 June 2001)

Meanwhile, in the 'CCTV doesn't work' news frame, several stories were critical of surveillance cameras because they had failed to prevent crimes committed by 'Them'. As one newspaper reported, 'Brixton's muggers and dealers may be getting away with offences because the area's ageing street lamps do not give enough light for decent CCTV footage' (*Evening Standard*, 15 October 2001). Similarly, stories focusing on the issue of 'displacement' described how picturesque villages (inhabited by 'Us') were being invaded by 'Them' ('thieves and yobs who desecrate England's garden') (*Evening Standard*, 23 May 2001). However, the vast majority of critical voices were found in stories reporting on the issue of speed cameras. The remainder of this chapter will explore this strategy of ideological polarization in more detail by examining newspaper reporting on this issue.

Speed cameras

The critical discourse on speed cameras can be broken down into the following ten themes.

1. Speed cameras are about revenue not safety

While speed cameras have been operational on UK roads for about a decade, in 2000 a new hypothecation system was introduced which allowed the police and local authorities to use the money raised by speeding fines to pay for and maintain speed cameras. It was the introduction of this hypothecation system that dominated newspaper reporting on speed cameras between 1 November 2000 and 1 November 2001. In a classic case of 'condemning of the condemners' (Sykes and

Matza, 1957), these stories claimed that the motives and behaviour of the law enforcers was worse than the law violation. The following extracts are fairly typical of newspaper reporting on this issue:

> Our argument is not that speed cameras are always and everywhere bad. Rather, it is that their use is disproportionate and represents a misdeployment of police resources. This is especially true of the latest scheme, which would allow part of the revenue from fines to be used to install more cameras. (*Daily Telegraph*, 14 August 2001)

> Roving round-the-clock speed cameras are to be used across London in a fresh onslaught on drivers. It is expected that there will be a 250 per cent rise in the number of prosecutions – to around 3.5 million – generating £200 million a year in fines, when the scheme is extended to other parts of the country. The mobile quick-response units, operated by specially trained police officers, are the next 'weapon' against drivers who persist in flouting the law. (*Evening Standard*, 19 October 2001)

> ENOUGH. Truly, enough. The Government is about to unleash a plague of speed cameras. (*Daily Telegraph*, 'Road Rage')

The first example is typical of many of the stories on speed cameras that begin with a disclaimer ('Of course speed cameras are a good thing, but ...') and then go on to argue the case against their introduction. As van Dijk (1998: 39) points out, 'in this way, the first clause emphasises the tolerance of the speaker, whereas the rest of the ... text following the *but* may be very negative'. The next two examples use a number of negative lexical items to describe the use of speed cameras that we would not find in descriptions of open-street CCTV systems. Thus, unlike CCTV systems operating in public space, which are portrayed in the newspapers as new 'crime-busting' initiatives, speed cameras are described as a 'the next weapon against drivers', or as a 'plague' that has been unleashed by the government on the poor unsuspecting motorist. By describing speed cameras as a 'weapon', these stories portray the speeding motorist as a 'victim' rather than an offender. The police and local authorities, on the other hand, are described as responsible agents, who are consciously, intentionally and cynically aware of what they are doing – using speed cameras 'in a blatant "revenue-raising" exercise' (*Evening Standard*, 19 October 2001).

2. Deterrence before entrapment

The second news theme called for speed cameras to be made more visible so that they would deter speeding motorists rather than entrap them:

> Police will have to inform motorists through local newspapers and radio stations of areas in which they are using mobile speed cameras. Fifteen forces have also been advised by the Department of Transport to post details on the Internet. (*Daily Telegraph*, 29 October 2001)

This news theme implies that those who break the law by speeding are not completely responsible for their actions because the government has used the cameras in a covert way to entrap the unsuspecting motorist. The logic of this argument is that cameras should be made more visible to allow speeding motorists to slow down when they see a speed camera before reverting to their normal speed, which presumably will be above the legal limit!

3. Speed cameras have no film in them

> A police force that recently demanded more 'openness' on the location of speed cameras today went a step further – admitting that none of its 'spy' devices had been loaded with film for eight months. (*Evening Standard*, 10 August 2001)

> As most motorists have already worked out, most speed cameras do not have any camera film in them most of the time. You can cruise past at 85mph, you may even get flashed, but there is no film in the speed camera to record your naughtiness. (*Daily Telegraph*, 22 March 2001: 9)

In the first category of speed camera stories ('Speed cameras are about revenue not safety') it was suggested that speed cameras 'could send the number of speeding tickets issued spiralling to 10 million a year, generating around £600 million in fines'. However, the two examples above suggest that most speed cameras don't work because they have no film in them. Meanwhile, while research has suggested that excessive speed contributes to a third of Britain's annual 3,400 road deaths (*Evening Standard*, 20 August 2001), the second article above describes speeding at 85mph as 'naughtiness', discursively shifting it from a criminal act to trivial deviance.

4. Resisting speed cameras

While the theme of resistance is a very rare occurrence in reporting on open-street CCTV surveillance systems, there were several stories that focused on this issue in relation to speed cameras:

> How to Beat the Speed Cameras (*Evening Standard*, 4 September 2001)
>
> Drivers are dodging controversial speed cameras by using a revolutionary device that alerts them in advance ... The makers say the device gives the driver ample time to slow down gradually rather than slamming on the brakes at the last minute and risking an accident

In the above article speeding motorists are offered advice on how to beat the speed cameras by deploying camera detectors. In this story, speed cameras are described as 'controversial' while detectors, which allow motorists to break the law, are described as 'revolutionary'. This article also seems to imply that the use of detectors is legitimate because detectors prevent accidents by allowing those who flout the law to slow down gradually rather than slamming on the brakes. But if motorists did not speed in the first place there would, of course, be no need to slam on the brakes. Other forms of resistance to speed cameras were reported including those below:

> Fast and Furious (*Daily Telegraph*, 20 August 2001)
>
> Four speed cameras have been wrecked on a 15-mile stretch of the A40. Detectives say they suspect Motorists Against Speed Cameras. That hardly narrows it down, since almost all motorists are against speed cameras. But they should not smash them, and we deprecate such criminal behaviour. The inventor of the Gatso speed camera used it in the 1950s to help him drive faster. It took four decades for a British government to become shameless enough to use the device to grab money unfairly from a fraction of drivers. No surprise that some fight back.

> We is Doing Our Bit for Society, Bruv (*Evening Standard*, August 2001)
>
> While we British are predictably supine in reacting to the pernicious menace of speed cameras, the Italians are said to take a more active approach. In parts of the south especially, young men have taken to driving past them at huge speed, apparently, and blowing them away with shotguns.

The first article begins by condemning the reported acts of vandalism but goes on to suggest that this behaviour is justified because of the government's 'shameless' use of speed cameras to grab money from motorists. The second article provides a 'humorous' approach to the resistance of speed cameras. Reporting on how young men in Italy have apparently used shotguns to blow away speed cameras, the author goes on to wonder whether it could be possible to persuade 'Yardie crack dealers' in the UK to do the same thing.

5. The camera never lies, but speed cameras do

In our sample of 392 CCTV stories, we failed to find a single story reporting how open-street city-centre CCTV systems had 'got it wrong' by, for example, wrongly identifying a particular suspect. However, as the articles below illustrate, speed cameras often get it wrong and this is described in great detail by the newspapers:

'Farce' as Tractor Clocked at 87mph (*Evening Standard*, 1 November 2000)
The owner of a vintage tractor has received a speeding ticket for driving his old vehicle on a motorway at 87mph – 72mph more than it's capable of travelling at. Garry Porter, whose tractor has a top speed of 15mph, received an apology from Northamptonshire police for the 'mistake'. The ticket was issued after speed cameras caught a Mercedes, believed to have the same numberplate as the tractor, travelling at 87mph near junction 15 of the M1.

Don't Smile You're on Camera (*Daily Telegraph*, 30 June 2001: 9)
Paul Watters, head of roads and transport policy at the AA, says: 'This flood of faulty notices is bringing the entire system into serious disrepute'. Some drivers have been accused of breaking a 30-mph limit even though they were on holiday abroad when the offence was said to have been committed … A vicar was accused of speeding in London while giving a sermon in Wales. A dairyman in Scotland has received numerous tickets for 'speeding' in his milk float.

These articles provide further examples of ideological polarization whereby negative opinions about cameras that monitor 'Them' (thieves, robbers, drug dealers, violent criminals, etc.) tend to receive very little attention, while negative opinions about cameras that target 'Us' (motorists) tend to be detailed, repeated and illustrated with concrete examples. Moreover, the significance of these incidents of speed cameras getting it wrong is blown out of all proportion. Thus according to these stories, these isolated incidents are 'bringing the entire system into disrepute'. They also fail to tell us exactly how many technical glitches make up the 'flood of faulty notices'.

6. Speed cameras can cause crime/accidents

In this category a number of articles in the Daily Telegraph suggest that speed cameras far from reducing law-breaking or accidents, can actually be seen as a cause of crime and accidents:

> 'Penalty Points for Sale' (*Daily Telegraph*, 8 September 2001)
> 'Can Speed Cameras Kill?' (*Daily Telegraph*, 8 September 2001)

In the first article, a representative of the Association of British Drivers condemns the illegal trade in penalty points, but goes on to argue that this practice 'is the inevitable result of misguided government policy'. He says, 'More and more safe motorists (i.e. speeding motorists) are in danger of losing their licence because of unreasonable speed limits and the senseless proliferation of speed cameras'. In the second article it is argued that speed cameras are forcing motorists to brake suddenly, which is resulting in road accidents.

7. Speed cameras erode civil liberties

While open-street CCTV surveillance systems are presented as a 'technological fix' for problems of crime and disorder, the introduction of speed cameras is said to erode civil liberties. The *Daily Telegraph* was so concerned about this issue that it launched 'Our Free Country' campaign, which was:

> Founded on the principle that there should be a presumption against coercion. There may be occasions when it's legitimate to limit someone's liberty, but the onus should always be on those who want to do the limiting. The Government's plan for a huge expansion in the number of speed cameras will drag our law still further away from this principle. (*Daily Telegraph*, 14 August 2001)

8. We need 'Bobbies', not cameras

In a recent documentary on speed cameras, the narrator of the pro-gramme asked the following question: 'As the cameras breed like rabbits are the real cops losing out to the Robocops?' (Channel Four, 6 July 2002). The 'Bobbies not cameras' news theme also appeared in our sample of newspapers:

'Criminals Gain from Police Cuts' (*Evening Standard*, 22 January 2001)
Violent criminals are escaping detection because traditional police traffic patrols have been dramatically scaled down, it was claimed today. New Home Office research shows motorists who commit serious traffic offences are frequently also involved in major crime ... The study ... shows a high proportion of drivers stopped for motoring offences are involved in crimes including violence, burglary, robbery, theft, drug offences and criminal damage. Now that an increasing number of drivers are instead caught on camera and processed automatically, however, their involvement with serious crime, is often being missed.

In this article the shift from 'traditional policing' to a reliance on speed cameras is seen as a bad move because it means that 'They' ('real criminals') are getting away with it while 'We' (speeding motorists) are being targeted.

9. Speed does not kill

Positive opinions about cameras that monitor 'Us' are forestalled by counter-arguments against such opinions (van Dijk, 1998). For instance, one of the main arguments in favour of speed cameras is, of course, that by deterring drivers from speeding they will save lives. However, to counter this argument one newspaper pointed to a Transport Research Laboratory Report, which stated that 'excessive speed was a definite causal factor in only 6 per cent of accidents' (*Daily Telegraph*, 24 February 2001: 2). Other articles made the same point:

Motor Mouth: Speed Cameras are Defrauding Motorists, says Mike Rutherford. What's More, No One Knows if They Work (*Daily Telegraph*, 18 August 2001)
Whether the cameras can, on their own, bring about a net reduction in road accident casualties is highly questionable ... On Thursday, the DoT assured me that a speed camera report will be published in October. That document must, at the very least, say what percentage of cameras are directly responsible for preventing death and injury ... But if the report does not make valid comparisons or fails to offer evidence that cameras are doing the job they're supposed to, it won't be worth the paper it's written on.

The article above questions whether speed cameras can reduce road accident casualties, and demands that the impending Department of

Transport report state what percentage of cameras are directly responsible for preventing death and injury. However, the same newspaper requires less convincing when it comes to the effectiveness of open-street CCTV surveillance systems. In one article, for example, it reported that 'CCTV cuts crime on estate by 45 per cent' (*Daily Telegraph*, 27 December 2000). The same goes for open-street CCTV systems in general, which, as Norris and Armstrong (1999: 63) have pointed out, were introduced throughout the country before any systematic evaluation of their effectiveness had been carried out.

10. Speed cameras don't target 'real' criminals
In the final group of speed camera stories it is argued that CCTV cameras should not be targeting 'Us' (speeding motorists); rather they should be targeting 'Them' ('real criminals'). This theme cropped up over and over again in speed camera stories:

> Scotland Yard has ordered a freeze on the number of speed cameras in the capital saying that the war on violent crime and burglary should take greater priority than stopping speeding motorists. (*Evening Standard*, 10 July 2001)

> The multiplication of safety cameras will widen still further the gulf between what the public want the police to do, and what the police themselves want to do. Most people would like the police to concentrate on catching dangerous criminals. (*Daily Telegraph*, 14 August 2001)

The ideological polarization between 'Us' ('law-abiding motorists') and 'Them' ('dangerous criminals') is perhaps most clearly illustrated in the examples above. This became the central discursive strategy in news reporting on speed cameras.

Conclusion

As we saw at the beginning of this chapter, Foucaldian notions of panopticism and synopticism have dominated theoretical discussions on surveillance and the media. This chapter began by suggesting that where trends towards both panopticism and synopticism are evident, they usually involve surveillance of the deviant 'other' rather than the powerful. Next the chapter examined newspaper reporting on visual surveillance, where the rapid growth in the use of speed cameras has presented the mass media (which are generally supportive of visual surveillance systems) with a problem. Unlike open-street CCTV systems, which target the deviant 'outcast', speed cameras target 'respectable citizens'. As the chapter has shown, the news media overcome this problem by developing a discursive strategy of 'positive self-presentation and negative other-presentation' (van Dyke, 1998: 61). Generally speaking, we find that cameras that monitor 'Them' (e.g. thieves, robbers, muggers, etc.) are good, while cameras that monitor 'Us' (e.g. motorists, workers, etc.) are bad. We return to the question raised earlier: have newspapers in the UK suddenly become critical of surveillance cameras? The answer in short is 'yes and no' depending upon whether they are reporting on cameras that target 'Us' or cameras that target 'Them'; because while cameras that target 'Us' are described as 'Big Brother tactics' (*Daily Telegraph*, 16 June 2001), cameras that target 'Them' are presented as a 'West End war on "Ibiza-style" yobs' (*Evening Standard*, 8 March 2001).

Note

1. The author gratefully acknowledges financial and research support from the European Commission's Fifth Framework RTD Project on surveillance entitled URBANEYE, which is part of a three year comparative project on the use of CCTV surveillance technology in seven European capital cities. Contract No. HPSE-CT2001-00094. Further details can be found at: http://www.urbaneye.net/

References

American Civil Liberties Union (2000) 'Court Rejects Michigan's Attempt to End ACLU Challenge to Urine Testing of Welfare Recipients', 18 April, http://www.aclu.org/news/2000/n041800a.html

Bannister, J., Fyfe, N. and Kearns, A. (1998) 'Closed Circuit Television and the City', in C. Norris, J. Moran and G. Armstrong (eds) *Surveillance, Closed Circuit Television and Social Control*, Aldershot: Ashgate.

Bauman, Z. (1992) *Intimations of Postmodernity*, London: Routledge.

Bauman, Z. (1997) *Postmodernity and its Discontents*, Cambridge: Polity Press.

Boddy, T. (1992) 'Underground and Overhead: Building the Analogous City', in M. Sorkin (ed.) *Variations on a Theme Park*, New York: Hill and Wang.

Boyne, R. (2000) 'Post-Panopticism', *Economy and Society*, 29(2), May, 285–307.

Brunsdon, C., Johnson, C., Moseley, R. and Wheatley, H. (2001) 'Factual Entertainment on British Television', *European Journal of Cultural Studies*, 4(1), 29–62.

Chibnall, S. (1977) *Law and Order News: An Analysis of Crime Reporting in the British Press*, London: Tavistock.

Colonna, T.E. (1998) 'Protection of Privacy in Personal Genetic Information', *West Virginia Journal of Law and Technology*, 2(2).

Davis, M. (1990) *City of Quartz*, London: Vintage.

Elias, N. (1978) *The Civilizing Process: The History of Manners*, Oxford: Blackwell.

Feeley, M. and Simon, J. (1994) 'Actuarial Justice: The Emerging New Criminal Law', in D. Nelken (ed.), *The Futures of Criminology*, London: Sage.

Fyfe, N.R. (1995) 'Law and Order Policy and the Spaces of Citizenship in Contemporary Britain', *Political Geography*, 14(2), 177–89.

Garland, D. (1996) 'The Limits of the Sovereign State: Strategies of Crime Control in Contemporary Society', *The British Journal of Criminology*, 36(4), Autumn, 445–71.

Gilliom, J. (1994) *Surveillance, Privacy and the Law: Employee Drug Testing and the Politics of Social Control*, Michigan: University of Michigan Press.

Haggerty, K.D. and Ericson, R.V. (2000) 'The Surveillant Assemblage', *British Journal of Sociology*, 51(4), 605–22.

Mathiesen, T. (1997) 'The Viewer Society: Michel Foucault's "Panopticon" Revisited', *Theoretical Criminology*, 1(2), 215–34.

Marx, G. (1992) 'The Engineering of Social Control: The Search for the Silver Bullet', in J. Hagan and R. Peterson (eds) *Crime and Inequality*, Stanford: Stanford University Press.

McCahill, M. (2002) *The Surveillance Web: The rise of visual surveillance in an English City*, Cullompton: Willan.

McCahill, M. and Norris, C. (2002) 'Literature Review: Working Paper Number 2', at http://www.urbaneye.net/results/ue_wp2.pdf

Muncie, J. (2001) 'Surveillance', in E. McLaughlin and J. Muncie (eds) *The Sage Dictionary of Criminology*, London: Sage.

Nelkin, D. and Andrews, L. (1999) 'DNA Identification and Surveillance Creep', *Sociology of Health and Illness* 21(5), 689–706.

Newburn, T. and Hayman, S. (2002) *Policing, Surveillance and Social Control: CCTV and Police Monitoring of Suspects*, Cullompton: Willan.

Norris, C and Armstrong, G. (1999) *The Maximum Surveillance Society: The Rise of Closed Circuit Television*, Oxford: Berg.

O'Malley, P. (1992) 'Risk, Power and Crime Prevention', *Economy and Society*, 21(3), August, 252–75.

Pratt, J. (2000) 'Emotive and Ostentatious Punishment, *Punishment and Society*, 2, 417–39.

Pratt, J. (2002) 'Critical Criminology and the Punitive Society: Some New "Visions of Social Control" – Western Gulags and Vigilantes', in R. Hogg and K. Carrington (eds), *Critical Criminology: Issues, Debates, Challenges*, Cullompton: Willan.

Reiner, R. (2002) 'Media Made Criminality: The Representation of Crime in the Mass Media', in M. Maguire, R. Morgan and R. Reiner (eds) *The Oxford Handbook of Criminology*, 3rd edn, Oxford: Clarendon Press.

Sparks, R. (1992) *Television and the Drama of Crime: Moral Tales and the Place of Crime in Public Life*, Buckingham: Open University Press.

Surette, R. (1998) *Media, Crime and Criminal Justice: Images and Realities*, Belmont: Wadsworth.

Sykes, G. and Matza, D. (1957) 'Techniques of Neutralization', *American Sociological Review*, 22.

van Dijk, T. A. (1998) 'Opinions and Ideologies in the Press', in A. Bell and P. Garrett (eds) *Approaches to Media Discourse*, Oxford: Blackwell.

Wazir, B. (2002) 'Lost Angeles', *The Observer Magazine*, 7 July, 26–31.

Chapter 11

Completing the 'half-formed picture'? Media images of policing

Rob C. Mawby

In everyday life, the police mark moral boundaries, the limits of the permissible, the threats of the unknown and dangerous, and the location of good and evil. In the mass media, the police take on gigantic, even phantasmagoric proportions. (Manning, 1997: 328)

Did you see *Crimewatch UK* on the telly last night? God it was good. Sometimes when I'm watching I think – ooooh that looks so exciting I wish I was a copper and then I remember – I am one. (Police Constable Kevin Goody, 'Fly on the Wall', *The Thin Blue Line*)

Setting the Scene

The appointment of a former Director General of the British Broadcasting Corporation (BBC) as the Labour government's special adviser on crime in July 2000 provided an interesting take on the relationship between policing and the media. Pondering how Lord Birt might draw on previous experience when approaching his new role, the broadcaster and barrister, Clive Anderson, surmised:

> ... he will have gained useful insights into the problems of law enforcement by commissioning such TV programmes as *Dalziel and Pascoe, City Central* and *The Cops*. The human aspects of policing, he will have understood from a close study of Ben Elton's sitcom *The Thin Blue Line* ... his knowledge of police work will extend north of the border with *Taggart* and *Hamish Macbeth* ... and programmes

such as the *Midsomer Murders* and *Inspector Wexford* will have made him an expert on policing in different parts of rural England. (Anderson, 2000)

Although Anderson concluded that Birt's appointment was 'tough on crime, tough on the criminal justice system', the implication of a connection between television representations and the realities of the policies and practices of policing is far from flippant or novel. Hurd, for example, writing about police drama series, argued that they worked ideologically by completing 'the "half-formed picture" that the viewer has of often unfamiliar sections of society' (1979:121). In pursuing this line, Hurd was drawing on Hall, who wrote that the mass media provide:

a) the basis on which groups and classes construct an 'image' of the lives, meanings, practices and values of other groups and classes;

b) the images, representations and ideas around which the social totality, composed of all those separate and fragmented pieces can be coherently grasped as a *'whole'*. (Hall, 1977: 340–1)

More recently, Loader (1997: 2–3) has posited that, partly through fictional television representations, the police remain 'a principal means by which English society tells stories about itself'. He argues that policing can provide 'an interpretive lens through which people make sense of, and give order to, their world' (Loader, 1997: 3). Taking this as a starting point, in this chapter it is my aim to examine: why policing images communicated through the media, particularly television, matter; the range of television images of policing and how they have been interpreted as informing us about policing and society; and, finally, the ways in which the police actively seek to communicate and influence their media image. However, it is first helpful to consider media images before the era of 'cops on the box' and the power of television.

From Self-published Pamphlet to the Global 'Box'

Media representations of policing have always been a key aspect of the 'crime and media' debate and, as Reiner argues, policing in Britain has always been as much a matter of image as of substance (Reiner, 1994; 2000a, ch.5; 2000b). This is to afford both an instrumental and a symbolic value to media images of policing. Television became the dominant medium in the second half of the twentieth century, but the practices and policies of policing have long been a subject of media interest. Before the introduction of Robert Peel's new police in the 1820s, the creators of the Bow Street Runners, Henry and John Fielding, used pamphlets and their newspaper, *The Covent Garden Journal*, to spread news of their crime-fighting successes in the 1750s, 'keeping their names before the public and the government' (Rawlings, 1995: 140). Following the establishment and spread of the modern police after 1829, the imagery of policing developed, aided by the growth of the media. In the 1840s, Britain experienced the establishment of a popular Sunday press, the spread of periodicals, the development of minor theatres and the rise of music halls (Williams, 1961: 72–3). These media were vehicles for projecting contrasting images of policing. On the one hand, the police were cultivated as one of Britain's 'best in the world' institutions, building the image of the celebrated 'British Bobby' as a national symbol which developed into an 'an indulgent tradition' (Emsley, 1992).[1] On the other hand, the police were satirized and ridiculed in ballad literature, in the music halls and in the pages of *Punch*, which first appeared in 1841. While *Punch* initially targeted the police with 'ridicule and contempt' (Ascoli, 1979: 119), this later softened to 'joking and jibes' (Emsley, 1992: 120). This ambivalent, developing image of the police and popular sentiment towards the institution were captured fittingly by the Gilbert and Sullivan operetta, *The Pirates of Penzance,* first performed in 1880. It portrayed the police with some affection, but also with contempt: the police were characterized as 'decent, dutiful, well-meaning and in-corruptible – even if not overbright' (Cannadine, 1992: 27).

Thompson (1995) has argued persuasively that communications media play a central role in the development and understanding of modern societies and their institutions. In Britain, as media forms developed, the image of the British police officer was established as a cultural icon that has become a 'powerful condensing symbol' for the nation (Loader, 1997: 16). Loader argues that within 'prevailing English "structures of feeling" the police figure as central to the production and reproduction of order and security' (Loader, 1997: 3).[2] This symbolic dimension of the police image increased in significance as media forms developed during the twentieth century, particularly in relation to television. In the mid-1950s, this became part of the mass media in the sense of being available to a mass audience, and the growing influence of television over the second half of the twentieth century is difficult to overstate. Frith has recently taken stock and points out that 'it has trans-formed political communication and the process of democracy. It has changed the ways in which news is gathered and made public. It is a source of new forms of cultural identity. It dominates the household world and has reshaped domesticity' (Frith, 2000: 33). In short, he concludes that we now take for granted that our knowledge of the world is first mediated by television (Frith, 2000: 33). Other influential commentators agree that television has become dominant, that it 'sets the stage for all the processes that intend to be communicated to society at large' (Castells, 1996: 336) and represents 'the emergence of a single nation-wide information system to which everyone has constant access' (Garland, 2001: 85).

Why Media Images of Policing Matter

In the context of the increasing presence of television, the portrayal of policing soon became an influential part of the television viewing content, as I will trace below. But do media images of policing matter and, if so, why?

As part of the wider theoretical debate about 'crime and the media', concerns have regularly been expressed about media images of policing. Robert Reiner has argued that analyses of media representations of law and order and policing have tended to be either 'hegemonic' or 'subversive' (Reiner, 2000a: 139–47; 2000b: 55; 2002: 376–7, 406–8). Proponents of the former perspective point to the police as being in a position to provide access to information, to select and to filter information. This places them in a position of dominance in relation to media agencies, which become 'propagators of a dominant ideology' (Reiner, 2000a: 139). In contrast, proponents of the latter perspective perceive the media as a threat to morality and authority, and fear that media representations undermine respect for the police service. Such analyses, as Reiner rightly maintains, are oversimplistic for such a complex relationship. However, within this general debate, it is clear that media images of policing are important and worthy of study for a number of reasons, both prosaic and symbolic.

First, people know the police through television, which is a rich source of policing images. Research has suggested that up to two-thirds of people find out about the police through the media rather than through personal contact (Skogan, 1990: 18–19; 1994, 13–14). At a local level, in 2001 West Yorkshire Police found that although crime had fallen by 5 per cent, according to a survey 36 per cent of people believed crime was rising and 51 per cent claimed to have formed this opinion via television viewing (*Police Review*, 26 October 2001). Following on from this first point, policing is a popular television subject and policing programmes attract sizeable viewing figures, regularly featuring in charts of the most watched programmes. For example, in 1997 the funeral of Diana, Princess of Wales, was the most watched programme of the year, with 19.29 million viewers, but it was closely followed by police dramas *Heartbeat* and *A Touch of Frost* with 18.35 and 18.22 million viewers respectively. *Frost* and *Heartbeat* again made the top five watched programmes in 1999 and the month-on-month figures for 2000 onwards show the frequent presence of series such as *Frost, Taggart, Dalziel and Pascoe, Heartbeat* and *The Bill*.

Third, policing programmes can inform debates about the nature and future of policing, and can influence policy and procedure. For example, Reiner has shown how the debate concerning whether the role of the police should be essentially 'service' or 'force' based can be plotted dialectically through police drama series (Reiner, 1994; see also Leishman and Mason, 2003, chapter 6, for an update of this dialectical discussion). Equally, factual programmes such as Roger Graef's 1982 observational documentary, *Police*, can highlight unacceptable policing practices and add to the pressure to implement change and reform.

Finally, policing is an index of the 'state of the nation' and media images of policing have a symbolic value as a vehicle for commenting on contemporary society. As Sparks says, the 'analysis of law and order as a public issue must include not only debates about specific policies or measures but also a consideration of its values as a talisman, as a potent index of the integrity of society as a moral order' (Sparks, 1992: 29). Television programmes concerning policing or using policing series as a vehicle to present messages about society are an important aspect of this.

Therefore media images of policing are significant for a number of interlinking reasons. They are important for reasons of transparency, for demonstrating and challenging the accountability of a public sector institution. They are a source of information on policing and 'vital for the attainment of that minimum of "consent" which is essential for the preservation of police authority' (Reiner, 2000a: 139). They also fulfil a symbolic role, providing a commentary on policing and on society, and offering interpretations of the police in society.

Television Images of Policing

Television images of policing are conveyed through a range of dramatic programmes, including those based on detectives, uniformed officers and elite squads, and also factual programmes including 'docusoaps', investigative documentaries and 'crimescarers'. Numerous images of policing are also conveyed daily through the news media. There are also drama-documentaries and docu-dramas, which blur the distinction between fictional and factual programming. The police, therefore, are represented through a number of different types of programme, some of which they cooperate with and influence and others which are beyond their control.

Fictional images

Within the body of literature and research addressing policing and the media, the work of Robert Reiner (1994, 2000a, 2000b, 2002) is prominent. In *The Politics of the Police* his chapter on the media presentation of policing analyses both factual and fictional images. Taking the crime genre of fiction, Reiner distinguishes between criminal tales and law enforcement stories and classifies the latter into 12 ideal types of representation across film, literature and television, providing a framework in which changing and contrasting policing images can be placed (Reiner, 2000a: 149–60). In conjunction with Sonia Livingstone and Jessica Allen, Reiner recently conducted a systematic analysis of changing representations of crime and criminal justice, through a historical contents analysis of films and newspapers (1945–91) and television programmes (1955–91). This comprehensive research provides an authoritative account of the way the police have been portrayed (Allen *et al.*, 1998, Reiner, 2000b: 60–1; Reiner *et al.*, 2001: 185–6; Reiner *et al.*, this volume). Their research confirmed that the only medium that has always represented the police as central characters in fiction has been television (Reiner, 2000b: 60). In all, the research found an 'increasing prevalence of professional police heroes, especially after the late 1960s' (Allen *et al.*, 1998: 67). The representation of the police became less positive over the whole period, but remained mostly positive. The police are represented most positively during the years 1945–63; in 1964–79 the image is more negative; from which there is some recovery in the final period, 1980–91. However, this masks a complex picture in which increasingly negative representations of policing coexist with the utopian images conveyed by programmes like *Heartbeat*[3] (Allen *et al.*, 1998; Reiner, 2000b: 62). Significantly, Reiner concludes that underlying the shifts in representation is 'a demystification of authority and law, a change in the conceptualisation of policing and criminal justice from sacred to secular' (Reiner, 2000b: 62).

The research undertaken by Reiner and his colleagues has resonance with a contents analysis study undertaken in the United States.

Researchers examined 1,321 fictional programmes screened between 1955 and 2001 to analyse how American television had presented images of US public officials (Lichter *et al.*, 1999, 2002). The studies concluded that law enforcers[4] retained a predominantly positive image from television's earliest days through to the present. Although police officers dominated the law enforcers group in terms of their numbers, they were mid-table in terms of role models. Citing Detective Andy Sipowicz of *NYPD Blue* (an alcoholic racist) as a prime example, typically 1990s portrayals of police officers were of 'mixed characters who are well-intentioned but have personal flaws or pursue their goals in a sometimes reprehensible manner' (Lichter *et al.*, 1999: 84). Although law enforcers usually achieved their goals (in 55 per cent of cases), the researchers found a long-term trend towards moral ambiguity, a 'greater criticism of human failings and institutional inadequacies while still portraying individual law enforcers in a generally sympathetic light' (Lichter *et al.*, 1999: 96; 2002: 15). This increasing moral ambiguity and the lack of certainty in state institutions emphasized in both the British and US research, are aspects I will return to in relation to specific drama series.

Seminal drama series

Moving from general to specific dramatic fictionalized portrayals of the police, Cooke notes that the police series has been one of the most popular genres on television for more than five decades (Cooke, 2001: 19). This tradition was established and maintained principally through three seminal police series whose programme runs overlapped. The first, which set the benchmark, was *Dixon of Dock Green* (BBC, 1955–76) starring Jack Warner as PC (later Sergeant) George Dixon. The programme created a symbolic representation of the 'British Bobby' that remains a reference point today. Well-intentioned, solid and honest police officers were projected as the guardians of a cohesive, settled neighbourhood. Dixon's image and that of policing was projected as at one with the postwar consensus that existed at a time when policing was not perceived as a controversial national issue (Loader and Mulcahy, 2001: 43–4). Although Dixon was originally welcomed as a realistic portrayal of policing (story lines drew on actual events recorded in police files and newspapers), in its later years it was criticized as irrelevant and outdated (Sparks, 1993: 88, Cashmore, 1994: 156). Despite this, *Dixon* remains a point of reference against which the current police service continues to be compared (Emsley, 1996: 170; Mawby, 2002a: 15–16).[5]

Dixon was a child of its fast-disappearing time and was eclipsed by *Z Cars* (BBC, 1962–78), which presented a grittier and updated vehicu-larized image of policing. It was set in a new town in the north of

England, an urban environment in which the police role was seen to be more problematic within a context of declining social cohesion. This context was quite different to *Dixon*'s portrayal of the policing of a settled London working-class community. Instead there existed an underlying potential for conflict between the police and the public (Laing, 1991). *Z Cars* has escaped much of the criticism aimed at *Dixon* concerning loss of relevance, partly through its portrayal of police officers with human failings and its attempts at social realism. *Z Cars* also kept in step with changing times by promoting its characters and spinning them off into other series such as *Softly Softly* and *Task Force*, which also reflected a trend from local to regional crime series and towards the activities of elite squads (Clarke, 1992: 236; Sparks, 1992: 26; 1993: 88).

The third key series was *The Sweeney* (ITV, 1974–78), which heralded a hardening of media representations of policing. In this construction of policing, violence may justify ends and rules are bent, but within parameters and only to secure justice (Clarke, 1992: 243; see also Hurd, 1979; Donald, 1985). The central characters, Inspector Jack Regan and Sergeant George Carter, are at odds not only with the criminal elements of society but with the rule-bound bureaucracy that is perceived as holding back the efficient fighting of crime (Hurd, 1979: 131–32, Leishman 1995: 145–6). They are alienated in an unforgiving world that since the days of Dock Green has become less consensual. The construction of policing has changed; the decent optimism of Dixon ('the police are there to protect the public and that's what we do … I've been proud to have been part of that') is replaced by the cynicism of Regan ('Try and protect the public and all they do is call you "fascist" … it is all bloody wrong my son') (Donald, 1985: 121; Clarke, 1992: 237, 242). These central characters were symbolic of the spirit of their respective times – the late 1950s and less settled mid-1970s.

Policing series in the 1970s were increasingly situated in a society that was questioning of policing and more generally of the powers of the state and its institutions, threatening an 'exhaustion of "consent"' (Hall *et al.*, 1978: 218–19). Crime series such as *The Sweeney* became 'an arena where the ideological and coercive work of the police was foregrounded as never before' (Cooke, 2001: 22). The genre was subjected to Gramscian Marxist analysis, which concluded that police series did ideological work in contributing to and validating the 'rightness' of a hegemonic order (Hurd, 1979; Donald, 1985; Clarke, 1992; see Tulloch, 2000: 34–8 for a review of this debate). For example, *The Sweeney* articulated sentiments that were present in the politicized law-and-order debate of the 1970s (Donald, 1985: 122), and Clarke argued that police series had a role in shaping the consensus and constituted 'sites on which ideological struggle can take place and in which the cultural formation can be shaped' (Clarke, 1992: 252). It was not, according to Clarke, that police series were consciously partisan, but that they were 'contained within the mode of reality of the state' (Clarke, 1992: 252). As Sparks (1992: 29) has noted, the 'growing assumption of a crisis of law and order and the problem of the alleged power of mass communication, especially of television, intersect in television crime drama'.

The three highlighted series mapped the terrain and set the standards for representations of British policing. Although other series followed in the 1980s and 1990s which developed the genre, few captured the imagination in quite the same way. The 1980s saw the introduction of *The Bill* (ITV, 1984–), whose lineage can be traced from *Dixon* and *The Sweeney* (Mason, 1992). It has retained its relevance through a series of metamorphoses (Leishman and Mason, 2003). There were also many detective-based drama series including the ever-popular *Inspector Morse*, and others such as *Bergerac* and *Taggart*. During the 1990s this trend continued, producing, among others, *Spender, A Touch of Frost, Wycliffe* and the *Midsomer Murders*. While they were a welcome revival of the classic detective series, these series put entertainment rather than accuracy or issues to the fore. Morse's Oxford, with its alarmingly high murder rate, had 'no Blackbird Leys estate. Neither do Morse's 1980s show any sign of having included a Miners' Strike, a Broadwater Farm, nor any of the consequent queries about the roles and powers of the police' (Sparks, 1993: 100).

There were exceptions to the focus on entertainment rather than issues, notably *Prime Suspect* and *Between the Lines*. *Prime Suspect* (ITV, 1991–96), with Helen Mirren as the senior detective officer, Jane Tennison, was a significant development in the portrayal of women police officers (Eaton, 1995; Brunsdon, 2000: 204–8; Creeber, 2001; Leishman and Mason, 2003). It illustrated the difficulties that women face in the management ranks of the police service and in the particularly masculine world of the Criminal Investigation Department (CID). This built on *Juliet Bravo* (BBC, 1980–85), which followed the travails of a woman uniformed police inspector encountering the routine sexism of the occupational culture (Sparks, 1992: 132, Leishman, 1995: 147). While these series have been criticized for simply placing female characters in traditional male roles, they are a significant step forward from series that marginalized or exploited women, as in the 1970s' *Charlie's Angels*. *Merseybeat* (BBC, 2001–) has seen the further development of the portrayal of women officers, the second series featuring prominent female characters including two probationers, a newly promoted sergeant and the station commander. The latter character, the liberal Superintendent Susan Blake, regularly exposed the sexism of the organization, but is also portrayed as a victim when she is raped in the police station car park ('Desperately Seeking', screened 23 July 2002).

The issue at the heart of the first two series of *Between the Lines* (BBC, 1992–94) was not sexism but corruption. It featured the activities of the Metropolitan Police's anti-corruption squad, the Complaints Investigation Bureau (CIB). Earlier treatments of police corruption had been primarily about the 'bad apple'. *Between the Lines* reinforced the 'good cop' image at one level in that it acknowledged the existence of corruption and limited the damage by showing what was being done to detect dishonest officers. At the same time, however, as Leishman (1995: 148–9) reports, it 'dealt with the politics of policing in a quite new way', involving recurrent manipulation and 'flexible morality ... at all levels of the hierarchy, from the street cops, through the management cops, to their political overseers'. The likelihood of a 'bad barrel' underlies *Between the Lines* and, in a typical twist, in the last episode of the first series, high-level corruption is revealed – the head of CIB is corrupt (though as we later discover, found 'not guilty' in court). The series portrayed law enforcement at its most ambivalent, demonstrating CIB's 'complicity in undermining democratic sanctions' (Wayne, 1998: 38) and constantly raising the issue 'of whether effective policing can be achieved without a necessary blurring of boundaries between policing and criminality' (Brunsdon, 2000: 208). Instead of providing reassurance that the police were capable of tackling individual and institutional corruption, the series laid out the complexities of policing contemporary society, taking in not only corruption, but also addressing other key areas of 1990s policing – public-order policing, drugs, racism, sexual harassment and discrimination, rule-bending and the increasing involvement of the police in firearms incidents. The question left hanging is – *quis custodiet ipsos custodies*? ('Who will guard the guards themselves?' Juvenal, VI: 347–8).

This question was picked up by the outstanding police drama series of 1990s, *The Cops* (BBC 1998–). The creation of Tony Garnett, this more than any other contemporary policing series exemplifies what Reiner identifies as the demystification of authority and law, the moral ambiguity of policing Britain at the end of the twentieth century (see also Billingham, 2000, ch. 1). In *The Cops*, a powerful and disturbing picture of policing and contemporary Britain is painted, but the series is also deeply rooted in previous portrayals.

The series was the subject of controversial police and media interest in the run-up to the screening of the first episode on BBC2 on 19 October 1998. The pre-publicity hailed it as 'one of the most controversial programmes of the decade' ('Coke-snorting TV "Cops" infuriate real-life force', *Independent on Sunday*, 4 October 1998) as it trailed police officers snorting cocaine, committing crime and brutalizing members of the public. The Greater Manchester Police force and Lancashire Constabulary had cooperated with the film-makers, but registered dismay at the results. They worried that the series, though a drama, was filmed in documentary style, and would have a negative impact on their reputation.[6] However, the *Police Review*'s editorial took a more measured approach, suggesting that although police officers were portrayed as 'lecherous, liberty-taking liabilities' the programme should be recognized for the drama it was – 'it's only TV and it's not real' (*Police Review* leader, 16 October 1998). Despite this voice of reason, Greater Manchester Police and Lancashire Police refused to cooperate with the making of the second series.

As for the series itself, it proved gripping and unsettling drama. Focusing on the policing of the fictional northern urban town 'Stanton', it followed the activities of a group of uniformed officers. It showed policing as a remorseless and thankless labour in which officers are continually challenged and compromised, not only by the situations they are placed in and the people they deal with, but also by management, by colleagues and the circumstances of their personal lives and beliefs. Police officers were seen engaging in a wide range of deviant behaviour including moonlighting, neglecting duties, illegal drugs use, brutality, fitting-up suspected criminals, committing perjury and practising racial discrimination. It was this completion of the 'half-formed picture' that the police service felt threatened by and which the media attention focused upon. However, the series is as striking for its depiction of contemporary Britain as for the questioning of the legitimacy of its policing. What is notable is the bleakness of the 'half-formed picture'. Despite moments of dark humour, *The Cops* portrays a society of little hope and dysfunctional communities where social deprivation is the norm and in which the police, often despised, are helpless. As Tony Garnett has said, 'we go out into the community with the police, live there with them and use their unique perspective to witness just how our society is working – or not. We will see problems, but propose no solutions'.[7] In this respect, *The Cops* is an expression of social and economic deprivation, of unremitting urban desolation, which attuned to other commentators' concerns about the state of *fin de siècle* Britain (see, for example, Danziger, 1996; Davies, 1997; and, more sociologically, Taylor *et al.*, 1996).

The Cops creates a world in which policing is a 'minefield of ambiguity' and a context where 'violence is countered with violence, where no-one is ever clearly "right" or "wrong"' (MacMurraugh-Kavanagh, 2000: 44–5). While this vision of the state of the nation was perceived as controversial, *The Cops* was following in earlier footsteps in providing a vehicle for playing out the condition of society. This has been a consistent feature of police series – the original creators of *Z Cars* were concerned more with using policing as a way of showing how people live than producing another show about the police. To them, 'the cops were incidental – they were a means of finding out about people's lives' (Laing, 1991). In this sense *The Cops* is the latest expression, if the darkest, of an established form.

It is not only in this respect that *The Cops* is evolutionary rather than revolutionary.[8] While the series did show officers involved in deviant behaviour as part of their everyday lives, rather than as exceptional situations, like *Z Cars* and latterly *The Bill*, it portrayed officers as humans with all their failings and occasional heroic actions. *The Cops* follows the lineage of previous police series. As Clarke observes (1992: 243), there is a linking of 'police heroes across time'. Just as Mason (1992: 24–7) traces Sergeant Dixon through to Sergeant Cryer and Jack Regan through to Inspector Frank Burnside in the case of *The Bill*, familiar police types are also found in *The Cops*. In addition to the continuation of the Dixon/Cryer/senior sergeant figure in the form of the flawed but reliable Sergeant Giffen, there are other standard police types on display. Just like its comedy cousin *The Thin Blue Line*,[9] *The Cops* has a bureaucratic station manager (Fowler/Newland), a reckless detective (Grim/Wakefield before returning to uniform), ethnic minorities (Asian and black officers Habib and Gladstone/Shundara and Kennett) and a hapless innocent (Goody/Jellico). *The Cops* also has an old-fashioned loose cannon, PC Roy Brammell. Nevertheless, despite the links with past portrayals, in keeping with a state-of-the-nation series, *The Cops* asked complex questions about contemporary Britain and police legitimacy. If, as Brunsdon has argued (2000: 196), the police series is 'a privileged site for the staging the trauma of the break-up of the post-war settlement', then *The Cops* is surely the police drama series' finest hour.

Factual images

In *The Thin Blue Line* episode 'Fly on the Wall', Inspector Fowler (Rowan Atkinson) briefs his team in preparation for a visit from a BBC television unit, and passes on the following words of wisdom:

We'll show those communists from the BBC that despite the pernicious influence of their puerile police dramas, the British Bobby still believes in the very highest of standards … Now you be careful with these media people Goody, they're all smiles until they pounce … Deceitful and underhand the lot of them, well I know their game, those Trotsky-ite BBC swine will have to get up pretty early to catch me with my trousers down.

Fowler's attitude encapsulates a number of key features of the policing and media debate, including the police service's obsession with its image, police distrust of media organizations and their representatives, and the proliferation of police images in the media (Chibnall, 1977; Crandon, 1990; ITC, 1996; Mawby, 1999; Perlmutter, 2000; Reiner, 2000a, b). These issues have been brought sharply into focus through fictional parodies of factual policing programmes. In addition to *The Thin Blue Line*'s memorable tribute to the making of an observational documentary, the series *Operation Good Guys* (BBC, 1997–) was premised on the basis of a film crew shadowing a (fictional) elite, but incompetent, group of officers. This blurring of factual and fictional styles was a notable feature of the presentation of policing from the mid-1990s, but equally the proportion of factual programmes on British television increased between 1989 and 1999 (Dovey, 2001: 134) and policing was a frequent and favoured subject.

Factual television programmes about policing historically can be categorized as, on the one hand, information-based documentaries that were broadly supportive of the police, often made with their full support and cooperation; and, on the other hand, investigative critical programmes that questioned police powers and practices and/or competence and integrity. Considered in these terms factual programmes can provide a counterbalance to dramatized portrayals of policing that often present the police as crime fighters, emphasizing and legitimating the role of the police as solvers of crime (described memorably by Peter Manning (1971: 155) as the 'impossible mandate'). In contrast, factual programmes are an opportunity to show alternative representations of policing, varying from the expertise of elite squads to the mundanity of routine police work. Alternatively, investigative factual programmes are opportunities to take to task the shortcomings and failures of an accountable public-sector organization. In their different ways these programmes contribute to the 'half-formed' picture of the British police.

However, policing and policing programmes are not always so clear-cut. A radically different approach to making factual programmes about the police was taken by Roger Graef with his groundbreaking 'fly-on-the-wall' documentary, *Police* (BBC, 1982). This watched Thames Valley Police, warts and all, and 'challenged the official version of police perfectibility by showing their mortality on television' (Graef, 1989: 10). The programme with its observational technique was innovative at the time, was perceived as damaging to the reputation of the police, but was subsequently acclaimed for its contribution towards changing policing policy in respect of procedures for rape complaints (Jones *et al.*, 1994: 111). The observational technique was subsequently repeated and has since become commonplace – so much so that when Graef returned to Thames Valley Police almost 20 years on to film *Police 2001* (BBC, 2001), the programme's impact was minimal. In an essentially sympathetic update, Graef concluded that the police were overburdened by paper-work, faced spiralling expectations and spent most of their time on order-maintenance activities that were not measured by performance indicators – 'failure is built into the job description'.

During the 1980s, a form of factual programme gained in popularity that became known as the 'crimescarer'. This type is characterized by a focus on real, unsolved crimes that are dramatically reconstructed and viewers are asked to provide information that may assist with detection. In the UK, crimescarers began with *Police 5* (ITV, 1962–90), but the most famous exponent is *Crimewatch UK* (1984–) (Schlesinger and Tumber, 1994; Fairclough, 1995). While *Crimewatch UK* has achieved a measure of respectability, others, including *Crime Stalker, Michael Winner's True Crimes* and *Crime Monthly*, have been criticized concerning style and content and their role in generating anxiety about crime (Home Office, 1989; Hill, 2000a). The police service, after initial suspicion, has sup-ported *Crimewatch UK*. From a policing perspective, during times of concern about crime and the ability of the police to control it, *Crimewatch UK* unambiguously demonstrates the police and public working successfully in partnership and presents a positive image of the police investigating and solving real crimes.

Crimescarers have also been criticized for the level of complicity between the police and programme-makers. This criticism remained persistent throughout the 1990s as the numbers of factual programmes increased. During this period, and particularly from the mid-1990s, crimescarers were subsumed within the dominant trends of 'Reality TV'[10] and the 'docusoap'[11] (Hill, 2000a; Kilborn *et al.*, 2001; Leishman and Mason, 2003). Although not restricted to the policing arena, fast cars, blue lights and the drama of ordinary and extraordinary law enforce-ment and crime control are a common component of these forms of factual programming. Kilborn *et al.* (2001), focusing on docusoaps, link the rise of factual programming to pressures on commissioners and schedulers to compete for market share and to provide accessible television. This, critics argue, has contributed to a move away from public service and towards consumer-oriented broadcasting, producing superficial entertainment vehicles rather than cutting-edge investigative programmes. These forms of factual programming have drawn criticism for their 'tabloidization', for their blurring of information-provision and entertainment, and for a level of complicity that can produce programmes that are little more than public relations productions (Kilborn *et al.*, 2001; Hill, 2000a, b).

It is no doubt correct that these currently dominant forms of factual programming have produced examples of more anodyne and less challenging television, presenting images of a caring and competent, if sometimes under-resourced, police service with little hint of institutionalized racism or serious corruption (Hill, 2000a: 231–3). However, it is interesting to note that these mediated images were presented at a time when drama series such as *The Cops* were producing questioning images of policing. Similarly, programmes that blurred fact and fiction, including subjects such as the Hillsborough stadium disaster (*Hillsborough*) and the Stephen Lawrence case (*The Murder of Stephen Lawrence, The Colour of Justice*), challenged official discourses. Therefore, while critics may fear dumbing-down and a loss of a critical edge, there remain programmes that confront and hold accountable public-sector organizations. Although, on balance, favourable representations of policing emerge through the media (Allen *et al.*, 1998; Lichter *et al.*, 1999, 2002), as Reiner (2000a: 162), observes, in respect of fictional images, for every *Heartbeat* there is an *LA Confidential*. Equally, in respect of factual programming, for every *999* there is a *Mersey Blues*.[12]

News Media Images and Police Promotionalism

Images of policing also arise on a daily basis through the news media. A substantial body of research and literature exists on the police–news media relationship (Chibnall, 1977, 1979; Hall *et al.*, 1978; Ericson *et al.*, 1989, 1991; Schlesinger and Tumber, 1994; Ericson, 1995; Crandon and Dunne, 1997; Mawby, 1999, 2002a, b; Reiner, 2000a: 140–7, 2000b, 2002). The literature focuses on diverse aspects of the relationship, but a number of key themes emerge. These suggest that news media images of policing help to legitimate police work, although the media have had an important 'watch-dog' role, acting against state agencies such as the police when propriety or justice are in doubt, for example, in the cases of miscarriages of justice. Despite this largely favourable picture, the police remain suspicious of their treatment by the media, although several content analysis studies have repudiated the basis of such suspicions (Crandon, 1990; Chermack, 1994). Influential commentators have suggested that the relationship is driven by the police, who as gatekeepers to information are in a position of dominance in relation to media agencies (Hall *et al.*, 1978; Ericson *et al.*, 1989; Ericson, 1995). This, it has been argued, enables them to use 'proactive publicity' for damage control and to 'promote and protect the image of their organization as accountable' (Ericson, 1995: 147–9).

Since these arguments were put forward, however, the media context in which both parties operate has changed; it is now infinitely more complex and accordingly more difficult for an agency such as the police to control (Mawby, 1999). To provide one example, the development of lightweight technologies for film-making has created a situation in which the number of potential news-gatherers has increased exponentially. Amateurs with camcorders have captured police malpractice from West Yorkshire to Los Angeles (Manning, 1996)[13] and, as Mathiesen (1997) has argued, it is the synopticon principle ('the many watch the few') as much as the panopticon ('the few watch the many') that now fulfils Foucault's vision of surveillance and its role in controlling society (Foucault, 1977).

What is beyond doubt, however, is that since the late 1980s the police service has become engaged in activities to promote and project the police image as never before. The police service has shown interest in concepts and practices more often associated with the private sector and commercial organizations. These activities take in corporate identity management (Wolf Olins, 1988; Heward, 1994) and marketing (Mawby and Worthington, 2002), together with the development of increasingly sophisticated structures and processes for police–media relations (Mawby, 2002a). While the police have always had a concern with protecting their reputation and projecting appropriate images, in the 1990s this took on greater significance as a new policing context emerged generated by a combination of managerialist government policy and widespread concern with police performance and misconduct. At the same time there existed an apparently insatiable demand for policing services within a general climate of anxiety over levels and fear of crime. Such pressures compelled the police to take measures to communicate effectively – in order to prove efficiency, economy and effectiveness, to maintain support and consent, and to demonstrate transparency and accountability. Police–media relations became a core aspect of this communications process.

Research conducted in the early 1990s suggested that the police service was showing uneven, but increasing interest in managing its media relations (Schlesinger and Tumber, 1992). Since then there have been significant steps towards increased coordination and organization. This is evident at both a national level and at the level of local forces. The Association of Chief Police Officers (ACPO) established a Media Advisory Group (ACPO MAG) in 1993 to fulfil a coordinating role and to disseminate advice to forces on policy and practice. In 1998 the establishment of the Association of Police Public Relations Officers (APPRO) signalled a further step towards professionalization. Also operating at a national level, the three main uniformed staff associations (ACPO, the Police Superintendents' Association and the Police Federation) actively promote the police through the media. At the local level, forces have developed media strategies and their press offices are now routinely managed and staffed by civilian communications specialists. These 'image workers' are increasingly media professionals, recruited for their specific skills and far removed from earlier incumbents, generally police officers or civilian support staff (Mawby, 2002b).

Although press offices were originally established for the purpose of conducting reactive and proactive press relations, the trend is now towards a broader role. The traditional 'Press Bureau' has given way to 'Media Services' departments that coordinate communications activities force-wide, including marketing and sponsorship, to promote and manage the image of the force. Press officers work at strategic and tactical levels, communicating with external agencies and also providing support to operational colleagues – backstage by enabling them to communicate more effectively, and frontstage by acting as a buffer between the media and operational officers. These specialists, therefore, are actively involved in both developing overarching communications strategies and in day-to-day news management and public relations activities. In short, police–media relations are now professional – they are guided by strategy and policy, they have their own processes, and they are managed by specialist communicators or conducted by police officers who have been trained and advised by specialists.

Embedded within police force strategies and processes for media relations is the prominent use of the language of 'openness'. Police forces are espousing 'open' communications with the objective of providing transparency, allowing the media and the wider public to be informed about policing policy and practice. Hence there is an implied legitimation purpose through mediated accountability. However, there remain fears that police–media relations activities may be deployed for motives of organizational advantage and, at worst, systematic misrepresentation to mask malpractice and deflect responsibility. Such fears promoted one prominent journalist to comment that 'criminal justice agencies often barely seem to have considered an appropriate way to inter-act with the media in a modern, democratic state' (Rose, 2001: 8). While it is neither unexpected nor unwelcome that media representatives should question police motives and competences, it is clear that the police service will continue to develop its operations in this area as communication becomes *the* key concept for police forces to address in the first decade of the new millennium (Wright, 2000).

And Finally …

The police service is an exceptional public-sector institution. It is responsible for coercive legitimate force, it is an accountable public service that must balance care and control, force and service. It is responsible for heroic work, but also has a track record of cock-up and corruption. For such an institution, image is of crucial importance in an increasingly mediated society. In the development of television as the dominant broadcast medium, images of policing have been constantly present, transcending forms and formats, crossing dramatic, factual and news programming. These have contributed to completing different 'half-formed' pictures of both policing and the state of the nation, variously presenting images of the police as heroic, reliable and effective, yet also repressive, corrupt and incompetent. Contrasting and conflicting images coexist, reflecting the complexity of policing in the early twentyfirst century. As the forms and functions of public policing become more contentious, policing programmes, at their best, will continue to address policing and wider issues, providing information, stimulating debate and also entertaining. What is clear, however, is that completing the half-formed picture of both modern policing and contemporary society is no longer straightforward, if it ever was. The picture is now blurred, lacking certainty and constantly open to reinterpretation.

Notes

1. This term appeared in *The Times* (20 January 1950) review of the 1950 film *The Blue Lamp*. It stated that the central characters (one of them was PC George Dixon) were not 'policemen as they really are but policemen as an indulgent tradition has chosen to think they are' (cited in Emsley, 1992: 114). This indulgent tradition has subsequently been perpetuated in the

public imagination by television cops such as Inspector Morse (for example, see Sparks, 1993; Thomas, 1997; Davis, 2001).

2. The term 'structure of feeling' was coined by Raymond Williams, who argued that meanings and values held by particular societies are kept alive by social inheritance and by embodiment, and although each generation may 'train' its successor, each new generation will develop its own 'structure of feeling' (Williams, 1961: 64–5).

3. *Heartbeat* (ITV, 1992–) is an interesting example because although it has become an enduringly popular drama about 'golden age' policing, the original market research on the programme provoked negative responses to the idea of it being another police drama series (Nelson, 1997: 76–7).

4. The law enforcers included court officials (judges and lawyers) and 'peace officers' (federal agents, local police and local sheriffs).

5. In May 2002, when the president of the Association of Chief Police Officers (and chief constable of Kent) dismissed the relevance of *Dixon* at the annual ACPO conference, there was no shortage of defenders of the myth. The chief constable of Merseyside, for example, spoke of his force's neighbour-hood policing officers thus – 'I would say *Dixon of Dock Green* has been resurrected and has come back with teeth' ('Police chief hails the Blyton bobby effect', *The Times*, 16 May 2002).

6. Lancashire Constabulary took measures to assess the impact of the programme on members of their public, and focus group research suggested that the series had not significantly influenced the image of the local police.

7. Quoted on *The Cops* website (www.worldproductions.com/wp/content/shows/cops/ info/history.htm).

8. Even the pre-launch furore surrounding *The Cops* echoed the oft-recounted story of the chief constable of Lancashire becoming apoplectic watching the first episode of *Z Cars* and demanding the withdrawal of the programme (Laing, 1991: 125).

9. The BBC screened two series of Ben Elton's comedy in 1995–96. Although a traditional British situation comedy, it was also a knowing satire of police types – the rule-bound station inspector who began each episode with a *Dixon of Dock Green*-type homily, the naive police constable, and the over-dramatic detective inspector who mixed his metaphors as he fought to keep anarchy off the mean streets of Gasforth. These officers parodied such contemporary policing challenges as dealing with anti-road protesters, fighting the war against drugs, and hosting a visit by a fly-on-the-wall television crew.

10. 'Reality TV' takes in a variety of programme types that mix entertainment and information. The term arose in the 1990s as a description of magazine-format programmes based on crime and accidents. It is characterized by the use of CCTV footage, reconstructions and expert testimonies, and would include programmes such as *Crimewatch UK*, *Police Camera Action*, *Blues and Twos* and *999* (Dovey, 2001).

11. The term 'docusoap' was coined in the mid to late 1990s for factual programmes which followed every day events in the lives of ordinary people, focusing on particular professions (e.g. driving instructors, police officers, vets, traffic wardens) or locations (airports, vets surgeries, hospitals). They differ from conventional observational documentaries in that their concern is primarily with entertainment rather than social commentary (Bruzzi 2001).

12. The 1999 BBC2 documentary series *Mersey Blues* shadowed the work of Merseyside Police's detectives. The charismatic Detective Chief Inspector Elmore Davies was portrayed as an affable wisecracking 'coppers' cop', respected by his team, providing leadership and boosting flagging morale. The dénouement of an episode called 'A Fair Cop' was the unveiling of Davies as a corrupt officer who was charged with passing confidential information to a known criminal in exchange for £10,000. He received a custodial sentence of five years and one of his co-accused was Mike Ahearne, one of the stars of *Gladiators*. Elly Davies, a modern TV cop – complex, ambiguous and ultimately flawed.

13. In 1991 officers of the Los Angeles Police Department were captured on video beating Rodney King. In 2001, in Wakefield, a student with a camcorder filmed an apparently unprovoked attack by a police constable on a member of the public (*Manchester Evening News*, 24 July 2001). Both these amateur videos were subsequently screened on national television news.

References

Allen, J., Livingstone, S. and Reiner, R. (1998) 'True Lies: Changing Images of Crime in British Postwar Cinema', *European Journal of Communication*, 13(1), 53–75.

Anderson, C. (2000) 'There's a Criminal Mind at Work – it's Written in the TV Listings', *The Independent*, 16 July, 23.

Ascoli, D. (1979) *The Queen's Peace*, London: Hamish Hamilton.

Billingham, P. (2000) *Sensing the City through Television: Urban Identities in Fictional Drama*, Bristol: Intellect Books.

Brunsdon, C. (2000) 'The Structure of Anxiety: Recent British Television Crime Fiction', in E. Buscombe (ed.) *British Television: A Reader*, Oxford: Clarendon Press, 195–217.

Bruzzi, S. (2001) 'Docusoaps', in G. Creeber (ed.) *The Television Genre Book*, London: British Film Institute, 132–4.

Cannadine, D. (1992) 'Gilbert and Sullivan: The Making and Unmaking of a British "Tradition"', in R. Porter (ed.) *Myths of the English*, Cambridge: Polity Press, 12–32.

Cashmore, E. (1994) *...And There Was Television*, London: Routledge.

Castells, M. (1996) *The Information Age: Economy, Society and Culture, vol.1: The Rise of the Network Society*, Oxford: Blackwell.

Chermack, S.M. (1994) 'Body Count News: How Crime is Presented in the Media', *Justice Quarterly*, 11(4), 561–82.

Chibnall, S. (1977) *Law-and-Order News: An Analysis of Crime Reporting in the British Press*, London: Tavistock.

Chibnall, S. (1979) 'The Metropolitan Police and the News Media', in S. Holdaway (ed.) *The British Police*, London: Edward Arnold, 135–49.

Clarke, A. (1992) '"You're Nicked!" TV Police Series and the Fictional Representation of Law and Order', in D. Strinati and S. Wragg (eds) *Come on Down? Popular Media Culture in Post War Britain*, London: Routledge, 232–53.

Cooke, L. (2001) 'The Police Series', in G. Creeber (ed.) *The Television Genre Book*, London: British Film Institute, 19–23.

Crandon, G. (1990) 'The Media View of the Police', *Policing and Society*, 6, 573–81.

Crandon, G.L. and Dunne, S. (1997) 'Symbiosis or Vassalage? The Media and the Law Enforcers – the Case of Avon and Somerset Police', *Policing and Society*, 8, 77–91.

Creeber, G. (2001) 'Cigarettes and Alcohol: Investigating Gender, Genre and Gratification in *Prime Suspect*', *Television and New Media*, 2(2), 149–66.

Danziger, N. (1996) *Danziger's Britain: A Journey to the Edge*, London: Flamingo.

Davies, N. (1997) *Dark Heart: The Shocking Truth about Hidden Britain*, London: Vintage.

Davis, H. (2001) 'Inspector Morse and the Business of Crime', *Television and New Media*, 2(2), 133–48.

Donald, J. (1985) 'Anxious Moments: The Sweeney in 1975', in M. Alvarado and J. Stewart (eds) *Made For TV*, London: Euston Films, 117–35.

Dovey, J. (2001) 'Reality TV', in G. Creeber (ed.) *The Television Genre Book*, London: British Film Institute, 134–7.

Eaton, M. (1995) 'A Fair Cop? Viewing the Effects of the Canteen Culture in *Prime Suspect* and *Between the Lines*', in D. Kidd-Hewitt and R. Osborne (eds) *Crime and the Media: The Post-modern Spectacle*, London: Pluto Press, 164–84.

Emsley, C. (1992) 'The English Bobby: An Indulgent Tradition', in R. Porter (ed.) *Myths of the English*, Cambridge: Polity Press, 114–35.

Emsley, C. (1996) *The English Police: A Political and Social History*, 2nd edn, London: Longman.

Ericson, R.V. (1995) 'The News Media and Account Ability in Criminal Justice', in P.C. Stenning (ed.) *Accountability for Criminal Justice*, Toronto: University of Toronto Press, 135–61.

Ericson, R.V., Baranek, P.M. and Chan, J.B.L. (1989) *Negotiating Control – a Study of News Sources*, Toronto: University of Toronto Press.

Ericson, R.V., Baranek, P.M. and Chan, J.B.L. (1991) *Representing Order – Crime, Law and Justice in the News Media*, Toronto: University of Toronto Press.

Fairclough, N. (1995) *Media Discourse*, London: Edward Arnold.

Foucault, M. (1977) *Discipline and Punish: The Birth of the Prison*, London: Allen Lane.

Frith, S. (2000) 'The Black Box: the Value of Television and the Future of Television Research', *Screen*, 41(1), Spring, 33–50.

Garland, D. (2001) *The Culture of Control: Crime and Social Order in Contemporary Society*, Oxford: Oxford University Press.

Graef, R. (1989) *Talking Blues*, London: Fontana.

Hall, S. (1977) 'Culture, the Media and the "Ideological Effect"', in J. Curran, M. Gurevitch and J. Woollacott (eds) *Mass Communication and Society*, London: Edward Arnold, 315–48.

Hall, S., Critcher, C., Jefferson, T., Clarke, J. and Roberts, B. (1978) *Policing the Crisis: Mugging, the State, and Law and Order*, London: Macmillan.

Heward, T. (1994) 'Retailing the Police: Corporate Identity and the Met', in R. Keat, N. Whitely and N. Abercrombie (eds) *The Authority of the Consumer*, London: Routledge, 240–52.

Hill, A. (2000a) 'Crime and Crisis: British Reality TV in Action', in E. Buscombe (ed.) *British Television: A Reader*, Oxford: Clarendon Press, 218–34.

Hill, A. (2000b) 'Fearful and Safe: Audience Response to British Reality Programming', *Television & New Media*, 1(2), 193–213.

Home Office (1989) *Standing Conference on Crime Prevention Report of the Working Group on the Fear of Crime*, London: Home Office.

Hurd, G. (1979) 'The TV Presentation of the Police', in S. Holdaway (ed.) *The British Police*, London: Edward Arnold, 118–34.

Independent Television Commission (1996) *Annual Performance Review*, London: ITC.

Jones, T., Newburn, T. and Smith, D. (1994) *Democracy and Policing*, London: Policy Studies Institute.

Kilborn, R., Hibberd, M. and Boyle, R. (2001) 'The Rise of the Docusoap: the Case of Vets in Practice', *Screen*, 42(4), Winter, 382–95.

Laing, S. (1991) 'Banging in Some Reality: the Original Z Cars', in J. Corner (ed.) *Popular Television in Britain*, London: British Film Institute, 125–44.

Leishman, F. (1995) 'On Screen – Police on Television', *Policing*, 11(2), 143–52.

Leishman, F. and Mason, P. (2003) *Policing and the Media: Facts, Fictions and Factions*, Cullompton: Willan.

Lichter, S.R., Lichter, L.S. and Amundson, D. (1999) *Images of Government in TV Entertainment*, Washington: Partnership for Trust in Government, http://www.trustingov.org/research/govtv/TVStudy.PDF

Lichter, S.R., Lichter, L.S. and Amundson, D. (2002) *Images of Government in TV Entertainment 1998-2001*, Washington: Partnership for Trust in Government (http://www.trustingov.org/research/govtv/mediarpt.PDF)

Loader, I. (1997) 'Policing and the Social: Questions of Symbolic Power', *British Journal of Sociology*, 48(1), March, 1–18.

Loader, I. and Mulcahy, A. (2001) 'The Power of Legitimate Naming, Part I: Chief Constables as Social Commentators in Post-War England', *British Journal of Criminology*, 41(1), 41–55.

MacMurraugh-Kavanagh, M.K. (2000) 'What's All This Then?: The Ideology of Identity in *The Cops*', in B. Carson and M. Llewellyn-Jones (eds) *Frames and*

Fictions on Television: The Politics of Identity Within Drama, Exeter: Intellect Books, 40–9.

Manning, P.K. (1971) 'The Police: Mandate, Strategies and Appearances', in J.D. Douglas (ed.) *Crime and Justice in American Society*, Indianapolis: Bobbs-Merrill, 149–93.

Manning, P.K. (1996) 'Dramaturgy, Politics and the Axial Media Event', *The Sociological Quarterly*, 37(2), Spring, 101–18.

Manning, P.K. (1997) *Police Work: The Social Organization of Policing*, 2nd edn, Illinois: Waveland Press.

Mason, P. (1992) *Reading The Bill: An Analysis of the Thames Television Police Drama*, Bristol: Bristol and Bath Centre for Criminal Justice.

Mathiesen, T. (1997) 'The Viewer Society: Michel Foucault's "Panopticon" Revisited', *Theoretical Criminology*, 1(2), May, 215–34.

Mawby, R.C. (1999) 'Visibility, Transparency and Police Media Relations', *Policing and Society*, 9, 263–86.

Mawby, R.C. (2002a) *Policing Images: Policing, Communication and Legitimacy*, Cullompton: Willan.

Mawby, R.C. (2002b) 'Continuity and Change, Convergence and Divergence: the Policy and Practice of Police-Media Relations', *Criminal Justice*, 2(3), 303–24.

Mawby, R.C. and Worthington, J.S. (2002) 'Marketing the Police: from a Force to a Service', *Journal of Marketing Management*, 18(9–10), 857–76.

Nelson, R. (1997) *TV Drama in Transition: Forms, Values and Cultural Change*, London: Macmillan.

Perlmutter, D. (2000) *Policing the Media: Street Cops and Public Perceptions of Law Enforcement*, London: Sage.

Rawlings, P. (1995) 'The Idea of Policing: A History', *Policing and Society*, 5, 129–49.

Reiner, R. (1994) 'The Dialectics of Dixon', in M. Stephens and S. Becker (eds) *Police Force, Police Service*, London: Macmillan, 11–32.

Reiner, R. (2000a) *The Politics of the Police*, 3rd edn, Oxford: Oxford University Press.

Reiner, R. (2000b) 'Romantic Realism: Policing and the Media', in F. Leishman, B. Loveday and S.P. Savage (eds) *Core Issues in Policing*, 2nd edn, London: Longman, 52–66.

Reiner, R. (2002) 'Media Made Criminality: the Representation of Crime in the Mass Media', in M. Maguire, R. Morgan and R. Reiner (eds) *The Oxford Handbook of Criminology*, 3rd edn, Oxford: Clarendon Press, 376–416.

Reiner, R., Livingstone, S. and Allen, J. (2001) 'Casino Culture: Media and Crime in a Winner-Loser Society', in K. Stenson and R.R. Sullivan (eds) *Crime, Risk and Justice: The Politics of Crime Control in Liberal Democracies*, Cullompton: Willan, 175–93.

Rose, D. (2001) 'What's In It for Us?', *Criminal Justice Matters*, 43, Spring, 8–9.

Schlesinger, P. and Tumber, H. (1992) 'Crime and Criminal Justice in the Media', in D. Downes (ed.) *Unravelling Criminal Justice*, London: Macmillan, 184–203.

Schlesinger, P. and Tumber, H. (1994) *Reporting Crime*, Oxford: Clarendon Press.

Skogan, W. (1990) *The Police and the Public in England and Wales: A British Crime Survey Report*, Home Office Research Study 117, London: HMSO.

Skogan, W. (1994) *Contacts Between Police and Public: Findings from the 1992 British Crime Survey*, Home Office Research Study 134, London: HMSO.

Sparks, R. (1992) *Television and the Drama of Crime*, Milton Keynes: Open University Press.

Sparks, R. (1993) 'Inspector Morse: The Last Enemy', in G.W. Brandt (ed.) *British Television Drama in the 1980s*, Cambridge: Cambridge University Press, 86–102.

Taylor, I., Evans, K. and Fraser, P. (1996) *A Tale of Two Cities. Global Change, Local Feeling and Everyday Life in the North of England: A Study in Manchester and Sheffield*, Routledge: London.

Thomas, L. (1997) 'In Love with Inspector Morse: Feminist Subculture and Quality Television', in C. Brunsdon, J. D'Acci and L. Spigel (eds) *Feminist Television Criticism: A Reader*, Oxford: Clarendon Press, 184–204.

Thompson, J.B. (1995) *The Media and Modernity: A Social Theory of the Media*, Cambridge: Polity Press.

Tulloch, J. (2000) *Watching Television Audiences: Cultural Theories and Methods*, London: Arnold.

Wayne, M. (1998) 'Counter-Hegemonic Strategies in *Between the Lines*', in M. Wayne (ed.) *Dissident Voices: The Politics of Television and Cultural Change*, London: Pluto Press, 23–39.

Williams, R. (1961) *The Long Revolution*, Harmondsworth: Penguin.

Wolff Olins (1988) *A Force for Change: A Report on the Corporate Identity of the Metropolitan Police*, London: Wolff Olins Corporate Identity.

Wright, A. (2000) 'Managing the Future: an Academic's View', in F. Leishman, B. Loveday and S.P. Savage (eds) *Core Issues in Policing*, 2nd edn, London: Longman.

Chapter 12

Film lawyers: above and beyond the law

Steve Greenfield and Guy Osborn

Introduction

The courtroom has a distinguished history as the focal point for memorable film drama, and is a theme that is still used for contemporary productions. In a more general sense, the law itself has also been considered a suitable and useful vehicle for filmic portrayals. There are a number of reasons for this. Perhaps most overtly, the law offers to a writer or director a surface upon which a tapestry can be woven and applied far beyond a mere 'story about legal processes'. It can serve as a touchstone for many wider issues, often moral and ethical, and also provides a way in to an appreciation of other themes and considerations (see for example the review of the existing literature in Greenfield *et al.*, 2001: 1–29). This chapter is concerned with cinematic legal films, essentially American films, and excludes films made directly for television. There is a whole host of material that is concerned with legal issues that fall outside of our limited parameters. This would par-ticularly include specific television series and theatrical works. In a televisual sense, perhaps the most well known British lawyer is John Mortimer's creation, Horace Rumpole. The various series involving Rumpole enjoyed long runs on the BBC and transferred successfully to the television screens across the Atlantic.[1] More recently we have seen legal, moral and ethical themes played out through television legal dramas such as *Kavanagh QC* and *Judge John Deed*.[2] This chapter has an American focus, and whilst there have been films that have concentrated on the British courtroom, these are in a minority. Previous analyses of British tropes include work on *Let Him Have It* (1991) and *In the Name of the Father* (1993), here concerned particularly with the problems of 'faction'.[3]

There is no particular reason to include or exclude types of work: film and the law constitutes a broad project. However, once we venture outside of feature films, different sets of criteria may need to be applied as part of the analysis and even access to the material may become a problem:

> The distinction between television and cinema films can be justified on a number of grounds, one of which is firmly rooted in pragmatism. Cinematic films are categorised, reviewed and generally readily available whilst television movies have far less longevity. (Greenfield *et al.*, 2001: 2)

This is also tied in closely to the question of genre and how we recognize and read the material in front of us. This moves us into areas of film theory and questions about the role of the audience and methods of interpretation. While these theoretical perspectives would no doubt add much to the study of legal films, much of the contemporary work, in the first instance is concerned with charting its boundaries and features. However, it is clear that there are distinctions in the ways in which films are viewed in different surroundings, although some of the technical aspects have been blurred through the vast improvements in home cinema equipment and the introduction of digital recordings.

This chapter considers a number of films and as noted above, these are largely American although some deal with British events. With the focus on the courtroom and with limitations of space and sets, law perhaps provided a pragmatic choice of foci, with the added bonus that the subject matter allowed considerable latitude and the development of sub-plots. Within a number of broad approaches there are several sub-genres or categories, such as court martial films, and also a number of identifiable threads that commonly appear.

There are a number of approaches to the study of law and film. This is of course an offshoot of the debate over the exact nature and breadth of the subject matter. This debate is outlined by Machura and Robson (2001); their collection included a chronological review of selected writings in the area since 1986 when the first critical and measured attempts to begin to map the area were made by Anthony Chase (1986a, b). This brief chapter seeks to introduce and examine some of the key questions that relate to the broader subject area and then considers the portrayal of lawyers in film. It concentrates largely on the criminal law, which tends to dominate the law film, although there are some notable examples that are concerned largely with civil law matters, including divorce (*Kramer v Kramer*, 1979) and personal injury cases (*The Verdict*, 1982). The personal injury trope has developed recently with an added twist of environmental issues in *A Civil Action* (1999) and *Erin Brockovich* (2000). Further examples include the area of employment law, and more importantly perception and treatment of those with HIV, in *Philadelphia* (1993). A recent offering, *Legally Blonde* (2001), covers legal education and professional ethics from a comedic perspective, although the key case is criminal in nature. These recent films demonstrate that law can be used in a number of ways and is a flexible basis on which to launch a number of themes. Our approach is thus as follows: firstly, to briefly consider why law is utilized within film and how the question of genre may be answered; secondly, we consider some broader issues about the portrayal of lawyers within film and draw out some significant elements of their portrayal.

Why, and What is, Law and Film?

For our analysis, law films are much more than just courtroom drama, and this latter 'group' is a distinctive sub-category. To classify law films as merely courtroom drama would be to exclude a whole host of films that are intimately concerned with either the process of law, such as *Twelve Angry Men* (1957); the administration and organization of lawyers, such as *The Firm* (1993) or *Devil's Advocate* (1997); or even the consequences of law, in *In The Name of the Father* (1993) or *Cape Fear* (1961, 1991). To adopt such a narrow definition of law, to consider only what happens within the confines of the courtroom, ignores wider perspectives on the role that law and lawyers play in society. One alternative approach that has been adopted is to focus on the courtroom but to extend its definition to encompass films such as *Judge Dredd* (1995) and *Cape Fear* (1961, 1991) (Greenfield and Osborn 1999). Law is much more than a set of procedural rules and this extended sphere of influence is reflected in film. For example, *Inherit the Wind* (1960) plays out, with the backdrop of law, the debate between evolutionists and creationists. Thus in one sense it can be classified as a law film because of the paraphernalia of a legal hearing however. But the essential subject matter is not essentially the specific alleged breach of statute but a broader philosophical debate.

Part of the reason for the fascination with law and screen lawyers is the essential conflict that can be identified and explored. This often manifests itself as a battle between good and evil – the helpless consumer and large corporation as in *A Civil Action* (1999) or more likely the state and the wrongly accused as in *Suspect* (1987). Apart from the relationship between individuals, there may be a tension between the formal process of law (a process that we see can make mistakes and appears to privilege procedure over the truth) and what we might construe as justice (the right result being seen to be done).

Good examples of this tension are shown in all the films that contain miscarriages of justice, such as *Let Him Have It* (1991), *In the Name of the Father* (1993), *The Hurricane* (1999), *To Kill a Mockingbird* (1962); and those where a miscarriage of justice is set to occur but for some timely intervention, such as *Suspect* (1987) or *A Time to Kill* (1996). Films portraying miscarriages of justice offer an additional dimension, that of redemption either of the individual or the system, and most seem to offer hope with justice triumphing, albeit belatedly. *To Kill a Mockingbird* (1962) portrays eventual justice but not for the wronged individual; similarly *Let Him Have It* (1991) has a bleak message concerning the death penalty, although the merits of the case against Derek Bentley (who was hanged in England in 1953) are not covered in sufficient critical detail (Greenfield and Osborn, 1996). The death penalty and its apparent brutality also feature in *Dead Man Walking* (1995) and are covered critically, as is incarceration, in numerous prison movies such as *I Am a Fugitive from a Chain Gang* (1932), *The Shawshank Redemption* (1994) and *Murder in the First* (1995) (Mason, this volume). Often though, notably in the miscarriage cases, law and lawyers or even judges (*The Hurricane*, 1999) are portrayed in a positive light, righting the previous wrongs. Blame is laid squarely at the door of individuals who have corrupted the system, whether this is judges (*And Justice for All*, 1979; *Suspect*, 1987) or the police (*The Hurricane*, 1999). Lawyers seem to escape lightly: they are rarely shown as wrong or blameworthy despite their inadequacies (*Twelve Angry Men*, 1957; *Just Cause*, 1995).

All of these films have a tension at their core, and we have previously argued that these binary themes are at the heart of good drama. They also occur naturally within the law, hence the appeal of the law as a vehicle for dramaturgical portrayal (Greenfield and Osborn, 1995). Examples of such depictions are manifold, and include Henry Fonda's portrayal of Abraham Lincoln in John Ford's *Young Mr Lincoln* (1939), where the law and justice interface is neatly played out against a backdrop of inner truth and mythical development. Ford's fascination with the law is neatly unpacked by Bohnke (2001), but on a very basic level the binary themes in *Young Mr Lincoln* might be seen as a stark depiction of choices that are presented throughout the film. Will it be the law or the woman, the cherry or the apple pie or, perhaps more importantly, law or justice, and life or death? It is this continual set of choices, which are presented to the viewer, that provide the vehicle to explain the progress of a green lawyer towards the Presidency. Ultimately, perhaps the choices are predetermined as the decisions that are made have to be seen through a gauze of our own preconceptions of his pre-ordained greatness as the cinema rewrites the history of an American icon.

As we observed above, the focus is the criminal justice system and this is a popular topic, from cop movies and gangster films through the legal process to incarceration. The prime reason for this is fairly obvious – civil law is deemed to be less exciting than criminal law. The point is clearly made by Friedman that law is a key component of modern society that invades our lives at nearly every juncture. Yet in terms of representations, not all areas of law are subject to treatment in popular culture:

> *Popular* legal culture, then, is (potentially) an important witness and source. Law and legal institutions are absolutely ubiquitous in modern society, and thus, quite naturally, in the media … Popular culture is therefore involved with law; and some of the more obvious aspects are exceedingly prominent in popular culture. But of course not *all* of law. No songs have been composed about the Robinson-Patman Act, no movies produced about the capital gains tax … there are also no songs, movies or TV programs about medicare, dog licenses, zoning laws, or overtime parking … On the other hand, television would shrivel up and die without cops, detectives, crimes, judges, prisons, guns and trials. (Friedman, 1989: 1587–8)

So, essentially, many aspects of law might be inherently boring, and particularly mundane civil aspects may well be unattractive to the film-maker unless the area taps into a wider moral or emotive issue, as with *Erin Brokovich* or *A Civil Action*. The criminal law has an added advantage in that it allows the stakes to be raised; when the liberty of the accused is at risk this obviously increases the desire of the viewer to see justice be done. Within an American context and with the spectre of capital punishment looming large, this becomes even more pertinent given the finality and impossibility of later redress. Interestingly, the issue of later redress may be seen in films that deal with the appellate process such as *In the Name of the Father* (1993) or *Amistad* (1997). This may give rise to a curious contradiction in that the legal process may be praised in film for finally achieving the 'right' result notwithstanding the fact that the very same legal system was responsible for the original injustice. In terms of the capital cases, films such as *My Cousin Vinny* (1992), *Young Mr Lincoln* (1939) and *Suspect* (1987) illustrate the backdrop of the ultimate punishment that adds to the drama and the need to find a just result.

As we have argued above, there is some problem in defining what a law film is, or potentially might be. It is easy to classify law film as just courtroom drama, but this approach fails to offer any explanation for 'difficult' films such as *Twelve Angry Men*. There are ways to include *Twelve Angry Men* (essentially by including the jury room as part of the courtroom) but such an approach doesn't enable us to deal with a whole category of films such as prison movies (O'Sullivan, 2001; Mason, Chapter 14 of this volume). Law and film scholars have at times attempted to tackle the thorny question of genre (Greenfield *et al.*, 2001) and part of this process is how far as legal theorists we wish to embrace the terminology of film studies, which of course, like the law, has its own modes of discourse:

> Genre, star and auteur are, like narrative and realism, important discourse systems working within and on behalf of the larger discourse system we call 'film studies' or 'cinematics'. A discourse is a mode of speech which has evolved to express the shared human activities of a community of people. So, for example, there is the distinctive discourse of the medical and legal professions, and there is the discourse of different academic disciplines. Film studies has, like other academic disciplines, developed its own language – its own discourse system – to make possible the identification and 'mapping' of that area of human activity and experience with which it is concerned. (Phillips, 1996: 164)

Even outside of a concordance with the view that all disciplines have their own tools via which they can be mapped (to use Phillips' phrase), it is certainly arguable that if we just concern ourselves with genre and its notion of compartmentalization, as lawyers we are well used to classification in any event. For example, the common law case method is based upon assumptions of groupings of material both on a macro level (the law of tort) and on a minor level (occupiers' liability at sports grounds within the wider area of tort), and taking this analogy further, some judges might even be seen as auteurs (Greenfield *et al.*, 2001: 15).

Starting from an assumption that genre (by which we mean a method to allow us to classify or group material into a more ordered framework) might provide a more legitimate framework for future inquiry and development within 'law and film studies', it becomes apparent that we need to decide what the genre is, before deciding what goes in to this category once selected. The Tarlton Law Library, with its highly impressive collection of law and popular culture artefacts, has its own filmography and argues that the only requirement for inclusion is based on an approach within which 'the intent of the collection is to depict the broad scope of the image of the lawyer in American and British Commonwealth popular culture'.[4] This is certainly a far more inclusive approach than merely classifying films within the genre of 'courtroom drama'; but does such an approach help us? Interestingly, the Tarlton Library also points out, when describing its collection, that while many of the films have little to do with the practice of law, it can be argued that the same applies to many courtroom dramas. This is the point alluded to earlier that the legal element may be a red herring in some ways, with a film actually being about something different. There are in fact academic arguments as to whether such a classification or typology of films serves any real purpose, especially when many films today might be seen as 'hyphenates' that sit astride traditional categorizations, and that boundaries are fluid:

> Lawrence Alloway (1971) on the other hand, writing in the context of late 1960s developments in genre theory, resists the temptation to establish 'classic' timeless dimensions in popular forms ... He insists on the transitional and ephemeral character of any particular period of genre production. Rather than attempting definitive accounts of particular genres or genre films he talks about 'cycles, runs or sets', so drawing attention to the shifts and differences which constitute 'internal successive modifications of forms'. (Cook and Bernink, 1999: 138)

So, while accepting that a framework is useful, we would baulk at imposing a restrictive one, both for reasons of choosing what such a narrow definition would allow us to do and for pragmatic reasons that a classification, or genre, is only useful in so far as there is a point to having such a classification. That said, to aid exposition we would adopt a definition along the lines of our suggestion in Greenfield *et al.* (2001: 24) of the category of *law film*: 'In order to qualify as a law film the following characteristic(s) must be present in some form: the geography of law, the language and dress of law, legal personnel and the authority of law'. On this basis films such as *Cape Fear* and *Judge Dredd* (1995) are fairly easily brought within the terms of our inquiry, whereas it might be more difficult to classify them as courtroom dramas without some creative thought; we have previously argued, for example, that the boat in *Cape Fear* is effectively a courtroom and the sidewalk is the courtroom for *Judge Dredd*, both stripped of their ceremonial trimmings.

To take a more recent example, does the film *Minority Report* (2001), by virtue of the fact that it concerns the criminal justice system of the future, become a law film? Within the film there is an absence of lawyers in terms of how we traditionally think of them, and there are no courtrooms. The film is ostensibly about a method of predicting murders via the 'Pre-Crime Department' and then stopping crimes before they are committed. This certainly raises some interesting legal points, not least about punishment for inchoate offences as no crime is actually committed (Joseph, 2001), but would it fall within the compass of a law film? Why not an old-fashioned Hitchcockian manhunt or a detective story? Why not a sci-fi thriller? On our analysis above, *Minority Report* would still classify as a law film, and therefore come within the ambit of our inquiry as the authority of law is explicit within the film. Although it may not appear as overtly legal as a 'traditional courtroom drama', its plot certainly is and it has a resonance with our own legal system in terms of corruption within the administration of justice, and there are in fact parallels with the objectives of pre-crime and some preventative governmental policy and legislative measures. For example, Paul Joseph (2001) offers the following US parallel:

> There is a growing belief that some violent sex offenders suffer from some sort of personality disorder or mental condition and that this produces a high probability that they will repeat their crimes. In response to this, some states have passed violent sexual predator laws … under these laws, the person in question upon appropriate legal findings, can be civilly committed for an unlimited term in a secure treatment facility until such time, if ever, that the person is no longer a danger to others.

While this example involves a different area, it is still clearly comparable to a degree with the 'pre-crime' punishment of *Minority Report*. Law films, however we define them, are concerned with the behaviour and activities of legal personnel, whether lawyers, judges or other figures. A key issue is to see whether there are any common themes or characteristics that can be drawn out of the films that we have identified. This piece is too brief to examine figures beyond that of lawyers so the pertinent question here is: 'what makes the screen lawyer'?

Above, Beyond and Before the Law

One key thread in many of the law films, especially those that have the element of a wrongly accused defendant, is the lawyer who triumphs against adversity. The lawyer must, against incontrovertible odds, act to defend his (generally the lawyer is a male figure, though there are some prominent examples of female lawyers – such as Cher in *Suspect* (1987) and Reese Witherspoon in *Legally Blonde* (2001)) client and deliver justice. This is often seen in tandem with the lawyer acting outside their traditional capacity or going beyond what a lawyer is procedurally permitted to do. This ties in to the binary theme of law and justice we alluded to earlier – that sometimes the lawyer might feel that he has to go beyond the law to achieve a higher notion of (subjective) justice. There are three distinct strands that we have identified here: physical defence of the client, acting as an investigator and ignoring professional codes of ethical conduct. The first example is, as to be expected, somewhat rarer though it features prominently in both *Young Mr Lincoln* and *To Kill a Mockingbird*. Both Lincoln and Finch physically prevent a lynch mob from delivering instant justice to their clients but they have a somewhat different approach. Lincoln uses 'kidology' and his own inexperience although he does offer to fight one of the ringleaders:

> **Lincoln**: All joking aside lets look at this matter from my side. Why you all know I'm just a fresh lawyer trying to get ahead but some of you boys act like you want to do me out of my first clients.

> *(laughter from the crowd)*

> I'm not saying that you fellas are not right maybe these boys do deserve to hang. But with me handling their case don't look like you'll have much to worry about on that score.

> *(more laughter from the crowd)*

> **Lincoln**: All I'm asking is to have it done with some legal pomp and show.

> *(crowd mutters)*

> **Man with rope**: We've gone to a heap of trouble not to have at least one hanging.

Lincoln: Sure you have Mac and if these boys had more than one life I'd say go ahead, maybe a little hanging might'ent do 'em any harm, but the sort of hanging you boys would give 'em would be so … so … permanent.

Lincoln has effectively disarmed the crowd with his humour mixed with the threat of violence. He then engages in a more philosophical debate about the role and function of law more generally which moves the debate onto a more serious plane:

Lincoln: Trouble is when men start taking the law into their own hands they's just as apt in all the confusion and fun to hang somebody who's not a murderer as somebody who is. And the next thing you know they're hanging one another just for fun. Until it gets to a place when a man can't pass a tree or look at a rope without feeling uneasy. We seem to lose our heads in times like this. We do things together that we might be ashamed to do by ourselves.

The crowd, overwhelmed by Lincoln's sheer personality, meekly depart, leaving the lawyer free to defend his clients in court. This scene is repeated in *To Kill a Mockingbird* with the defence lawyer again having to repel the threat of a lynching, although he is helped, in no small measure, by his young daughter who identifies one of the protagonists. This type of approach is clearly limited to particular circumstances generally related to period and/or geography, but there are more examples of lawyers taking physical steps as part of the investigation essentially because of flaws in the investigative process. This might involve the lawyer acting as detective to track down the 'smoking gun' evidence that has been overlooked by the other parties, or even becoming a vigilante, in a flagrant breach of legal ethical codes of conduct. This often, but not always, boils down to the lawyer acting as a superhero.

There are myriad instances of this. For example, *In the Name of the Father* (1993) shows the lawyer for the Guildford Four seemingly single-handedly overturning the case for the Crown. Of course, this coup is further complicated by the fact that it is based upon real-life events, and that the superhero antics may be criticized on the basis that they do not reflect actuality. The problem of 'faction' approaches has been covered in depth elsewhere (Greenfield and Osborn, 1996) and does illustrate the difficulties that are created by basing films on true stories if we hope to find 'the truth' from these depictions.

In other films this superhero status is even more marked. As we note above, in *Young Mr Lincoln*, Abraham Lincoln is portrayed as a rookie lawyer who has never taken on a murder trial before, who is asked to defend two boys up against the seemingly incontrovertible evidence of the murder of Scrub White, with their mother as one of the key witnesses who is likely to condemn them both for fear of having to choose between them (the binary theme again). Notwithstanding his junior status, Lincoln locates the smoking-gun evidence (the literal rabbit out of the hat), in the form of a farmer's almanac. Crucially he is prepared to go beyond the law to achieve the right result – to privilege result over process. The comedy *My Cousin Vinny* (1995) parodies this approach well with the barely qualified lawyer having to conceal his background in order to defend his cousin on a murder charge. Similarly in *Suspect*, Cher carries out an active investigation into the crime to unmask the real perpetrator and prove her client's innocence. She is prepared to collude with a juror in order to achieve what she sees as justice for her client. In all these cases the possibility/probability is of the death penalty being the result and the odds are stacked against the lawyer. In these films we see melodramatic use made of courtroom antics as if to emphasize the fact that it is justice rather than law that needs to be seen to be done. There are no qualms about making the process look foolish and so, on one level, demeaning the process of law.

Similarly, Atticus Finch is perceived by many as a fine example of what they would like to become as a lawyer. Both the Harper Lee novel and the film *To Kill a Mockingbird* are often cited as classic pleas for tolerance with actor Gregory Peck held up as an ethical role model. However, as has been noted elsewhere (Greenfield, 2001), this picture is a little misleading, as is further noted by Simon:

> At the climax of Harper Lee's novel, the hermit Boo Radley emerges from seclusion and kills the villainous Bob Ewell. He does so in defense of Finch's children whom Ewell was trying to kill. Then in the novel's final pages, a fascinating development, invariably ignored by its lawyer admirers, occurs. Finch and Heck Tate, the sheriff, agree to lie to the town by saying that Ewell died accidentally by falling on his knife … in other words the novel concludes with Atticus Finch engaging in what today could only be called obstruction of justice. (Simon, 2000: 2)

Simon argues that what Tate is exhibiting here is 'moral pluck', a notion that combines elements of transgression and resourcefulness and has as its aim the vindication of justice (Simon, 2000: 3). This notion of moral pluck is certainly demonstrated in a number of legal films, perhaps most notably in *Cape Fear*. Interestingly, Gregory Peck, Academy Award winner for his role in *To Kill a Mockingbird*, is one of the common actor factors in the two versions of *Cape Fear*, although as Thain (2001) notes there are a series of critical differences between the two versions. Moral pluck arises when Max Cady's lawyer Sam Bowden (Nick Nolte as lawyer to Robert De Niro in the 1991 film) is shown to have withheld evidence on the basis that had he not done so, Cady would have received a far more lenient sentence notwithstanding the horrific injuries he inflicted upon the victim. The text from this is reproduced in Greenfield (2001: 38), and the principal issue was the duty that a lawyer has to represent his client – Bowden, by failing to disclose this evidence, was not acting in his client's best interests and therefore was in breach of the American Bar Association Rules with respect to professional conduct. Could it be permissible for Bowden to make such a (subjective) judgement given that he was striving for what he thought was justice?

Similar considerations run through films such as *The Verdict* (1982), although here the unethical act is one that furthers the lawyer's redemption, (and ultimately the clients). In short, everyone's happy except the judge and the defendants, although the lawyer (played by James Mason) for the hospital at one point, symbolically removes his hand from the doctor's as if to indicate his disapproval for his actions. After all, he's only doing his job even if at times this included planting a spy in Frank Galvin's office and apparently leaning on his expert witness. This law/justice interface is underpinned by a philosophical consideration of whether a 'bad' act can be outweighed by a wider moral objective. It is of course questionable whether the legal figures in *The Verdict* and *Cape Fear* are indeed heroic given the numerous flaws that they exhibit. However, we would argue that both can be read on a superhero level, and even De Niro's figure might be seen as in some ways heroic – the convict who betters himself through books and goes in search of justice (albeit vigilante based) as that has been denied to him.

Sometimes, the superhero idea may work on a different level, and might still illustrate some of the vexed ethical and procedural questions that are often at the heart of legal films. In terms of perceptions of law and lawyers, *Legally Blonde* provides a positive vehicle to tackle some of these issues. The initial premise of the film is that of using the law, or more specifically the acquisition by Elle (Reese Witherspoon) of a law degree from a top law school (Harvard) in order to win back the affections of her boyfriend, who feels that his association with a 'Marilyn' rather than a 'Jackie' will inhibit his ability to become a senator by the time he is 30. The film certainly begins as a satire on the law school admission process and does try to illustrate that image can be deceptive

(Elle achieves a phenomenally high score in her Law School Admission Test, notwithstanding her somewhat gaudy admission 'video'). In fact, the whole issue of portrayal of the law school and the environment of legal education is satirized within the film and has been subject to critical comment (Asimow, 2001; Joseph, 2001b).

The real interest for our purposes comes later in the film when, Elle having been sexually harassed by one of her law school professors during an internship with his firm, ends up defending a client on a murder charge. Asimow (2001) argues that the rules, that the film cites to allow this, do not in fact permit such a move: the rule (Massachusetts Rule of Court 3.03) only allows senior law students, who have undertaken some specific training, to represent either the state or an indigent client in limited circumstances. However, Elle does get the killer to confess in the courtroom in a (slight) variation on the well-worn theme (*A Few Good Men*, 1992; *Young Mr Lincoln*, for example). Denvir (2001) makes a very interesting point about the respective differences of approaches between Elle and her law-school professor, that intuition and facts rather than procedure are all:

> Elle and Callahan exhibit diametrically opposed attitudes to law and life. Elle sees the practice of law as a cooperative enterprise between lawyer and client, based on mutual respect, trust, and loyalty. Lawyers must be smart, but it's an intuitive intelligence which counts most. Callahan, on the other hand, sees law as a solo enterprise, fuelled by competition, logic, and ruthless pursuit of success. As he puts it, 'You have to know what you want and what to do to get it'.

Again we see the binary theme writ large. Elle may, in fact, be an example of a true superhero(ine); she does not fall into the 'trap' of Lincoln or Finch because she operates both within the law and within her own and her profession's ethical codes in order to achieve the 'right result'. Here, we have the superhero(ine) who fulfils the function of both ethical probity and courtroom brilliance. Further to this, the transformation from blonde bimbo to top of the class at Harvard Law School illustrates a (perhaps unrealistic) truly democratic educative process – a change as surprising in its own way as the redemption of Frank Galvin in *The Verdict*.

Conclusion

The brief orientation above has attempted to illustrate particular issues with respect to the filmic depiction of the law. We have outlined the rationale as to why the law is chosen as a site for film, drawing upon both the dramaturgical aspects of the law and legal process and the subtext of the law being a useful cloak under which many other themes can be played out. Furthermore, we have outlined some of the key issues of definition, and in particular, flagged the thorny issue of the application of genre theory and the need, or otherwise, of classification to further useful research. Lastly, we cover one particular theme that runs through many law films, especially in the criminal sphere, to illustrate one of the key tensions at the heart of law films and the portrayals of lawyers in film – the ethical dilemma or the tension between law and justice that is played out as a battle between right and wrong or the quest for justice.

Lawyers are at the centre of law films and it is interesting that judges and juries are rarely given major roles, with notable exceptions such as *Twelve Angry Men*. We have argued above that lawyers are given great versatility, they are not confined to the courtroom, and Lincoln is a fine example of a lawyer delivering justice to all and sundry beyond the courtroom. There is no doubt that the lawyer is the crucial figure at the expense of others and therefore it becomes important to identify the characteristics of the portrayal. In one sense, when it comes to race and gender, what the lawyer isn't may be important (Greenfield *et al.*, 2001). Perhaps the overwhelming question is whether or not our justice figure gets a good review. We do see lawyers with weaknesses: Galvin's alcoholism (*The Verdict*), Bowden's adultery (*Cape Fear*), Riley's loneliness (*Suspect*), McDeere's greed (*The Firm*), Lomax's arrogance (*Devil's Advocate*), Miller's homophobia (*Philadelphia*), but what comes shining through is redemption, on a personal level tied into the delivery of justice for the client. Galvin wins his case and is seen at the end of the film rejecting the advances of Charlotte Rampling and drinking coffee, basking in the against-all-odds victory. Bowden reclaims his family from the clutches of Cady and justice is delivered through Cady's death. Riley exposes judicial corruption, has her client acquitted and enjoys a romantic liaison that she was seen pining for. McDeere rediscovers his priorities and refuses to participate in the activities of his employers despite the rewards on offer. Lomax gives his life to prevent the devil achieving greater power (through law!) and Miller conquers his bigotry while achieving justice for Beckett.

In all of these examples we see lawyers coming good, even those who we might not much like or approve of at the beginning. Even those who are seriously flawed (Bowden and Galvin) act for the 'right' reasons to set right injustice. No easy route is followed and to deliver justice they must tread a difficult path. The reward? Justice (but whose?) and personal redemption. In this sense lawyers do benefit from being generally portrayed in a benevolent fashion. They rarely are shown as 'dishonest' or occupy the role of the 'baddie' except in opposition to the superhero. Where our central figure is concerned, our lawyer is often a complicated character that is difficult to categorize as good/bad but rather we can see how they deliver a positive end result (justice), which then reflects the lawyer (the deliverer of justice) in a good light.

Notes

1. The first Rumpole story, *Rumpole of the Bailey*, was commissioned from John Mortimer by the BBC as part of the Play for Today television series and published under the title *Rumpole and the Confession of Guilt*. It was broadcast in 1975 and the Rumpole series ran for seven series between 1979 and 1992.
2. *Kavanagh QC* ran between 1995 and 1999, for some 28 episodes, starring John Thaw. *Judge John Deed* features Martin Shaw as something of a contemporary maverick judge. It started in January 2001 with a pilot episode followed by a first series in November 2001 and a second series in 2002. A third series is scheduled to be filmed in 2003.
3. See for example Greenfield and Osborn (1996). There is of course some debate about what makes a film British or American and here we are considering not the place of manufacture but rather the geographical setting. We are also currently engaged in a project examining an older British Film, *Eight O'Clock Walk* (1953).
4. See www.law.utexas.edu/lpop/lpop.htm

References

Asimow, M. (2001) 'Legally Blonde Shines in the Classroom, Falls Flat in the Courtroom', *Picturing Justice*, at http://www.usfca.edu/pj/blonde_asimow.htm.

Bohnke, M. (2001) 'Myth and Law in the Films of John Ford', *Journal of Law and Society*, 47–63.

Chase, A. (1986a) 'Towards a Legal Theory of Popular Culture', *Wisconsin Law Review*, 527–69.

Chase, A. (1986b) 'Lawyers and Popular Culture: A Review of Mass Media Portrayals of American Attorneys', *American Bar Foundation Research Journal*, 297.

Cook, P. and Bernink, M. (eds) (1999) *The Cinema Book*, 2nd edn, London: British Film Institute.

Denvir, J. (2001) 'First Thing, Let's Kill All the Law Professors!', *Picturing Justice*, at http://www.usfca.edu/pj/blonde_denvir.htm

Friedman, L. (1989) 'Law, Lawyers and Popular Culture', *The Yale Law Journal*, 98, 1579–606.

Greenfield, S. (2001) 'Hero or Villain? Cinematic Lawyers and the Delivery of Justice', *Journal of Law and Society*, 25.

Greenfield, S. and Osborn, G. (1995) 'Where Cultures Collide: the Characterisation of Law and Lawyers in Film', *International Journal of the Sociology of Law*, 23(2), 107–30.

Greenfield, S. and Osborn, G. (1996) *Pulped Fiction?* Cinematic Parables of (In) Justice University of San Francisco Law Review Vol 30 No 4 1181.

Greenfield, S., Osborn, G. and Robson, P. (2001) *Film and the Law*, London: Cavendish.

Joseph, P. (2001a) 'Minority Report: is the Future Now?' *Picturing Justice*, at http://www.usfca.edu/pj/minorityreport_joseph.htm

Joseph, P. (2001b) *Legally Blonde*: It's a crime. Picturing Justice at http://www.usfca.edu/pj/blonde.htm

Machura, S. and Robson, P. (2001) 'Law and Film', *Journal of Law and Society*, Special Issue.

O'Sullivan, S. (2001) 'Representations of Prison in Nineties Hollywood Cinema: From *Con Air* to *The Shawshank Redemption*', *Howard Journal of Criminal Justice*, 40(4), 317–34.

Phillips, P. (1996) 'Genre, Star and Auteur; an Approach to Hollywood Cinema', in J. Nelmes (ed.) *An Introduction to Film Studies*, London: Routledge.

Simon, W. (2000) 'Moral Pluck: Legal Ethics in Popular Culture', *Stanford Public Law and Legal Theory Working Paper*, Series No.17.

Tarlton Law Library (2000) *Law in Popular Culture – Feature Films*, Austin, Tex.: Tarlton Law School.

Thain, G. (2001) 'Cape Fear – Two Versions and Two Visions Separated by Thirty Years', *Journal of Law and Society*, 40.

Chapter 13

British justice: not suitable for public viewing?

Daniel Stepniak

Introduction

Whether television cameras ought to be permitted to record proceedings in British courtrooms has been hotly debated for decades. Arguments for and against have been refined and widely publicized. Periodic suggestions that British courts ought to undertake an experiment with such coverage have only served to reinforce the notion that it is possible to establish conclusively, once and for all, whether the perceived dangers of courtroom televising can be avoided, and whether the purported benefits can be established.

The debate's almost morbid preoccupation with titillating, high-profile, televized American trials of OJ Simpson, Louise Woodward, the Menendez Brothers, Lorena Bobitt and others, has served to reinforce two widely held views regarding this issue: first, that it is a conflict between the apparently incompatible and irreconcilable interests of the media and of the administration of justice; and second, that the televising of courts is an American aberration – for which reason alone it must be opposed.

This chapter re-examines the rationale for why television cameras were initially banned from English courtrooms; evaluates the reasons why the prohibition has been retained; and finally, in the light of recent developments, considers why the continuing ban may no longer be appropriate nor desirable.

The Statutory Ban

Section 41 of the Criminal Justice Act 1925 prohibits both the taking and publishing of photographs in courtrooms and even in precincts of court buildings (*In re St Andrew's, Heddington* [1977] 3 WLR 286) in England and Wales. Section 29 of the Criminal Justice Act 1945 imposes a similar prohibition with respect to courts in Northern Ireland. While section 41(2)(a) of the 1925 Act defines a 'court' as 'any court of justice, including the court of a coroner', the prohibition has been held not to apply to the House of Lords, courts in Scotland (Lord Hope, 1994), and Public Inquiries set up under the Tribunals of Inquiry (Evidence) Act 1921. These exceptions have proven to be significant, and are discussed further below.

The provision has been held to also prohibit the use of television cameras (*Re Barber* v *Lloyds Underwriters* [1987] 1 QB 103, 105). The appropriateness of the prohibition extending to television has been questioned for a number of reasons. First, it appears inappropriate because the 1925 prohibition was enacted 11 years before television broadcasts began, and even before television had been invented (Dockray, 1988: 597). Secondly, and perhaps more significantly, the discernible reasons for the 1925 prohibition on photography, as discussed below, appear to be largely unrelated to the reasons why the desirability of permitting television cameras to record and broadcast court proceedings continues to be questioned. Thus Susan Prince notes that 'the Act was instigated to correct a different mischief from that which it extends to today – merely stopping the publication of photographs in newspapers' (Prince, 1998: 84). Finally, not only the extension of this prohibition to television but its continuing existence after 77 years appears incongruous in light of its categorization as 'an experiment' (Sir William Joynson-Hicks, Home Secretary, 1924–1925).

Explanations for the Statutory Prohibition

So why was section 41 of the Criminal Justice Act 1925 enacted?

1. Historical explanation

Explanations of why cameras came to be banned from English and Welsh courtrooms inevitably refer to the public outcry over the *Mirror's* publication of a photograph, taken at the Old Bailey of Judge Bucknill in the process of passing a sentence of death on Frederick Seddon. Although this photograph was published on 15 March 1912, it continued to be cited in parliamentary debates as evidence of the need for a ban on photography. For example, 12 years after it was published, Lord Darling (1924) made the following remarks about the photograph in the House of Lords:

> There was a dreadful case some time ago, in which a photograph was taken at the Old Bailey of a Judge passing sentence of death. That photograph was published – a most shocking thing to have taken, or to have published, dreadful for the Judge, dreadful for everybody concerned in the case. (*House of Lords Debates*, Vol. 56, column 313)

As the infamous photograph was apparently taken without the consent of court officials and at a time of growing opposition to press courtroom photography, it could be said that the media only had itself to blame for the ban. For example, television producer Nick Catliff has explained the imposition of the statutory prohibition in the following terms: 'Following several rather sordid attempts by the press to take sneak photographs in court, all cameras were outlawed' (Catliff, 1999: 1). However, such an explanation would appear to be more appropriate in explaining the banning of cameras from American courtrooms.

The media's presence in a number of early-1930s, high-profile American cases, such as the trial of the kidnapper and murderer of famous aviator Charles Lindbergh's son (*State v Hauptmann* 180 A. 809 (1935)), served to create a circus-like atmosphere (Stepniak, 1998: 35). It was the disruption of those trials, particularly by photographers and film crews recording footage for movie newsreels, that led the American Bar Association to amend its Canons of Professional and Judicial Ethics to prohibit photographic coverage of court proceedings. Canon 35, which since 1937 had prohibited courtroom photography, was amended in 1952 to also prohibit the use of television cameras and to spell out clearly the justification for the ban:

> Proceedings in court should be conducted with fitting dignity and decorum. The taking of photographs in the courtroom, during sessions of the court or recesses between sessions, and the broad-casting or televising of court proceedings are calculated to detract from the essential dignity of the proceedings, distract the witness in giving his testimony, degrade the court and create misconceptions with respect thereto in the minds of the public and should not be permitted. (House of Delegates of the American Bar Association, 1952: 427)

In *Estes* v *Texas* 381 US 532 (1965), the US Supreme Court appeared to endorse this basis for prohibiting camera coverage by ruling television camera recordings to be distracting and disruptive and consequently, inherently prejudicial to a fair trial.

Even with respect to the American ban, the 'media only has itself to blame' explanation only provides a partial explanation. Ample evidence exists to suggest that media excesses and disruptions of trials weren't the only reasons why the American Bar Association opposed the broadcast of court proceedings in the early 1930s. The objection also appeared to reflect a sentiment held by members of the legal profession – that visual reporting of proceedings by the media changed 'what should be the most serious of human institutions … into an enterprize for the entertainment of the public … Using such a trial for the entertainment of the public or for satisfying its curiosity shocks our sensibilities' (American Bar Association Committee on Professional Ethics and Grievances, 1932).

Similar sentiments held by English authorities arguably provide the overriding reason for why cameras were and remain barred from British courts. In seeking an explanation for the imposition of the 1925 prohibition in England and Wales we must look to the alarm expressed by authorities at the growing level of public interest in media reports of gruesome or salacious cases – a trend apparently fuelled by the newly introduced publication of courtroom photographs and sketches to accompany press reports of proceedings (Dockray, 1988: 594). While the criticism of press reports of judicial proceedings extended beyond the publication of photographs, courtroom photography was singled out for particular attention because it constituted a novel intrusion into the relative privacy of court proceedings, and because published photographs 'were seen as having limited public benefit and their only purpose was to excite the public's morbid curiosity' (Prince, 1998: 84).

Dockray argues that 'it was precisely because photographs attracted interest in such unwholesome matters as proceedings in court that they were suppressed in 1925' (Dockray, 1988: 597). He suggests that 'it was the cumulative effect of … three highly charged cases … in 1922' that provided the final impetus for the enactment of a statutory ban (Dockray, 1988: 596). Two of the cases were criminal cases in which death sentences were passed, while the third was a divorce case. The publication of the sordid details of the evidence in the divorce case and the high level of media and public interest in the criminal cases appeared to reinforce earlier calls for restrictions on courtroom reporting and on photographic coverage in particular.

Disapproval by authorities of the media's facilitation of an increased public interest in and commentary on judicial proceedings provides a tenable if incomplete explanation of why cameras were banned from British courtrooms. It arguably also explains why the statutory prohibition remains in spite of: technological advances that have eliminated fears of distraction and disruption; the consistently favourable experiences and evaluations of experiments with cameras in courts in other jurisdictions; and the prohibition's apparent inconsistency with the principle of open justice and its emphasis on publicity.

2. Prohibition in spite of technological advances

Thanks to technological developments, concerns that the presence of cameras may disrupt proceedings and distract participants – concerns largely responsible for the initial prohibition of cameras in courts in the United States and for the retention of the statutory ban in England and Wales – no longer exist. Over 20 years ago American courts ruled that audiovisual recording technology had advanced to the point where, in the absence of evidence to the contrary, the presence of cameras in court could no longer be presumed to be inherently physically disruptive and thus prejudicial to a fair trial (*Re: Petition of Post-Newsweek Stations, Florida* 370 So 2d 764 (1979); *Chandler* v *Florida* 449 US 560, 576 (1981)). Not only is modern audiovisual recording equipment unobtrusive, its utilization for other purposes increasingly means that the recording of proceedings for broadcast need no longer even involve the presence of additional cameras or personnel in the courtroom. Increasingly, the recording of court or tribunal proceedings means utilizing the courts' own unobtrusive audiovisual equipment, tapping into the courts' own recording processes or simply using the courts' own recordings – as is the case in the International Criminal Tribunal for the Former Yugoslavia (Mason, 2000); numerous courts which post their own audiovisual recordings of proceedings on the Internet; and as has been the case in the Shipman Inquiry, which is discussed below.

3. Prohibition in spite of the favourable experiences of other jurisdictions

In 1989, after studying overseas experiences with cameras in courts for over 12 months, a working party of the Public Affairs Committee of the General Council of the Bar (of England and Wales) released a report titled *Televising the Courts* (the Caplan Report) in which they concluded that 'that the benefit of televising outweighs the arguments against it' (Caplan Report, 1989: 35, paragraph 4.13) and recommended that legislation be amended to allow a televising of court proceedings under strict controls, for a trial period of two years (Caplan Report, 1989: 49, paragraph 7.1, recommendation iv).

Deeming objections to the televising of courts to be 'based largely on fears which, in practice, are revealed to be unfounded, and in part upon an emotive reaction to television' (Caplan Report, 1989: 47, paragraph 6.1), the Working Party urged that even inherent risks could be 'effectively removed or controlled by the rules of coverage and the trial judge's discretion and … are not a justification for banning the camera altogether' (Caplan Report, 1989: 46, paragraph 6.1).

Such conclusions relating to risks and fears together with findings with respect to the availability of 'non-intrusive technology' led the working party to 'see no legitimate reason in 1989 in continuing to exclude the major source of news for the great majority of the population' (Caplan Report, 1989: 46–7, paragraph 6.1).

In 1990 the working party's proposals were endorsed by the Bar Council, which sponsored a private members bill (Courts (Research) Bill 1991), to amend section 41 of the Criminal Justice Act 1925. Though vigorously debated in the House of Commons (*House of Commons Debates*, Vol. 186, 549–67 and 578–615), the Bill failed.

It is important to underline that the Caplan Report's favourable findings were consistent with those of every known study and evaluation of this issue (Stepniak, 1994, 1998; Mason, 2000). Repeatedly and inevitably, studies and experiments have revealed no significant detrimental impact on courtroom participants or on the administration of justice, and have deemed potential dangers capable of being addressed through appropriate regulations. It should also be stressed that such findings are not confined to American jurisdictions and courts. Studies undertaken in Canada, New Zealand and Australia (Stepniak, 1998) – where media reporting is subject to contempt and *sub judice* laws akin to those in Britain – have similarly been favourable.

4. Prohibition in spite of inconsistency with the principle of open justice

Many of the arguments relied on by those determined to retain the courtroom ban on cameras appear to be incompatible with the accepted notion of open justice. As Susan Prince has posited, 'Section 41 appears *prima facie*, to conflict with the common law principle of open justice which was articulated in *Scott v Scott*' (Prince, 1998: 89).

According to Judge Ellison, the purpose of section 41 is 'clearly to afford necessary privacy to judges and others concerned from un-welcome intrusions or feelings of such which is an essential for the proper conduct of proceedings' (*In Re St Andrews Heddington* [1977] 3 WLR 286, 289). Judge Ellison went on to explain that:

Justice could not be properly administered if judges or witnesses suffered the pressures, embarrassment and discomfort of being photographed whilst playing their particular role with the expectation that every sign, mood or mannerism or observation should later be displayed to the public media. (pp. 289–90)

Yet in the leading English authority on the public administration of justice – the House of Lords decision in *Scott* v *Scott* ([1913] AC 417) – Lord Atkinson stressed that the principle of open justice required precisely such pressures and inconveniences to be tolerated:

The hearing of a case in public may be, and often is, no doubt, painful, humiliating, or deterrent to both parties and witnesses, and in many cases, especially those of a criminal nature, the details may be so indecent as to tend to injure public morals, but all this is tolerated and endured, because it is felt that in public trial is to be found, on the whole, the best security for the pure, impartial and efficient administration of justice, the best means of winning for it public confidence and respect. (p. 463)

Unless *Scott* v *Scott* is to no longer be considered good law, it seems curious that so much of the debate about cameras in courts is taken up with arguments over whether cameras and broadcasts do or not have the effects that Lord Atkinson lists as the costs of open justice. Those opposed to the televising of proceedings inevitably raise fears of potential consequences such as witnesses and parties being deterred from bringing actions or testifying in court, and participants in trials being affected by an awareness of being observed by the public. For example, in seeking to protect the 'dignified administration of justice' and 'calm, rational atmosphere' of trials from television, Robin Day (1995: 12–13) appears to overlook the recognized costs of open justice or chooses to minimize such costs via a form of open justice that severely undervalues the importance of publication.

Although open justice is often equated with courts being open to the public, the principle entails much more than merely permitting the public to observe judicial proceedings. Indeed, it is undoubtedly publicity, rather than open court doors, that defines open justice. It is significant to note that in extolling the indispensable virtues of open justice, Jeremy Bentham emphasized publicity rather than open court doors – declaring publicity to be 'the very soul of justice … the surest of all guards against improbity' (Bowring, 1843: 305, 316–17) and observing that 'Without publicity, all other checks are insufficient: in comparison of publicity, all other checks are of small account … (Bentham, 1827: 524). He went so far as to suggest that 'It is to publicity, more than to every-thing else put together, that the English system of procedure owes its being the least bad system … instead of being the worst' (Bowring, 1843: 305, 316–17).

There are those who continue to argue that opening courts to both the public and the press and publishing reasons for decisions is all that is required by the principle of open justice. In doing so they are ignoring the realities of public access to courts. The Caplan Report described what the concept of open justice in England and Wales meant in practice:

> … those members of the public who have the time, the resources and the will to travel to a particular court may succeed on arrival in gaining access to the proceedings they wish to observe if space in the public gallery permits. For those who do not or cannot go to court [which is clearly the vast majority of the population], or who cannot gain access even if they do go, their understanding and knowledge of what transpires in court depends exclusively on the reports in the print media and if a television reporter is present, on that reporter's account to camera outside the court building of what he observed. (Caplan Report, 1989: 5, paragraph 1.6)

As open justice clearly no longer depends on public attendance of proceedings, public scrutiny and informed debate relies almost entirely on the media. In *Richmond Newspapers Inc v Virginia* (448 US 555 (1980)), the Supreme Court of the United States acknowledged the role performed by the media:

> Instead of acquiring information about trials by firsthand observation or by word of mouth from those who attended, people now acquire it chiefly through the print and electronic media. In a sense, this validates the media claim of functioning as surrogates for the public. (per Brennan J at 573)

However, while courts have recognized the crucial role played by the media, they have been rather more reluctant to embrace and ac-commodate the audiovisual media, preferring to practically confine reporting to the press or press-like coverage. This attitude is confronted by the reality that television is by far the most relied on source of public information. Thus Walker and Brogarth note that 'given the fact that television is the main source of information about public affairs for most people, broadcasting should be viewed as more important than a press presence' (Walker and Brogarth, 1989: 638).

The need for courts to be willing to accommodate courtroom reporting by the audiovisual media is made all the more important by a discernible reduction in press coverage of courts. As, Susan Prince notes:

> With pressure on space, many newspaper reports of cases or proceedings have been truncated, and over the length of the trial or enquiry there may be many days when little is reported at all. In consequence the public rely on the television more than the press, radio and all other branches of the media for a comprehensive insight into the workings of government and information about what is going on in local as well as global communities. (Prince, 1998: 90)

It could further be said that those who are satisfied by an 'open court doors' interpretation of open justice not only overlook the principle's emphasis on publicity, but fail to consider adequately why courts are required to be administered openly. By apparently confining the principle's purpose to ensuring impartial and fair administration of justice through public scrutiny, they understate the significance of the principle's crucial role in maintaining public confidence in the judiciary through its facilitation of the meaningful public scrutiny required for informed public debate. As Lord Scarman observed in *Harman* v *Secretary of State for Home Department* ([1983] 1 AC 280), the purpose of subjecting the administration of justice to public scrutiny and making evidence and argument publicly known is 'so that society may judge for itself the quality of justice administered in its name, and whether the law requires modification'(at p. 316).

The principle of open justice seeks to promote public confidence in the judiciary through its insistence on public administration of justice, and through the resulting informed debate. However, as Susan Prince suggests:

> [I]t seems that public confidence in the English system is manifested through reliance on those undertaking the judicial role and principles of due administration of justice, rather than through a public knowledge of the working of the courts and the resolution of proceedings. However with concerns over miscarriages of justice and other concerns and criticisms coming to the fore, it is arguable that public confidence in the administration of justice has

weakened and that means a strengthening public accountability and transparency need to be sought. (Prince, 1998: 87)

As Professor Clive Walker (1996) observes, media reporting of courts requires a balancing of the interests of the administration of justice and the right to a fair trial on the one hand, with the interests flowing from the open and publicized administration of justice, on the other. In this respect Walker identifies a move away from the traditional English approach of leaving this conflict to be resolved by the courts themselves, and towards greater reliance on open justice, freedom of speech and the public's right to receive information. Walker suggests that such a trend, in part imposed by technology and the imposition of international rights and standards on the administration of British justice, points to a move away from reliance on restrictions on publication as manifest in contempt and *sub judice* laws to balance the sometimes conflicting interests.

The Scottish Experiment

Although the prohibition specified in section 41 of the Criminal Justice Act 1925 does not apply to Scotland, prior to 1992 cameras were effectively banned from Scottish courts by a rule of practice flowing from the courts' inherent powers to control their own proceedings. Sensing that this practice would not survive, Lord Hope, the Lord President of Scotland, decided to retain control by taking the initiative:

> It seemed to me that it was unlikely, given the pace of modern development, that the practice which had existed hitherto would survive, or at least would continue to command public respect and confidence, until my retirement. I decided that, if there were to be changes, I would rather that they occurred early during my time as Lord President when I was in a position, by taking the initiative, to control events. (Lord Hope, 1994: 3)

Consequently, Lord Hope requested that a judge undertake informal consultations and an examination of available technology and prepare a report on the question of courtroom televising in Scotland. The findings and recommendations of the report formed the basis for the Directions on the Televising of Court Proceedings, set out in a practice note, which Lord Hope formally issued on 7 August 1992 (reproduced in *BBC, Petitioners No.1* 2000 JC 419). The effect of these Directions was to replace the total prohibition on courtroom cameras with limited access, determined by 'whether the presence of television cameras in the court would be without risk to the administration of justice' (paragraph b). Although the Directions reiterated a prohibition on camera access to civil and criminal proceedings at first instance (unless for later broadcast as educational or documentary programmes), they elicited much media interest and led Lord Hope to conclude that:

> detailed guidelines were required to lay down the procedures to be followed ... when seeking consents from witnesses, jurors and other participants in court proceedings ... and the terms on which the proceedings in any given case might be filmed for televising. (Lord Hope, 1994: 9)

The resulting protracted and tense discussions (described by BBC producer Nick Catliff as a 'ritualistic dance' (Catliff, 1994)) and the stringent and legalistic nature of the resulting guidelines caused a number of media networks to lose interest. The BBC's willingness to persevere and risk extravagant amounts of time and money to an undertaking without any guarantees bore testimony to its commitment to courtroom televising.

The first case to ever be filmed in a British court was a shoplifting and assault trial in the Edinburgh Sheriff Court. It was recorded by BBC Television on 31 May 1993, and broadcast in April 1994. Subsequently, numerous other proceedings were also recorded for broadcast. For example, BBC Scotland recorded and broadcast two, one-hour documentaries on the behind the scenes workings of Scottish courts. The investiture ceremony of a new judge of the Scottish Criminal Court of appeal was also broadcast. However, perhaps the most significant resulting recordings were those by the BBC 2 for *The Trial*, a five-part documentary series that utilized footage of Scottish criminal trials and was broadcast to much acclaim nationally in late 1994 and overseas in subsequent years. According to its producer, the series 'took almost 2 years to make at a cost of £180,000 an hour, which is almost as much as Eastenders, 3 times the price of Top Gear and six times that of BBC Sport' (Catliff, 1999: 1).

Though the strictness of the guidelines resulted in relatively few broadcasts, the experiences were vital in reassuring British authorities and the public of the viability and desirability of courtroom televising. For instance, the feared 'playing up to the cameras did not materialize' (Bawdon, 1994: 10). The feedback from those involved was largely favourable – a judge noted that he was 'happy' with the experience (Fisher, 1995: 480), a Queen's Counsel indicated that he would like to 'do it again' (Fisher, 1995: 480) and another advocate observed that participants 'soon forgot the cameras were there' (Webster, 1994). Even Lord Hope was reported to have been 'reassured' by what was televized (Fisher, 1995: 480). Several years later, Nick Catliff, the producer of *The Trial* series recounted that:

> The reviews were very kind. It was good telly, it got a huge amount of press coverage and was watched by healthy audiences. Many commentators noted that it was sober, responsible and balanced … very BBC. Furthermore, the BBC was delighted. We got what we wanted out of the project. The courts were pleased too … Our presence hadn't caused chaos, there were no complaints that the administration of justice had been interrupted, the practitioners looked highly competent, the sheriffs looked suitably wise and none of the judges was visibly asleep on the bench – although it has to be said one clerk of the High Court did nod off on camera. Most importantly for us, we seemed to have fulfilled our own public service brief and to have delivered what the Lord President has asked for; namely educated and informed a lot of people about what happens in court. (Catliff, 1999: 1)

Criticisms of the broadcasts, on the other hand, tended to relate less to the recording process (Fisher, 1995: 480) or the impact of the broadcast (Bawden, 1994; Purves, 1994) and instead appeared to reflect the concerns held by some members of the legal profession and commentators regarding the undesirability of broadcasts fuelling public interest in the details of court proceedings. Such criticism led the *Evening Standard* to observe: '… there is a large element of snobbery in the resistance to trial television – a belief that what the general public is avidly interested in must in some respect be base' (*Evening Standard*, 1 August 1994).

The televising of *The Trial* series resulted in some 8 million people viewing Scottish courtroom proceedings on television – at a time when British courts in England, Wales and Northern Ireland remained closed to cameras. It was also during the early 1990s that British television viewers began to watch broadcasts of overseas trials. For example, several court TV programmes were broadcast on Channel 4 and on the Sky Channel.

The largely favourable responses to the Scottish experiment and the popularity of the broadcasts of overseas trials renewed and strengthened calls for the legalization of courtroom televising, largely on the grounds that such broadcasts would be of public educative value. In

1993 and 1994 the BBC engaged in discussions with Lord McKay, the Lord Chancellor, who was said to have been a keen observer of the Scottish broadcasts and quite receptive to the idea of courtroom television. However, just as the pro-televising movement appeared to be gaining momentum, it was ironically two American trials, the broadcasts of which attracted the largest viewing audiences in Britain, that turned public opinion against cameras in British courts and appeared to strengthen opposition by the legal profession and authorities.

The OJ Simpson Case

The BBC 2 broadcasts of OJ Simpson's pre-trial hearing were watched by 4 million Britons. As for the trial itself, the weekly reviews broadcast by the BBC were viewed by an average of 1 million viewers. In addition the live weekday evening coverage by Sky News, from January until October 1995, was watched by an estimated 7 million viewers.

In contrast to the Scottish broadcasts, the negative public reaction to the broadcast of the OJ Simpson case was said to have 'brought a pendulum swing in the opposite direction' (Hamilton-Rump, 1996). Thus the OJ Simpson case was reported to have caused the Lord Chancellor to 'go cold on the idea' (Verkaik, 1995: 14). Similarly, Lord Browne-Wilinson, who had previously expressed support for courtroom televising, changed his position (Day, 1995: 11).

Public disapproval of the televising of the OJ Simpson case had the most damaging impact on moves to allow cameras into British courts. It is summed up by media commentator Robin Day, who while conceding that there were many reasons for why the trial 'became a deplorable circus' noted that 'these problems and difficulties were intensified and magnified by the continuous presence of the television camera, and by the awareness in that LA courtroom of the huge audience outside' (Day, 1995: 11).

The Louise Woodward Case

Two years after the OJ Simpson trial, the televized Boston murder trial of English nanny Louise Woodward added a nationalistic element to public opposition to the adoption of the widely criticized American style of court reporting that televising of court proceedings represented. Somewhat ironically, Britons watched the broadcasts of the trial in unprecedented numbers. On 31 October 1997, immediately following Louise Woodward's televized sentencing, the Lord Chancellor's Department issued a press release referring to the 'widespread live television coverage of the case and verdict' and spelling out the Lord Chancellor's reasons for not being able to 'countenance the televising of court proceedings'.

Even though Louise Woodward mounted a campaign to highlight 'the dangers of allowing television cameras into courtrooms' (Landesman, 1998), and in doing so helped ensure continuing public opposition, as the 1990s drew to a close, support for the admission of cameras into British courts continued to be heard. Jonathan Caplan QC, Chairman the Working Party that in 1989 had recommended the abolition of the prohibition on cameras in court, was one of a number of prominent lawyers to argue that in view of British contempt-of-court laws and other legal restrictions on media reporting, the excesses of the media coverage of the OJ Simpson case could not be replicated in Britain (Day, 1995: 11–12). While the Lord Chancellor continued to oppose the broadcast of court proceedings, in 1998 the Lord Chancellor's Department appeared to signal a relaxation of the absolute prohibition of cameras in the precincts of courts when it advized that 'when approved by the trial judge, a fixed, non-recording CCTV link between the courtroom and the media annex (established at high profile trials) would not contravene s.41' (Wicksteed, 1998).

The broadcast of Scottish court proceedings had provided the authorities, legal profession and the British public with an opportunity to adjudge whether statutory prohibitions on cameras ought to be removed. The OJ Simpson and Louise Woodward cases appeared to undo the positive assessment of the Scottish experiment and to confuse the debate through their American legal contexts. It took another British court not bound by section 41 of the Criminal Justice Act 1925 to reignite the debate and refocus its application to British courts and media reporting laws, and to the potential benefits of televising courts of appeal.

The Augusto Pinochet Appeals

In late 1998, the Law Lords permitted cameras to record their findings in the three hearings regarding Augusto Pinochet, the former president of Chile. This was not the first time that the House of Lords had permitted cameras to broadcast its judicial and not just legislative work. In 1989 the BBC was permitted to record and broadcast the formal proceedings following the hearing of an appeal during which the Lords of Appeal

Law as members of the Appellate Committee report their opinions to the House in the chamber of the House of Lords. In his detailed and instructive outline of the televising of the Law Lords, Joshua Rozenberg notes that 'in giving this consent, the law lords demonstrated that they did not consider themselves to be a court for the purposes of [section 41 of the Criminal Justice Act 1925]' (Rozenberg, 1999: 178). Subsequently in 1992 the BBC sought permission to record hearings and to broadcast such footage as part of a documentary. As Rozenberg explains, the rationale for such a request was that if the Law Lords were not a court for the purposes of section 41, they could allow their judicial hearings to be televized either on the basis of the same inherent power that permitted the Scottish courts to admit cameras, or alternatively on the basis that the Appellate Committee is a committee of the House of Lords and the proceedings of some House of Lords committees are permitted to be broadcast (Rozenberg, 1999: 178). While the Law Lords were prepared to accede to such a request, the conditions they sought to impose – in particular, editorial control – were not acceptable to the BBC. It appears that due to an earlier ITV programme, the Law Lords were conscious of how broadcasters could make 'judges look silly' (Rozenberg, 1994: 190).

The Law Lords were not as agreeable in 1996, when the BBC next sought permission to record the proceedings of a murder appeal for news broadcasts. Extracts from the letter by Lord Goff, the senior Law Lord, in reply to the application, are set out by Rozenberg (1999: 179–80) and provide an invaluable insight into the Law Lords' views on open justice and court reporting. Although the Law Lords denied the BBC's request to record and broadcast the proceedings of the Appellate Committee, they indicated that they had 'had no wish to prevent broadcasters from televising their judgments given in the chamber' (Rosenberg, 1999: 180). Consequently, the proceedings in the Jamie Bulger case (*Thompson and Venables* [1998] AC 407) were not broadcast, but the judgment was.

Due to the level of public interest in the judicial proceedings relating to the extradition of Augusto Pinochet, the BBC sought and gained permission to broadcast live the Law Lords' judgments on whether General Pinochet had immunity from arrest and extradition (*Ex parte Pinochet Ugarte (No 1)* [1998] 3 WLR 1456). To make the broadcast more meaningful to viewers and listeners, the five Law Lords departed from traditional practice and presented oral summaries of their judgments.

In the second Pinochet appeal, to facilitate the broadcast of their ruling, the appeal committee departed from traditional practice by assembling in the chamber and reporting to the House (*Ex parte Pinochet Ugarte (No 2)* [1999] 2 WLR 272).

While the Law Lords did not accede to calls for the third *Pinochet* hearing to be televized, they once again permitted the judgment to be televized live (*Ex parte Pinochet Ugarte (No 3)* [1999] 2 WLR 827). This time the innovation was the televized speech by Lord Browne-Wilkinson in which he briefly summarized the effect of the decision.

In 1999 the televising of courts issue also returned to Scottish courts, albeit in the Netherlands.

The Lockerbie Trial And Appeal

The trial of the Lockerbie bombers, held in the Netherlands but under Scottish law, with two Libyans accused of mass murder, large numbers of distantly located relatives of the victims, in the absence of a jury, and with largely professional witnesses, appeared to be particularly suitable for television broadcast (Rozenberg, 1999: 183–4; Hogan and Mason, 1999; Catliff, 1999).

It was not only an opportunity to allow the world to see Scottish justice in action, but also to test the implications for courtroom televising of Article 10 of the European Human Rights Convention – in particular whether prohibiting or restricting courtroom broadcasts impinged on the guaranteed 'freedom of expression', couched in terms of 'freedom to … receive and impart information and ideas without interference by public authority' (Article 10 (1)). A crucial question was whether restricting or prohibiting the broadcast of court proceedings would be held to be justified on the grounds that associated duties and responsibilities subject the freedoms:

> … to such formalities, conditions, restrictions or penalties as are prescribed by law and are necessary in a democratic society, in the interests of national security, territorial integrity or public safety, for the prevention of disorder or crime, for the protection of health and morals, for the protection of the reputation or rights of others, for preventing the disclosure of information received in confidence, or for maintaining the authority and impartiality of the judiciary. (Article 10 (2))

The Lockerbie trial also provided an opportunity to revisit and possibly review Lord Hope's directions, which had governed the televising of Scottish courts since 1992.

In urging the Scottish judiciary to permit the BBC to film the trial, Alistair Bonnington, the BBC's legal advisor in Scotland, stressed that the absence of a jury appeared to remove a key obstacle to the broadcast of trials (Hogan and Mason 1999). Nick Catliff, who in the early 1990s had filmed over 20 trials under Lord Hope's guidelines, also argued that the guidelines needed to be amended for the Lockerbie trial. In particular, he noted that: 'The guidelines currently embargo any footage until after a trial is over. This rule was designed to prevent jurors from going home in the evening and seeing news coverage of the trial in which they were sitting. But in the Lockerbie trial there will be no jury' (Catliff, 1999). The international attention, and the trial's location in the Netherlands, also prompted comparisons with the International Crimes Tribunal for the Former Yugoslavia, located in The Hague. By recording its own proceedings and providing media networks with the footage, the Tribunal had successfully, and without any detrimental impact to the conduct of hearings, ensured that the world could view its proceedings (Mason, 2000). Nick Catliff observed: 'Imagine how bizarre it will be if Lockerbie takes place out of sight of the world while nearby in The Hague war crimes trials are being filmed regularly' (Catliff, 1999).

As attempts to gain consent to televize the Lockerbie trials through administrative channels failed, the BBC and other broadcasters presented a petition to the *nobile officium* seeking the consent of the court to televize the entire proceedings of the trial, live. They sought consent for the broadcasting of edited portions of the trial proceedings in news broadcasts and other broadcasts, or for the compiling and broadcasting after the end of the trial of one or more documentary programmes on the trial, utilizing parts of the proceedings of the trial. Observing that 'what was sought was no more than a judicial determination that in the particular circumstances of this unique case the petitioners should be permitted to televize the proceedings', Lord Macfadyen refused the application on 7 March 2000 (*BBC, Petitioners No.1* 2000 JC 419). In concluding his opinion Lord Macfadyen stated:

I am of the opinion that the prohibition of broadcasting of current proceedings in criminal cases at first instance, formulated in paragraph (c) of the Lord President's Directions [prohibiting 'the televising of current proceedings in criminal cases at first instance ... under any circumstances'], based as it is on the settled practice of the court and supported by the sanction that such broadcasting would be regarded as a contempt of court, is properly to be regarded as 'prescribed by law'. Its purpose is to protect the rights of others, in particular the rights of the accused to a fair trial. It may therefore, well within the available margin of appreciation, be regarded as 'necessary in a democratic society'. I therefore take the view that any restriction on the petitioners' right to receive and impart information effected by refusal of the prayer of the petition is a restriction which is legitimate in terms of Article 10(2). I therefore do not consider that in refusing the prayer of the petition I would be acting in a way which is incompatible with a Convention right.

The petitioners' subsequent appeal to the Appeal Court, High Court of Justiciary, was not successful (*BBC, Petitioners No.2* 2000 JC 521). Once again, legal argument on the 'freedom of communication' clause of the European Human Rights Convention was not accepted.

Noting that 'justice must be seen to be done. But it never is thanks to our ban on cameras in courts', Geoffrey Robertson QC described the Scottish judiciary's denial of permission to televize the Lockerbie trial as 'foolish'. However, he saw some hope in that 'the new Human Rights Act has a "freedom of communication" clause which might open the way to TV coverage of tribunal inquiries and some court proceedings' (Robertson, 2000).

However, on the 9 January 2002 Lord Cullen, the Lord Justice General for Scotland and chair of the bench of five judges appointed to hear the appeal, which was due to begin on 23 January 2002, granted BBC Television permission to broadcast and provide an Internet stream of the appeal proceedings. As noted on the Scottish Courts webpage, 'A number of websites throughout the world provided streaming video live. The proceedings were broadcast live (in both English and Arabic) over the Internet by the BBC.' (http://www.scotcourts.gov.uk/index1.asp) The appeal was broadcast live and unedited on the Internet via the BBC website (http://news.bbc.co.uk/1/hi/world/1766508.stm).

With the exception of new evidence from witnesses, the recording and broadcast of which was prohibited under Lord Hope's August 1992 directives, the Appeal was broadcast in its entirety. The appeal decision was also recorded and broadcast live on both the Internet via the BBC website and television on 14 March 2002.

While some legal commentators, such as Professor Jim Murdoch, have stressed that the decision to permit the live broadcast of the Lockerbie appeal, though 'an important step', 'should not be seen necessarily as establishing a new precedent' (BBC News, 9 January 2002), the Lockerbie appeal broadcasts do appear to have coincided with some reform proposals by Scottish legal authorities. In a 19 February 2002 speech (Boyd, 2002) the Lord Advocate, Colin Boyd QC, suggested that broadcasts of proceedings could be used to counter the inaccuracies and sensationalism of existing media reporting. Advocating greater cooperation between the courts and the media, he emphasized the potential benefits of greater audiovisual coverage. In the end, the broadcast of the Lockerbie appeal may not herald the advent of regular broadcasting of Scottish proceedings. But it did serve to illustrate the appropriateness of broadcasting certain proceedings and a willingness by the Scottish authorities to employ and further develop Lord Hope's 1992 directions.

The Shipman Inquiry

Concurrently with the Lockerbie trial and appeal, the issue of courtroom broadcasting also came under close scrutiny following media applications to broadcast the Manchester hearings of the Shipman Inquiry (Shipman Inquiry Webpage). Such applications were able to be considered as the statutory prohibition on cameras in courts does not apply to public inquiries set up under the Tribunals of Inquiry (Evidence) Act 1921.

In March 2001, shortly after the Inquiry had begun its investigations into 'the most prolific serial killer in British criminal history', the BBC and others unsuccessfully sought permission to record and broadcast the proceedings. Though Dame Janet Smith, the Chairman of the Inquiry, permitted the filming of file footage and of an application on 10 May 2001, she continued to deny permission to record and broadcast the hearings. In response to a request to provide full reasons for her refusals to permit the hearings to be recorded and broadcast, Dame Janet, delivered a ruling on 11 June 2001 (http://www.the-shipman-inquiry.org.uk/ruling_20010611.asp). In the ruling Dame Janet outlined the arguments for and against the broadcasting of proceedings (paragraphs 4–6), considered the decisions on this issue of other inquiries (paragraph 7) and dismissed arguments based on Article 10 of the European Convention on Human Rights (paragraph 10). Dame Janet explained that after inviting 'the opinion of those most likely to be affected', she had decided that there would be no broadcasting of phase 1 of the hearings (when relatives of victims were expected to testify). She also decided that phase 2 (when a variety of persons would give evidence) should also not be broadcast, noting: 'I have come to the conclusion that the additional distress and anxiety which is likely to be suffered by non-professional witnesses outweighs the public interest in seeing the faces and hearing the voices of witnesses' (paragraph 8). As to phase 3 (considering what monitoring of procedures for prescribing, dispensing, collecting, etc. of controlled drugs reveal about Shipman) she observed: 'I very much doubt that there would be sufficient interest to warrant the broadcast of Phase 3' (paragraph 8).

In response to the 27 July 2001 application by Geoffrey Robertson QC on behalf of the media company CNN, Dame Janet issued a further ruling on 25 October 2001 (http://www.the-shipman-inquiry.org.uk/ ruling_20011025.asp) in which she granted CNN permission to broadcast the inquiry hearings. As well as seeking permission to broadcast the inquiry hearings by taking a 'feed' from the inquiry's own cameras or alternatively installing its own cameras, CNN had asserted it had a right to film and broadcast the Inquiry proceedings – particularly by virtue of Article 10 of the European Convention on Human Rights.

As to the asserted right, Dame Janet reviewed freedom of expression under the common law of England and Wales and under the European Convention on Human Rights. Significantly, Dame Janet concluded that Article 10 did not apply or give CNN a presumptive right to film or broadcast the proceedings of the inquiry (paragraph 67).

As to its request for permission to film and broadcast, Dame Janet reiterated her prohibition on the broadcasting of phase 1, but with some reservations agreed to permit the broadcast of phase 2 hearings, 'provided it can be done without jeopardising the process of investigation or disrupting the hearings' (paragraph 92). Uncertain as to whether this was possible, Dame Janet proposed to proceed in stages.

Consequently on 20 September 2002 Dame Janet issued a statement (Dame Janet Smith, 2002) announcing that 'Following a pilot project during Stage 1 of Phase 2 of the Inquiry, Dame Janet Smith, the Chairman, has decided that broadcasting of public hearings may continue during the remainder of Phase 2'. This notice spells out the extent to which Dame Janet retains control and regulates the broadcasting. For example, that: 'Dame Janet may rule that any part of the evidence should not be broadcast and that permission to broadcast may be withdrawn temporarily or permanently if it is interfering with the work of the Inquiry'. To be permitted to broadcast, broadcasters must be approved by Dame Janet and sign a protocol (Second Protocol Governing the Recording or Broadcasting of The Shipman Inquiry) which *inter alia* states that sound and image are provided on a switched-feed basis from the inquiry's voice-activated cameras and sets out the rules covering the filming and broadcasting. The Shipman Inquiry experience with broadcasting should prove invaluable to the determination of appropriate regulations for future courtroom televising.

Crystal Ball Gazing

The above outlined recent developments in the United Kingdom's experience with the broadcasting of judicial proceedings don't make it clear how much longer the prohibition on cameras in courts is likely to remain in force. However, they do provide a clear indication of the most likely developments.

Likely developments need to be considered in the light of the ongoing reform of the legal and judicial reforms, in large measure flowing from Lord Woolf's *Access to Justice Report* (Lord Woolf, 1996), which appear to be weakening the government's opposition to cameras in court. In fact, the most recent developments suggest that the government is about to approve a pilot project which if deemed successful by Parliament would lead to a lifting of the statutory ban. In December 2000, the Lord Chancellor's office indicated that the government was considering permitting cameras to record appeal court cases, judicial reviews and Law Lords' hearings. In October 2002 the BBC presented the Lord Chancellor's Department with a technical feasibility study on potential filming in certain courtrooms of the Royal Courts of Justice. On 7 March 2003, several broadcasting companies and other interested parties met with some judges and staff from the Lord Chancellor's Department to discuss and develop rules for a pilot program of recording and broadcasting cases which come before the Court of Appeal. A submission based on the outcome of this meeting is to be prepared and presented to the Lord Chancellor and senior judges for approval. Responses to the proposal are also to be sought from the Law Society and the Bar. It is anticipated that during the ensuing pilot program only judges and lawyers participating in appeal cases will be filmed, while trial proceedings will remain closed to cameras.

The use of audiovisual technology in British courts is also increasingly making the blanket prohibition on cameras untenable. As Rozenberg notes, the authorities already tolerate security cameras, video links to media annexes, and audiovisual recording by transcription services (Rozenberg, 1999: 184). Livenote technology, which enables 'verbatim court reporting in real time that can be viewed via the Internet' (Stepniak and Mason, 2000: 72), had been utilized extensively by British courts.

Considering which broadcasts elicited the greatest informed acclaim and criticism, and with the above-mentioned Lord Chancellor's proposal to undertake a pilot project in mind, I join those who foresee and would welcome the regular televising of appeal hearings in British courts. At the same time, I retain significant reservations about the desirability of a blanket approval for the televising of proceedings at first instance.

Nick Catliff is clearly right in identifying judicial control as the crucial ingredient in courtroom televising (Catliff, 1999: 1). When judges permit courtroom televising, not on the basis of whether the inconvenience and disturbance are likely to be minimal, but because the particular circumstances suggest that it is in the interest of the administration of justice to do so, broadcasting of proceedings will indeed enhance open justice. Consequently, when it comes to the relaxation of the current prohibition I wholeheartedly agree that 'only if the judges can be persuaded that televising the courts is a good idea, and that they can retain a sensible degree of control, will any progress be made' (Catliff, 1999: 1).

References

American Bar Association Committee on Professional Ethics and Grievances (1932) 'Formal Opinion 67 (March 21, 1932)', *American Bar Association Journal*, 18, 550.

BBC News, 9 January 2002; at http://news.bbc.co.uk/1/hi/uk/scotland/1751960.stm

Bentham, J. (1827) *Rationale of Judicial Evidence.*

Bawdon, F. (1994) 'TV on Trial', *English Law Society Gazette*, 91(46), 10.

Bowring, J. (ed.) (1843) *Works of Jeremy Bentham*, Vol. 4.

Boyd, C., QC (2002) 'The Media, The Public And The Judicial Process: The Kenneth Younger Memorial Lecture', Playfair Library, Old College, University of Edinburgh, 19 February.

Caplan Report (1989) *Televising the Courts: Report of a Working Party of the Public Affairs Committee of the General Council of the Bar.*

Catliff, N. (1994) 'His Lordship regrets that this particular case ...', *The Times*, 15 November, 29.

Catliff, N. (1999a) 'The Trial And The British Experience', Cameras in the Courtroom Conference, Southampton Institute, 12 February.

Catliff, N. (1999b) 'Lockerbie: A Trial for Television', *The Guardian*, 22 February.

Darling, Lord (1924) 56 *House of Lords Debates*, 5 s., column 313 (26 February 1924).

Day, R. (1995) 'Injustice Seen to be Done', *The Spectator*, 30 December, 11–13.

Dockray, M. (1985) 'In Camera', *New Law Journal*, 135, 6234, 1254.

Dockray, M. (1988) 'Courts on Television', *Modern Law Review*, 51(5), 593–604.

Evered, J. (1997) 'Televised Justice: Considered Proposals for the Controlled Use of Television Cameras in the United Kingdom Courts', *Contemporary Issues in Law*, 23.

Fisher, L. (1995) 'Through the Camera Lens: When Justice is Not Seen to be Done', *The Australian Law Journal*, 69(7), 477.

Hamilton-Rump, D. (1996) Memorandum from the Head of Administration of The General Council of the Bar to the author, dated 31 January 1996.

Hogan, D. and Mason, P. (1999) 'Let the People See the Lockerbie Trial', *The Times*, 9 February, 21.

Hope, Lord (1994) 'Television in the Scottish Courts', unpublished paper, delivered at Meeting of Chief Justices and Attorneys-General of the European Union (Lisbon), May 1994, in D. Stepniak (1998) *Electronic Media Coverage of Courts: A Report Prepared for the Federal Court of Australia*, Melbourne: Federal Court of Australia, Appendix 22.

House of Delegates of the American Bar Association (1952) 'Proceedings of the House of Delegates: Mid Year Meeting, February 25-26, 1952', *American Bar Association Journal*, 38, 425.

Joynson-Hicks, Sir William (1924-1925) 188 *House of Commons Debates*, 5 s., column 849 (20 November 1925).

Landesman, C. (1998) 'Courage of Her Conviction', *The Australian*, 11 September, 13.

Mason, P. (2000) *Report on the Impact of Cameras at the International Criminal Tribunal for the Former Yugoslavia*, International Criminal Tribunal for the Former Yugoslavia.

Prince, S. (1998) 'Cameras in Court: What Can Cameras in Parliament Teach Us?', *Contemporary Issues in Law*, 92, 82–99.

Purves, L. (1994) 'Where is the Justice When TV Moves In?' *The Times*, 15 November.

Robertson, G., QC (2000) 'Court on Candid Camera', *Evening Standard*, 28 September.

Rozenberg, J. (1994) *The Search for Justice*, London: Hodder & Stoughton.

Rozenberg, J. (1999) 'The Pinochet Case and Cameras in Court', *Public Law*, 178–84.

Second Protocol Governing the Recording or Broadcasting of The Shipman Inquiry, http://www.the-shipman-inquiry.org.uk/ruling_20020920.asp

Shipman Inquiry Webpage, http://www.the-shipman-inquiry.org.uk/home.asp

Scottish Courts Webpage, http://www.scotcourts.gov.uk/index1.asp

Smith, Dame Janet (2002) 'Media Information', 20 September, at http://www.the-shipmaninquiry.org.uk/mediainfo.asp?from=w&ID=56

Stepniak, D. (1994) Why shouldn't Australian Court Proceedings be Televised? *University of New South Wales Law Journal*, 17(2), 345–82.

Stepniak, D. (1998) *Electronic Media Coverage of Courts: A Report Prepared for the Federal Court of Australia*, Melbourne: Federal Court of Australia.

Stepniak, D. and Mason, P. (2000) 'Court in the Web', *Alternative Law Journal*, 25(2), 71–4.

Verkaik, R. (1995) 'Cameras Cross Pacific – the USA's Trial Broadcasters are Making a Pitch to Televise UK Hearings', *The Law Society's Gazette*, 92(19), 14.

Walker, C. (1996) 'Fundamental Rights, Fair Trials and the New Audio-Visual Sector', *Modern Law Review*, 59, 517–39.

Walker, C. and Brogarth, D. (1989) 'Televising the Courts', *Justice of the Peace*, 153, 637.

Webster, S. (1994) 'Year-long Struggle Allows TV Only Restricted View of the Courtroom', *The Independent*, 16 November.

Wicksteed, M. (1998) Memorandum from Chief Press Officer, Lord Chancellor's Department to the author, dated 21 October 1998.

Woolf, Lord (1996) *Access To Justice: Final Report To The Lord Chancellor On The Civil Justice System in England and Wales*, Lord Chancellor's Department, July 1996, at http://www.open.gov.uk/lcd/civil/final/contents.htm

Cases

BBC, Petitioners No. 1 2000 JC 419, www.scotcourts.gov.uk/opinions/MCF0203.html

BBC, Petitioners No. 2 2000 JC 521, http://www.scotcourts.gov.uk/opinions/60_00.html

Chandler v *Florida* 449 US 560, 576 (1981)

Estes v *Texas* 381 US 532, (1965)

Ex parte Pinochet Ugarte (No 1) [1998] 3 WLR 1456

Ex parte Pinochet Ugarte (No 2) [1999] 2 WLR 272

Ex parte Pinochet Ugarte (No 3) [1999] 2 WLR 827

Harman v *Secretary of State for Home Department* [1983] 1 AC 280

In re St Andrew's, Heddington [1977] 3 WLR 286

Re Barber v *Lloyds Underwriters* [1987] 1 QB 103, 105

Re: Petition of Post-Newsweek Stations, Florida 370 So 2d 764 (1979)

Richmond Newspapers Inc v *Virginia* 448 US 555 (1980)

Scott v *Scott* [1913] AC 417

State v *Hauptmann* 180 A. 809 (1935)

Thompson and Venables [1998] AC 407

Note

The author wishes to thank everyone who provided advice, research assistance and comments. In particular he acknowledges the generous assistance and helpful advice of Joshua Rozenberg, Alistair Bonnington and Mike Wicksteed, and the valuable contribution of his research assistant Suzie Ward.

Chapter 14

The screen machine: cinematic representations of prison

Paul Mason

The development of the prison as a penal sanction altered the symbolism of punishment, replacing the visible punitive measures of gallows and guillotine with something more nebulous. Whereas the spectacle of public execution depended upon 'the theatrical representation of pain' (Foucault, 1979: 14), the prison concealed punishment behind high walls and razor wire: 'the dominant apparatus of punishment' (Hale, 1981: 51). This shrouding of modern penality in secrecy is, in part, to blame for the occasionally ill-informed public knowledge about the British prison system. Successive sweeps of the British Crime Survey reveal that the public are unacquainted with numerous aspects of the criminal justice system (Chapman *et al.*, 2002) and rely on the media for their information. Levenson (2001) notes that the Survey reports that just 6 per cent of the public consider their principal source of information to be inaccurate.

Relatively little work has been undertaken on the effect of media representations of prison on public attitudes. However, several commentators have suggested that media coverage of prisons, both in Britain and elsewhere, has contributed to the public misinformation about prison. Consider the following:

- 'Selective, simplified and skewed' depictions of prison in the media have led to public misunderstandings about the relative effectiveness of custodial and non-custodial offences (Walmsley, 2000: 8).

- The ostensible public familiarity with the prison is based upon its symbolism rather than hard facts about prison population and prison routine. This symbolism is fed by media images of the penal system (Levenson, 2001).

- The media, and in particular television and Hollywood, continue to represent 'the vilest aspects of prison life', leading the public to conclude that prison reform is unachievable (Cheatwood, 1998: 210).

- The expansionist penal policy in the United States, and specifically the growth of the super-maximum security jail, was legitimated by the media-constructed notion of 'a "worst of the worst" section of the prison population in need of draconian measures of control and restraint' (O'Sullivan, 2001: 318).

- Any attempt by the prison film to argue for reform is problematic, as such representations and narratives are redefined 'as more sophisticated examples of the cheap exploitation movies, higher class entertainment but sensational nonetheless' (Nellis, 1982: 44).

- The media have reduced rational debate about the aim and role of prison to entertainment, thus 'corroding our doubts and worries about the prison solution' (Mathiesen, 2000: vii).

- '… soundbites, spin, sensation and celebrity have become core characteristics of media output across the ever-blurring boundaries between factual news, news-responsive drama, drama-documentary, dramatic reconstructions, and reality TV' (Leishman and Mason, 2002, chapter 7), highlighted by media-led campaigns to free fictional British soap opera characters who have been imprisoned unfairly, and the BBC prison-reality TV show *The Experiment*, broadcast in 2002.

- Audiences of prison films tend to accept as true those parts of a film that are beyond their experience. 'Perhaps we didn't really believe that convicts danced to Elvis's guitar, but who doubted that grizzled cons on Death Row played mournful tunes on harmonicas. And while we may be skeptical of the mole-like tunnelling abilities of the average prison inmate, we do tend to assume that escape is uppermost in his mind at all times' (Querry, 1976: 7).

It is also interesting to note that media representations of prison may not only affect public perceptions but also prison practitioners. At least two Director Generals of the prison service have admitted that their experience of prison was formed by media representations. In 1992, Derek Lewis confessed that prior to taking the post as head of the prison service, 'his knowledge of prison life came from the media and the BBC comedy programme *Porridge*' (*The Times*, 26 December 1992: 6). More recently, the current Director General, Martin Narey, said that the BBC prison documentary *Strangeways* 'played a big role in my deciding to apply to join the prison service' (cited in Levenson, 2001: 14). In 1995, Channel Four News were leaked a Prison Service memo outlining government plans for increased prison expenditure for security and public relations. This followed extensive media coverage of prison escapes from Parkhurst and Whitemoor; and the suicides at Wold and Feltham Remand Centre as well as the alleged suicide of Fred West at Winson Green.

While prison escapes, riots and the seemingly ever-increasing prison population are keenly reported by the British news media, an equally pervasive source of prison imagery is the prison film. Cheatwood calls it 'the primary medium that has created and supported popular images of what incarceration is' (1998: 210). Nellis is surely right when he suggests that imprisonment 'is difficult to imagine but easy to misinterpret and any study of the ways in which it has been misinterpreted in modern times must take account of prison movies' (1982: 11).

The Prison Film: Issues of Genre and Oversight

Cinematic representations of prison can be traced back as far as the early 1900s, to the film *Why Am I Here?* (1913), since when more than 300 prison films have been made. Among the B-movie fodder and exploitative dross are some of cinema's greatest moments. The extraordinary *I Am a Fugitive from a Chain Gang* (1932) depicts the harrowing real-life experience of James Allen (played by Paul Muni) who, having been wrongly convicted, escapes the horrors of a Georgia chain gang only to live in constant fear of being recaptured. In the film's final scene, Allen says a last goodbye to the woman he loves, Helen (Helen Vinson):

Helen: But you could've written. It's been almost a year since you escaped.

Allen: But I haven't escaped. They're still after me. They'll always be after me. I've had jobs but I can't keep them, something happens, someone turns up. I hide in rooms all day and travel by night: no friends, no rest, no peace. Keep moving, that's all that's left for me. Forgive me, Helen. I had to take a chance to see you tonight, just to say goodbye.

Helen: Oh, Jim. It was all gonna be so different.

Allen: It is different. They've made it different. *(Hears a noise and, startled, whispers.)* I've gotta go.

Helen: I can't let you go like this. Can't you tell me where you're going? *(Shakes his head.)* Will you write? *(Shakes head again.)* Do you need any money? *(Shakes head, backing away from her and staring wildly.)* But you must, Jim. How do you live?

He disappears into the darkness and hisses.

Allen: I steal.

The prison film has often explored the sheer physical brutality of prison, in films such as *Brute Force* (1947), *Midnight Express* (1978), *McVicar* (1980) and *Scum* (1979), for example. As well as tense, protracted negotiations between warden and inmate in *Riot in Cell Block Eleven* (1954) and Burt Lancaster tending to his canaries in *Birdman of Alcatraz* (1962), the prison film is best remembered for inmates battling with the prison authorities: Paul Newman as Luke Jackson doing two years' hard time in *Cool Hand Luke* (1967). For his nonconformity, Steve McQueen in the title role of *Papillon* (1973) does two lengthy spells in solitary confinement; while Paul Crew (Burt Reynolds) refuses to throw the cons versus guards football game in *The Mean Machine* (1974), even though his sentence will be increased and his life made a misery by the warden. Prison films veer wildly from the ridiculous: *Lock Up* (1989) (Stallone does 'Rambo' in a prison yard) and *Chained Heat II* (1993) (Bridget Nielsen prances about as a leather-clad lesbian prison warden) to the sublime: Gerry Conlon fighting for his freedom, wrongly accused of the Guildford pub bombing in *In the Name of The Father* (1993); Kevin Bacon and Christian Slater fighting against Alcatraz and the authorities in *Murder in The First* (1995) and Andy Du Fresne (Tim Robbins) and Red (Morgan Freeman) ingeniously escaping and wreaking revenge on Warden Norton (Bob Gunton) in *The Shawshank Redemption* (1994).

Despite these outstanding examples, two issues surrounding the prison film remain unresolved. Firstly, there is a surprising dearth of literature on the media representation of incarceration. With the exception of a list of prison films (Crowther, 1989), film and cultural studies appear to have overlooked the genre. There are several useful contributions from prison commentators (Querry, 1973, 1975; Root, 1981; Nellis and Hale, 1981; Nellis, 1988; Wilson, 1993) and a handful of criminologists with an interest in crime, media and popular culture have written on the subject (Cheatwood, 1998; Mason, 1994, 1996, 1998a, b, 2000; Rafter, 2000; O'Sullivan, 2001). This is perhaps surprising given some of the outstanding examples of the genre and their critical success: *I Am A Fugitive From A Chain Gang* was nominated for three Academy Awards, *The Birdman of Alcatraz* and *The Green Mile* (1999) for four and *In The Name of the Father* and *The Shawshank Redemption* for seven. *Cool Hand Luke* won three Oscars, *Midnight Express* won two and *Dead Man Walking* (1995) won one. As Nellis argues 'no other type of crime film – the gangster movie, the police procedure movie and the characteristically English murder mystery-has claimed such impressive credentials in its bid for genre status' (Nellis, 1981: 6). And yet, what defines the prison film genre is problematic and this may partially explain why so relatively little has been written on it.

'Prison film' is not a recognizable genre in the way that 'gangster film', 'musical' or 'western' is used and yet most of us would describe *Midnight Express, The Birdman From Alcatraz* and *Papillon* as 'prison films'. Maybe it is not the problem of defining the prison film that has prevented a successful demarcation, but the futility of the exercise. It has been argued that debating whether *Angels With Dirty Faces* (1938) can be classed as a 'crime film', a 'gangster film' or a 'prison film' achieves very little. It may allow 'a sort of bibliographic classification of the history of film' (Tudor, 1995: 4), but beyond that its usefulness is limited. It is also argued that this kind of classification of cinema is often avoided as it leads to 'the laying down of rules and regulations that will arbitrarily restrict the freedom of … critics to talk about anything they want' (Buscombe, 1995: 12). However, to trace the history of the prison film would seem to require an understanding of the phrase for both writer and audience.

Any discussion of what a prison film is cannot avoid incorporating notions of *genre,* a complex term afforded different levels of significance in film criticism. At a simple level genre is a useful basic delineation of films into categories like 'western', 'horror film' and 'thriller'. The fundamental difficulty with genre analysis concerns defining the genre itself:

> To take a genre such as a western, analyse it, and list its principal characteristics is to beg the question that we must first isolate the body of films that are westerns. But that can only be isolated on the basis of the 'principal characteristics' which can only be discovered from the films themselves after they have been isolated. (Tudor, 1995: 5)

This circular predicament in which genre critics find themselves stems from the notion that certain films can be viewed as classic examples of a genre, from which the essence is distilled, allowing for discussion about 'early examples of', 'neo' and 'quasi' versions and 'decline of'.

As well as the difficulties inherent in the term 'genre', the biggest problem with prison films is deciding what proportion of a film should be based inside a prison before it is classed as a 'prison film'. As Nellis points out, 'scenes of imprisonment occur in all different types of … film … like *A Man For All Seasons*, swashbuckling melodramas like *The Count Of Monte Cristo* and even in westerns, *There Was A Crooked Man* for example (1981: 6). Conversely, a film about prison does not necessarily have to be set in one. David Hayman's film *Silent Scream* (1990) concerns the suffering and mental anguish brought on by incarceration, yet this is not predominantly set in prison. *We're No Angels* (1955), *Breakout* (1975), *In The Name Of The Father* and *Sleepers* (1996) could all be seen as concerned with prison, yet a significant part of each film takes place outside the prison walls. Furthermore, Laurel and Hardy in *The Hoose Gow* (1929), Elvis Presley's *Jailhouse Rock* (1957) and *Porridge* (1978), though all mainly set within the walls of a prison, are merely star vehicles with prison as a backdrop.

This discussion is taken up by O'Sullivan (2001), who suggests that there has been little consideration given to films that may be on the margins of the genre. He suggests that Rafter (2000) is rather simplistic and arbitrary in her definition of the prison film as:

> … essentially fantasies, films that purport to reveal the brutal realities of incarceration while actually offering viewers escape from the miseries of daily life through adventure and heroism … prison movies enable us to believe, if only briefly, in a world where long-suffering virtue is rewarded. (Rafter, 2000: 117)

Indeed, two of the films O'Sullivan discusses, *Con Air* (1997) and *American History X* (1998), are certainly on the margins of the genre, and he terms these 'prison-related films of nineties Hollywood cinema' (O'Sullivan, 2001: 322).

Cheatwood argues his definition on pragmatic grounds, suggesting that 'in the public, the "prison problem" tends to be identified with adult, male, civilian facilities' (1998: 211) and hence determining what constituted a prison film was 'not as difficult as it might seem' (1998: 211). Having considered these problems, the discussion of prison films that follows is based upon the following definition: an English-language film that concerns civil imprisonment and that is mainly set within the walls of a prison or uses prison as a central theme. Like Cheatwood's, this is partly a practical definition, excluding prisoner-of-war films despite Nellis's accurate assessment of the shared scepticism towards the captor and the conditions of incarceration between the two bodies of film. The majority of the discussion will concern male prisons, which reflects the partiality of the genre rather than the author.

Chronology and Cliché: Prison Film History and Themes

Since the early 1900s, the prison film has offered both diversity and congruence. As Nellis states, 'there are probably no more than a dozen different plots in all the prison films that have been made' (Nellis, 1981: 6). These include escape, riot, inmate and prison officer violence, wrongful conviction and so on. Rafter charts these common prison narratives as far back as the Oscar-winning MGM release *The Big House*, illustrating reccurences of prison-film leitmotifs in films 50 years apart:

> Convicts in *Each Dawn I Die* use the weekly movie as an occasion to knock off their enemies, as they do half a century later in *In The Name of the Father*. When Paul Newman joins a chain gang in *Cool Hand Luke*, he busts rocks in a tradition that began with *The Whipping Boy* (1922) and was perpetuated by *I Am A Fugitive from a Chain Gang*. Graphic scenes of life behind bars became *de rigeur*, one of the elements audiences expect to find in prison movies. (Rafter 2000: 121)

As well as these well-worn prison clichés, there are several other themes worthy of consideration, and these are discussed below. It is useful however, to trace the chronology of the prison film.

A Brief History of (Doing) Time

It would be helpful to provide an historical taxonomy of the prison film in a similar vein to Mason's work on British television's depiction of prison (Mason, 2000) or Reiner's dialectical analysis of the British police drama (Reiner, 1994; Leishman and Mason, 2003; Mawby, Chapter 11 of this volume). However, cinematic representations of prison are not easily classified nor do they follow any linear pattern. This is due partly to the limited number of plots and characters that comprise the genre, but also to the variation in the number of prison films that have been made across the decades. Cheatwood (1998), however, attempts something approaching such an analysis, in which he traces the prison film through 'the depression era' of the 1930s, the 'rehabilitation' era from 1943 to 1962, 'confinement' from 1963 to 1980 and finally, contemporary prison films, which he terms the 'administration era'. However, Cheatwood's taxonomy is rather forced and falls foul of the problems mentioned above. Claiming, for example, that *Cool Hand Luke* is part of the 'confinement era' where 'toughness and the image of the Bad Dude have replaced loyalty and the Square John as primary values' (Cheatwood, 1998: 223) is surely to miss the point that *Cool Hand Luke* is about the horrors of a chain gang in Southern America, owing much, in spirit at least, to *I Am A Fugitive From A Chain Gang*, made 30 years previously and in what Cheatwood terms the 'depression era'. Indeed, he himself highlights the fundamental difficulty of his analysis when discussing *The Shawshank Redemption*:

> One lead character is innocent, the warden is corrupt, and the guards are brutal all of which places it in the Big House era ... The other lead character is guilty of his crime and, although he rejects the label of rehabilitation, eventually confronts himself and recognises what he has done wrong. That, of course, is a key feature of the rehabiltation era. (Cheatwood, 1998: 226)

Such an 'anomaly' (Cheatwood, 1998: 226) merely confirms this categorization as half-baked and decontextualized. Brian Winston's critique of content analysis springs to mind:

> it is arguable that any one of the examples given in the study can be read differently, and different inferences drawn from those given with such authority. (Winston, 1990: 56)

Despite the fundamental flaws in Cheatwood's classification, his first era – prison films of the 1930s – does have some basis. The 1930s remains the most prolific decade for the production of prison films, with over 60 being made. The decade provided quality and quantity. As well as *I Am A Fugitive From A Chain Gang*, prison films of the 1930s included the Oscar-nominated *The Criminal Code* (1931) and *The Big House* (1930), the latter described by *Variety* as 'not a two-dollar talkie but a virile, realistic melodrama' (cited in Walker, 1997: 71). Nellis notes:

> the failure of prison to rehabilitate, together with scenes of admission to prison and solitary confinement have become integral to the narrative and iconography of subsequent prison

films, and have helped to give *The Big House* its status as a minor classic. (Nellis, 1981: 15)

Some of subsequent legends of Hollywood starred in prison films during the 1930s, including James Cagney (*The Mayor of Hell*, 1933; *Angels With Dirty Faces*; *Each Dawn I Die*, 1939); Edward G. Robinson (*Two Seconds*, 1932; *The Last Gangster*, 1937); and George Raft (*Each Dawn I Die*; *Invisible Stripes*, 1939).

Prison films were influenced by the Hays Code on film production during the 1930s, which led to what Parker terms a 'negotiated struggle and eventual convergence' (Parker, 1986: 146) between the film industry and the institutional regulators, producing repeated cinematic narratives in which crime never pays. Thus the exciting criminal character whom the Catholic Church feared would be emulated by the young, male film audience was replaced by 'a blander racketeer' (Parker, 1986: 150). The US government issued the following statement in 1936:

> It is not unnatural for the boys of a country which has recently lost its frontier to be excited and stimulated by tales of danger and thrilling adventure. But it is certainly not right for such a spirit to be fanned up artificially by the engines of a sensational press ... by the movies and by the other modern instruments of mob excitement. (US Department of Justice 1936; cited in Parker, 1986: 149)

From this point the film industry portrayed the causes of crime as poverty and slum housing: social problems of the Great Depression in America. Roffman and Purdy (1981) identify three 'character prototypes' (1981: 15) during this period: the fallen woman, the gangster and the convict.

Both Roffman and Purdy and Parker (1986) argue that the prison film during this time was 'the ultimate metaphor of social entrapment, where the individual disappears among the masses in an impersonal institution' (Roffman and Purdy, 1981: 26). In films such as *I Am A Fugitive From A Chain Gang*, *Criminal Code* and *The Big House* the protagonist is either an innocent man wrongly convicted, framed or with strong mitigating circumstances. Where a crime has been committed, in films like *The Last Mile* (1932), *20,000 Years in Sing Sing* (1932) or *San Quentin* (1937) the convict, usually a gangster, makes good, only to suffer an unjust death while in prison (Cheatwood, 1998). As Roffman and Purdy argue, such films reflected the dejection of the recession in 1930s America:

... the films' evocation of innocence living in subjugation and terror clearly reflects the despair of the nation faced with incomprehensible social and economic upheaval ... the cells and bars and chains eloquently re-create the sense of frustration and restriction in a land of lost opportunity. (Roffman and Purdy, 1981: 28)

During the 1940s, prison films declined both in number and in quality, although the period did produce James Cagney in *White Heat* (1949) and the *film noir* of *Brute Force*, Jules Dassin's bleak representation of prison life. Among this film's many scenes of brutality is the death of a prison informer: a group of inmates carrying blow torches force him into the pit of a drop hammer. Naturally, the hammer falls and the guards need to find a new informant.

Apart from several notable prisoner-of-war films, prison films of the 1950s included the development of women protagonists in prison narratives (Nellis, 1981) in films such as *Caged* (1950) and *I Want To Live* (1958). The former's tagline, 'Will she come out a woman or a wildcat?', although not actually the case in *Caged*, highlighted the tendency for films about women in prison to err on the side of cheap exploitation films, particularly in the 1970s with films such as the Women's Penitentiary series, *Women in Cages* (1971), and *The Big Doll's House* (1971), *The Big Bird Cage* (1972). Further series of these continued to appear throughout the 1980s and 1990s with sub-Benny Hill titles like *Chicks in Chains* (1982) and *Bimbo Penitentiary* (1992).

Prison film production continued to decline in the 1960s, when Hollywood produced only 15 prison films (Cheatwood, 1998). Among these, however, was *Birdman of Alcatraz*, based upon the true story of Robert F. Stroud, who had spent 42 years in solitary confinement; and *Cool Hand Luke*, in which Paul Newman plays Lucas Jackson, sentenced to hard labour on a chain gang for knocking the heads off parking metres. The archetypal British comedy *Two Way Stretch* (1960) and the excellent *The Pot Carriers* (1962) were also made, perhaps paving the way, in tone at least, for the very successful television prison comedy *Porridge*, broadcast in the 1970s and starring Ronnie Barker.

In cinema, the 1970s continued to produce few prison films of note, besides the run of women's prison exploitation films, and comedies such as the Burt Reynolds vehicle *The Mean Machine* (poorly remade in 2001 with seemingly most of the cast of *Lock, Stock and Two Smoking Barrels*, 1998). Nellis (1981) suggests that true stories provided the narratives for several prison films during this period, notably *The Sugarland Express* (1974), *Straight Time* (1978) and *Midnight Express*, based on Billy Hayes's account of life in, and escape from, a Turkish prison. Both *Midnight Express* and *Papillon* highlighted conditions in prisons outside America: in the case of *Papillon*, Devil's Island in French Guiana.

Stock prison narratives continued throughout the 1980s: violence (*Scum*; *Stir*, 1980; *Lock Up*, 1989); escape (*McVicar*; *Escape From New York*, 1981); and corruption and miscarriage (*Fast Walking*, 1981; *An Innocent Man*, 1989). However, there were some interesting and challenging prison films made. *The Kiss of the Spider Woman* (1985), in which William Hurt won an Academy Award for his portrayal of Luis Molina, a homosexual window-dresser, explored the relationship between Luis and Valentin (Raul Julia), a macho political prisoner, in a South American jail. Also, *Brubaker* (1980), in which Robert Redford played the eponymous warden, attempting prison reform against a backdrop of corruption at local and government level.

Brubaker was one example of a retrospective prison film: set in an earlier decade, in the case of *Brubaker*, the 1960s. More recent examples include the two Frank Darabont films *The Shawshank Redemption*, set in the 1940s, and *The Green Mile*, concerning a death-row prison officer in the 1930s. The 1980s also witnessed the emergence of prison films looking forward rather than back, in science-fiction prison films such as *Escape From New York* and the mindless *Prison Ship* (1984). This continued into the 1990s with *Wedlock*, in which inmates could not stray more than 100 yards from an unknown partner without their electronic collars exploding; *Fortress* (1992) and *No Escape* (1994). Cheatwood (1998) notes how these futuristic prisons are run by faceless, mechanistic wardens: in *No Escape*, the warden is a hologram, while in *Fortress* he is part robot.

Recent years have seen a re-emergence of the prison film, both in production terms and in popularity. *The Shawshank Redemption* in particular, while saying nothing new about prison, has become the best known and most popular prison film of all time, voted second in the top 250 films of all time,[1] ahead of films like *Citizen Kane* (1941), *Star Wars* (1977) and *Psycho* (1960). Other prison films that have proved popular with critics and audiences in recent years, although placed firmly within existing prison film narratives, have included Jim Sheridan's controversial retelling of the Guildford Four's imprisonment in *In The Name of the Father*; the powerful *Murder In The First*, in which young lawyer James Stamphill (Christian Slater) takes on the administration of Alcatraz and brutal prison warden Milton Glenn (Gary Oldman); and the Academy Award-winning *Dead Man Walking*, in which a nun (Susan Sarandon) befriends a man on death row (Sean Penn).

Themes of the Genre

The brief chronology above highlights some of the more obvious themes of the prison film: escape, riot, violence, wrongful conviction and so on. Rafter (2000) identifies several stock characters, plots and themes in her trawl of the genre. However, two broader issues arising from a study of the prison film have been under-investigated: the notion of prison as a machine and the consequent relationship between Foucault's account of the prison and the disappearance of punishment as spectacle.

Grinding rogues honest: the prison machine

A central tenet of the prison film is the representation of the prison as a machine: the 'system' with its impenetrable sets of rules and regulations which grind on relentlessly. The effect of such a mechanistic depiction of punishment is to highlight both the individual fight for survival and the inherent process of dehumanization that comes with incarceration in the system. The monotony and regulation of prison life is most often depicted by the highly structured movement of prisoners. From prison films of the 1930s and 1940s like *Numbered Men* (1930), *The Criminal Code* (1931), *San Quentin* (1937), *Men Without Souls* (1940) and *Brute Force* through to recent films like *Dead Man Walking* and *The Shawshank Redemption*, shots of inmates trudging along the huge steel landings, up and down stairwells to and from their cells has been used to convey the system within prison:

> Rows of cell doors open simultaneously and hundreds of prisoners tramp in unison to the yard. In the cavernous mess hall, they sit down to eat the mass-produced fodder their keepers call food. The camera tracks along a row of prisoners to reveal faces mainly individuated by the manner in which they express their revulsion at the meal. (Roffman and Purdy, 1981: 26, on a scene from *The Big House*)

One of the most memorable examples of this depiction of routine came in *I Am A Fugitive From a Chain Gang*. After his first night's sleep in the camp, James Allen (played by Paul Muni) awakes to the sound of the chains that bind the inmates together being pulled along the bunks and out of the dormitory. With heads bowed, the inmates sit with their legs over the bunks waiting for the chains to disappear out of sight, after which they stand up and march out of the dorm and onto trucks where they are transported to the mines to hammer rocks. All of this is accompanied by the deafening sound of rattling chains and guards shouting abuse at the men.

Many prison films continually repeat shots of inmates doing the same tasks, which acts both as a link between scenes and as a reminder to the audience of the mundane regime of prison. In *San Quentin* (1937) for example, we are regularly shown the massive exercise yard filled with inmates; in *The Pot Carriers* inmates are frequently seen lining up to collect food; and in *McVicar* many of the conversations take place as prisoners walk either up or down stairwells or from their cells. This uniformity in movement not only underlines the highly structured routine of the prison but extends the machinery image further. The motion of inmates, in contrast to the solid silence of the walls that contains it, mirrors the workings of a machine – prisoners are the cogs that whir around, driving the huge mechanism of punishment unswervingly onward.

Indeed, in some films the camera pans round the prison interior, dwelling on landings, stairwells, bars and cell doors, stressing the quasi-industrial nature of the prison. In *Wedlock* (1991) the audience follow new inmate Magenta (Rutger Hauer) around the high-tech maximum security prison to which he has been sent. The camera sweeps around the dripping silver pipes, huge fans and metal columns accompanied by an insistent humming noise. *Two Way Stretch*, *Midnight Express* and *Silent Scream* (1990) also feature lengthy internal shots of the prison, and prison films featuring Alcatraz (*Alcatraz Island*, 1937; *The Birdman of Alcatraz*; *Escape From Alcatraz*, 1979); and two TV movies, *Alcatraz: the Whole Shocking Story*, 1980, and *Six Against The Rock*, 1987) all dwell on their grim surroundings.

As well as the machine's physical presence, the prison film shows its inflexible rules: 'I know 'em. There the same in all Pens. They tell you when to eat, when to sleep, when to go to the privy' (Robert F. Stroud (Burt Lancaster) in *The Birdman of Alcatraz*). Although used primarily to illustrate injustice, the hard-and-fast prison rules serve to emphasize the unyielding processing of inmates through the penal system. This is expressed through seemingly trivial regulations: for example, no inmate may touch the prison radio in *The Ladies They Talk About* (1933); no talking during hard labour in (among many others) *Road Gang* (1936), *Papillon* and *Scum* (1979); inmates to refer to each other only by their prison name in *Wedlock*; and so on. Breach of such regulations is often punished by long periods of solitary confinement, a penalty often represented as harsh given the original offence (*Papillon* and *Murder In The First*, for example).

The injustice suffered by inmates at the hands of the prison machine is used by some films to make political points. This was particularly true of films made in the 1930s, such as *Hell's Highway* (1932) and *Blackwell's Island* (1939), which emphasized the brutality of prisons and chain gangs robbing men of their individuality and freedom:

> … the evil in the men's prisons appears to have been transformed into some larger entity. More often than not, that larger entity takes the form of a political or big city 'machine'. The effect of this was to encourage the audience to … vent whatever animosity they might be able to muster on … the 'system' that seemed, to the thirties audience, to control the very life of every honest, hard working (or unemployed) man in America. (Querry, 1976: 159)

The representation of the prison as a machine in cinema is fundamental to the prison film. For it is from this idea that the other themes flow: escape from the machine, riot against the machine, the role of the machine in processing and rehabilitating inmates, and entering the machine from the free world as a new inmate.

On entering prison

One method frequently employed by prison films to stress the systematic nature of the prison experience is the emphasis on its effect on inmates; in particular, the dehumanizing process that turns men into prisoners, numbers and statistics. This process begins with the routine that new inmates first go through when they enter the prison. When Gerry Conlon is first taken to prison in *In The Name Of The Father*, he hands over his clothes, which are placed in a box by a stern-looking prison officer. Stripped naked, he is then hosed down in cold water and covered with delousing powder. His clothes are replaced by prison-issue uniform and he is pushed into his cell. The dehumanizing process begins. A similar process occurs in both *Numbered Men* (1940) and *The Shawshank Redemption*, but versions of this routine are present in nearly all prison films. Their significance centres on the prison's control of the body. Inmates stripped, examined and washed accentuate the transformation from outsider to insider. There are also parallels with public executions. Executions at the gallows and guillotine were visible displays of the sovereign's ultimate control over his subjects. This mastering of the body of the condemned, while not ending in the taking of it, is present in the routine on entry to prison. Perhaps most symbolic is the cutting of hair, seen in *The Loneliness Of The Long Distance Runner* (1962), *Papillon* and *Midnight Express*, historically an attack on liberty and personal autonomy and, of course, visually the most noticeable difference between inmate and free man. The speed and mechanical implementation of these rules regarding the entry of a new inmate is the first, and perhaps therefore the most striking, example of the regulated institutional nature of prison that the viewer sees. The machine begins to roll.

This new-inmate procedure has an additional function to highlighting the process of turning men into prisoners. As viewers, we have limited knowledge of prison and hence when a character enters prison, we too share their ignorance and fear. As an audience we are subjected to the harsh regime of prison life, stern officers and claustrophobic cells. Cinema is often aware of our ignorance, using it to elicit sympathy for the new inmate: the naivety of 'Red' Kennedy (Humphrey Bogart) in falling for an inmate prank in *San Quentin* and freshly convicted James Rainbow trusting a well-known tobacco baron in *The Pot Carriers*, for example.

As part of the new arrival, inmates often meet with a violent introduction from guards. Chain gang films like *Road Gang* (1936) and *I Was A Fugitive From A Chain Gang*, depict guards whipping inmates new to the regime of hard labour. In *The Mean Machine* Paul Crew (Burt Reynolds) is beaten by head guard Captain Kennauer and in *Murder In The First* Henry Young (Kevin Bacon) has his foot sliced with a razor by Chief Warden Glenn (Gary Oldman).

The spectacle of punishment

Foucault's (1979) account of the development of modern penality and the consequent disappearance of punishment as spectacle replaces 'the *mise-en-scene* of the public execution' (Sparks 1992: 34) with a process of correction carried out in secret. Prison negated the visible punitive measures of gallows and guillotine and replaced it with something more nebulous: punishment itself was concealed behind giant grey walls; prison – 'the dominant apparatus of punishment' (Hale, 1982: 51). This withdrawal of visible modes of punishment from contemporary society is not a fact accepted by all. Sparks (1992) contends that Foucault's account of modern penality 'tended to neglect the survival of the demand for retribution in modern culture' (Sparks, 1992: 34). He argues that a version of the spectacle 'persists vigorously' (Sparks, 1992: 35) in televisual and cinematic representations of crime and punishment. Hale (1982) also argues that despite the loss of a focus for the public appetite to watch punishment, the appetite remains: 'the desire to observe punishment does not disappear – it cannot. As it breaks against the walls of prison like a wave, it flows back and is absorbed in numerous images of the punitive' (Hale, 1982: 54). Hale's argument is that a desire exists in modern culture to see punishment carried out. With the absence of public punitive displays and with prison 'wrapped in an impenetrable veil of secrecy' (Cohen,1985: 57), this desire to see translates into 'fantasies of punishment' (Hale 1981: 62). Hale identifies the prison film as one such fantasy, an idea supported in Querry's (1975) work:

> Should we decide to think about our prisons we find that we are quite ignorant about them, and that we are forced to call upon the powers of our imaginations – or the imaginations of someone else – to help us with the details of an institution about which we really know very little. (Querry, 1975: 147)

Sparks' and Hales's arguments are flawed, however. Hales's proposition based on audience yearning to witness punishment relies on the assumption that the public want to *see* others punished, an assumption he does not justify. He submits no evidence in the argument relating to notions (explicit or otherwise) of systematic needs and processes leading to this 'desire' to see punishment. Furthermore, such a theory reduces audience motives for watching to one simplistic, homogenous need: a view that is dubious at best.

Sparks' argument is far more convincing but it, too, is problematic. In explaining his position, Sparks cites two aspects of crime and punishment in the mass media: first, vigilante characters such as Clint Eastwood's 'Dirty Harry' and the *Death Wish* films with Charles Bronson. These, he argues are moral tales with 'immense public salience' (Sparks, 1992: 35). It seems that Sparks identifies a parallel between the monarchic power over the body of the wrongdoer described by Foucault and the revenge killings of Eastwood and Bronson: the gallows and guillotine replaced by the .44 Magnum. Consequently, Sparks submits, 'it is not possible to argue' (p. 35) with Foucault's standpoint that the spectacle of punishment has disappeared from modern penality. This is an interesting viewpoint: a parallel may exist in terms of the eventual death of the offender administered by the law enforcer. To equate monarchical power to that of the vigilante, however, requires a considerable jump.

As discussed above, the visual nature of punishment involved the public. Sparks' assertion that spectacle still exists is based upon a supposed parallel between crowds at public executions and those at the cinema. As with the position of Hale, this relies on an assumption about audience: that those who go to see films like *Dirty Harry* (1971) and *Death*

Wish (1974) do so to see the villains receive their comeuppance, just as the masses flocked to the gallows. Although this may be one reason for viewers watching such films (notwithstanding the lack of statistical evidence), it is hardly exclusive. Other reasons exist for watching such films, not least the actors themselves. *Dirty Harry* and later *Magnum Force* (1973) allowed Eastwood to develop the character first seen in westerns like *A Fistful of Dollars* (1964) and *The Good, The Bad and The Ugly* (1966). To use vigilante films as an illustration of how spectacle still plays a part in modern penality is to ignore these difficulties.

As a second example, Sparks cites the recounting of the Moors murders in the mass media as Gothic horror. This, he argues, illustrates the existence of visible punishment in real events which 'assimilate them to fictional and dramatic conventions' (Sparks 1992: 35). This is not punishment, however. Events such as the Moors murders, the Fred and Rosemary West murders at Cromwell Street, or more recently events in Soham centre on the killings, not the punishment. If tabloids and broadsheets alike reported on what happened to the Wests or Hindley while in prison, then perhaps such reports could be seen as an exhibition of punishment. However, the lurid accounts of such crimes in the media refer to the killings themselves, not the punitive acts of the state.

Prison Films and Reform

And so we return to the initial premise of this chapter: that any account of prison must include representations of prison in film. One may well ask whether the prison film has done anything more than simply entertain:

> If one could total up all the hours of screen time that have been devoted to imprisonment, all the years of effort that have been put into making prison films, and if one could count all the people that had seen them, one might be tempted to wonder if it had all been worth it. (Nellis and Hale, 1981: 44)

One could argue that it has been worth it, if only because particular prison experiences have come to light as a direct result of their retelling in cinematic form. However, the question remains whether the prison film ever created 'an atmosphere more conducive to prison reform' (Nellis and Hale, 1981: 44). There are perhaps two reasons for this failure. The first concerns some of the films that comprise the genre – those prison films that used the horrors of imprisonment for titillation and shock value, indifferent to any wider reformist stance. Consequently those prison films with a genuine reform agenda are viewed as simply more refined versions of their crass counterparts. The second reason for the prison film's failure to encourage reform is more political: that the only reason any prison film contributes to the penal debate is because passages already exist for it to happen. In the case of *I Am A Fugitive From A Chain Gang*, Nellis (1981) points out the publicity at the time concentrated on how un-American chain gangs were and how they resembled the barbarous acts of nations given a bad press at the time, such as the French on Devil's Island. Hence the billboard poster advertising the film:

> Watch the crowds as they come out! Women ... with tears in their eyes ! Men ... ready to fight! (cited in Querry, 1975: 28)

Despite the apparent failure of the prison film to change the penal system, its popularity is unquestionable. Root (1981) argues that the attraction of the prison film lies in something intangible:

> It isn't immediately obvious why prison films should occupy such a prominent place with the film going public. Most prison films ... don't have glamorous locations, rarely involve inter-national stars and usually have very little sex in them. (Root, 1982: 14)

The appeal of films concerning prison lies in a combination of factors. These include the 'deterrent factor' – making the audience think twice before committing a crime; the 'graphic and extreme sadism' (Root, 1982: 14), particularly prevalent in films like *Scum* and *Midnight Express*; and the identification with revolt against authority as we are encouraged to revolt with the hero, against (mostly) his inhumane treatment: to stop the prison machine. As Rafter comments, 'Sassy and truculent, the heroes of prison movies remain defiant even in the face of threats or inducements that would sway an ordinary mortal' (Rafter, 2000: 124).

Perhaps most appealing to the audience is the fact that the prison film opens up the world of the prison. The audience have the opportunity to share in the criminal world, to move in circles of illegality from the safety of their cinema seats. This viewer experience is positively encouraged by the film: the audience is locked up with the inmates, hears of the escape plan, talks to the officers and exercises in the yard. It is perhaps in this that the real appeal of prison film lies.

Whatever its appeal, and however little the prison film may

contribute to reform, Nellis is right when he suggests that prison film audiences should remember the real prisoners and prison conditions and that we are failing as a society if, when consuming prison narratives as entertainment, we 'look without wanting to act, without wanting to know more or without wanting to know *why*' (Nellis and Hale, 1981: 48).

Note

1. Internet Movie Database audience poll 2002, at http://us.imdb.com/ top_250_films

References

Buscombe, E. (1995) 'The Idea Of Genre in the American Cinema', in B. Grant (ed.) *Film Genre Reader II*, Austin: University of Texas Press.

Chapman, B., Mirrlees-Black, C. and Brawn, C. (2002) *Improving Public Attitudes to the Criminal Justice System: the Impact of Information*, London: HMSO.

Cheatwood, D. (1998) 'Prison Movies: Films About Adult, Male, Civilian Prisons: 1929-1995', in F. Bailey and D. Hale (eds) *Popular Culture, Crime and Justice*, Belmont: Wadsworth, 209–31.

Cohen, S. (1985) *Visions of Social Control*, Cambridge: Polity Press.

Crowther, B. (1989) *Captured On Film – the Prison Movie*, London: BT Batsford.

Foucault, M. (1979) *Discipline and Punish: the Birth of the Prison*, Harmondsworth: Penguin.

Hale, C. (1981) 'Punishment and the Visible', in M. Nellis and C. Hale (eds) *The Prison Film*, London: Radical Alternatives To Prison.

Leishman, F. and Mason, P. (2003) *Police and the Media: Facts, Fictions and Factions*, Cullompton: Willan.

Levenson, J. (2001) 'Inside Information: Prisons and the Media', *Criminal Justice Matters*, 43, Spring, 14–15.

Mason, P. (1994) Like It or Lump It? Prisons, Porridge and Television', *The Legal Executive*, August, 17–18.

Mason, P. (1995) 'Prime Time Punishment: the British Prison and Television', in D. Kidd-Hewitt and R. Osborne (eds) *Crime And The Media: the Post-modern Spectacle*, London: Pluto Press.

Mason, P. (1998a) 'Systems and Process', *Images*, at www.imagesjournal.com// issue06/features/prison.htm

Mason, P. (1998b) 'Men, Machines and the Mincer: the Prison Movie', *Picturing Justice*, at www.usfca.edu/pj/articles/Prison.htm

Mason, P. (2000) 'Watching the Invisible: Televisual Portrayal of the British Prison 1980-1991', *International Journal of the Sociology of Law*, 28, 33–44.

Mathiesen, T. (2000) *Prison on Trial*, 2nd edn, Winchester: Waterside Press.

Nellis, M. (1975) *The American Prison As Portrayed in the Popular Motion Pictures of the 1930s*, unpublished PhD thesis, University of New Mexico.

Nellis, M. (1988) 'British Prison Movies: the Case of *Now Barabbus*', *Howard Journal of Criminal Justice*, 27, 2–31.

Nellis, M. and Hale, C. (1981) *The Prison Film*, London: Radical Alternatives to Prison.

O'Sullivan, S. (2001) 'Representations of Prison in Nineties Hollywood Cinema: From *Con Air* to *The Shawshank Redemption*', *Howard Journal of Criminal Justice*, 40(4), 317–34.

Parker, J. (1986) 'The Organizational Environment Of The Motion Picture Sector', in S. Ball-Rokeach and M. Cantor (eds) *Media, Audience and Social Structure*, Beverly Hills: Sage.

Querry, R. (1973) 'Prison Movies: an Annotated Filmography 1921–Present', *Journal of Popular Film*, 2, Spring, 181–97.

Querry, R. (1975) *The American Prison as Portrayed in the Popular Motion Pictures of the 1930s*, unpublished PhD thesis, University of New Mexico.

Rafter, N. (2000) *Shots in the Mirror*, Oxford: Oxford University Press.

Reiner, R. (1994) 'The Dialectics of Dixon: the Changing Image of the TV Cop', in M. Stephens and S. Becker (eds) *Police Force, Police Service*, London: Macmillan, 11–32.

Roffman, P. and Purdy, J. (1981) *The Hollywood Social Problem Film: Madness, Despair and Politics from the Depression to the Fifties*, Bloomington: Indiana University Press.

Root, J. (1981) 'Inside', *The Abolitionist*, 10, London: Radical Alternatives To Prison.

Sparks, R. (1992) *Television And The Drama Of Crime: Moral Tales and the Place of Crime in Public Life*, Milton Keynes: Open University Press.

Tudor, A. (1995) 'Genre', in B. Grant (ed.) *Film Genre Reader II*, Austin: University of Texas Press.

Walker, J. (ed.) (1997) *Halliwell's Film Guide*, London: Harper Collins.

Walmsley, R. (2000) 'The World Prison Population Situation: Growth, Trends, Issues and Challenges', Plenary paper at The Association of Paroling Authorities International Conference, Ottawa, at http://www.apaintl.org/Pub-Conf2000-PlenaryWalmsley-En.html

Wilson, D. (1993) 'Inside Observations', *Screen*, 34(1), 76–9.

Winston, B. (1990) 'On Counting The Wrong Things', in M. Alvarado and J. Thompson (eds) *The Media Reader*, London: British Film Institute.

Index